GENDER IN HISTORY

Series editors:
Lynn Abrams, Cordelia Beattie, Pam Sharpe and Penny Summerfield

The expansion of research into the history of women and gender since the 1970s has changed the face of history. Using the insights of feminist theory and of historians of women, gender historians have explored the configuration in the past of gender identities and relations between the sexes. They have also investigated the history of sexuality and family relations, and analysed ideas and ideals of masculinity and femininity. Yet gender history has not abandoned the original, inspirational project of women's history: to recover and reveal the lived experience of women in the past and the present.

The series Gender in History provides a forum for these developments. Its historical coverage extends from the medieval to the modern periods, and its geographical scope encompasses not only Europe and North America but all corners of the globe. The series aims to investigate the social and cultural constructions of gender in historical sources, as well as the gendering of historical discourse itself. It embraces both detailed case studies of specific regions or periods, and broader treatments of major themes. Gender in History titles are designed to meet the needs of both scholars and students working in this dynamic area of historical research.

Distant sisters

Manchester University Press

OTHER RECENT BOOKS
IN THE SERIES

The state as master: gender, state formation and commercialisation in urban Sweden, 1650–1780 Maria Ågren

Love, intimacy and power: marriage and patriarchy in Scotland, 1650–1850 Katie Barclay
(Winner of the 2012 Women's History Network Book Prize)

Men on trial: performing emotion, embodiment and identity in Ireland, 1800–45 Katie Barclay

Modern women on trial: sexual transgression in the age of the flapper Lucy Bland

The Women's Liberation Movement in Scotland Sarah Browne

Modern motherhood: women and family in England, c. 1945–2000 Angela Davis

Women against cruelty: protection of animals in nineteenth-century Britain Diana Donald

Gender, rhetoric and regulation: women's work in the civil service and the London County Council, 1900–55 Helen Glew

Jewish women in Europe in the Middle Ages: a quiet revolution Simha Goldin

Women of letters: gender, writing and the life of the mind in early modern England Leonie Hannan

Women and museums 1850–1914: modernity and the gendering of knowledge Kate Hill

The shadow of marriage: singleness in England, 1914–60 Katherine Holden

Women, dowries and agency: marriage in fifteenth-century Valencia Dana Wessell Lightfoot

Catholic nuns and sisters in a secular age: Britain 1945–90 Carmen Mangion

Medieval women and urban justice: commerce, crime and community in England, 1300–1500 Teresa Phipps

Women, travel and identity: journeys by rail and sea, 1870–1940 Emma Robinson-Tomsett

Imagining Caribbean womanhood: race, nation and beauty contests, 1929–70 Rochelle Rowe

Infidel feminism: secularism, religion and women's emancipation, England 1830–1914 Laura Schwartz

Women, credit and debt in early modern Scotland Cathryn Spence

Being boys: youth, leisure and identity in the inter-war years Melanie Tebbutt

Women art workers and the Arts and Crafts movement Zoë Thomas

Queen and country: same-sex desire in the British Armed Forces, 1939–45 Emma Vickers

The 'perpetual fair': gender, disorder and urban amusement in eighteenth-century London Anne Wohlcke

DISTANT SISTERS
AUSTRALASIAN WOMEN AND THE
INTERNATIONAL STRUGGLE FOR THE
VOTE, 1880–1914

⇌ James Keating ⇌

Manchester University Press

Copyright © James Keating 2020

The right of James Keating to be identified as the author of this work has been asserted by them in accordance with the Copyright, Designs and Patents Act 1988.

Published by Manchester University Press
Oxford Road, Manchester M13 9PL
www.manchesteruniversitypress.co.uk

British Library Cataloguing-in-Publication Data
A catalogue record for this book is available from the British Library

ISBN 978 1 5261 4095 1 hardback
ISBN 978 1 5261 6711 8 paperback

First published 2020
Paperback published 2023

The publisher has no responsibility for the persistence or accuracy of URLs for any external or third-party internet websites referred to in this book, and does not guarantee that any content on such websites is, or will remain, accurate or appropriate.

Typeset by Deanta Global Publishing Services

For Katie Grant

Contents

LIST OF FIGURES AND TABLES	*page* viii
ACKNOWLEDGEMENTS	x
LIST OF ABBREVIATIONS	xii

	Introduction: Leading the empire, leading the world?	1
1	For God and home and every land: Suffrage internationalism in the World's Woman's Christian Temperance Union	28
2	'My heart ... yearn[s] for a genuine voting Australian woman!': Australasian suffragists and the international suffrage movement	64
3	The business of correspondence: Politics, friendship, and intimacy in suffragists' letters	98
4	Shaking hands across the seas: The Australasian women's advocacy press	133
5	Suffragists on tour: Exporting and narrating the female franchise	170
	Conclusion	203
	BIBLIOGRAPHY	213
	INDEX	245

List of figures and tables

Figures

1.1	The sixth South Australian Woman's Christian Temperance Union convention, Adelaide, 1894. (SLSA, Pictorial Collection, B56711)	page 44
1.2	The Woman's Temple, La Salle and Monroe Streets, Chicago, c. 1900. (*Rand, McNally & Co.'s Pictorial Chicago: Containing Views of Principal Buildings, Residences, Streets, Parks, Monuments, etc.*, Chicago: Rand, McNally, 1901)	52
2.1	The board of the International Council of Women, Berlin, 1904. (*Der Tag*, 11 June 1904, n.p., ATL, MS-Papers-4331)	86
3.1	Sir John Hall, 1894. (SLNSW, PXA1023/102)	105
3.2 and 3.3	Signed portrait of Anna Howard Shaw, c. 1910. (SLNSW, PXA1023/214)	112
3.4	The interior of the Women's Christian Temperance Union exhibit at the New Zealand International Exhibition, Christchurch, 1906. (CM, ARC2008.144.43)	113
4.1	Print runs of Australasian women's advocacy newspapers, 1888–1910	138
4.2	B. E. Minns, *Just Out of Reach*, 1891. (SLNSW, SV/80)	150
5.1	Elizabeth Nicholls' organising tours for the WCTU of Australasia, 1893–1901	185
5.2	Mr & Mrs A. R. Nicholls and Family, 1898. (*Our Federation*, 15 November 1898, n.p.)	193

LIST OF FIGURES AND TABLES

Tables

2.1	Australasian attendance at ICW congresses, 1893–1914	*page* 70
2.2	Australasian attendance at IWSA conferences, 1902–13	71
2.3	Australasian attendance at World's WCTU conventions, 1891–1913	74
4.1	Composition of Australasian women's advocacy newspapers, 1901–02	142
4.2	Geographical location of news and editorial in Australasian women's advocacy newspapers, 1894–95	153
4.3	Geographical location of news and editorial in Australasian women's advocacy newspapers, 1901–02	154
4.4	Subject matter of news and editorial in Australasian women's advocacy newspapers, 1894–95	156
4.5	Subject matter of news and editorial in Australasian women's advocacy newspapers, 1901–02	156

Acknowledgements

This book bears my name, but it only exists because of the support of my unfailingly generous friends and colleagues. It has been my privilege to spend years thinking, talking, and writing about suffragists in Australia and New Zealand. Along the way I have accumulated considerable debts, and I am grateful to everyone who helped me here. I began training as a historian at Victoria University of Wellington, where Steve Behrendt and Simone Gigliotti's teaching ignited my passion for the discipline, and Evan Roberts guided me into the world of higher research. Later, Jim McAloon proved an astute advisor. I can think of no better person to have spent so much time debating New Zealand's 1890s with. The idea for this book sprang from discussions with Charlotte Macdonald who, like many of the aforementioned, remained a source of guidance long after I left Wellington.

In Lisa Ford and Ian Tyrrell at the University of New South Wales (UNSW) Sydney, I could not have found two sharper critics or more careful readers. Both path-breaking scholars, they took a chance on me when I moved to Australia, giving liberally of their time to discuss my ideas, share their knowledge, and set me straight when that was required. Lisa's probing questions have profoundly shaped my instincts as a writer and historian, and her incisive commentary invariably pushed me in new directions. Likewise, Ian's curiosity and intellectual generosity sustained this project for many years. It is my good fortune to have spent so much time learning from such exemplary historians.

Beyond these mentors, my work has been enriched by countless conversations with scholars who took the time to share their expertise and lend their support. When I began my research, Patricia Grimshaw – without whose scholarship it could not have been conceived – provided encouragement and inspiration in equal measure. Zora Simic pushed me to think about feminisms in new ways, both as a teacher and as a historian. Her deep knowledge of feminist histories and her formidable library informed much of this work. Tony Ballantyne and Fiona Paisley read an early iteration of this manuscript, and their perceptive commentaries have helped me to improve it immeasurably. During the time I spent writing and rewriting this, Isobelle Barrett Meyering, Genevieve Dashwood, Meg Foster, Matt Haultain-Gall, Liam Kane, and Briony Neilson were friends and scholars from whose example I drew so much.

Many others, including those already named, read or discussed parts of this book, shaping my thinking and honing my arguments. Alan Atkinson, Georgine Clarsen, Kate Laing, Grace Millar, Sumita Mukherjee,

ACKNOWLEDGEMENTS

Melanie Nolan, Katie Pickles, Yves Rees, Alecia Simmonds, Megan Smitley, the Sydney Feminist History Group, Richard White, Angela Woollacott, and Maureen Wright discussed my research and shared generously of their own, for which I am very grateful. In Sydney, I am lucky to live among many talented emerging scholars, who did me the enormous favour of reading my drafts and allowing me to learn alongside them. My heartfelt thanks to Helen Bones, Jac Dalziell, James Dunk, Jarrod Hore, Rohan Howitt, Emma Kluge, Danielle Thyer, and Cheryl Ware.

Historians rely on cultural institutions, and during the writing of this book I have benefitted from the assistance of many librarians and archivists. As well as those who preserved the histories of their activism, my gratitude to the staff who helped me explore these stories at the Alexander Turnbull Library; the Auckland War Memorial Museum; the British Library; Girton College Library; the Hocken Collections; the State Libraries of New South Wales and South Australia; the University of Auckland Library; the University of Melbourne Archives; the UNSW Library; Wellington Central Library; the Women's College Archive at the University of Sydney; and the Women's Library at the London School of Economics. Especial thanks to Sarah Murray, curatorial manager at the Canterbury Museum, for going beyond the call of duty to ensure I could read Kate Sheppard's papers after the damage wrought by the earthquakes of 2011. I am also very grateful for the State Library of New South Wales' David Scott Mitchell Fellowship, which provided me the time and space to read, write, and return to the archive.

Sections of Chapter 2 appeared in '"An utter absence of national feeling": Australian women and the international suffrage movement, 1900–14', *Australian Historical Studies*, 47:3 (2016), 462–81, and of Chapter 3 in '"The defection of women": The New Zealand Contagious Diseases Act repeal campaign and transnational feminist dialogue in the late nineteenth century', *Women's History Review*, 25:2 (2015), 187–206. I would like to thank the editors and reviewers of both journals for their comments on my manuscripts.

Finally, I want to acknowledge the people without whom I could not have completed this book. First, my parents, John and Nancy Keating, whose support I have always enjoyed. While writing this manuscript I began to appreciate how their histories shaped my notions about place, identity, and distance. I hope that they might see something of themselves in its pages. Linda Forbes and Don Grant's generosity has been a constant throughout the life of this work. To my first reader, Katie Grant, whatever I write would be an understatement. I can only say that her love, warmth, and curiosity are the wellsprings from which I have drawn most deeply. This book is for her.

List of abbreviations

ATL	Alexander Turnbull Library
AWLL	Auckland Women's Liberal League
AWMM	Auckland War Memorial Museum
AWPL	Auckland Women's Political League
AWS	*Australian Woman's Sphere*
BWTA	British Women's Temperance Association
CM	Canterbury Museum
ICW	International Council of Women
IWSA	International Woman Suffrage Alliance
LNA	Ladies' National Association for the Repeal of the Contagious Diseases Acts
MLIA	Manchester Libraries, Information and Archives
NCW	National Council of Women
NUWSS	National Union of Women's Suffrage Societies
NZH	*New Zealand Herald*
SAR	*South Australian Register*
SLNSW	State Library of New South Wales
SLSA	State Library of South Australia
SMH	*Sydney Morning Herald*
UAL	University of Auckland Library
UMA	University of Melbourne Archives
WCTU	Woman's Christian Temperance Union
WFL	Women's Franchise League [New Zealand]
WFPA	Women's Federal Political Association
WL	The Women's Library at the London School of Economics
WPA	Women's Political Association of Victoria
WSL	Womanhood Suffrage League of New South Wales
YWCA	Young Women's Christian Association

Introduction: Leading the empire, leading the world?

On 10 October 1902, the Melbourne feminist newspaper *Australian Woman's Sphere* featured 'An Open Letter to the Women of the United States'.[1] It was written by the paper's editor, the newly elected secretary of the International Woman Suffrage Committee, Vida Goldstein, fresh from her first overseas journey, a six-month tour of America. The letter, published three months after the passage of the Commonwealth Franchise Act 1902 – which granted white Australian women the right to vote and stand for Federal Parliament – ostensibly offered Goldstein's 'impressions of the woman suffrage movement in the United States'. Yet Goldstein quickly turned to the celebration of her newfound status as an enfranchised citizen. 'Australia', she declared, 'leads the way in the suffrage movement, for she is the only country in the world which has endowed its women with national suffrage.' Belying its title, her effusive column did not convey the magnitude of her compatriots' victory to the *Sphere*'s handful of American subscribers. Instead, Goldstein drew parallels with the United States to reinvigorate her embattled Victorian counterparts in their struggle for the franchise at state elections. Like all rights, Goldstein reminded her readers, enfranchisement conferred responsibilities. 'Women in the land of the Southern Cross', she explained, were 'indebted' to suffragists in Britain and America. As a result, her readers were obliged to 'use our right of suffrage so that the men of other nations will soon want to follow the example of the Australian champions of women's enfranchisement'.[2]

Goldstein's rhetoric would have been familiar to anyone who had observed the spate of turn-of-the-century antipodean suffrage celebrations. Ten years earlier, in 1893, after New Zealand became the first self-governing colony in the British Empire to enfranchise all adult women, Kate Sheppard found herself in a similarly expansive mood. Days before voting in her first general election, she used her platform as one of the campaign's pre-eminent figures to urge women to translate their newfound rights into political power, reminding them that 'the eyes of the world are on the women of New Zealand'. Whereas Goldstein drew Pacific parallels, Sheppard – uncharacteristically – emphasised the day's imperial resonance: 'the 28th of November, 1893, will be a memorable day in the history of the British Empire ... here, in our beautiful land, is the problem to be solved as to whether the women of the mighty domain that for over fifty years has been worthily governed by a woman can as worthily govern themselves.'[3] For Goldstein and Sheppard – suffrage leaders, newspaper editors, and members of international women's organisations – the 'struggle for freedom' was not geographically limited, nor did it end with voting rights.[4] Enfranchisement, they insisted, obliged women to reform settler society and, in doing so, to exemplify the virtues of political citizenship for the benefit of disenfranchised women across the world.

As both women knew, the Australasian colonies were conspicuous in their early enfranchisement of white women. The cascade of electoral reform began in New Zealand in 1893. It was followed by South Australia (1894), then Western Australia (1899), the Commonwealth of Australia and New South Wales (1902), Tasmania (1903), Queensland (1905), and Victoria in 1908. The expansion of antipodean suffrage was unique, but it was neither unprecedented nor universal. By 1893, women voted on the Isle of Man and in pockets of the western United States, and would likewise do so in Finland (1906) and Norway (1907) before Victoria. Furthermore, Australasian suffrage was racially delineated. New Zealand, which enfranchised Māori and Pākehā (European) women alike in 1893, restricted 'aliens' – non-British nationals, primarily those the state deemed 'non-white' – from voting. In one of Australia's founding injustices, the Commonwealth Franchise Act 1902 disenfranchised most 'aboriginal natives of Australia Asia Africa or the Islands of the Pacific'.[5] The suffragists were not silent witnesses to the racialisation of Australian citizenship but aided in its construction, decrying the composition of electorates that included 'blackfellows and naturalised aliens' before white women.[6] Notwithstanding New Zealand's more inclusive suffrage, Māori women – because of the campaign's urban nature, its institutions' disinclination to cultivate their support, and their parallel commitment to the Kotahitanga movement to establish a Māori parliament (in which they enjoyed full political rights from 1897) – were poorly represented in the suffragists' ranks.[7] Mirroring settler women's lack of interest in their Indigenous counterparts beyond the Christian missions established to 'protect' and convert Aboriginal people, Indigenous voices were absent from the Australian campaigns. As many scholars have noted, these exclusions must be considered alongside the combination of legislative prohibition and bureaucratic obstruction that circumscribed the voting rights of Indigenous Australians until 1965.[8]

Even in its exclusions, then, the spread of women's suffrage was an Australasian phenomenon that followed a paradigm established by the colonial labour movement. Led by white, middle-class women with significant enclaves of working-class support, and fortified by a Protestant temperance vision, suffragists from Perth to Invercargill enlisted male political sponsors and drew on a common tactical arsenal – adapted from British and American literature that filtered through organisational and informal networks – to engender public support for their demands.[9] Despite local variations, in each case, after relatively short campaigns, suffrage bills were passed by inchoate colonial parliaments amid the transition to a formal party system.

This book takes these regional parallels seriously. It uses them as a basis to explore the rise of suffrage internationalism, one of the dominant strands within the fin-de-siècle international women's movement, alongside peace activism and the campaigns against regulated prostitution and the 'white slave traffic'. Suffrage was neither the first nor the most enduring of these, but as an inherently parochial demand, it most intimately connected grassroots activists with a new world of cross-border networking and transnational solidarity. Focusing on the decades before and after 1890 – a transitional period when proto-feminist networks crystallised into formal international organisations – it documents the individual and institutional connections that allowed Australasian suffrage leaders like Sheppard and Goldstein, as well as the thousands of ordinary women who constituted the women's movement, to think and act in a transnational context. Just as importantly, it seeks to understand the impediments that made pre-war internationalism a fraught and frustrating endeavour.

Despite the Australasian suffragists' proximity to each other, scholars have shown little interest in the shared history of their campaigns for the vote. Such inattention is surprising, not only in the context of historians' fascination with settler women's 'remarkably supranational … mental and actual geographies', but because the suffragists situated themselves in a Tasman world.[10] In 1892, the South Australian Mary Lee responded magnanimously to an erroneous report that New Zealand had enfranchised adult women: 'We, S.A., N.S.W. [New South Wales], & the other colonies have been racing each other in the noble ambition to be the first to reach the desired goal, women's suffrage. New Zealand has won … her victory is ours.' Then, as now, trans-Tasman ties were competitive and collegial. Weeks later, on discovering that New Zealand's 1892 Electoral Bill had actually been defeated, Lee was 'not sure if I am glad or sorry.

I certainly have from the first set my heart on S.A. leading the way in this Reform. I fear I am selfish about it.' Echoing Lee, in 1893 the New South Wales Labor politician Arthur Rae ended a letter to the Sydney suffrage leader Rose Scott with an exhortation: 'don't let South Australia beat us!'[11]

In addition to losing the sense of simultaneity that exhilarated these activists, the proliferation of state and national histories fixated on who won the vote first and most completely has also obscured how the suffragists fitted within an international movement for the expansion of women's political rights. Sheppard and Goldstein's desire to exercise the vote on behalf of disenfranchised women across the globe was instilled as much by interactions with overseas suffragists as by their personal ambitions. On learning of the New Zealanders' victory, Lee's compatriot, Mary George, reminded them of their duty 'to help forward the cause in other lands'. Ten years later, Vida Goldstein returned home to Melbourne carrying a diary crammed with messages from admirers like New York suffragist Mary Garrett Hay: 'we are glad "Little Australia" crossed the waters to see us, and now we will look for great things across the seas.'[12]

Historians have recognised these connections in their accounts of the suffrage campaigns. However, despite the popular acknowledgement of the suffragists' regional and international connections, we have yet to substantiate the range and significance of the personal, ideological, and organisational bonds that inspired and informed antipodean suffrage activism with multi-archival research. Instead, moments like Goldstein's Oval Office meeting with President Theodore Roosevelt in 1902 or Sheppard's 'triumphal' return to the United Kingdom as an enfranchised woman in 1894–95 form the basis of a largely celebratory historiography.[13] Within this canon, the sources of the suffragists' transnational consciousness, the extent to which ordinary women shared their enthusiasm, and the limits of the suffragists' intercolonial and international networks remain opaque. Australian and New Zealand historians have framed the settler colonies as 'world leader[s] in democratic practice' whose suffragists committed themselves to the global expansion of women's political rights.[14] Building on this scholarship, *Distant Sisters* contends with the reality that, for all their endeavour, antipodean women played a circumscribed role in the international struggle for women's suffrage.

Heeding Australian historian Angela Woollacott's reminder that 'amorphous' declarations of internationalism must be contextualised by the investigation of 'historically specific and evolving ... relationships', this book examines the transnational networks developed, sustained, and severed by New Zealand and Australian suffragists from the advent of organised suffrage activism in the mid-1880s until 1914, when the outbreak of the First World War drew a curtain on women's international organising.[15] It is not a recapitulation of the well-documented domestic suffrage campaigns, but a history of antipodean suffragists' cross-border interactions as they fought to win the vote at home and simultaneously struggled to negotiate old colonial identities alongside the new demands of national and international citizenship.[16] To break the fetters of national history and follow the traffic of information, goods, and bodies between, across, and through nations, it focuses on women from three emblematic British colonies: New South Wales, New Zealand, and South Australia.

Sheppard and Goldstein's compatriots did not always realise their lofty ambitions. Still, in revealing the fragility of international connections, their stories enrich the scholarship on transnational organising that has energised feminist history since the 1990s. For all its insights, this project remains preoccupied with successful endeavours.[17] Belying the promise of transnational history, subjects from the transatlantic centre still eclipse women at the margins. As Ellen Carol DuBois observed, a comprehensive history of women's transnational activism requires historians to explore 'feminism's byways as well as its mainstreams, its dissidents as well as its representative voices', devote equal attention to its heartlands and hinterlands, and explain why some networks proved more durable than others.[18] By scrutinising the personal and organisational records of antipodean women's participation in the first international women's movement, *Distant Sisters* deepens our understanding of the suffragists and troubles the reflexive celebration of transnational activism. In doing so, it provides a clearer account of the operation of the women's reform networks that encircled the globe in the late nineteenth century, stressing the contingent nature of cross-border organisation as well as the limits of women's internationalism before the First World War.

Situating the suffragists: Australasia at the fin-de-siècle

The campaigns for the extension of women's political rights in Australia and New Zealand emerged alongside the demands for manhood suffrage that echoed across the Tasman after Britain granted the colonies responsible government in the 1850s. Europeans had explored the region since the seventeenth century, but settlement only began in 1788, when Britain established New South Wales as a penal colony. Colonisation started twenty years later in New Zealand and was shaped by the humanitarian discourse which then prevailed in British political and missionary circles. It was conceived not as a site of penal reform but as a free settlement, and its incorporation into the British Empire coincided with the signing of a treaty between the

Crown and Māori at Waitangi in 1840. The treaty, which owed as much to Māori strength as the enlightened instructions carried by Lieutenant-Governor William Hobson, moulded the colony's development and would, in time, contribute to its settlers' sense of distinctiveness from their Australian counterparts.[19] From 1825, New South Wales (which gradually expanded to incorporate the eastern two-thirds of the Australian continent and New Zealand) was divided into a series of colonies. The first to separate was Van Diemen's Land (renamed Tasmania in 1856), then the free settlements of South Australia (1836) and New Zealand (1840), followed by Victoria (1851) and Queensland (1859). The six colonies and Western Australia, which was founded from the territory that lay beyond New South Wales' western border in 1829 and did not achieve self-government until 1890, were administered by appointed governors. Devolution circumscribed gubernatorial power and saw the creation of bicameral colonial parliaments and, in New Zealand, a series of short-lived provincial councils (1853–76). These bodies passed legislation pertaining to domestic affairs, subject to Britain's seldom-used veto, and proved receptive to working men's calls for greater democracy. As a result, they were elected under an increasingly generous franchise which, by the late 1870s, included all adult men in New Zealand and most white men in the Australian colonies.[20]

Despite their neglect in the scholarship on Australasian women's internationalism, the years bookending 1900 were a period of rare intensity. Historians have long been fascinated by fin-de-siècle decades, but the 1890s hold a special place in Australian and New Zealand history.[21] Before the federation of the Australian colonies into the Commonwealth of Australia in 1901 – New Zealand attended the Federation conventions of 1890–91, but thereafter withdrew from the process – Tasman relations remained robust. Since the early nineteenth century, capital, goods, and ideas had circulated in a common market, animated by the 'perennial interchange' of migrants. Close relations saw companies and trade unions operate on both sides of the Tasman and meant that from the mid-1880s, the eastern Australian colonies and New Zealand suffered a depression.[22] Economic turbulence, alongside shared labour unrest and the cultural resurgence associated with the Federation movement, heightened the settlers' political consciousness and whetted their appetite for progressive reform. Amid the decade's tumult, the 'nervous nineties' are remembered as the years when feminism 'acquired critical mass'.[23] Across the region, those who had pondered the woman question coalesced in the organised suffrage movements that unfolded between the mid-1880s and 1908. While the rise of colonial women's movements is well understood, we must better apprehend how the circulatory forces that modernised the Victorian world – the steamship, railway, telegraph, and cheap newsprint – affected Australasian women's presence on the international stage.[24]

If 1880 is a logical beginning to the story of Australasian suffrage internationalism, the First World War serves as its natural conclusion. Federation did not terminate this flourishing Tasman world. However, the creation of the Commonwealth accelerated the erosion of the cultural, financial, and organisational ties that once bound the region. So too did Australasia's tightening economic connections with Britain, which, ironically, occurred as the colonies became Dominions, the appellation reflecting their self-governing status and increased prominence in imperial affairs.[25] However, as *Distant Sisters* explores, these new settler nations did not fill the void. The rush of 'civic enthusiasm' which had prompted Federation soon abated and, in the short term, the states, rather than the federal government, retained responsibility for most domestic affairs.[26] Likewise, the conclusion of the suffrage campaigns did not immediately sever activists' intercolonial bonds. Yet, as we shall see, by 1905 the once vibrant Australasian women's advocacy press had disappeared. At the same time – having deliberated Tasman federation a decade before the Commonwealth was established – the region's Woman's Christian Temperance Unions (WCTUs), formerly a force for intercolonial dialogue, grew apart.[27] Enfranchised Australasian women lived in an ever more connected world, but their diminished Tasman networks were only gradually replaced by ties to women further afield.

Instead, as the century progressed, many former suffragists turned inward. With their political coalitions irrevocably fractured, a problem exacerbated by the demise of feminism's unifying causes and figures, as well as the challenges their successors faced in using the vote to transform society, antipodean women seemed to relinquish their place on the international stage almost as soon as they had taken it up. When the first international women's movement entered its wartime hiatus, antipodean accents were seldom heard anywhere outside the World's WCTU conventions. Yet while the union remained a force for internationalism, its domestic membership slumped. Similarly, the National Council of Women of New Zealand and that of South Australia, once each respective territory's peak women's organisation and representative on the world stage, had lain dormant for almost a decade. A new generation of feminists would take their place in the more diverse and less centralised interwar international women's movement, yet in 1914 it was clear that antipodean suffragists' moment in the sun had passed.

Histories of women's suffrage: Colony, nation, world?

As a book that bridges the gaps between colony and nation, metropole and periphery, and empire and world, *Distant Sisters* sits between myriad historiographies. Beyond reviving a regional approach to the history of the woman question, it draws on and historicises the corpus produced by Australasian feminist historians. At the same time, in challenging the ideational limits of national histories of women's enfranchisement and the Anglo-American narratives that still shape the historiography of the international women's movement, it applies spatial approaches from British imperial history to uncover how women distant from the movement's Atlantic centres nevertheless lived at the heart of complex cross-border political networks.

Although most histories of antipodean women's suffrage are now encapsulated within the nation, the movement's earliest chroniclers situated themselves within broader frames. Histories of the colonial campaigns, written within months of their authors' enfranchisement, first appeared in European and North American periodicals. Convinced that history could be used as a political weapon, victorious suffragists used their pages to spread inspirational stories 'for the benefit of women in other countries'.[28] These attempts to disseminate a suffrage narrative centred on women's agency did not pass unchallenged. Instead, critics used these channels to subordinate suffragist activism to the masculine business of parliamentary politics. Foremost among these was the former New Zealand cabinet minister and Agent-General in the United Kingdom, William Pember Reeves. *State Experiments in Australia and New Zealand* (1902), his history of the colonies' progressive social and economic legislation, ignored the suffrage campaigns. Instead, he insisted that Australasian politicians had 'spontaneously' gifted women the vote. Published at a moment of international interest in antipodean progressivism, *State Experiments* sold well in Britain and America and, outside feminist circles, his gift narrative was widely accepted.[29]

Ironically, given Reeves' disdain for the suffragists, *State Experiments* offered a model for a Tasman history of women's enfranchisement. Yet, by the 1920s, with the vote won in the United States and much of Europe and the international women's movement increasingly focused on peace and economic rights (even as women elsewhere continued to fight for the vote), those writing women's histories in Australasia narrowed their scope. Seeking to inscribe their forebears' triumphs into emerging national narratives, feminists wrote for domestic audiences. This 'collusive relationship' between feminism and nationalism characterised the interwar years as women bargained for the unabrogated benefits of citizenship with their 'maternal service' to the nation.[30] In the same vein, when post-war historians revisited the suffrage movements, they wrote campaign histories that unfolded in colonial legislatures.[31]

Seeking to refashion a national past to liberate their communities, the feminist historians who upended established narratives of nation-making in the 1970s continued to overlook the cross-border exchanges that shaped the suffragists' activism. Inspired by another imported ideology, Women's Liberation, the first generation of explicitly feminist historians in Australia and New Zealand endeavoured to connect the region 'with a worldwide story of power struggles between women and men'. Despite this ambition, Ann Curthoys observes that – like many on the left – her cohort wrote unabashedly national histories, seeking to effect domestic change.[32] Collectively, they questioned what they could salvage from suffrage-era feminism. Thus, their work tended to assume or ignore suffragists' connections to the outside world, rather than making them a subject of investigation.[33] Attitudes towards the suffragists softened, although they were seldom the subject of comparative analysis. After all, for those occluded from the canon, the nation remained a battleground.[34]

Since the turn of the millennium, suffrage historians have 'reconceive[d] ... their project as an international one'.[35] Like the antipodean suffragists, Australian and New Zealand historians were forerunners in this endeavour. Gathered a century after New Zealand's first election under universal suffrage, delegates at the 'Suffrage and Beyond' conference advocated the reconceptualisation of the women's suffrage campaigns as an 'international protest movement'. Seeking to transcend transatlantic myopia, they recommended returning to the conduits of the suffragists' 'fundamental internationalism': the temperance movement, the Second International, and suffragette militancy. Antipodean stories, as Patricia Grimshaw envisaged, lay at the heart of this enterprise, offering the chance to reorient the field away from the Atlantic and towards feminism's nineteenth-century frontiers: Australia, New Zealand, and the American Midwest.[36]

Sandwiched between Mineke Bosch's history of the International Woman Suffrage Alliance (IWSA) and Leila Rupp's ground-breaking *Worlds of Women*, 'Suffrage and Beyond' presaged a sea-change in Western feminist history. Within a decade, a plethora of histories documented the proto-feminist dialogue nurtured within nineteenth-century friendship circles and their crystallisation into formal organisations, like the IWSA and the International Council of Women (ICW). Collectively, these scholars stressed that women, in their drive for social and political reform, considered their labours in transnational perspective. Their work explicated the interplay between feminism, nationalism, and internationalism, illuminating a world of conferences populated by Euro-American elites pursuing what they considered to be universal goals: peace, prohibition, and the eradication of gendered moral double standards.[37] Still, suffrage fits uneasily in such company. Unlike these 'indissolubly transnational' issues, the fight for political citizenship is better understood as a series of battles fought in specific colonial or national contexts.[38] While acknowledging this paradox, historians continue to emphasise the movement's global character, bringing into focus the connections that suffrage campaigners forged with like-minded women across the world as a new century dawned.[39]

Today, those of us interested in the cross-border currents that animated women's fin-de-siècle reform movements sit atop this 'mountain of scholarship, precariously dangling our legs over the precipice'.[40] Yet, while Rupp opened new vistas, most studies of the suffrage movement's international dimensions – especially those documenting the period before the First World War – retain a familiar, Atlanticist bias. Two decades after 'Suffrage and Beyond', and notwithstanding numerous reminders that more might be done to expand its remit, suffrage scholarship has yet to internalise its transnational ideals.[41] The irony here is that Australian historians of women and gender have long been primed to fill this lacuna. Australasia's settler colonial origins have made its historians acutely aware of the need to grapple with a connected past, a push that has been led by feminist historians.[42] Motivated by the mobility of their subjects – whether they were actors seeking stardom in Edwardian London and golden-age Hollywood or missionaries drawn to Asia by the promise of soul-saving and the prospect of adventure – these scholars produced exciting histories of cultural exchange. Focusing equally on unruly life stories and sweeping histories of organisations like the World's WCTU and Pan-Pacific Women's Association, their work has provided an escape from 'the death grip of the national' in favour of an analytical approach attentive to individuals, movements, and ideas that transcended state borders.[43]

In spite of such trailblazing work on the myriad forms taken by women's cross-border organising after 1918, the suffragists remain trapped in an anachronistic national frame. Tellingly, surveys of Australian women's international activism elide the years between Vida Goldstein's tour of the United States and the outbreak of the First World War.[44] In New Zealand, the picture is cloudier. In retrospect, the 1993 suffrage centenary appears not as a new beginning in the writing of suffrage history, but rather its zenith. The subsequent lack of attention has meant that pre-war women's internationalism remains all but invisible.[45] There are, of course, exceptions. Following her call to reorient suffrage studies, Grimshaw and others have illuminated the shared racial imagination that saw the coincidence of white women's enfranchisement and the political marginalisation of indigenous peoples across the Pacific.[46] Probing deeper into the colonial past, Australian and New Zealand historians alike have traced settler women's contributions to the debates about women and citizenship that echoed across the Western world after the 1848 Seneca Falls Convention.[47] Above all, historians have lavished attention on the suffrage diaspora, seeking to upend ingrained assumptions about core–periphery relationships by documenting the efforts of seasoned activists who travelled to 'teach feminists in the Imperial "heartland"' in the 1910s.[48] Research exploring these few women's privileged status in Edwardian Britain is valuable, but the problem of periodisation remains. As has been noted of the Atlantic world, little detailed scholarship on internationalism bridges the gap between the Victorian feminism of the Australasian suffrage movements and the rise of post-suffrage women's movements in the twentieth century.[49]

Paradoxically, while the suffragists continue to be lauded as the epitome of the democratic spirit that distinguished the settler nations of Australia and New Zealand from the rest of the world, they have been viewed in isolation and overlooked in the drive to globalise Australasian histories. For some, this oversight is a product of the former Dominions' inferiority complex. New Zealand, Canada, and Australia possess 'parallel historiographies', but as Katie Pickles argues, the prevalence of insiders writing national histories, an aversion to referencing unfamiliar scholars, and the difficulty of marketing small nations' histories abroad have inhibited the publication of comparative histories.[50] However, the avalanche of transnational scholarship published in the past decade alone suggests that such 'cultural cringe' might be a thing of the past.

Instead, as this book contends, the difficulties inherent in the Australasian suffragists' ambition to lead the global suffrage movement account for the absence of connected histories of women's enfranchisement. First, Australian and New Zealand suffragists' interactions with one another and the rest of the world resist easy categorisation. Projects that celebrate the claims to international leadership made by, and about, women like Goldstein in the aftermath of colonial and national enfranchisement disregard the suffragists' strained relations with the international suffrage movement. The focus on women who travelled overseas to describe their successes has obscured the fact that many leading suffragists either died or retired soon after winning the vote, or did not feel inclined to embark on overseas tours. Those who arrived during the late nineteenth-century lull in the Atlantic campaigns often found local conditions too hostile and their hosts too introspective to make the headway they had enjoyed in the colonies. Their successors reached more receptive audiences in the 1900s, yet as Britain's Edwardian suffrage era ended with the intensification of suffragette militancy in 1912, they too retreated from the cause.[51]

As the stories recounted in this book make clear, travel could be as frustrating as it was pleasurable. The experience mixed sociability and solidarity with first-hand knowledge of the structural impediments within international organisations that marginalised antipodean women or circumscribed the discussion of women's enfranchisement. Yet travel was not the only entry into the Anglophone suffrage community. Like most British world networks, these were based on the dissemination of printed texts, which allowed ordinary women to feel part of a global movement. Here, the emergence of a Tasman women's advocacy press that existed in symbiosis with British and American titles might be taken as powerful evidence of transnational suffrage dialogue. However, a closer look at its content and circulation cautions against viewing these newspapers as reliable vectors for suffrage internationalism.

Finally, by the twentieth century, the former colonies' reputation as progressive innovators had diminished, both as other countries surpassed them and as women discovered the limitations of electoral politics. In contrast with Kate Sheppard's ebullience in 1893, Isabel Napier, New Zealand's representative at the ICW's 1904 congress, fretted about the future. Like Sheppard, she affirmed the 'eternal verities' of internationalism and believed that New Zealanders were still responsible for refuting anti-suffragists' 'prognostications of evil'. However, as she admitted, enfranchised women's divisions had been 'intensified by the bane of party government and petty class jealousies'. Contradicting the colony's 'indefatigable Premier', Richard Seddon, a reluctant convert to suffrage who nevertheless 'boasts of its success wherever he goes', Napier warned her audience that possessing the vote without legislative representation was no better than wielding a 'blunt weapon'.[52] In the Australian states where the vote was won later, these frustrations took longer to surface. Nevertheless, they collectively suggest a more ambivalent relationship between Australasian suffragists and their overseas counterparts than some might have expected, but also make it a more compelling subject of inquiry.

In this spirit, rather than replace tired nationalist mythologies about women's enfranchisement with refreshed internationalist versions, *Distant Sisters* follows the connections suffrage activists made between the local and the global in their pursuit of the vote but, crucially, delineates their limits. Although New South Wales, New Zealand, and South Australian suffragists' interests extended beyond the British Empire, this book employs analytical approaches devised by twenty-first-century imperial historians, particularly the turn towards spatial analysis. Rejecting conceptions of empire centred on exchanges between colony and metropole, scholars like Tony Ballantyne, Alan Lester, and Zoë Laidlaw have emphasised that imperial interactions transpired within networks that linked sites scattered across the globe.[53] United by a conviction of the efficacy of tracing connections beyond political borders, these scholars have unravelled the dynamics of imperial knowledge production and social formation. Advocating for this spatial approach, Ballantyne argues that studying networks – whether they comprised journalists and editors, convicts and slaves, or even suffragists and social reformers – allows historians 'to recover the mobility and exchanges that were so central in the constitution of both metropolitan and colonial cultures'. To supersede radial imaginations of empire with tools that would help recapture a connected past, historians devised a set of metaphors: webs, networks, entanglements. Influenced by social geography, they are intended to reimagine empire as a malleable structure, forged from disparate parts connected in different ways across space. Used carefully, such metaphors allow historians to consider 'metropole and colony, or colony and colony, within the same analytical frame ... without privileging either'.[54]

Whatever the merits of re-examining the suffragists with regional or transnational lenses, this book also reckons with a growing unease at the ascendance of panoramic approaches to the past. Because of the novelty of national history and the rapidity with which transnational approaches have been adopted, these concerns are acute in Australasia.[55] While acknowledging the benefits of studying lives and events that did not coincide with national borders, some fear that the ascendance of spatial metaphors amounts to a stultifying new orthodoxy. The dependence on transnational tools, critics argue, has produced sweeping histories that disregard local specificities, normalise extraordinary lives, and omit the disconnections, failures, and experiences – especially those of indigenous peoples – that fall outside their remit.[56] Yet, rather than retreat from connected histories, this book contends that the opposite is required. In common with a wave of globally oriented women's histories grounded in local research, it is written with the conviction that the study of colonial women's lives and their familial and community ties offers valuable opportunities to further conceptualise regional and international networks. After all, as Fiona Paisley has noted, antipodean internationalist women, marginalised by gender *and* distance, provide a perfect vantage point for historians working to discover 'the potential and limits of the international'.[57]

It seems clear, then, that scrutinising the personal and organisational records of antipodean suffragists and determining their place in local, regional, and international women's movements will enrich our understanding of their lives. Such a project does not assume that transnational organisations automatically imbued local suffrage campaigning with a wider resonance. Nor does it uncritically celebrate events like Kate Sheppard's and the South Australian journalist Catherine Helen Spence's respective British and American tours as examples of the suffragists' internationalist spirit in action. Rather, it elucidates the bounds of the suffragists' networks and seeks to understand the disconnections that shaped their experience. Individuals and organisations forged transnational connections for many reasons. Together, they reveal a more entangled history of Tasman and transnational suffrage activism than has previously been written. However, this book is not a history of unbridled connection. While the Australasian presence is vital to understanding the early international women's movement, to develop an accurate picture of its operation historians must acknowledge the frustrations that conspired to keep the 'most fully enfranchised' women in the world on its margins.[58]

Approaching Australasia's suffragists

Piecing together the networks that pervaded Australasian suffragists' organising requires reckoning with another battleground of feminist and post-colonial scholarship: the archive. Here, historians confront the institutional 'bond between history making and nation making'. In the case of women's enfranchisement, which has become a byword for a history of antipodean egalitarianism – especially in New Zealand, where suffrage artefacts are accorded the status of constitutional documents – the sway of the national is remarkably strong. Unpicking the tangle of personal and organisational ties between mobile subjects requires scholars to first employ mobile research methods and then subvert the nationalistic 'logic of the archive'.[59]

At Girton College, Cambridge, one can pore over Sheppard's speeches, stored among boxes of ephemera sent to Helen Blackburn, the editor of *Englishwoman's Review*. Nineteen thousand kilometres away, Blackburn's scribbled responses to Sheppard are held by the Canterbury

Museum.⁶⁰ Their letters, alongside thousands of others held by repositories from Adelaide to Amsterdam, lie at the heart of *Distant Sisters*. The largest of these collections, the archive preserved by Rose Scott, a central figure in the New South Wales suffrage movement, encapsulates the tension between abundance and silence that frustrates women's historians. Scott's life, and the lives of her New Zealand and South Australian counterparts, are reasonably well documented. Whereas, whether through the lack of interest shown by archival institutions, the personal or familial desire for privacy, or simple ignorance of their possessions' value, much less remains of the suffragists across the rest of Australia – an absence that dictates the contours of this book.⁶¹

For all the allure of Scott and Sheppard's voluminous archives, it is vital not to beget histories preoccupied with women who had the means to travel and indulge in prolonged correspondence. As historians are painfully aware, few of their contemporaries could 'place ... in posterity's hands the documents necessary to engage posterity's feeble attention'. Such silences make it difficult to tell the stories of working women – seamstresses in Adelaide and Dunedin and schoolteachers in Sydney – who agitated for the vote.⁶² At the same time, as Ballantyne warns, reading the colonial archive as an undifferentiated site of 'lettered governance' risks flattening our understanding of materials, like those preserved by the suffragists, collected outside the auspices of the state. Nevertheless, reflecting the biases of colonial repositories, women's organisations, and subsequent scholars, the 'faintest traces' in the archive that this work draws on are those left by indigenous women.⁶³ Thus, it is even harder to find documentary traces of the few Māori who joined the New Zealand campaign for parliamentary suffrage or the many who joined the Kotahitanga movement. In Australia, where Rebecca Mead's argument that the frontier suffrage campaigns reflected settlers' desire to 'defend their brave new worlds against resentful indigenes' rings truest, Aboriginal women were excluded from the movement's formal structures altogether. Even those few activists who considered Indigenous rights in the interwar years operated from the assumption that Aboriginal women could not advocate for themselves.⁶⁴ While cognisant of these limits, this book goes beyond the study of emblematic individuals and reveals how the tendrils of internationalism touched all those associated with the suffrage movement, elite and ordinary alike. In this endeavour, it is vital to pay close attention to 'unfashionable' organisational histories.⁶⁵

Few of the Australasian WCTU's 8,000 members, or the thousands of members of women's associations who paid for the pleasure of affiliation with international organisations like the ICW and IWSA, have extant papers. Nevertheless, the records of these mass-membership organisations attest to their quotidian ties to 'worlds of women'. Here, as ever, the local and international intertwined. From their formation, WCTU branches followed edicts from their Chicago headquarters instructing that 'every document issued should be filed away', while the ICW's colonial affiliates shared their Northern Hemisphere leaders' commitment to posterity.[66] *Distant Sisters* draws on this vast archive of local, colonial, and international reports and minutes. Reading them in conversation with one another for the first time, it substantiates previous assertions of the suffragists' 'fundamental internationalism' and qualifies what such sentiments meant for the sedentary readers of working-class Louisa Lawson's iconoclastic newspaper, *Dawn* (1888–1905), as well as the peripatetic few who graced the international conference circuit.[67]

This book takes a bipartite approach to the history of Australasian women's participation in, and retreat from, the international suffrage moment. The first section considers the organisational dimensions of suffrage internationalism, focusing on the international women's associations that emerged in the 1880s. Chapter 1 concerns the WCTU, then the world's largest women's organisation and a common denominator in all seven colonial suffrage campaigns. Tracing relations within the union's local, intercolonial, and international networks through a study of branches in two port cities, Auckland and Adelaide, it explores how cross-border connections influenced antipodean members' activism before and after their enfranchisement. The chapter situates the WCTU in a moment of flux, explaining the disjuncture between the everyday internationalism that propelled Australasian women to embrace the union's mimetic rituals at the same time as members elsewhere in the world retreated from the global suffrage cause. The promise and frustrations of international organising in pursuit of the vote also lie at the heart of Chapter 2. Turning from evangelical internationalism to the broader-based ICW and IWSA, it explains why Australasian women's early enfranchisement ultimately led to little more than a marginal position in the pre-war international women's movement. Bookended by Vida Goldstein's 1902 tour of the United States and her post-war refuge in the world of Christian Science, it charts the rise and fall of Australasian suffragists' influence on the world stage. Discounting traditional explanations that distance kept antipodean women on the international periphery, the chapter focuses on the repercussions of national representation – the cornerstone of liberal internationalism – for women on the cusp of old colonial and imperial identities and the newfound responsibilities of national citizenship.

Whereas the opening chapters concern the organisational dimensions of suffrage internationalism, the second half of the book examines the communication networks that enabled Australasians to consider themselves part of an international women's movement. Chapter 3 explores the politics and practice of suffragists' letter writing. It finds that Australasian women's intercolonial and international circuits of discussion were smaller, more functional, and more frustratingly incomplete than previously described. Scrutinising cultures of correspondence, it explores the intimate practices that bound the international women's movement. At the same time, it juxtaposes tropes of epistolary friendship against the disruptive possibilities of letter writing at a moment when cracks emerged in the relationship between enfranchised and disenfranchised feminists in the English-speaking world. Chapter 4 turns from private correspondence to mass communication, detailing the rise of the Australasian women's advocacy press. Soon after *Dawn*'s launch, a Tasman newspaper market flourished, rivalled only by the British and American feminist press in its variety and proliferation. Examining the filaments that connected writers, editors, and readers, the chapter shows how cooperative production and communal consumption engendered transnational solidarity, if not always collective action. It also probes the racial, geographic, and ideological limits of Australasian publications, finding that the worldview presented to readers was neither as expansive nor as cosmopolitan as its producers and later historians have claimed.

Ties between suffragists were not only constituted discursively but forged and sustained by mobile activists. Chapter 5 centres on three journeys: Catherine Spence's 1893–94 tour of North America, Kate Sheppard's return to the United Kingdom in 1894–95, and the suffragist and temperance advocate Elizabeth Webb Nicholls' missionary expeditions throughout Australia's federal decade. Reassessing their adventures, it unsettles heroic narratives about the women who travelled to teach their metropolitan sisters and complicates typologies of political tourism that normalise the experiences of hyper-mobile elites. Concluding in the 1920s, when feminists began to reassess the suffragists' legacy, *Distant Sisters* ends with an exploration of the shame felt by women like Australian novelist Miles Franklin and New Zealand journalist Jessie Mackay at their forebears' inability to fulfil their promises of international leadership. In retracing the networks that allowed enfranchised Australasian women to envisage a future of international leadership and led them to issue heartfelt apologies in globally circulated publications, it emphasises the fragility of liberal internationalism, the sense of hope that allowed the movement to flourish, and how such connections altered women's lives, elite and ordinary alike.

While indebted to a generation of Australasian historians' insistence on understanding and explaining antipodean history in a global context – a process that has refigured colonial and national histories on both sides of the Tasman – this book contends that the opposite is also true. Australian and New Zealand suffragists provide an ideal platform from which to interrogate familiar national and international histories. The stories of their search for connection – from the quotidian experiences of WCTU members in dusty colonial towns to the adventures of the movement's globetrotting luminaries – unsettle the creeping primacy of the nation in antipodean suffrage history. At the same time, they reveal much about the obstacles facing those who thought and acted across borders at the turn of the twentieth century. Attending to their histories not only casts new light on both settler nations' founding myths but also offers a productive challenge to celebratory accounts of global connection at the fin de siècle.

Notes

1 Applying the term feminism to turn-of-the-century debates about the woman question is, strictly speaking, an anachronism. Feminism did not enter the Australasian vernacular as a term to describe efforts to expand women's rights until the 1910s. Even then, the term was contested by those within the movement. However, following Nancy Cott's and Linda Gordon's discussion of applying the term retrospectively to describe women's civic and political activities without 'attributing transhistorical content to feminism', I follow the understanding that 'feminism is a critique of male supremacy, formed and offered in the light of a will to change it, which in turn assumes a conviction that it is changeable'. N. F. Cott, 'What's in a name? The limits of "social feminism;" or, expanding the vocabulary of women's history', *Journal of American History*, 76:3 (1989), 826; L. Gordon, 'What's new in women's history', in T. De Lauretis (ed.), *Feminist Studies/Critical Studies* (Bloomington: Indiana University Press, 1986), p. 29. See also L. Delap, 'The "woman question" and the origins of feminism', in G. Steadman Jones and G. Claeys (eds), *The Cambridge History of Nineteenth-Century Political Thought* (Cambridge: Cambridge University Press, 2011), pp. 319–48.
2 *Australian Woman's Sphere (AWS)*, 10 October 1902, p. 218.
3 *Prohibitionist*, 25 November 1893, p. 3. While women across the British Empire took heart from Australasia's successful suffrage movements, articulating notions of imperial citizenship was unusual for Sheppard and her contemporaries. As Sharon Crozier-De Rosa has pointed out, antipodean suffragists, despite benefitting from their status as imperial citizens, usually insisted on broader international identity. Only in the 1910s would conservative groups, like the Australian Women's National League, draw consistently on the rhetoric of imperial duty, seeking to shame women

voters into acting as a bulwark against domestic and international radicalism by acting as loyal British-Australians. See S. Crozier-De Rosa, 'The national and the transnational in British anti-suffragists' views of Australian women voters', *History Australia*, 10:3 (2013), 51–64; S. Crozier-De Rosa, *Shame and the Anti-Feminist Backlash: Britain, Ireland and Australia, 1890–1920* (New York: Routledge, 2018), pp. 93–111.

4 *AWS*, 10 October 1902, p. 218.

5 *Commonwealth Franchise Act 1902* (Cth), s. 4. Māori were included in the Commonwealth electorate. The decision was both a shibboleth from the early Federation conventions at which New Zealand delegates had made Māori citizenship a precondition of their agreeing to join the Commonwealth and a testament to the settler notion that Māori were 'racially superior' to Aboriginal people. A. Woollacott, *Settler Society in the Australian Colonies: Self-Government and Imperial Culture* (Oxford: Oxford University Press, 2015), pp. 203–4. New Zealand's Electoral Act 1893 nevertheless entrenched a system of indigenous parliamentary seats, established in 1867, that separated those the state deemed Māori from the general electorate until 1975 (when Māori were permitted to choose between the Māori and general electoral rolls). T. Ballantyne, 'The state, politics, and power, 1769–1893', in G. Byrnes (ed.), *The New Oxford History of New Zealand* (Melbourne: Oxford University Press, 2009), pp. 115–17, 122–4.

6 J. Keating, 'Review article: *Mary Lee*; *How Australia Led the Way*; *You Daughters of Freedom*', *Australian Journal of Biography and History*, 2 (2019), 140–1; see, for example, *Evening News*, 16 July 1895, p. 6; 5 March 1898, p. 5; *AWS*, October 1900, cover page; *Sydney Morning Herald* (*SMH*), 11 September 1901, p. 5.

7 In 1936, 59.3 per cent of the Pākehā population was urban, compared with 11.2 per cent of Māori. Before then, reliable figures about urban Māori are hard to obtain, but the percentage of Māori dwelling in towns and cities *c*. 1890 would have been much lower. M. King, *The Penguin History of New Zealand* (Auckland: Viking, rev. edn, 2004), p. 473. See also A. Ballara, 'Wāhine rangatira: Māori women of rank and their role in the women's Kotahitanga movement of the 1890s', *New Zealand Journal of History*, 27:2 (1993), 127–39; M. Johnson, 'Chiefly women: Queen Victoria, Meri Mangakahia, and the Māori Parliament', in S. Carter and M. Nugent (eds), *Mistress of Everything: Queen Victoria in Indigenous Worlds* (Manchester: Manchester University Press, 2016), pp. 228–45; T. Rei, *Maori Women and the Vote* (Wellington: Huia Publishers, 1993).

8 Following convention, when referring to Aboriginal Australians and Torres Strait Islanders I capitalise Indigenous, but not when referring to the original inhabitants of other continents. The history of Indigenous people's voting rights in Australia is complicated, reflecting settler uncertainties regarding their status as British subjects and twentieth-century efforts to preclude them from exercising their franchise. These restrictions varied over time and by location, but largely ended by 1962 at the federal level and 1965 in the states. J. Cooper, 'In the beginning were words: Aboriginal people and the franchise', *Journal of Australian Studies*, 42:4 (2018), 428–44; N. G. Parkinson, 'Impersonating a voter: Constructions of race, and conceptions of subjecthood in the franchise of colonial New South Wales, *c*. 1850–1865', *Journal of Imperial*

and *Commonwealth History*, 47:4 (2019), 652–75. Much has been written about the ignorance on the part of the white women's movement of their Indigenous counterparts. For a survey of this literature, see J. Carey, '"Wanted! A real white Australia": The women's movement, whiteness and the settler colonial project, 1900–1940', in F. Bateman and L. Pilkington (eds), *Studies in Settler Colonialism: Politics, Identity and Culture* (Basingstoke: Palgrave Macmillan, 2011), pp. 122–39.

9   J. Curtin, 'New Zealand: A country of firsts in women's political rights', in S. Franceschet *et al.* (eds), *The Palgrave Handbook of Women's Political Rights* (London: Palgrave Macmillan, 2019), pp. 129–35; S. Scalmer, 'The history of social movements in Australia', in S. Berger and H. Nehring (eds), *The History of Social Movements in Global Perspective* (London: Palgrave Macmillan, 2017), pp. 335–40.

10 A. Rees, 'Rebel handmaidens: Transpacific histories and the limits of transnationalism', in A. Clark *et al.* (eds), *Transnationalism, Nationalism, and Australian History* (Singapore: Palgrave Macmillan, 2017), p. 51; P. Mein Smith *et al.*, *Remaking the Tasman World* (Christchurch: Canterbury University Press, 2008).

11 State Library of New South Wales, Sydney (hereafter SLNSW), MLMSS186/13/535–41, Mary Lee to Lady Mary Windeyer, 23 September 1892; SLNSW, AL34, Lee to Windeyer, 11 October 1892; SLNSW, MLA2272/73, Arthur Rae to Rose Scott, 20 December 1893.

12 *New Zealand Herald* (*NZH*), 12 October 1893, p. 5; SLNSW, M2309, Vida Goldstein, Autograph Book January–June 1902, p. 41.

13 J. Adams, *Women and the Vote: A World History* (Oxford: Oxford University Press, 2014), p. 119; J. Devaliant, *Kate Sheppard: A Biography* (Auckland: Penguin Books, 1992), pp. 132–43; C. Wright, '"A splendid object lesson": A transnational perspective on the birth of the Australian nation', *Journal of Women's History*, 26:4 (2014), 12–36; C. Wright, *You Daughters of Freedom: The Australians Who Won the Vote and Inspired the World* (Melbourne: Text Publishing, 2018).

14 Wright, 'A splendid object lesson', 12, 25.

15 A. Woollacott, 'Australian women's metropolitan activism: From suffrage, to imperial vanguard, to Commonwealth feminism', in I. C. Fletcher *et al.* (eds), *Women's Suffrage in the British Empire: Citizenship, Nation, and Race* (London: Routledge, 2000), p. 208.

16 See especially B. Brookes, *A History of New Zealand Women* (Wellington: Bridget Williams Books, 2016), 113–44; P. Grimshaw, *Women's Suffrage in New Zealand* (Auckland: Auckland University Press, rev. edn, 1987); S. Magarey, *Passions of the First Wave Feminists* (Sydney: UNSW Press, 2001); A. Oldfield, *Woman Suffrage in Australia: A Gift or a Struggle?* (Cambridge: Cambridge University Press, 1992).

17 J. Carlier, 'A forgotten instance of women's international organising: The transnational feminist networks of the Women's Progressive Society (1890) and the International Women's Union (1893–1898)', in O. Janz and D. Schönpflug (eds), *Gender History in a Transnational Perspective: Biographies, Networks, Gender Orders* (New York: Berghahn, 2014), pp. 78–9.

18 E. C. DuBois, *Woman Suffrage and Women's Rights* (New York: New York University Press, 1998), p. 172.

19 Ballantyne, 'The state, politics, and power', pp. 101–5; R. Hill, 'Settler colonialism in New Zealand', in E. Cavanagh and L. Veracini (eds), *The Routledge Handbook of Settler Colonialism* (London: Routledge, 2016), pp. 391–408.

20 Tasmania was an exception, delaying manhood suffrage until 1900. Ballantyne, 'The state, politics, and power', pp. 112–23; A. Brett, 'Colonial and provincial separation movements in Australia and New Zealand, 1856–65', *Journal of Imperial and Commonwealth History*, 47:1 (2019), 51–6.

21 D. Denoon et al., *A History of Australia, New Zealand and the Pacific* (Oxford: Blackwell, 2000), pp. 190–247. See especially M. Bellanta, 'Rethinking the 1890s', in A. Bashford and S. Macintyre (eds), *The Cambridge History of Australia, Volume 1: Indigenous and Colonial Australia* (Melbourne: Cambridge University Press, 2013), pp. 218–41; J. Docker, *The Nervous Nineties: Australian Cultural Life in the 1890s* (Melbourne: Oxford University Press, 1991); M. Hearn, '"Originally French but afterwards cosmopolitan": Australians interpret the fin de siècle', *Journal of Australian Studies*, 43:3 (2019), 365–80; S. Magarey et al. (eds), *Debutante Nation: Feminism Contests the 1890s* (Sydney: Allen and Unwin, 1993); B. Scates, *A New Australia: Citizenship, Radicalism and the New Republic* (Cambridge: Cambridge University Press, 1997). In New Zealand, there is less of a consensus that the 1890s constituted a moment of social and political ferment. Nevertheless, for some historians, the era was marked by democratisation, ideological contestation, and change. See, for example, J. Binney with V. O'Malley, 'The quest for survival, 1890–1920', in A. Anderson et al. (eds), *Tangata Whenua: An Illustrated History* (Wellington: Bridget Williams Books, 2014), pp. 290–310; E. Olssen, *Building the New World: Work, Politics and Society in Caversham 1880s–1920s* (Auckland: Auckland University Press, 1995), pp. 155–206; B. Brookes et al. (eds), *Sites of Gender: Women, Men & Modernity in Southern Dunedin, 1890–1939* (Auckland: Auckland University Press, 2003).

22 R. Arnold, 'The Australasian peoples and their world, 1888–1915', in K. Sinclair (ed.), *Tasman Relations: New Zealand and Australia, 1788–1988* (Auckland: Auckland University Press, 1987), pp. 53–62.

23 Bellanta, 'Rethinking the 1890s', p. 220; Brookes, *A History of New Zealand Women*, pp. 122–70.

24 For an overview of these forces and their effects on the Victorian world, see J. Osterhammel, *The Transformation of the World: A Global History of the Nineteenth Century*, trans. P. Camilleri (Princeton: Princeton University Press, 2014) and the essays in Emily S. Rosenberg (ed.), *A World Connecting, 1871–1945* (Cambridge: Belknap Press, 2012).

25 Australia was accorded Dominion status in 1901 and New Zealand in 1907. J. Belich, *Paradise Reforged: A History of the New Zealanders from the 1880s to the Year 2000* (Auckland: Allen Lane, 2001), pp. 53–87; J. Belich, *Replenishing the Earth: The Settler Revolution and the Rise of the Anglo-World, 1783–1939* (Oxford: Oxford University Press, 2009), pp. 206–9, 364–8; A. Loughheed, 'International transactions and foreign commerce', in W. Vamplew (ed.), *Australians: Historical Statistics* (Sydney: Fairfax, Syme, and Weldon, 1987), pp. 188–96; Mein Smith et al., *Remaking the Tasman World*, pp. 81–5.

26 C. Holbrook, '"What sort of nation?" A cultural history of Australians and their Federation', *History Compass*, 15:11 (2017), 4–6.

27 The WCTU was spelt 'Woman's' in America and Australia and 'Women's' in New Zealand. Ever adaptable, World's WCTU president Frances Willard ruled 'it is

not necessary to use the singular form of the word, and many prefer the plural'. F. E. Willard, *Do Everything: A Handbook for the World's White Ribboners* (Chicago: Woman's Temperance Publishing Association, 1895), p. 108.

28 *Prohibitionist*, 9 December 1893, p. 3. See, for example, *Englishwoman's Review*, 16 July 1894, pp. 166–9; C. H. Spence, 'South Australia's victory for adult suffrage', *Canadian Magazine*, 5:3 (1895), 276–7; M. E. Wolstenholme, 'Le mouvement féministe en Australie', *Revue Politique et Parlementaire*, 15 (January–March 1898), 520–45. These texts, and subsequent accounts written by Sheppard, Goldstein, and William Sidney Smith – the New Zealand WCTU's publisher and an important ally in the suffrage movement – trouble Jad Adams' assertion that those who wrote the histories of women's enfranchisement were not usually 'the people who did the most for women's suffrage'. Adams, *Women and the Vote*, pp. 4–5; V. Goldstein, *Woman Suffrage in Australia* (London: International Woman Suffrage Alliance, 1908); K. Sheppard, *Woman Suffrage in New Zealand* (London: International Woman Suffrage Alliance, 1907); W. S. Smith, *Outlines of the Women's Franchise Movement in New Zealand* (Christchurch: Whitcombe & Tombs, 1905).

29 W. P. Reeves, *State Experiments in Australia and New Zealand, Volume 1* (London: Grant Richards, 1902), pp. 103–42; R. Dalziel, 'Presenting the enfranchisement of New Zealand women abroad', in C. Daley and M. Nolan (eds), *Suffrage & Beyond: International Feminist Perspectives* (Auckland: Auckland University Press, 1994), pp. 46–51; T. McKenzie, 'William Pember Reeves, 1857–1932', *Kōtare: New Zealand Notes & Queries*, 7:3 (2008), 46.

30 M. Lake, 'Feminist history as national history: Writing the political history of women', *Australian Historical Studies*, 27:106 (1996), 157. The extent to which maternal citizenship was a diminution of the suffragists' goals or a pragmatic politics that allowed feminists to achieve radical ends remains contested, but I follow Marilyn Lake's argument that maternalist rhetoric presaged the extension of antipodean 'state socialism' to white women. M. Lake, 'State socialism for Australian mothers: Andrew Fisher's radical maternalism in its international and local contexts', *Labour History*, 102 (2012), 55–70; Magarey, *Passions of the First Wave*, pp. 171–92. For examples of these interwar women's histories, see L. Brown et al. (eds), *A Book of South Australia: Women in the First Hundred Years* (Adelaide: Women's Centenary Council of SA, 1936); F. S. Eldershaw (ed.), *The Peaceful Army: A Memorial to the Pioneer Women of Australia, 1788–1938* (Sydney: Women's Executive Committee and Advisory Council of Australia's 150th Anniversary Celebrations, 1938); H. M. Simpson, *The Women of New Zealand* (Wellington: Department of Internal Affairs, 1940).

31 Even the most comprehensive of these, Patricia Grimshaw's *Women's Suffrage in New Zealand*, drew primarily on colonial sources to rebut Reeves' gift theory and prove that the Electoral Act 1893 was the result of both parliamentary politics and an extra-parliamentary campaign for women's enfranchisement. See also J. E. Cobb, 'The women's movement in New South Wales, 1880–1914' (PhD thesis, University of New England, 1966); W. M. Ross, 'Votes for women in Western Australia', *Western Australian Historical Society Journal and Proceedings*, 4:4 (1952), 44–54; D. Scott, 'Woman suffrage: The movement in Australia', *Journal of the Australian Royal Society*, 53:4 (1969), 299–322.

32 A. Curthoys, 'We've just started making national histories and you want us to stop already?', in A. Burton (ed.), *After the Imperial Turn: Thinking with and Through the Nation* (Durham: Duke University Press, 2003), pp. 79-80; G. Millar, 'Women's lives, feminism and the *New Zealand Journal of History*', *New Zealand Journal of History*, 52:2 (2018), 139-40.

33 A. Summers, *Damned Whores and God's Police: The Colonization of Women in Australia* (Melbourne: Penguin Books, 1975), p. 358; Cobb, 'The women's movement', pp. 182-3.

34 See, for example, Oldfield, *Woman Suffrage in Australia*; S. Coney, *Standing in the Sunshine: A History of New Zealand Women Since They Won the Vote* (Auckland: Viking, 1993). Two exceptions are J. Allen, 'The "feminisms" of the early women's movements, 1850-1920', *Refractory Girl*, 17 (1979), 10-16; and I. Tyrrell, 'International aspects of the women's temperance movement in Australia: The influence of the American WCTU, 1882-1914', *Journal of Religious History*, 12:3 (1983), 284-304.

35 A. Sneider, 'The new suffrage history: Voting rights in international perspective', *History Compass*, 8:7 (2010), 692.

36 E. C. DuBois, 'Women suffrage around the world: Three phases of suffragist internationalism', in Daley and Nolan (eds), *Suffrage & Beyond*, pp. 252-74; P. Grimshaw, 'Women's suffrage in New Zealand revisited: Writing from the margins', in Daley and Nolan (eds), *Suffrage & Beyond*, pp. 25-41.

37 M. Threlkeld, 'Twenty years of *Worlds of Women*: Leila Rupp's impact on the history of US women's internationalism', *History Compass*, 15:6 (2017), 1-13. Highlights of this scholarship include N. Berkovitch, *From Motherhood to Citizenship: Women's Rights and International Organizations* (Baltimore: Johns Hopkins University Press, 1999); M. Bosch with A. Kloosterman (eds), *Politics and Friendship: Letters from the International Woman Suffrage Alliance, 1902-1942* (Columbus: Ohio State University Press, 1990); M. H. McFadden, *Golden Cables of Sympathy: The Transatlantic Sources of Nineteenth-Century Feminism* (Lexington: University Press of Kentucky, 1999); L. J. Rupp, *Worlds of Women: The Making of an International Women's Movement* (Princeton: Princeton University Press, 1997); I. Tyrrell, *Woman's World/Woman's Empire: The Woman's Christian Temperance Union in International Perspective, 1880-1930* (Chapel Hill: University of North Carolina Press, 1991).

38 J. Hannam, 'International dimensions of women's suffrage: "At the crossroads of several interlocking identities"', *Women's History Review*, 14:3-4 (2005), 550; I. Tyrrell, *Reforming the World: The Creation of America's Moral Empire* (Princeton: Princeton University Press, 2010), pp. 75-6.

39 See, for example, L. Edwards and M. Roces (eds), *Women's Suffrage in Asia: Gender, Nationalism and Democracy* (New York: Routledge, 2004); Fletcher et al. (eds), *Women's Suffrage in the British Empire*; A. L. Sneider, *Suffragists in an Imperial Age: U.S. Expansion and the Woman Question, 1870-1929* (New York: Oxford University Press, 2008).

40 J. Reinisch, 'Introduction: Agents of internationalism', *Contemporary European History*, 25:2 (2016), 196. Recent collections on turn-of-the-century women's internationalism include B. Bush and J. Purvis (eds), 'Connecting women's histories: The local and the global', Special Issue, *Women's History Review*, 25:4 (2016); F. de Haan *et*

al. (eds), *Women's Activism: Global Perspectives from the 1890s to the Present* (Oxford: Routledge, 2013); Janz and Schönpflug (eds), *Gender History in a Transnational Perspective*; C. Midgley et al. (eds), *Women in Transnational History: Connecting the Local and the Global* (London: Routledge, 2016); I. Sharp and M. Stibbe (eds), 'Women's international activism during the inter-war period, 1919–1939', Special Issue, *Women's History Review*, 26:2 (2017).

41 See, for example, L. Edwards and M. Roces, 'Introduction: Orienting the global women's suffrage movement', in Edwards and Roces (eds), *Women's Suffrage in Asia*, pp. 1–23; M. Sinha, D. J. Guy, and A. Woollacott, 'Introduction: Why feminisms and internationalism?', *Gender & History*, 10:3 (1998), 345–57. Most recently, the introduction to the *Journal of Women's History*'s special issue on the Nineteenth Amendment borrowed Daley and Nolan's title, yet the papers within largely eschewed the original's outlook. E. Camiscioli and J. H. Quataert, 'Editorial note: Suffrage and beyond: Celebrating women's history', *Journal of Women's History*, 32:1 (2020), 7–10. Early exceptions include books by Richard Evans and Ross Evans Paulson, while new work suggests that the dominance of transatlantic histories is ending. R. J. Evans, *The Feminists: Women's Emancipation Movements in Europe, America and Australasia 1840–1920* (London: Croon Helm, 1977); S. Mukherjee, *Indian Suffragettes: Female Identities and Transnational Networks* (Oxford: Oxford University Press, 2018); R. E. Paulson, *Women's Suffrage and Prohibition: A Comparative Study of Equality and Social Control* (Glenview: Scott, Foresman, and Company, 1973); A. Stevenson, 'Imagining women's suffrage: Frontier landscapes and the transnational print culture networks of Australia, New Zealand, and the United States', *Pacific Historical Review*, 87:4 (2018), 638–66.

42 S. Berger and S. Scalmer, 'The transnational activist: An introduction', in S. Berger and S. Scalmer (eds), *The Transnational Activist: Transformations and Comparisons from the Anglo-World Since the Nineteenth Century* (Cham: Palgrave Macmillan, 2018), p. 20. Despite the prominent roles that New Zealanders played in interwar organisations like the British Commonwealth League and Pan-Pacific Women's Association, with few exceptions the country's historians have paid little attention to women's overseas activism. See A. J. Laurie, 'A transnational conference romance: Elsie Andrews, Hildegarde Kneeland, and the Pan-Pacific Women's Association', *Journal of Lesbian Studies*, 13:4 (2009), 395–414; D. Page, 'Women and nationality: Feminist organisations in the inter-war period', in B. Brookes et al. (eds), *Women in History: Essays on European Women in New Zealand* (Wellington: Allen and Unwin/Port Nicholson Press, 1986), pp. 157–75; F. Paisley, 'Performing "New Zealand" Māori and Pākehā delegates at the Pan-Pacific Women's Conference, Hawai'i, 1934', *New Zealand Journal of History*, 38: 1 (2004), 22–38.

43 J. J. Matthews, 'Modern nomads and national film history: The multi-continental career of J. D. Williams', in A. Curthoys and M. Lake (eds), *Connected Worlds: History in Transnational Perspective* (Canberra: ANU Press, 2005), p. 167. See, especially, Curthoys and Lake (eds), *Connected Worlds*; D. Deacon et al. (eds), *Transnational Ties: Australian Lives in the World* (Canberra: ANU Press, 2008); D. Deacon et al. (eds), *Transnational Lives: Biographies of Global Modernity, 1700–Present* (New York: Palgrave Macmillan, 2010); F. Paisley, *Glamour in the Pacific: Cultural Internationalism*

and *Race Politics in the Women's Pan-Pacific* (Honolulu: University of Hawai'i Press, 2009); Tyrrell, *Woman's World*; A. Woollacott, *To Try Her Fortune in London: Australian Women, Colonialism and Modernity* (New York: Oxford University Press, 2001); A. Woollacott, *Race and the Modern Exotic: Three 'Australian' Women on Global Display* (Melbourne: Monash University Press, 2011).

44 B. Caine, 'International links', in B. Caine et al. (eds), *Australian Feminism: A Companion* (Melbourne: Oxford University Press, 1998), pp. 158–67; M. Lake, 'Women's international leadership', in J. Damousi et al. (eds), *Diversity in Leadership: Australian Women, Past and Present* (Canberra: Australian National University Press, 2014), pp. 71–90; N. Campo and M. Lake, 'International activism and organisation', *The Encyclopedia of Women & Leadership in Twentieth Century Australia*, http://womenaustralia.info/leaders/biogs/WLE0200b.htm (accessed 27 August 2018). In *You Daughters of Freedom*, Clare Wright considers these years through a national lens, focusing on the reception of Australian activists in Britain between 1905 and 1911.

45 Since 1993, women's histories have seldom featured in the *New Zealand Journal of History*, the country's premier site for historical debate, and suffrage not at all. As Grace Millar notes, Barbara Brookes' *A History of New Zealand Women* (2016) may prove transformative, but it too overlooks pre-war feminists' international endeavours. Millar, 'Feminism and the *NZJH*', 134–41.

46 P. Grimshaw, 'Settler anxieties, indigenous peoples, and women's suffrage in the colonies of Australia, New Zealand, and Hawai'i, 1888 to 1902', *Pacific Historical Review*, 69:4 (2000), 553–72; Sneider, *Suffragists in an Imperial Age*; A. Stevenson, 'Harriet Clisby's "Sketches of Australia": Travel writing and colonial refigurations in Boston's *Woman's Journal*', *Women's History Review*, 27:5 (2018), 837–57; Stevenson, 'Imagining women's suffrage', 638–66.

47 J. Coleman, *Polly Plum: A Firm and Earnest Woman's Advocate, Mary Ann Colclough 1836–1885* (Dunedin: Otago University Press, 2017); Woollacott, *Settler Society in the Australian Colonies*; C. Wright, *The Forgotten Rebels of Eureka* (Melbourne: Text Publishing, 2013).

48 S. Crozier-De Rosa and V. Mackie, *Remembering Women's Activism* (New York: Routledge, 2019), p. 46; Hannam, 'International dimensions', 554; B. Caine, 'Vida Goldstein and the English militant campaign', *Women's History Review*, 2:3 (1993), 363–76; M. Lake, *Progressive New World: How Settler Colonialism and Transpacific Exchange Shaped American Reform* (Cambridge, MA: Harvard University Press, 2019), pp. 136–68; C. Millar, 'The making of a feminist: Bessie Rischbieth encounters the English suffragettes', *Lilith*, 12 (2003), 78–94; R. Nicholls, *The Women's Parliament: The National Council of the Women of New Zealand 1896–1920* (Wellington: Victoria University Press, 1996), pp. 89–95; A. Nugent, 'Nellie Alma Martel and the Women's Social and Political Union, 1905–09', *Hecate*, 31:1 (2005), 142–59; L. Trethewey and K. Whitehead, 'Beyond centre and periphery: Transnationalism in two teacher/suffragettes' work', *History of Education*, 32:5 (2003), 547–59; Wright, *You Daughters*.

49 L. Delap and M. DiCenzo, 'Transatlantic print culture: The Anglo-American feminist press & emerging "modernities"', in A. Ardis and P. Collier (eds), *Transatlantic Print Culture, 1880–1940* (London: Palgrave Macmillan, 2008), p. 53.

50 K. Pickles, 'Transnational history and cultural cringe: Some issues for consideration in New Zealand, Australia and Canada', *History Compass*, 9:9 (2011), 657–73. These inhibitions are not all unique to Britain's former settler colonies. See S. Pedersen, 'Comparative history and women's history: Explaining convergence and divergence', in A. Cova (ed.), *Comparative Women's History: New Approaches* (Boulder: Social Sciences Monographs, 2006), pp. 128–32.

51 Wright, *You Daughters*, pp. 461–3.

52 *International Council of Women Report of Transactions during the Third Quinquennial Term Terminating with the Third Quinquennial Meeting, Volume II* (Boston: International Council of Women, 1909), pp. 60–4.

53 For a comprehensive survey of this scholarship, see Z. Laidlaw, 'Breaking Britannia's bounds? Law, settlers, and space in Britain's imperial historiography', *The Historical Journal*, 55:3 (2012), 807–30; G. Curless *et al.*, 'Editors' introduction: Networks in imperial history', *Journal of World History*, 26:4 (2015), 705–32.

54 T. Ballantyne, *Webs of Empire: Locating New Zealand's Colonial Past* (Wellington: Bridget Williams Books, 2012), p. 49; T. Ballantyne, 'Rereading the archive and opening up the nation state: Colonial knowledge in South Asia and beyond', in Burton (ed.), *After the Imperial Turn*, pp. 112–13; T. Ballantyne, *Entanglements of Empire: Missionaries, Māori, and the Question of the Body* (Auckland: Auckland University Press, 2015), p. 17; A. Lester, 'Imperial circuits and networks', *History Compass*, 4:1 (2006), 124, 133.

55 In 2019, for example, Alison Bashford observed that 'for historians taught and researching from an Australian base, "transnational" is now an orthodoxy [so entrenched that] … the nation no longer holds any historiographical monopoly'. Bashford, 'On nations and states: A reflection on "Thinking the Empire Whole"', *History Australia*, 16:4 (2019), 638–9. I discuss such concerns further in J. Keating, 'Piecing together suffrage internationalism: Place, space, and connected histories of Australasian women's activism', *History Compass*, 16:8 (2018), 6.

56 R. J. Anderson, 'Te kāinga tapu: Māori cultures of travel, 1888–1918' (MA thesis, University of Auckland, 2018), pp. 9–14; Curthoys, 'Stop already?'; N. Green, *The Limits of Transnationalism* (Chicago: University of Chicago Press, 2019), pp. 52–5; A. Simmonds *et al.*, 'Testing the boundaries: Reflections on transnationalism in Australian history', in Simmonds *et al.* (eds), *Transnationalism, Nationalism and Australian History*, pp. 1–14.

57 F. Paisley, 'The spoils of opportunity: Janet Mitchell and Australian internationalism in the interwar Pacific', *History Australia*, 13:4 (2016), 577, 590; F. Berry, '"Home allies": Female networks, tensions, and conflicted loyalties in India and Van Diemen's Land, 1826–1849', *Journal of World History*, 26:4 (2015), 757–84.

58 Wright, 'A splendid object lesson', 13.

59 Ballantyne, *Webs of Empire*, pp. 178–89; Rees, 'Rebel handmaidens', p. 53. The 1893 suffrage petition is one of three 'constitutional documents' on display at the National Library of New Zealand. 'He tohu: About', *The National Library of New Zealand*, https://natlib.govt.nz/he-tohu/about (accessed 2 May 2019).

60 See, for example, Girton College Library, Cambridge, P396.3/18, 'Address on the subject of woman suffrage, Wellington, February 1889'.

61 The records left by leading suffragists like Anna Stout and Margaret Sievwright in New Zealand and Maybanke Wolstenholme, Louisa Lawson, and Lady Mary and Margaret Windeyer in New South Wales are fragmentary, while most women and organisations that fought for the vote (the WCTU aside) in Victoria, Queensland, Western Australia, and Tasmania have few extant papers.

62 M. Nolan and C. Daley, 'International feminist perspectives on suffrage: An introduction', in Daley and Nolan (eds), *Suffrage & Beyond*, p. 14; J. Malcolm, 'A house of one's own', *New Yorker*, 5 June 1995, p. 65. On these women see, for example, A. Cooper et al., 'The landscape of gender politics: Place, people and two mobilisations', in B. Brookes et al. (eds), *Sites of Gender*, pp. 43–9; K. Deverall, 'They did not know their place: The politics of Annie Golding and Kate Dwyer', *Labour History*, 87 (2004), 31–48. Laura Schwartz offers a model of how to write these histories in *Feminism and the Servant Problem: Class and Domestic Labour in the Women's Suffrage Movement* (Cambridge: Cambridge University Press, 2019), see especially pp. 25–8, 59–89.

63 T. Ballantyne, 'From colonial collection to tribal knowledge base: Herries Beattie, Ngāi Tahu Whānui and the many lives of an archive', *Journal of Colonialism and Colonial History*, 20:2 (2019), 7–8; A. L. Stoler, *Along the Archival Grain: Epistemic Anxieties and Colonial Common Sense* (Princeton: Princeton University Press, 2010), 1; L. Patterson and A. Wanhalla, *He Reo Wāhine: Māori Women's Voices from the Nineteenth Century* (Auckland: Auckland University Press, 2017), pp. 1–9; A. Wanhalla, *Matters of the Heart: A History of Interracial Marriage in New Zealand* (Auckland: Auckland University Press, 2013), p. 14.

64 R. Mead, *How the Vote was Won: Woman Suffrage in the Western United States 1868-1914* (New York: New York University Press, 2004), pp. 13–14; F. Paisley, 'White settler colonialisms and the colonial turn: An Australian perspective', *Journal of Colonialism and Colonial History*, 4:3 (2004), paras 17–18.

65 Threlkeld, 'Twenty years of *Worlds of Women*', 7.

66 *Minutes of the National Woman's Christian Temperance Union at the Eighteenth Annual Meeting* (Chicago: Woman's Temperance Publishing Association, 1891), pp. 219–25; F. de Haan, 'A "truly international" archive for the women's movement (IAV, IIAV now Aletta): From its foundation in Amsterdam in 1935 to the return of its looted archives in 2003', *Journal of Women's History*, 16:4 (2004), 148–72.

67 DuBois, 'Suffrage around the world', 254.

1

For God and home and every land: Suffrage internationalism in the World's Woman's Christian Temperance Union

Early on 18 February 1898, Lillian Stevens, vice-president of the American Woman's Christian Temperance Union (WCTU), wired its Chicago headquarters from Manhattan. 'The unfavorable change came about seven o'clock. Service here Sunday; Evanston [Illinois] Thursday. God pity and comfort us.'[1] Her terse dispatch announced the death of Frances Willard, the World's WCTU's president, 'one of the most formidable and powerful political figures' in the United States and, arguably, the most famous woman in the world.[2] Since assuming the American presidency in 1879, Willard had been the subject of a cult of adoration. Her death from influenza, aged fifty-nine, elevated her to virtual sainthood, as members rushed to celebrate her 'beautiful life'.[3] The following week was a blur of activity. Mimicking the memorialisation of her fellow Illinoisan, Abraham Lincoln, a funeral train carried Willard's casket west, stopping for mourners to glimpse their beloved 'chieftain'. Before her interment, Willard lay in state at the Woman's Temple, a Chicago office building she envisaged as the union's 'Westminster Abbey, its West Point and its gold mine all in one'. Inside, thousands of women filed through a hall 'heavy with the perfume of a million flowers' to pay their final respects.[4]

Willard's funeral triggered a series of commemorations that unfolded across the empire she had built over the previous twenty-five years. Despite repeated promises to visit Australia and New Zealand, Willard never left the Northern Hemisphere.[5] Nevertheless, she was a vivid presence for the WCTU's antipodean members. From the union's formal arrival in Australasia in 1885, photographs of Willard had passed between branches, as had her innumerable speeches, circular letters, instructional manuals, and newspaper columns. After her death, a hastily written biography and two memorial editions of the American WCTU's newspaper, *Union Signal*, circulated the globe, filled with descriptions of her funeral.[6] In the following months, these served as touchstones for antipodean women, who staged miniature commemorations modelled on the original. In August 1898, the Auckland union held a memorial service beneath 'large framed photos of Miss Willard ... decorated with snowdrops and violets'. Four months later, the Adelaide WCTU congregated around a 'framed photo of Late Miss Willard draped in White and Heliotrope'.[7] Both services took their cue from the Chicago 'reception room' into which mourners had passed beneath 'purple and white bunting' to contemplate 'a large picture of Miss Willard ... decorated with white carnations'.[8]

Frances Willard's funeral services are a quintessential example of the infectious spirit and homogenising effect of the WCTU's internationalism. The belated Auckland and Adelaide commemorations were staged in modest halls rather than the grand Woman's Temple. Nevertheless, they demonstrated the adaptability that underpinned the union's growth. Ian Tyrrell, the union's foremost chronicler, characterises its rise as a form of American 'organizational imperialism'.[9] Established amid the 1873-74 Women's Crusade, a Midwestern anti-saloon campaign that catapulted women to leadership positions in the temperance movement, the WCTU concentrated on building a national presence. However, its members were soon swept along by the 'wave of world evangelisation' that transformed late nineteenth-century Protestantism.[10] Prompted by Willard's 1883 tour of the West Coast, which inspired her to take a trans-Pacific view of her mission, the union sent emissaries overseas. Their proposition was simple: a vision of a world liberated 'from the evils of alcohol and sexual subordination' allied with a model for reform.[11] Recognising that such goals required more than earnest 'parlour meetings', Willard divided the union's 'home protection' agenda into departments – ranging from food reform to franchise work – overseen by branch, regional, national, and world's superintendents. Like all successful international organisations, the World's executive permitted local idiosyncrasies, but its distinct structure enabled an early form of 'transnational collective activism'.[12] Seventy years before historians devised radial metaphors to describe the relationship between Britain and its colonies, Luella McWhirter, president of the Indiana WCTU, described the organisation thus: 'the Union is the hub; from it goes out the department spokes and all are symmetrically enclosed in the rim of the World's W.C.T.U.'[13]

Suffrage activism, more than any other aspect of the WCTU's agenda, challenges McWhirter's affirmation of the union's organisational and ideological coherence. In Australia and New Zealand, the union's centrality to the women's suffrage campaigns has been thoroughly documented. Whatever its exact role in each colony, historians agree that between the

1880s and 1900s, the union channelled suffrage propaganda and ideas about women's emancipation between branches and to and from that great 'rim', the World's WCTU.[14] Indeed, the WCTU's omnipresence in the Australasian suffrage campaigns has led historians to normalise the form it took in the colonies and to conclude that the processes that directed Frances Willard's memorial services helped members in their trailblazing campaigns to win the vote. However, as this chapter contends, the WCTU's role in the internationalisation of the women's suffrage movement was more complex and less coherent than has previously been described.

In *Woman's World/Woman's Empire* (1991), Tyrrell devotes a chapter to 'women, suffrage, and equality'. His work has a broad ambit, illustrating the 'ebb and flow of ideas, institutions, and personnel across national boundaries' rather than delving into the intricacies of the union's structure and its effects on members' activities.[15] By contrast, histories of the Australasian campaigns examine the colonial unions' organising strategies in depth, but gloss over their local mechanics and international influences. Yet, the World's WCTU was not a monolithic organisation composed of national and colonial representatives. Rather, it functioned as a complex, multi-tiered network, comprised of branches, colonial unions, and intercolonial and international executives, all of which operated simultaneously, if not always in unison.

Despite gesturing at the union's organisational hierarchy, historians have overlooked how the politics of suffrage campaigning unfolded in the union's local, intercolonial, and global 'layers'. Mirroring developments in imperial history, feminist historiography has emphasised the importance of drawing connections between local and global activism. Nevertheless, little of this work offers a blueprint for transcending the nation to consider all three categories in a single analytical frame.[16] Elizabeth Harvey's examination of the 'layered networks' that connected nineteenth-century imperial philanthropists is an exception. Guided by her argument that the 'layered nature' of transnational networks must be revealed to understand their operation, this chapter explores the relationships between local, intercolonial, and international suffrage activism in the WCTU. Separating these layers allows historians to substantiate nineteenth-century networks by showing how individual and organisational connections 'permeated various spheres: the local, national/intercolonial ... and imperial'.[17] Applying her approach to the WCTU casts the singularity of its antipodean chapters into relief. Furthermore, it reveals the forces that prevented Australasian members from propagating the methods that expedited their enfranchisement through its international channels.

Rather than privileging elite individuals' experiences, a risk of top-down approaches, the chapter begins with a comparison of branch life in Auckland and Adelaide. While the WCTU's success is attributed to the power of local democracy, embodied in the quiet radicalism of the parlour meeting, few historians have considered its fundamental unit, the branch.[18] Comparing the records of two branches integral to their respective suffrage campaigns, the first section explores how the WCTU's celebrated internationalism manifested in members' lives. Branch papers, as Anne Firor Scott argues, allow historians to fathom the 'gap between what the most articulate leaders wished to accomplish and what timid members of local groups were willing to undertake'.[19] These records contain selective accounts of ephemeral exchanges but still reveal much about members' plans and preoccupations. Rather than considering either city as a microcosm of their respective colonies, this chapter uses local records to illuminate the union's international hierarchies and to explain how previously hidden trans-Tasman links shaped members' experiences. Branch archives also testify to the importance of place and space in shaping members' activism. Locating each chapter within the social and physical geographies of its respective colony, the section concludes by explaining why Auckland members developed a more cosmopolitan outlook than their Adelaide counterparts and how members' differing fields of vision informed their suffrage activism.

Although the rhetoric of international solidarity echoed at WCTU meetings in Auckland and Adelaide, such sentiments dissipated soon after members' enfranchisement. Given union leaders' insistence that local work constituted an 'insignificant' component of the World's WCTU's 'mighty force', the rapidity with which members retreated from suffrage activism is surprising.[20] Their waning concern with the fortunes of external suffrage campaigns is only partly explained by self-interest. While political citizenship presented new challenges, union members remained invested in its other international campaigns, like the humanitarian response to the Armenian massacres of 1894–97, even when such endeavours were far removed from their quotidian existence.[21] Examining the union's intercolonial and international 'layers' reveals that despite the alacrity with which branches pursued the vote, ambivalence about women's enfranchisement pervaded the WCTU's upper echelons. Contradicting claims that the WCTU fortified intercolonial suffrage sentiments, the union's Australasian records reveal why interest in the movement's progress in other colonies dwindled.[22] Although the Australasian body began life with the demand for women's suffrage in

1891, members were reluctant to permit central intervention in colonial or state matters, which tempered its founders' enthusiasm for the reform.

Finally, switching focus to the World's WCTU, the last section uncovers the tensions that stymied Australasian members' attempts to discuss women's enfranchisement at its showpiece international conventions. World's WCTU missionaries legitimised and popularised suffrage activism among middle-class evangelicals in Australasia. Nevertheless, within a few years of their arrival, the pursuit of political citizenship had become a contentious subject in the American union and its sister organisation, the British Women's Temperance Association (BWTA). Willard's inner circle regarded women's enfranchisement as part of a 'blessed trinity of movements' – alongside prohibition and 'labor's uplift' – that constituted the union's core work, yet by the 1890s a new conservatism gripped the World's membership.[23] Whereas women in the antipodes embraced her famous axiom, 'Do-Everything', WCTU leaders elsewhere struggled to convince their compatriots that suffrage did not jeopardise temperance work. By focusing on the World's WCTU's triennial conventions, this chapter reveals how the union marginalised suffrage activists, and ultimately extinguished antipodean members' interest in suffrage as a universal project.

Global influences, local work: The WCTU in Auckland and Adelaide

Over the past fifty years, New Zealand and Australian historians have produced a comprehensive picture of the WCTU's operation, participation in women's suffrage movements, and place in colonial society. So much so that in 1975 Anne Summers complained that the union's meticulous record-keeping had fuelled an ahistorical inflation of its perceived importance in the women's movement.[24] Although a more balanced approach to the history of women and religion emerged over the following decade, prompting renewed interest in the WCTU, historians have not delved into the union's prodigious branch records to examine members' beliefs, experiences, and mentalities.[25] These sources offer the opportunity to go beyond filling gaps in the WCTU's past. Rather, scrutinising nodes within the union's vast whole can reveal much about the operation of the networks that linked geographically isolated communities of women with the late nineteenth-century world.

Examining the local and global mechanics of the Australasian women's suffrage movement through two urban WCTU branches yields a partial history. As everywhere, the WCTU was not the only organisation committed to winning votes for women in Auckland or Adelaide. The Women's Suffrage League played a greater role in the South Australian suffrage campaign, while the Auckland union's efforts faltered until the formation of the Women's Franchise League (WFL) in 1891. Both suffrage leagues mobilised working-class women more effectively than the WCTU.[26] Nevertheless, among the leadership at least, multi-memberships were common, and where the campaign for the vote was concerned, the divisions between these groups were minor. Furthermore, unlike the suffrage leagues, the WCTU enjoyed formal international ties. Thus, an examination of the union offers a unique opportunity to see how policies designed to encourage 'universal' work interacted with local priorities. Finally, the union was the most robust of the contemporary women's political organisations. While suffrage leagues disintegrated after winning the vote, WCTU branches remained intact, allowing a comparison of how members' attitudes to the international suffrage movement changed after their own enfranchisement. The WCTU's longevity has also ensured that its institutional history is well preserved. Here, as ever, the local and international intertwined. From their formation, branches received edicts from Chicago reminding them that 'every document issued should be filed away'.[27] The Auckland and Adelaide branches were unusually attentive to these instructions. A comparison with the Sydney branch, the oldest in Australasia, would have proved illuminating, but its records are sparse, making it difficult to draw useful conclusions.[28]

Despite their concurrent suffrage campaigns, Auckland and Adelaide were far from identical. By the end of the century, Adelaide was a bustling colonial capital and the third largest city in Australasia. With a population exceeding 133,000 in 1891 the city, home to almost half of South Australia's residents, was the heart of colonial life.[29] New Zealand had twice South Australia's population, but its residents were more scattered. From the 1860s, urban dwellers were divided between Auckland, Wellington, Christchurch, and Dunedin. In 1886, Auckland became New Zealand's largest city, boasting 57,000 residents. By Australian standards Auckland remained small, but its population doubled by 1906, a trajectory that saw it dwarf the southern cities.[30] Whereas Adelaide was home to the South Australian legislature, with the relocation of the colonial parliament to Wellington in 1865, Auckland lay several days' travel from the seat of government. As both branch archives show, the cities' demographics and proximity to political power had surprising effects on WCTU members' outlook and the scope of their activism.

Auckland's and Adelaide's WCTU branches were the first and last founded by Mary Clement Leavitt on her tour of Australasia. Beginning in Hawai'i in November 1884, Leavitt's 'round-the-world' mission lasted seven years and covered 97,308 miles across six continents.[31] The World's WCTU's first evangelist travelled alone, a vanguard of the roving missionary force envisaged when the United States union decided to globalise its agenda in 1883. Women had served as overseas missionaries since the creation of the American Board of Commissioners for Foreign Missions in 1810, but the World's WCTU represented a new stage in American cultural expansion. Whereas its short-lived predecessor, the International Woman's Temperance Union (1876), was designed as a confederation of national delegations, Frances Willard envisioned the World's union as a 'cohesive international force'. The terminological shift from 'international' to 'World's' signified her universalist ambition. Co-opting the principles that underpinned the success of the American union, the new organisation had a centralised bureaucracy and a global missionary corps, led by seasoned American evangelists and funded by local donors. Over the following decade, the efficacy of Willard's vision was borne out. By 1900, the union boasted half a million members across fifty countries.[32] However, in 1884 the World's WCTU remained a letterhead organisation. The first test of its adaptability lay before Leavitt in the Pacific.

Keenly aware of the stakes, Leavitt fretted about her prospects when she reached New Zealand in 1885. In *Union Signal* she described an underwhelming reception, attributing locals' coolness to their taste for alcohol 'which is far stronger and more universal than in any part of the United States'.[33] In hindsight, Leavitt's complaint appears misplaced. Her visit was an unalloyed success. When she arrived, Auckland – like most Australasian cities – already hosted branches of British and American temperance organisations.[34] Yet, despite the appeal of temperance for evangelical women, such organisations seldom prioritised their interests. In 1880, for example, women were excluded from Melbourne's International Temperance Conference.[35] Among the audiences Leavitt reached in 1885–86, the WCTU's articulation of a gendered consciousness centred on the home that linked global and local reform causes was refreshing. After several weeks in Auckland, she inaugurated a branch and enlisted 'more than eighty ladies'.[36] Over the following seven months she travelled south, establishing seven branches before anointing a local successor, Anne Ward, who founded seven more, boosting the WCTU's membership to 528 by 1886.[37]

Sixteen months after landing in Auckland, Leavitt concluded her Australasian tour in Adelaide, establishing a union on 8 April 1886. Reflecting the importance of personal relationships within the union, and the filaments that already connected Australasian branches, Leavitt appointed W. E. Rice of the Auckland branch as Adelaide's inaugural president.[38] Unlike in Auckland, Leavitt worked rapidly, leaving South Australia after five days. Rather than continue Leavitt's mission, the branch's twelve members waited for another round-the-world missionary visit.[39] Jessie Ackermann's arrival in June 1889 electrified the union. Whereas Leavitt had arrived exhausted by two years of uninterrupted work, Ackermann – described by the press as 'a lady in the prime of her life; tall, of good figure' and, crucially, in possession of a 'clear, ringing voice' – landed fresh from stopovers in New Zealand and Tasmania.[40] Within months of her arrival the Adelaide branch boasted 124 members, part of a recruitment drive that saw the union's South Australian membership swell to 1,112 during her visit.[41]

Over the following decade, the WCTU fell victim to its success. In Leavitt and Ackermann's absence, a lack of charismatic leadership was compounded by the onset of an economic depression. Between 1886 and 1891, Auckland's population fell for the first time since the mid-1860s' repatriation of thousands of imperial soldiers garrisoned in the city, as people left in search of work. After peaking at 165 in 1886, WCTU membership plummeted, plateauing at sixty-five members over the next decade.[42] Adelaide endured a more dramatic reverse. By 1894 its membership had halved, and it declined further throughout the 1890s. Branch fortunes reflected trends in their respective unions. From its peak in 1893, the South Australian WCTU suffered a decade of attrition. Members attributed the collapse to the depression, overlooking the fact that by forming twenty-one branches in two months Ackermann had overextended their resources. By 1902 its membership had declined from 1,832 members to 637, accounting for half of the 2,000 women who left the union across Australia.[43] By contrast, New Zealand's membership exploded from 700 to 1,610 between 1897 and 1900 as the depression eased and the advent of universal suffrage gave the temperance movement new political resonance.[44]

The Auckland and Adelaide unions occupied the same position in the WCTU's hierarchy, yet branch autonomy varied between the cities. In 1886, New Zealand's fifteen branches formed a colonial union. South Australia's twenty-three branches followed suit in 1889. Each branch paid dues to their respective colonial union, which served as a forum to discuss policy, coordinate campaigns, pool resources to contract speakers or purchase literature, and liaise with the World's WCTU. By 1891, the Adelaide branch also sat beneath the Australasian WCTU, a loose federation encompassing Australia's five colonial unions that ostensibly committed its members to combine their 'forces and funds' in the pursuit of the 'national' 'prohibition of the traffic in liquor, vice and opium, and the legal suppression of Gambling and Sabbath desecration'.[45] Despite its hierarchical structure, the WCTU's success, as Alan Atkinson argues, stemmed from its compatibility with the 'networks of family and neighbourhood which were the stuff of women's lives'.[46] Although members could not be compelled to follow central orders, this interpretation exaggerates the predominance of local concerns. In practice, New Zealand's scattered population afforded its branches greater freedom. The Auckland WCTU lay 400 kilometres from its nearest neighbour, and the New Zealand executive only met annually. By contrast, the proliferation of branches in Adelaide's suburbs – by 1895, thirteen branches lay within seven kilometres of the Adelaide union's rooms – led to the formation of 'district' executives in 1892. As contemporaries noted, the bureaucratism that underpinned its rise could easily 'dissipate the energies of the union'.[47] While Auckland members enjoyed their freedom from central oversight, district and colonial executives took charge of matters that lay beyond South Australian branches' territory. As a result, Adelaide members' horizons were limited to the leafy confines of the inner city.

In both cities, WCTU branches were enmeshed in local reform networks, yet Auckland's smaller population and the absence of competing branches gave the union a more prominent role in city life. From 1885, Auckland members sat on the city's peak temperance body and shared its newspaper, the *Leader* (1885–88).[48] In women's political circles, these connections were intimate. The union's leaders belonged to an influential Protestant feminist nexus that steered public debate on the 'woman question'. Within a decade, they had founded the WCTU, the Young Women's Christian Association (YWCA) (1885), the Auckland WFL (1891), and the Auckland Women's Political League (AWPL) (1894).[49] Although the WCTU was non-denominational, Methodists dominated its leadership, as they did in Adelaide. There, the WCTU was similarly entangled in the city's temperance circles, yet while Adelaide boasted more members per capita, the union was never the focal point of their political life. Like their Auckland counterparts, Adelaide branch members joined organisations like the Ladies' Social Purity Society (1883), the YWCA (1884), and the Women's Suffrage League (1888). These organisations' leaders – Mary Lee, Rosetta Birks, and Catherine Helen Spence – collaborated with the WCTU but remained outside its ranks, alienated by its overriding commitment to prohibition.[50]

Although the Auckland and Adelaide branches occupied different social and political positions, their records evince a similar quotidian experience for members. Under Frances Willard's leadership, the WCTU codified its operations, issuing manuals advising members on everything from recruitment to meeting protocol.[51] At her instruction, the Auckland and Adelaide unions held monthly gatherings that resembled church services. Meetings began by reading scripture selected by the American union and closed with a rendition of the union's hymn, the temperance doxology. Achievements were celebrated 'in the American fashion', with members waving their handkerchiefs in a 'Chautauqua salute', while the devout observed a noontide prayer hour, taking solace in joining a continuous 'chain of prayer encircling the world'. These tendrils of internationalism reached all members, who read aloud from each edition of *Union Signal*.[52] The intimacy of communal reading forged bonds between those present and, combined with the sharing of texts, helped women imagine themselves as part of the WCTU's colonial, national, and international 'layers'.[53] Signifiers of international identity were visual as well as textual. At the Auckland union's inaugural convention, members gathered before a Union Jack crossed with the 'Stars and Stripes', hung above the WCTU motto 'union is strength'. Such displays were commonplace. As Phillida Bunkle observes, affirmations of international connections constituted the 'highpoint' of WCTU gatherings, from branch meetings to Australasian conventions.[54]

Women in both branches were also united by a shared racial identity. Although the union did not officially discriminate on racial grounds, it is unlikely that either branch accommodated indigenous members. In Australia, unlike most WCTU outposts, Aboriginal women were considered 'too foreign ... to be active subjects of temperance'. Only in 1899, for example, did the South Australian union attempt interracial outreach, giving its superintendent for 'work among foreigners' responsibility for Indigenous women.[55] The situation was more complicated in Auckland. In 1891, branch and colonial president Annie Schnackenberg – a fluent Māori speaker – sent a banner emblazoned with Māori text to the World's WCTU's Boston convention, a 'classic colonialist move' designed to distinguish the settlers abroad.[56] However, Māori women's enfranchisement in 1893 drove the union to extend its intercultural engagement beyond appropriation. It swiftly employed bilingual organisers and by 1899 had enlisted 112 Māori members – 8 per cent of its membership.[57] Just four years after Schnackenberg delighted in Frances Willard's inability to read the New Zealand banner, her compatriots boasted that 'our WCTU work among Maoris has been sent all over the world'. Nevertheless, union members' attempts to incorporate 'our dark-skinned sisters' within their mission were far from beneficent.[58] Such efforts rested on what Maria Valverde terms their 'racialization of drink', whereby members deemed 'native races' easily corruptible by white men's drinking habits because they lacked the discipline to 'govern their consumption'.[59] Furthermore, the existence of segregated branches indicated an underlying tension in the union's project. So too did union leaders' desire to see Māori branches 'adapt themselves to the new methods of their pakeha friends', specifically to mould girls into domestic servants – an ambition many Māori resisted, considering it tantamount to 'slavery'.[60]

Mobility shaped Australasian WCTU members' identities as much as race and the participation in global rituals. Travelling members' easy assimilation into distant branches provided a practical demonstration of the 'universal sisterhood' evoked by the World's leadership.[61] As Catherine Bishop has argued of businesswomen, 'onward mobility' within Australasia has been underestimated. As well as the financial incentives that drove Bishop's subjects, Christian organisations like missionary training institutes and the WCTU enabled women to join the traffic that linked the Australasian settlements.[62] Equipped with letters of introduction, members had access to like-minded communities across the region, and attended meetings wherever they could. In 1888, 'bearing a letter of commendation', Auckland branch stalwart Hannah Main joined a WCTU meeting during a stay in Sydney and returned with 'greetings [for] the friends in Auckland'.[63] The existence of uniform departments opened avenues for inter-branch correspondence and allowed members to request the latest British and American literature.[64] Migrants settled easily into new branches and maintained correspondence with former colleagues or reported in person if they returned 'home'. Helen Dewar of the Auckland union moved to Queensland in the 1890s. After settling in Mount Morgan, she served as president of the local WCTU for three years. Dewar returned to Auckland in 1897, but her reputation remained such in Queensland that the press published original obituaries on her death in 1931.[65]

Such stories were common. Despite its isolation within New Zealand, Auckland was a gateway to the Pacific. By 1885 the city's leaders had secured its inclusion on the route to San Francisco, and Auckland doubled as a branch connection for the 'All-Red' route linking Britain's oceanic territories.[66] While these connections drew overseas visitors, the WCTU's cross-border network turned stopovers into prolonged stays. Although the neighbouring AWPL took a similar interest in world affairs, it received just one international visitor in the 1890s.[67] By contrast, the WCTU hosted twenty-three overseas guests and welcomed recruits from Queensland, New South Wales, and California. Such proximity to arterial shipping routes allowed Main to return to Sydney five times in the fifteen years after 1888, forming warm ties with the city's union members.[68]

Others followed suit, forging links with branches in Queensland, New South Wales, and South Australia.[69] Aucklanders not only incorporated WCTU business into their private travel but financed journeys they believed would enhance union work. In 1900, for example, the branch presented Mary Powell, New Zealand's delegate to the World's WCTU's Edinburgh convention, a 'gift of money' to allow her to travel 'from place to place to gain knowledge of temperance work'.[70]

Travel was woven into the fabric of the Auckland union, but it barely features in the Adelaide branch records. Although neither branch retained itemised financial records, between 1890 and 1893 Adelaide reported an average annual income of £115, compared with just £21 in Auckland.[71] Such assiduous fundraising allowed the Adelaide branch to pay delegates to attend all four Australasian WCTU conventions in the 1890s. Aside from these official trips, the branch minutes record few women whose experiences matched those of the peripatetic Aucklanders. Like dozens of their compatriots, in the early 1890s sisters Edith and Clara Goode joined the London Missionary Society in China but communicated little about their new lives to the Adelaide branch. Another missionary, Minnie Billings, left Adelaide for British New Guinea in 1894, but like the Goodes, she left no trace in the union's records.[72]

Intercolonial visitors, so often welcomed in Auckland, are also absent from the Adelaide minutes. During the 1890s, only two women identified as visitors from outside South Australia attended Adelaide meetings. A comparison with the Sydney union, which entertained six intercolonial guests between 1888 and 1890, suggests that Adelaide's low visitor numbers were exceptional.[73] However, the dearth of intercolonial visitors was not a product of the city's isolation. Although Adelaide was not on the All-Red route, it was well serviced by intercolonial and intercontinental steamers. Instead, it resulted from the branch's proximity to the South Australian WCTU's headquarters, which welcomed twenty-five 'visitors from England and from other colonies' in the 1890s. While the easiest way to meet the New Zealand WCTU's president, Annie Schnackenberg, was to attend an Auckland meeting, the Adelaide union lacked a similar lure. Consequently, visitors attended the colonial executive's meetings, barred to the union's rank and file, rather than frequenting branch gatherings.[74]

Taken together, regular visits by overseas members and the lack of competing branches broadened Aucklanders' political horizons. Alongside the local activism that sustained the WCTU, the Auckland union regularly debated subjects of international significance, ranging from temperance campaigns across the world to the scourge of British military prostitution in India and the Armenian massacres of 1894–97.[75] These discussions seldom engendered political action. However, considered alongside Aucklanders' frequent travel, they reinforced members' conviction that despite their geographical isolation they were integral participants in the WCTU's international layer.

Until the formation of the South Australian WCTU in 1889, the Adelaide branch had a similarly cosmopolitan atmosphere. Formerly a hothouse for a cadre of ambitious social reformers, the colonial union's expansion dispersed its best and brightest across the city, leaving a rump to devote their energies to community concerns, while the South Australian executive monopolised the time of visiting activists. Both branches took inspiration from the United States, or at least the dynamic, outward-facing, evangelical idea propagated by *Union Signal*, but only Auckland members discussed their work with like-minded women from across the world. As the following sections explore, differences in members' outlook and relationship to the WCTU's intercolonial and international 'layers' had distinct implications for their suffrage campaigns and dictated how members treated their disenfranchised 'sisters' after winning the vote.

Local suffrage campaigns and the limits of the WCTU's internationalism

In New Zealand and South Australia, the WCTU emerged alongside the organised campaigns for women's enfranchisement. Although Mary Clement Leavitt arrived at a propitious moment, the colonial unions' transition from temperance advocacy to political agitation belies the fact that she seldom mentioned the ballot. Nevertheless, as one of the earliest women's organisations with an overt political agenda in either colony, the WCTU was a broad church. Whereas women's literary clubs had incubated suffrage movements before the arrival of the WCTU in most cities, women in Auckland and Adelaide lacked alternatives. Soon after Leavitt's departure, members discovered Frances Willard's Do-Everything policy. Debuted in 1881 to expand the American union's remit beyond temperance to an expansive Christian socialism that embraced causes from women's suffrage to wage equality and ameliorative labour legislation, Do-Everything became a guiding principle in Australasia.[76] Inspired by Willard, Australasian WCTUs became more immediately 'involved … in the political processes that helped to define (white) women as citizens' than their American counterparts.[77] Colonial members' conversion to suffrage activism was sudden, and it owed much to her redefinition of political action as an extension of 'true womanhood'.[78] Yet despite professing their commitment to further the cause in other countries, after winning the vote Auckland and Adelaide members soon forgot these promises. Expanding the discussion of local branches' position within the World's WCTU, this section examines the rise and fall of suffrage internationalism in Auckland and Adelaide, situating members' ambivalence toward women's enfranchisement as a universal project within a wider debate about the vote across the union's multi-layered hierarchy.

Adelaide WCTU members first deliberated women's enfranchisement in 1887, when their vice-president, Serena Lake, asserted that 'female suffrage' would soon be implemented in Victoria. They took no further action until 1889, when Jessie Ackermann toured Australia persuading members that a 'final solution to the liquor traffic' would not be realised by 'moral suasion' alone. Following her lead, delegates at the union's colonial convention established a franchise department and resolved to 'petition our Legislature to enfranchise the women of South Australia'.[79] A year later, however, in her role as South Australian suffrage superintendent, Lake complained of labouring 'under the burden of an unpopular department'.[80] Although the WCTU's balance sheets did not 'reflect the enormous human capital' at its disposal, decisions about expenditure hint at its priorities. South Australian members' literature budget reflected their ambivalence over the suffrage campaign. Of the £68 worth of leaflets the union held in 1893, less than a pound's worth concerned suffrage activism.[81]

The South Australian WCTU's suffrage resolution was predated by the formation of the Women's Suffrage League. Established in 1888, the League was predicated on the conviction that disenfranchisement was 'a propelling motor on the down grade of womanhood'.[82] Within the WCTU, the Adelaide branch was considered a hotbed of suffragist sentiment – a reputation that rested on its association with the League. Instead of conducting an assertive campaign, the branch directed members to join its sister organisation.[83] As a result, the Adelaide union's minutes record little discussion of suffrage. Members like Lake and Hannah Chewings held prominent roles in the League but seldom discussed their work at WCTU meetings. Through the tireless advocacy of its secretary, Mary Lee, the Women's Suffrage League circulated dozens of petitions demanding women's enfranchisement in South Australia between 1889 and 1892, all without the Adelaide WCTU's assistance. Only when victory neared in 1894 did its members dedicate themselves to the campaign, collecting 1,427 of the 11,600 signatures presented in support of the successful Adult Suffrage Bill.[84]

Despite the strict temperance agenda set by Leavitt, the Auckland WCTU debated women's enfranchisement from its formation. Literature from the American WCTU's western suffrage campaigns had circulated in New Zealand since 1885. In 1886, the Auckland branch collected hundreds of signatures for the colony's first organised women's suffrage petition.[85] Despite these initiatives, Auckland members ceased canvassing in 1888 at the behest of the New Zealand WCTU, which sought a colony-wide approach. At the request of Kate Sheppard, the colonial union's franchise and legislation superintendent, Auckland members resumed petitioning in 1891, this time contributing to a centralised effort that made women's enfranchisement a colony-wide issue.[86]

Initially progress was slow; of the 10,085 signatories to the 1891 petition, just 397 came from Auckland.[87] As in Adelaide, the formation of an independent suffrage organisation galvanised the WCTU's campaign for voting rights. The Women's Franchise League was established in Dunedin in April 1892 as WCTU leaders sought to mobilise working-class women, to whom prohibition proved unpopular. Local success prompted its founders to create satellites across the colony. Inaugurated in June 1892, within months the Auckland branch boasted 101 members, who helped collect 2,479 signatures in favour of women's enfranchisement that year, a figure they doubled in 1893. As elsewhere in the colony, WFL leaders insisted on their separation 'from any temperance or Christian organisation'.[88] Silence on temperance was a tactical compromise. The League shared personnel, objectives, and meeting rooms with the Auckland WCTU. Its president, Amey Daldy, 'the matriarch of the nineteenth-century Auckland feminist community', led the union's suffrage department and recruited at its meetings. When Premier Richard Seddon met a League delegation in 1893, all four women were also WCTU members.[89] As a matter of political expediency, Daldy eventually resigned her WCTU office, yet the organisations remained entangled. In September, the 'secular' WFL began its franchise celebrations with the temperance doxology. Soon after, confused WCTU members requested 'a clear definition' of the 'position of League to Union'.[90]

After celebrating their enfranchisement in September 1893, Auckland members followed the New Zealand WCTU executive's exhortation to exemplify the virtues of women's political citizenship and assist suffragists elsewhere in the world. Eager to mobilise voters before the December general election, Sheppard warned that 'the eyes of the world are on the women of New Zealand, to see whether Women's Suffrage is to be for good or evil'.[91] Branch members already knew of overseas interest in their achievement. In 1892, the temperance newspaper *Prohibitionist* published a series of congratulatory letters from women overseas, sent after *Union Signal* erroneously reported that New Zealand had instituted the universal franchise.[92] The following October, Annie Schnackenberg read aloud from letters received after the passage of the 1893 Act. The sentiments expressed by the South Australian WCTU secretary, Mary George, were common: 'on the use made of [the vote] ... in your colony will depend the progress of the measure in other lands to a great extent.'[93] Suffused with a sense of obligation to assist the WCTU's suffrage campaigns in other countries, over the next few years Auckland members shared their success with the stream of Australian visitors that attended local meetings, while travellers relayed their experiences to overseas audiences.

One such woman, Agnes Berry, fortified the Adelaide union's push for enfranchisement. In May 1893, Berry accompanied her husband and WFL co-founder, Joseph Berry, to assume the ministry at Pirie Street Methodist Church. On the recommendation of the Auckland branch, Agnes was appointed secretary of the Adelaide WCTU, while Joseph preached in favour of women's enfranchisement.[94] After winning the vote, Auckland members found themselves in demand as suffrage speakers whenever they travelled. In 1894, Hannah Main was introduced as a representative of 'the emancipated sisters of her colony' at the Australasian WCTU's triennial convention and spoke repeatedly on suffrage in Sydney.[95] Louisa Ardill of the Sydney union repaid the favour in 1895, elaborating on her compatriots' suffrage activism to an Auckland audience 'pleased to hear of the near approach of the franchise being granted to our sisters in NSW'.[96] The following year, another Auckland member, Helen Dewar, explained the New Zealand suffrage campaign at the request of delegates at the Queensland WCTU's annual convention.[97]

In contrast to the Auckland union, enfranchisement encouraged insularity rather than internationalism among Adelaide members. If they were enthusiastic about promoting women's suffrage in other colonies, such sentiments were seldom recorded. Although Hannah Chewings, a pillar of union life, met suffragists in Melbourne, Sydney, and Brisbane and established the Queensland Women's Suffrage League in 1889, the branch never formally discussed her activities, presumably because they occurred in her capacity as a member of the South Australian league.[98] Aside from brief debates preceding South Australian elections, the union's minutes are devoid of references to women's enfranchisement after the colonial campaign concluded in 1894.

South Australian members' apparent indifference to the struggle in other colonies was also a product of the compromise the executive brokered with hard-line prohibitionists. In 1894, Elizabeth Webb Nicholls justified the union's focus on the franchise by reassuring members that 'we

1.1 The South Australian WCTU gathered in Adelaide for their sixth annual convention in 1894. Despite winning the vote three months later, they collectively appeared to take little interest in the prospect of women's enfranchisement elsewhere in the world. (SLSA, Pictorial Collection, B56711)

can afford to let other questions stand aside till this is settled, for it will give us power to deal with so many'.[99] Although Nicholls, elected as president of the Australasian WCTU that year, used her platform to campaign for women's enfranchisement across Australia, local members refused to let 'other questions stand aside' any longer. The coincidence of women's integration into the South Australian electorate and, in the short term at least, the diminution of their desire to maintain international connections was not limited to the WCTU. Whereas the Women's Suffrage League positioned itself as a kindred spirit with 'the workers in this cause in the Old Country', forging ties with Britain's National Society for Women's Suffrage, its successor, the Woman's League, narrowed its focus to colonial politics.[100]

Adelaide members' reluctance to assist suffrage campaigns outside the colony revealed tensions between local aspirations and international ideals. Nicholls, it seems, was one of the few South Australians for whom women's enfranchisement did not augment her 'sense of difference' from the rest of the continent.[101] In 1893, for example, Joseph Kirkby, an honorary WCTU member, teased his Sydney audience that South Australians were '25 years in advance of New South Wales'. Although

South Australian women had 'lost' the race to win the vote, Kirby downplayed the achievement by casting aspersions on New Zealand's racially inclusive electorate, joking that 'the Maoris had stolen a march upon them in the matter of women's franchise'.[102] Responding in kind, Leonard Isitt, a preacher closely associated with the New Zealand WCTU, told a packed Adelaide Town Hall in 1894 that 'the light [of progress] had come to [New Zealand] first, as did the morning sun'. Only in time would it 'spread to the colonies of the west'.[103]

In their approach to federal enfranchisement, South Australian WCTU members adopted a similarly distant attitude to women in straggling states. Asked to support the Victorian suffragist Vida Goldstein's trip to the International Woman Suffrage Conference in 1902, South Australians gave little. Catherine Helen Spence spoke for many when she noted archly, 'she [is] not from an enfranchised state'.[104] The sense that a worthier compatriot had been overlooked was palpable. Months later, the state union's secretary, Mary George, admitted, 'we never took any interest much in the passing of the Suffrage for the Federal Parliament. We looked upon it as a foregone conclusion.' Such an attitude was again on display in 1903, when an Australasian WCTU pamphlet exhorting women to vote 'for the first time in our history' arrived in Adelaide. Upset that the text failed to recognise that 'we have been enfranchised for nine years', the colonial executive forbade its distribution, fearing 'it would subject us to ridicule'.[105]

Auckland members' budding internationalism distinguished them from their more insular Adelaide counterparts in the 1890s, yet such sentiments had all but vanished by 1900. In the years following their 1893 victory, Auckland members debated the prospects of women's enfranchisement across the British Empire. At the same time as Helen Dewar and Hannah Main lectured on women's enfranchisement at WCTU meetings across the English-speaking world, suffrage slipped from Auckland members' minds.[106] As with the WFL's successor, the Auckland Women's Political League, union members increasingly discussed the vote as a tool to ameliorate their daily lives rather than their obligations to exemplify their political citizenship to aid suffragists overseas.[107]

Tensions between the community activism that sustained branch life and the idea of cooperation in pursuit of common goals lay at the WCTU's core. Although the union's centralised structure encouraged inter-branch collaboration, members sometimes struggled to see the relationship between local and international work. From the outset, Frances Willard recognised this dilemma. She had a flair for rituals that allowed women the world over to express their religious convictions while inculcating a sense of connection among the union's scattered membership. In 1891, the World's WCTU orchestrated a worldwide day of prayer. Women across Australasia participated, as they did on Willard's death in 1898, and again the following year when the World's WCTU solicited donations to repay the debt on the Woman's Temple. Then, antipodean members were eager to have their names 'engraved on the marble wall of Willard Hall ... so that visitors may see that we are part of the organisation which brings blessing to so many lives'.[108]

Paradoxically, the most effective of Willard's rituals, the Polyglot Petition, hinted at the limits of Do-Everything as the basis of international organisation. The petition, written in 1884, asked world leaders to prohibit all intoxicants, a universal solution to a problem that '[made] misery for all the world'. As Willard admitted, 'it is not supposed that it will produce any strong impression upon any Government'.[109] Rather, the petition, signed by a million women from fifty countries when it was presented to US President Grover Cleveland in 1895, was the tangible goal around which the union 'organize[d] such a latent sentiment as internationalism'. The exercise encouraged women, regardless of their existing political rights, to sublimate their domestic struggles into a global identity, united by their labours to protect the home from the scourge of 'his Satanic Majesty ... King Alcohol'.[110] Yet, unlike prohibition, the campaign for political citizenship was difficult to frame in universal terms. Rather, it is better understood as a series of battles fought in colonial or national contexts. Such a programme was ill-suited to an organisation formed to surmount geopolitical barriers.[111] In establishing the World's WCTU, Willard framed the campaign against intoxicants as a fight that could not be won in one country alone. She could not afford women's enfranchisement similar status. For this reason, the Auckland and Adelaide branches' struggle to sustain their suffrage internationalism should not be viewed in isolation. Instead, it must be considered alongside the ideological and structural barriers that prevented the union's two supra-colonial layers, the Australasian and World's WCTUs, from placing the vote at the heart of their work.

Federations of suffragists? Women's enfranchisement in the Australasian and World's Woman's Christian Temperance Unions

Considered from most vantage points within Frances Willard's empire, Australasian members placed unusual emphasis on women's enfranchisement. Ironically, while Willard had advocated the expansion of the American union's remit to include women's enfranchisement since 1876, her message proved more palatable in Australasia than anywhere else in the world. In contrast to the colonial unions' rapid conversion to suffrage campaigning, the WCTU's supranational hierarchies struggled to accommodate suffragists. The WCTU of Australasia was established in 1891, its members anticipating Federation and seeking a voice for women in the Commonwealth. Although womanhood suffrage lay at the heart of this vision, colonial unions soon withdrew from their lofty national agenda. Within the World's WCTU, debating suffrage was more fraught. Its leaders expressed their pride in antipodean members' enfranchisement but feared upsetting the union's equilibrium by affording enfranchised women a platform at international conventions. To the chagrin of those like Elizabeth Nicholls, who emphasised the WCTU's unity of purpose and believed that Australasian women had much to offer their disenfranchised sisters, suffragists in the WCTU were forced to join new organisations to advance the international fight for women's political citizenship.

Those present at the Australasian WCTU's inauguration seemed certain that it would play an important role in the suffrage campaigns unfolding across the continent. Held in Melbourne while the Victorian WCTU members collected signatures for a 'monster' petition seeking the state franchise, the meeting was pervaded by a sense of optimism about the union's political activism. Describing the proceedings for *Union Signal*, Catherine Wallace, the American expatriate superintendent of the intercolonial franchise department, reported that 'a stranger might almost have suspected that the Australasian WCTU was a meeting for the advancement of woman suffrage'.[112] Despite delegates' enthusiasm, the ambitious agenda enshrined in their constitution ignored political rights. There is no record of their deliberations, making it difficult to determine whether the omission reflected their anxiety about committing to suffrage activism before it had been agreed to by all five colonial unions, or whether they simply neglected to amend the American original.[113]

Despite the constitutional wrinkle, readers of Wallace's report might have assumed the Australasian WCTU would lead women's struggle to win the vote. In the following months, Wallace advanced her vision, emulating the American union's drive for uniformity through the distribution of instructional literature. Her 1891 *Manual of the Franchise Department* sought to standardise the techniques that enabled Victorian members to collect 30,000 signatures demanding the vote. Wallace encouraged branches to form franchise departments, distribute propaganda, write to local newspapers, organise public debates, circulate petitions, and relay intelligence to colonial and intercolonial superintendents.[114] The *Manual* received a mixed reception. Although the South Australian union experimented with petitioning, collecting 12,000 signatures in 1894, the tactic was not widely adopted. Rather than a cause for optimism, as Jessie Ackermann reflected, the failure of the Victorian petition to achieve immediate results convinced many that making such appeals whilst 'shorn of the power of citizenship is like casting pearls before – honourable gentlemen! Results – nil!'[115]

Wallace's tract resonated more in New Zealand. Impressed by the work of Kate Sheppard, the union's colonial franchise superintendent, Wallace posted her a copy and confided, 'I wish you were here … to direct the work.'[116] In the years that followed, Sheppard's activism, particularly her renewed commitment to public petitioning as 'the only effectual method of making … a protest' and her popular 'Hints to District Franchise Superintendents', bore the American's imprimatur. Published in 1892, Sheppard's column distilled the *Manual* into a series of pithy imperatives – 'influence personal friends', 'watch progress of [the] movement in other places, and supply information to the Union' – that dictated the New Zealand campaign.[117]

Although informal suffrage dialogue thrived, Wallace and Sheppard's camaraderie did not precipitate substantive collaboration between the colonial unions. As its title suggested, Jessie Ackermann envisaged the Australasian union as a supranational organisation, and she invited the New Zealand union to affiliate in 1891. After protracted debate, the New Zealanders refused, explaining that the time and expense of travel – its delegates to the Melbourne convention spent six weeks away from home – as well as their existing ties to the World's WCTU outweighed any 'advantages offered by federation'.[118] Nevertheless, the Australasian executive persisted. That August, the Victorian president, Mary Love, visited Auckland and 'spoke in the strongest terms of the advisability and advantages in federating with Australia'.[119] Three years later, the Australasian secretary, Flora Harris, held out hope that 'we may yet induce them to unite with us'. Harris, like many of her compatriots, considered the New Zealand suffrage campaign 'an object lesson to all the colonies'.[120] In this spirit, the Australasian executive asked Sheppard to lead the intercolonial suffrage department in 1894. Sheppard declined, as she did requests to lecture on the vote in Sydney that year.[121] Her refusals signalled the end of the union's attempts to foster formal trans-Tasman collaboration on the vote.

Catherine Wallace's term as suffrage superintendent marked a high point in the Australasian WCTU's contribution to the colonial suffrage campaigns. Despite her prominence in the New South Wales campaign, Wallace's successor, Lady Mary Windeyer, took a quiescent approach to the Australasian superintendency. The union's triennial conventions remained forums for suffragists to share their progress, and published summaries of these discussions allowed convention debates to filter down to grassroots activists. Yet, whatever its sympathies, the executive refused to fund suffrage initiatives. Although Wallace's *Manual* was one of the few WCTU pamphlets written for an Australian audience, it was never reprinted. Despite reporting a £96 surplus, the executive refused to publish Wallace's 'excellent' valedictory speech in 1894.[122] Furthermore, while Elizabeth Nicholls lectured on women's suffrage as Australasian WCTU president between 1897 and 1903, members deemed these speeches a 'special feature' of her presidency. They were undertaken at her initiative, underwritten by donations from her audiences, and not repeated by the union's paid organisers.[123]

Resistance to using Australasian funds to support colonial suffrage activism was not merely an exercise in prudence. Local branches coalesced into colonial unions but resisted further centralisation. In 1893, Nicholls' plan to send a 'national' delegation to the World's WCTU convention in Chicago unravelled when the colonial unions opted to retain separate representation.[124] Four years later, the Victorian union derailed the Australian bid to host the World's convention in Brisbane by submitting a rival application on the grounds that Melbourne was 'better suited' for the event.[125] The following year, Nicholls launched *Our Federation* (1898–1903) to provide members with a forum 'in which all departments of our work ... [could] be discussed'. However, parochial sentiment undermined the enterprise, with colonial unions refusing to preference the newspaper above their existing publications.[126] By the late 1890s, the prospect of Federation provided members with an arena to pursue common goals. Nevertheless, the Federal franchise was never formally discussed at Australasian conventions. In 1897, the WCTU's Australasian executive urged delegates at the Australasian Federation Conference to include equal voting rights in the draft constitution. Their letter was a token gesture. It was neither raised at that year's convention, nor did its signatories orchestrate a response from their members on the issue.[127] When, five years later, the Commonwealth Parliament began deliberating the Federal franchise, it was the colonial unions rather than the Australasian executive that took the initiative and petitioned members to give women the vote in advance of the successful Commonwealth Franchise Act.[128]

Internationalism without suffrage

Despite emphasising that the WCTU's international links shaped colonial women's movements, the union's historians have been inattentive to the place of Australasian women in its global hierarchy. Because antipodean members readily took up the fight for the vote, and their rhetoric matched that of the union's charismatic leaders, it is assumed that their suffrage activism sat neatly within the broad church of the World's WCTU. However, Australasian members' suffrage activism coincided with a moment of crisis in the union's British and American strongholds. Unbeknownst to its colonial membership, the Anglo-American backlash against Do-Everything made suffrage increasingly contentious. Although members' unease with 'national' cooperation constrained the Australasian franchise department, it remained a forum for members to exchange ideas. By contrast, the World's department barely functioned. Paradoxically, while WCTU missionaries had politicised Australasian evangelical women, the World's union gave them little chance to share their success overseas. As Australasian delegates to World's conventions discovered, the union provided few official channels for suffragists to collaborate, a structural impediment that dampened members' enthusiasm for propagating their ideas and methods beyond the Tasman world.

Tensions over the inclusion of suffrage activism in the WCTU's agenda had long dogged the World's union. After a few years as a skeleton adjunct to the American union, the World's WCTU began life in earnest in 1891. Months earlier, Frances Willard met Lady Isabella Somerset, president of the BWTA and – in 1898 – her successor as World's president. The pair's friendship was the axis upon which the union revolved. Yet their quest to realise a 'temperance millennium' by internationalising the WCTU undermined their respective national causes.[129] Seeking to popularise the Do-Everything policy, Willard and Somerset lectured across Britain between 1892 and 1894. Rather than embracing Willard, however, BWTA members resented the association's Americanisation.[130] The alliance almost cost Somerset the presidency when, in 1893, her executive resigned, protesting the inclusion of political rights on the association's agenda. Under her successor, Rosalind Howard (1903–21), BWTA delegates passed annual resolutions demanding women's enfranchisement, although suffrage activism never became a primary concern for rank-and-file members.[131]

Suffrage was as contentious in the United States. In 1881, Frances Willard had, by force of personality, persuaded a sceptical membership to endorse women's enfranchisement. Yet, while national delegates acquiesced, state unions equivocated. In 1906, the American WCTU reported that only thirteen state branches had done 'a large amount of [suffrage] work'.[132] By then, years of slow growth and the emergence of competitors with mainstream political support, such as the Anti-Saloon League (1893–1933), had engendered a sense of malaise in its ranks. Mourning their declining influence in an era of increasing specialisation, conservative members feared Willard's ambition had not only eclipsed the union's commitment to prohibition but threatened its survival.[133] Conflict over the union's direction crystallised in the dispute over the Woman's Temple. The decision to build a permanent headquarters reflected Willard's desire for economic independence and to inscribe the union's virtues at the centre of her hometown, and the capital of America's Gilded Age heartland, Chicago. However, for her critics, Willard's outsized statement about the WCTU's place in the city's commercial heart signalled her desire to transcend the 'middle-class, Christian framework of home and family' on which she had built her career.[134]

Despite concerted opposition to the project, financing began in 1887, at the height of Chicago's construction boom. Five years later the tower was complete, but, amid a recession, it attracted few tenants. Already uncomfortable with Willard's drift toward 'gospel socialism', her detractors decried the 'alignment of religious virtues with financial profits'. The battle over the Temple became acrimonious, exacerbated by Willard's absences in Britain.[135] Stung by such criticism, and the implicit suggestion that Do-Everything had run its course, in 1897 an ailing Willard used her final national address to rally her supporters. During the speech, in large part an explication of her Christian socialism, Willard 'dedicate[d] the little I have' to the Temple.[136] That year, delegates endorsed her vision for the last time. As well as sending shockwaves across the world, her death precipitated the union's retreat from pre-eminence in the American women's movement. At their first national gathering after Willard's death, delegates voted to disaffiliate the union from the Temple. The decision symbolised a narrowing of the WCTU's ambit, paving the way for a decline – if not toward 'single-issue prohibitionism', then certainly toward a reprioritisation of moral issues above social and political reform.[137]

The failure of the Woman's Temple is usually considered a domestic affair. However, the crisis of confidence that engulfed the WCTU had wider ramifications, and not only because the American executive sought donations from as far afield as Auckland and Adelaide to repay its debts.[138] The arguments the Temple precipitated over the American union's direction coincided with the ascendancy of Frances Willard's first monumental project, the World's WCTU, and clearly shaped its growth. Scarred by domestic battles over the vote, and fearful of jeopardising temperance work, Willard and Somerset avoided making suffrage a feature of their World's agenda. Although a franchise department was established at the inaugural World's convention in 1891, delegates

1.2 Chicago's Woman's Temple was a symbol of Frances Willard's Do-Everything policy. Just months after the Temple staged her public funeral, it was cut loose by the union, signalling a return to a narrow focus on intoxicants. (*Rand, McNally & Co.'s Pictorial Chicago: Containing Views of Principal Buildings, Residences, Streets, Parks, Monuments, etc.*, Chicago: Rand, McNally, 1901)

approached the subject gingerly, if at all. Despite Willard and Somerset's convictions, suffrage activism remained absent from their agenda-setting presidential speeches. Furthermore, the refrain at World's gatherings that no department was 'obligatory upon any Union' reassured conservatives that suffrage remained subordinate to the union's temperance mission.[139]

Consequently, those interested in learning more about the union's suffrage campaigns were dismayed by World's conventions. As a rule, the triennial gatherings drew up to a thousand women, making them 'too unwieldy to allow of any discussion on individual departments'. Instead, as a convenor of the 1897 convention noted, 'the real views are discussed & really settled in the Executive'.[140] All departments were essentially ceremonial, then, but franchise work suffered particular neglect. Unlike its counterparts, the franchise department produced few written reports, and its superintendents seldom attended meetings. The department's status reflected the lack of interest taken by national affiliates, including enfranchised New Zealanders and Australians. Although Kate Sheppard served as associate World's franchise superintendent between 1900 and 1906, perhaps recognising the lack of enthusiasm for the topic, she neither attended a meeting nor wrote anything for the union and refused several invitations to accept the superintendency on a permanent basis after 1903.[141]

Sheppard had perhaps internalised the World's WCTU's caution around political reform. However, to other Australasian members, the World's executive's conservatism remained a source of dismay. After attending the 1900 World's convention, Nicholls complained that delegates were not given formal opportunities to discuss the vote.[142] Seven years earlier, when Willard addressed the 1893 convention, attentive New Zealanders might have noticed that she spoke more enthusiastically about the possibilities of using municipal suffrage as a temperance measure than she did about the union's role in the first successful national women's suffrage campaign.[143] Certainly, Australasian members were unlikely to have overlooked the fact that, while they received congratulations from overseas branches, they never heard directly from revered leaders like Willard or Somerset.

On the occasions when enfranchised members used the WCTU to share their methods, such exchanges occurred informally, rather than through the World's union. For example, in 1895, a year after voting in her first general election, Isabel Napier, New Zealand's delegate to the World's convention, uttered nothing about the achievement in public. Yet it was not reticence that held her back. Several years later, Napier's report on the status of New Zealand women before the 1904 Congress of the International Council of Women (ICW) 'took the Berlinese by storm'. As a result, she found herself besieged with requests for advice on 'franchise and temperance advocacy'.[144] The same was true in her native Scotland, where she resettled soon after. Contrasting her time at the World's convention, Napier found in the BWTA-affiliated Scottish Christian Union an audience eager for more openly politicised visions of women's organising. She quickly began lecturing on her experiences in New Zealand – 'that picturesque ... land of democracy' – and, within two years, established the union's first suffrage department.[145]

The World's WCTU treated women's enfranchisement with caution throughout the early twentieth century. Every three years, its massed delegates dutifully recognised the vote as the key to 'the success of all moral reforms' but fell short of demanding women's enfranchisement.[146] When the First World War began, differences in members' political privileges were stark. New Zealanders and South Australians had voted for twenty years, but most of the forty-five World's affiliates remained decades away from equal suffrage. During the interwar years, local unions led suffrage campaigns in Canada, South Africa, China, and Japan, but the subject remained off limits at World's conventions.[147] Ultimately, this constrained discourse on women's enfranchisement pushed suffragists to join specialist organisations like the IWSA, formed in 1904. The Alliance's origins, discussed in the next chapter, lay in the ICW's equivocation over the vote. However, Carrie Chapman Catt, its founder and the president of the National American Woman Suffrage Association, was also a longstanding WCTU member. Her time in the union convinced her of the need for a dedicated organisation, freeing suffragists from the compromises that broad-based institutions required. More importantly, it taught her of the merits of creating an international forum for women working toward similar goals to build friendships, discuss ideas, and share information.[148] For its part, the WCTU welcomed the addition to 'the great chain of organizations for the betterment of the world', not least because the diminished pressure for World's conventions to debate a contentious subject would smooth obstacles to its growth, a trajectory that saw it reach 766,000 paying members during the global temperance movement's interwar zenith.[149]

Established as organised women's movements emerged in New Zealand and Australia, the WCTU was, from the beginning, integral to all seven colonial suffrage campaigns. Like all the union's work, suffrage must be seen through the prism of its local, intercolonial, and international hierarchy. While branch members' lives were enriched by the WCTU's global vision, expressed through their participation in quotidian rituals like the noontide prayer hour, the links between local and international work were rarely as straightforward. As the differences between the cosmopolitan Auckland branch and its Adelaide counterpart demonstrate, understanding the context of members' work is vital. Suffragists and their writings travelled freely along informal channels, allowing Auckland's enfranchised members to forge relationships with like-minded women from Queensland to California. At the same time, examining the local mechanics of suffrage internationalism within the WCTU illuminates the ambivalence toward women's enfranchisement in its intercolonial and international layers. Although suffrage activism was fundamental to Willard's ideology, it was embraced more completely in Australasia than in her homeland and remained marginal to the World's WCTU's agenda. Haunted by premonitions of the union's moral and material decline, its leaders abandoned the Do-Everything policy as it reached its apotheosis in the antipodes. Precisely because voices like Nicholls' were so seldom heard at World's conventions, historians examining the WCTU from the inside out have paid little attention to the relinquishment of suffrage by its international leadership, a decision that paralleled the union's decline as a force in the American women's movement.

However, as Chapter 2 explores, the shift from the WCTU's broad-based internationalism to smaller, specialised networks, like Catt's Alliance, did not guarantee Australasian women a voice on the world stage. Lacking the qualms of its sister organisation, the IWSA recruited pillars of the WCTU's colonial suffrage campaigns, like Kate Sheppard in New Zealand and Madge Donohoe in New South Wales, as standard-bearers of enfranchised womanhood. Nevertheless, as a new organisation not rooted in the realities of local reform work, the Alliance lacked the strong, sentimental appeal of the WCTU's internationalism. Instead, it was a vanguard of a professionalising women's movement that established new norms for international engagement, most obviously in its insistence that national delegations constituted the bedrock of women's international organisation. As Australian and New Zealand suffragists discovered, such prescriptions proved as restrictive to their efforts to propagate the secrets of their success as the World's WCTU's pragmatic conservatism.

Notes

1 *Union Signal*, 24 February 1898, p. 2.
2 R. White, *The Republic for Which It Stands: The United States during the Reconstruction and the Gilded Age, 1865–1896* (New York: Oxford University Press, 2017), p. 5.
3 A. A. Gordon, *The Beautiful Life of Frances E. Willard* (Chicago: Woman's Temperance Publishing Association, 1898).
4 *Minutes of the Second Biennial Convention of the World's Woman's Christian Temperance Union* (Chicago: Woman's Temperance Publishing Association, 1893), p. 83; *Union Signal*, 3 March 1898, p. 2; 10 March 1898, pp. 6–7.
5 *Australasian Woman's Christian Temperance Union, Minutes of the Second Triennial Convention* (Sydney: n.p., 1894), p. 26; State Library of South Australia, Adelaide (hereafter SLSA), SRG186/748, Frances Willard to Elizabeth Webb Nicholls, 13 May 1896.
6 WCTU branches were established in Sydney (1882) and Invercargill (1884), but neither appears to have been bound into the union's official structures until the arrival

of its first 'round-the-world' missionary, Mary Clement Leavitt, in 1885–86. Gordon, *Frances E. Willard*; *Union Signal*, 3 March 1898, pp. 1–9; 10 March 1898, pp. 1–20.

7   *White Ribbon*, 1 August 1898, p. 3; SLSA, SRG186/435/4, Adelaide Woman's Christian Temperance Union Minute Book 1898–1904, 2 December 1898.

8   *Union Signal*, 17 March 1898, p. 12.

9   Tyrrell, *Woman's World*, p. 17.

10 R. Bordin, *Woman and Temperance: The Quest for Power and Liberty, 1873–1900* (Philadelphia: Temple University Press, 1981), pp. 15–26; C. Clark and M. Ledger-Lomas, 'The Protestant international', in A. Green and V. Viaene (eds), *Religious Internationals in the Modern World: Globalization and Faith Communities since 1750* (New York: Palgrave Macmillan, 2012), pp. 27–32.

11 I. Tyrrell, 'The Woman's Christian Temperance Union and internationalism', *Women and Social Movements, International*, https://search.alexanderstreet.com/view/work/bibliographic_entity%7Cbibliographic_details%7C2476955 (accessed 5 May 2018).

12 M. J. Buhle, *Women and American Socialism, 1870–1920* (Urbana: University of Illinois Press, 1981), p. 63; D. della Porta and S. Tarrow, 'Transnational processes and social activism: An introduction', in D. della Porta and S. Tarrow (eds), *Transnational Processes and Global Activism* (Oxford: Rowman & Littlefield, 2005), pp. 2–3.

13 *Twenty-Fifth Annual Meeting of Woman's Christian Temperance Union of the State of Indiana* (n.c.: n.p., 1898), p. 73.

14 This scholarship is too numerous to list in its entirety, but comprehensive accounts include E. Warne, *Agitate, Educate, Organise, Legislate: Protestant Women's Social Action in Post-Suffrage Australia* (Melbourne: Melbourne University Press, 2017), pp. 13–44; Grimshaw, *Women's Suffrage in New Zealand*; Oldfield, *Woman Suffrage in Australia*; Tyrrell, *Woman's World*, pp. 221–41.

15 Tyrrell, *Woman's World*, pp. 1–10, 221–41.

16 See, for example, Ballantyne, *Webs of Empire*, pp. 246–82; Bush and Purvis (eds), 'Connecting women's histories'; and the essays in Midgley *et al.* (eds), *Women in Transnational History*.

17 E. Harvey, '"Layered networks": Imperial philanthropy in Birmingham and Sydney, 1860–1914', *Journal of Imperial and Commonwealth History*, 41:1 (2013), 120–42.

18 A. Atkinson, 'Federation, democracy and the struggle against a single Australia', *Australian Historical Studies*, 44:2 (2013), 272; S. M. Marilley, 'Frances Willard and the feminism of fear', *Feminist Studies*, 19:1 (1993), 123–46. A telling exception is R. Smith, *The Ladies Are At It Again: Gore Debates the Women's Franchise* (Wellington: Victoria University Department of Women's Studies, 1993).

19 A. F. Scott, *Natural Allies: Women's Associations in American History* (Urbana: University of Illinois Press, 1991), p. 85.

20 *Minutes of Fifth Annual Convention of the Woman's Christian Temperance Union of South Australia* (Adelaide: Vardon and Pritchard, 1893), p. 86.

21 Alexander Turnbull Library, Wellington (hereafter ATL), 79-057-08/03, Auckland Women's Christian Temperance Union Minute Book 1889–98, 26 August 1896; *Woman's Christian Temperance Union of South Australia, Minutes of Eleventh Annual Convention* (Adelaide: A. & E. Lewis, 1899), p. 14.

22 Oldfield, *Woman Suffrage in Australia*, 15.
23 Willard, *Do Everything*, p. 5.
24 Summers, *Damned Whores and God's Police*, p. 351.
25 A. O'Brien, 'Sins of omission? Women in the history of Australian religion and religion in the history of Australian women: A reply to Roger Thompson', *Australian Historical Studies*, 27:108 (1997), 126–33.
26 Cooper et al., 'The landscape of gender politics', pp. 15–49; Denise George, *Mary Lee: The Life and Times of a 'Turbulent Anarchist' and Her Battle for Women's Rights* (Adelaide: Wakefield Press, 2018), pp. 126–30, 150–3.
27 *Minutes of the National WCTU at the Eighteenth Annual Meeting*, pp. 219, 225.
28 Auckland's are the only uninterrupted set of nineteenth-century New Zealand union records. The South Australian WCTU records are more comprehensive, but as the colony's sole branch until 1889, Adelaide's records are its most expansive. Although it was founded in 1882, the Sydney union lacks complete records until 1920. M. C. Leavitt, *Report Made to the First Convention of the World's Women's Christian Temperance Union* (Boston: Alfred Mudge & Son, 1891), p. 6.
29 J. B. Hirst, 'Adelaide and the country, 1870–1914' (PhD thesis, University of Adelaide, 1970), p. 1.
30 B. Schrader, *The Big Smoke: New Zealand Cities, 1840–1920* (Wellington: Bridget Williams Books, 2016), pp. 369–74.
31 Leavitt, *Report Made to the First Convention*, p. 62.
32 A. A. Gordon, *The World's Woman's Christian Temperance Union* (Chicago: Ruby I. Gilbert, 1900), pp. 11–12; Tyrrell, 'The WCTU and internationalism'; Tyrrell, *Reforming the World*, p. 76.
33 *Union Signal*, 11 June 1885, p. 8.
34 Brookes, *A History of New Zealand Women*, pp. 122–5.
35 S. Piggin and R. D. Linder, *The Fountain of Public Prosperity: Evangelical Christians in Australian History 1740–1914* (Melbourne: Monash University Publishing, 2018), p. 18.
36 The Auckland union was larger than most of its American contemporaries. In 1886, the American WCTU had 4,681 branches, each with an average of nineteen members. *NZH*, 31 January 1885, p. 6; *Minutes of the National Woman's Christian Temperance Union at the Thirteenth Annual Meeting* (Chicago: Woman's Temperance Publication Association, 1886), p. 126.
37 *Minutes of the New Zealand Women's Christian Temperance Union at the First Annual Meeting* (Wellington: Lyon & Blair, 1886), pp. 13–21.
38 Leavitt, *Report Made to the First Convention*, p. 8.
39 *Second & Third Years Report of the Women's Christian Temperance Union of South Australia* (Adelaide: T. S. Carey & Co., 1888), p. 2.
40 *Christian Colonist*, 14 June 1889, p. 5.
41 *Minutes of First Annual Convention of the Woman's Christian Temperance Union of South Australia, Held in Adelaide, August 13, 1889* (Adelaide: George Hassell, 1890), p. 20.
42 M. McKinnon et al. (eds), *Bateman New Zealand Historical Atlas: Ko Papatuanuku e Takoto Nei* (Auckland: David Bateman, 1997), plate 57; ATL, 79-057-08/03, Auckland

WCTU Minute Book 1889–98; *White Ribbon*, 1 April 1896, p. 10; 1 March 1897, p. 10; 1 March 1898, p. 13; 1 March 1900, p. 12.

43 *Minutes of the Fifth Annual Convention of the WCTU of South Australia*, p. 38; *Australasian WCTU Minutes of the Second Triennial Convention*, p. 64; *Australasian Woman's Christian Temperance Union, Minutes of the 6th Triennial Convention* (Brisbane: Outridge Printing Co., 1906), p. 36.

44 A. R. Grigg, 'Prohibition and women: The preservation of an ideal and a myth', *New Zealand Journal of History*, 17:2 (1983), 153.

45 A sixth union, the WCTU of Western Australia, joined after its formation in 1892. *The Woman's Christian Temperance Union of Australasia, Minutes & Proceedings of First Intercolonial Woman's Christian Temperance Union Convention* (Melbourne: J. J. Howard, 1891), p. 3.

46 Atkinson, 'Against a single Australia', 272.

47 *Report of the National Women's Christian Temperance Union of New Zealand Fifth Annual Meeting* (Dunedin: Munro, Hutchinson, & Co., 1890), p. 22; *Minutes of Fourth Annual Convention of the Woman's Christian Temperance Union of South Australia* (Adelaide: Hussey & Gillingham, 1892), p. 35; *Brisbane Courier*, 13 May 1897, p. 4.

48 K. Dreaver, 'Women's suffrage in Auckland, 1885–1893' (MA thesis, University of Auckland, 1985), pp. 11–12.

49 S. Coney, *Every Girl: A Social History of Women and the YWCA in Auckland* (Auckland: Auckland YWCA, 1986), pp. 8, 18, 30–6.

50 D. Wiles, 'As high as heaven: The Woman's Christian Temperance Union in South Australia, 1886–1915' (BA Hons thesis, University of Adelaide, 1978), pp. 11–12; SLNSW, A2272/261, Mary Lee to Rose Scott, 25 March 1897; SLSA, PRG88/7/92, Catherine Helen Spence to Alice Henry, 14 February 1908.

51 M. O. Lamme, 'Shining a calcium light: The WCTU and public relations history', *Journalism & Mass Communications Quarterly*, 88:2 (2011), 245–66.

52 SLSA, SRG186/435/3, Adelaide WCTU Minute Book 1889–98, September 1892; SLSA, SRG186/106/4, 'Readings for monthly meetings of W.C.T.U.'; ATL, 79-057-08/03, Auckland WCTU Minute Book 1889–98; *Alliance and Temperance News*, 1 October 1890, pp. 12–13; *White Ribbon*, 1 March 1898, p. 4; *Woman's Christian Temperance Union of New South Wales, Annual Report of the 20th Convention* (Sydney: n.p., 1902), p. 31.

53 S. Liebich, 'Connected readers: Reading networks and community in early twentieth-century New Zealand', *Mémoires du Livre/Studies in Book Culture*, 2:1 (2010), 5–6.

54 *NZH*, 20 March 1886, p. 5; P. Bunkle, 'The origins of the women's movement in New Zealand: The Woman's Christian Temperance Union, 1885–1895', in P. Bunkle and B. Hughes (eds), *Women in New Zealand Society* (Auckland: Allen and Unwin, 1980), pp. 57–8.

55 M. Valverde, '"Racial poison": Drink, male vice, and degeneration in first-wave feminism', in Fletcher *et al.* (eds), *Women's Suffrage in the British Empire*, p. 38. The Australasian union followed suit in 1900. *WCTU of South Australia Minutes of Eleventh Annual Convention*, p. 14; P. Grimshaw, 'Colonising motherhood: Evangelical social reformers and Koorie women in Victoria, Australia, 1880s to the early 1900s', *Women's History Review*, 8:2 (1999), 334.

56 *Prohibitionist*, 27 February 1892, p. 3; Paisley, 'Performing New Zealand', 22–38.

57 *White Ribbon*, 1 May 1895, pp. 5–6; 1 April 1899, p. 13. See also F. Harsant, *They Called Me Te Maari* (Christchurch: Whitcoulls Limited, 1979).
58 *Union Signal*, 14 November 1895, p. 10.
59 Valverde, 'Racial poison', p. 35.
60 Brookes, *A History of Women in New Zealand*, p. 171; Hocken Collections, Dunedin, MS-0273-1, ARC-0021, *White Ribbon*, 15 August 1908, p. 1.
61 Tyrrell, *Woman's World*, pp. 114–21.
62 C. Bishop, 'Women on the move: Gender, money-making and mobility in mid-nineteenth century Australasia', *History Australia*, 11:2 (2014), 38–59; H. Morrison, *Pushing Boundaries: New Zealand Protestants and Overseas Missions 1827–1939* (Dunedin: Otago University Press, 2016), pp. 41, 80–1.
63 SLNSW, MLMSS3641, Sydney WCTU Minute Book 1882–92, 1 February 1888.
64 See, for example, SLSA, SRG186/435/3, Adelaide WCTU Minute Book 1889–98, 4 May and 5 July 1888; ATL, 79-057-08/03, Auckland WCTU Minute Book 1889–98, 25 November 1891.
65 *Telegraph* [QLD], 18 May 1931, p. 9; *Queenslander*, 21 May 1931, p. 55.
66 F. Steel, 'Via New Zealand around the world: The Union Steam Ship Company and the trans-Pacific mail lines, 1880s–1910s', in P. Ahrens and C. Dixon (eds), *Coast to Coast: Case Histories of Modern Pacific Crossings* (Newcastle: Cambridge Scholars Publishing, 2010), pp. 62–5.
67 University of Auckland Library, Auckland (hereafter UAL), MSS2009/6/1-2, Auckland Women's Political League Minute Books 1892–98 and 1899–1911.
68 ATL, 79-057-08/03, Auckland WCTU Minute Book 1889–98, 21 August 1889, 8 March 1893, 11 April 1894; ATL, 79-057-08/04, Auckland WCTU Minute Book 1898–1902, 12 October 1898; SLNSW, MLMSS3641, Sydney WCTU Minute Book 1882–92, 1 February 1888; *NZH*, 9 July 1902, p. 5.
69 *Brisbane Courier*, 2 June 1888, p. 6; 31 August 1889, p. 4; 28 October 1894, p. 3; *Morning Bulletin*, 3 July 1896, p. 6; *SMH*, 14 April 1897, p. 5; ATL, 79-057-08/03, Auckland WCTU Minute Book 1889–98, 13 April 1893, 23 October 1895, 9 June 1897.
70 ATL, 79-057-08/04, Auckland WCTU Minute Book 1898–1902, 31 January 1900.
71 Author's calculations from South Australian WCTU convention reports 1890–93 and New Zealand WCTU convention reports 1888–94.
72 *Chronicle of the London Missionary Society*, March 1893, pp. 65–7; SLSA, SRG186/435/3, Adelaide WCTU Minute Book 1889–98, 29 November 1894.
73 SLSA, SRG186/435/4, Adelaide WCTU Minute Book 1898–1904, 25 November 1898; SLNSW, MLMSS3641, Sydney WCTU Minute Book 1882–92.
74 Author's calculation from South Australian WCTU convention reports 1890–1900. SLSA, SRG186/1/2, Minute Book of Colonial Executive Committee (South Australian WCTU Minute Book) 1895–1900, 11 June 1896.
75 See, for example, ATL, 79-057-08/03, Auckland WCTU Minute Book 1889–98, 2 October 1889, 19 February 1890, 13 September 1893, 11 April 1894.
76 Do-Everything was a dynamic agenda, but the clearest articulation of Willard's vision came at the 1893 World's convention, in a speech that Lady Henry Somerset delivered

on her behalf. *Minutes of the Second Biennial Convention of the World's WCTU*, pp. 37–130.
77 Warne, *Agitate, Educate, Organise, Legislate*, p. 5.
78 C. D. S. Gifford, 'Frances Willard and the Woman's Christian Temperance Union's conversion to woman suffrage', in M. S. Wheeler (ed.), *One Woman, One Vote: Rediscovering the Woman Suffrage Movement* (Troutdale: New Sage Press, 1995), pp. 120–6.
79 *Advertiser*, 10 June 1889, p. 6; SLSA, SRG186/435/2, Adelaide WCTU Minute Book 1887–91, 7 July 1887; *Minutes of First Annual Convention of the WCTU of South Australia*, p. 18.
80 *Second & Third Years Report of the WCTU of South Australia*, p. 63.
81 Wiles, 'The WCTU in South Australia', p. 26; SLSA, SRG186/181, South Australian WCTU Colonial Literature Department Record Book 1893–1903.
82 *South Australian Woman's Suffrage League. Report, 1891* (Adelaide: G. Hassell, 1891), p. 3.
83 *Second & Third Years Report of the WCTU of South Australia*, pp. 29, 63–4; SLSA, SRG186/435/2, Adelaide WCTU Minute Book 1887–91, 6 September 1889; SLSA, SRG186/435/3, Adelaide WCTU Minute Book 1889–98, 5 February 1892.
84 *Minutes of Sixth Annual Convention of the Woman's Christian Temperance Union of South Australia* (Adelaide: G. Hassell & Son, 1894), p. 63.
85 Grimshaw, *Women's Suffrage in New Zealand*, pp. 37–9; *NZH*, 20 March 1886, p. 5.
86 N. Perryman, *How We Won the Franchise in New Zealand* (Wellington: New Zealand Women's Christian Temperance Union, 1924), pp. 6–7.
87 *Prohibitionist*, 26 March 1892, p. 3.
88 Dreaver, 'Women's suffrage in Auckland', pp. 30, 47; Grimshaw, *Women's Suffrage in New Zealand*, p. 51; *Prohibitionist*, 13 August 1892, p. 3.
89 *NZH*, 2 June 1892, p. 3; 13 June 1893, p. 5.
90 ATL, 79-057/08/03, Auckland WCTU Minute Book 1889–98, 8 June 1892, 8 March 1893, 27 September 1893; *NZH*, 11 March 1893, p. 4; 23 September 1893, p. 5.
91 *Prohibitionist*, 25 November 1893, p. 3.
92 *Union Signal*, 17 December 1891, p. 4; *Prohibitionist*, 22 October 1892, p. 3; 28 January 1893, p. 3.
93 ATL, 79-057/08/03, Auckland WCTU Minute Book 1889–98, 11 October 1893.
94 ATL, 79-057/08/03, Auckland WCTU Minute Book 1889–98, 13 April 1893; *Eighth Annual Report of the Adelaide Woman's Christian Temperance Union* (Adelaide: G. Hassell & Son, 1894), p. 1; *Minutes of Fifth Annual Convention of the WCTU of South Australia*, p. 13.
95 *Freeman's Journal*, 7 April 1894, p. 19; *SMH*, 30 April 1894, p. 6; *Evening News*, 1 May 1894, p. 2; *NZH*, 2 June 1892, p. 3.
96 ATL, 79-057/08/03, Auckland WCTU Minute Book 1889–98, 11 April 1895; *NZH*, 11 April 1895, p. 5.
97 *Worker*, 5 October 1895, p. 3; *Brisbane Courier*, 25 September 1896, p. 2.
98 *Evening Journal*, 9 February 1889, p. 5.
99 *Minutes of Sixth Annual Convention of the WCTU of South Australia*, p. 29.

100 SLSA, SRG690, Woman's League Minute Book 1895–97; *South Australian Register (SAR)*, 21 March 1891, p. 18; *Report of the Women's Suffrage League of South Australia* (Adelaide: W. K. Thomas & Co., 1894), p. 6.
101 J. Hirst, 'South Australia and Australia: Reflections on their histories', in R. Foster and P. Sendziuk (eds), *Turning Points: Chapters in South Australian History* (Adelaide: Wakefield Press, 2012), pp. 118–30.
102 *White Ribbon Signal*, 16 October 1893, p. 3.
103 *SAR*, 23 May 1894, p. 3.
104 *AWS*, December 1901, p. 128; January 1902, p. 136; February 1902, pp. 144–5; SLSA, PRG88/7/10, Spence to Henry, 27 October 1901.
105 SLNSW, MLA2272/724, George to Scott, 22 August 1902; SLSA, SRG186/1/3, South Australian WCTU Minute Book 1900–4, 17 December 1903.
106 ATL, 79-057-08/03, Auckland WCTU Minute Book 1889–98, 23 May 1894, 11 July 1894, 25 July 1894, 11 April 1895; *White Ribbon*, 1 June 1903, p. 2; 15 November 1903, pp. 2–3.
107 See UAL, MSS2009/6/1, AWPL Minute Book 1892–98.
108 SLSA, SRG186/889, 'To officers of local unions: Miss Willard's first personal appeal', 15 June 1891; SLSA, SRG186/1/1, South Australian WCTU Minute Book 1889–95, 30 December 1890; SLSA, SRG186/1/2, South Australian WCTU Minute Book 1895–1900, 15 June 1899; ATL, 79-057-08/04, Auckland WCTU Minute Book 1898–1902, 15 March 1899; *Minutes of Fifth Annual Convention of the WCTU of South Australia*, p. 34.
109 Gordon, *Frances E. Willard*, p. 154; *Minutes of the Second Biennial Convention of the World's WCTU*, p. 83.
110 Tyrrell, *Woman's World*, pp. 39–41; F. E. Willard, *Home Protection Manual: Containing an Argument for the Temperance Ballot for Woman* (New York: The Independent Office, 1879), p. 6.
111 Hannam, 'International dimensions', 550.
112 *Union Signal*, 30 July 1891, p. 10.
113 The Tasmanian WCTU did not begin working for women's suffrage until 1892.
114 C. P. Wallace, *Manual of the Franchise Department* (Melbourne: Dunn & Wilkinson, 1891).
115 J. Ackermann, *Australia from a Woman's Point of View* (London: Cassell & Company, 1913), p. 213. Ackermann's criticism was not the final word on the petition. The most enduring of the public celebrations of the Victorian suffrage centenary in 2008 is Melbourne's imposing 'Great Petition' sculpture, located near the State Parliament, which has inscribed petitioning at the heart of public memories of the movement. Crozier-De Rosa and Mackie, *Remembering Women's Activism*, pp. 43–4.
116 Canterbury Museum, Christchurch (hereafter CM), ARC176.53/55, Catherine Wallace to Kate Sheppard, 18 August 1891.
117 *Prohibitionist*, 27 February 1892, p. 3; 7 May 1892, p. 3.
118 The decision was not unanimous. The West Taieri WCTU, which provided two of New Zealand's three delegates to the 1891 convention – Caroline Fulton and Mary Kirkland – arranged to federate with the Australian union before the national executive intervened. Hocken Collections, ARC-0379, AG613/021, Catherine Henrietta

Elliot Fulton diary 1891, 28 April–25 June; *Prohibitionist*, 29 August 1891, p. 3; *NZH*, 25 March 1892, p. 6.
119   ATL, 79-057/08/03, Auckland WCTU Minute Book 1889–98, 19 August 1891.
120   *WCTU of Australasia Minutes of the Second Triennial Convention*, p. 64.
121   CM, ARC176.53/228, M. E. Kirk to Sheppard, 18 January 1894; SLNSW, MLMSS3641, NSW WCTU Executive Minute Book 1892–94, 14 March 1894.
122   *WCTU of Australasia Minutes of the Second Triennial Convention*, pp. 16, 73.
123   *WCTU of Australasia Minutes of the Fourth Triennial Convention*, pp. 63, 66.
124   SLNSW, MLMSS3641, NSW WCTU Executive Minute Book 1882–94, 4 January 1893; *Minutes of the Second Biennial Convention of the World's WCTU*, p. 229.
125   SLSA, SRG186/1/2, South Australian WCTU Minute Book 1895–1900, 6 September 1895; University of Melbourne Archives, Melbourne (hereafter UMA), 101/85, Box 77/231/2, Margaret Press to Nicholls, 26 September 1895; UMA, 101/85, Box 77/231/2, Agnes Slack to Nicholls, 5 November 1895; *Mercury*, 25 March 1896, p. 3.
126   UMA, 101/85, Box 77/231/2, Nicholls to the WCTU of Australasia, 24 August 1896; UMA, 101/85, Box 15/241/1, Woman's Christian Temperance Union of Australasia Executive Council Minutes 1891–1909, 4 May 1903; *WCTU of Australasia Minutes of the Fourth Triennial Convention*, pp. 63–6.
127   *Official Report of the National Australasian Convention Debates, First Session: Adelaide 1897* (Sydney: University of Sydney Library, 1999), p. 69.
128   *Commonwealth of Australia, Parliamentary Debates, House of Representatives*, no. 1, 22 April 1902, p. 11847; *Commonwealth, Parliamentary Debates, House of Representatives*, no. 1, 24 April 1902, p. 11953.
129   R. Bordin, *Frances Willard: A Biography* (Chapel Hill: University of North Carolina Press, 1986), pp. 109, 181–213.
130   F. Willard, 'Address at Exeter Hall, January 9, 1893', in C. D. S. Gifford and A. R. Slagell (eds), *Let Something Good Be Said: Speeches and Writings of Frances E. Willard* (Urbana: University of Illinois Press, 2007), pp. 170–7.
131   M. Barrow, 'Teetotal feminists: Temperance leadership and the campaign for women's suffrage', in C. Eustance et al. (eds), *A Suffrage Reader: Charting Directions in British Suffrage History* (London: Leicester University Press, 2000), pp. 75–84; *Journal: Official organ pro tem of the British Women's Temperance Association*, June 1893, pp. 7–8; August 1893, p. 16..
132   Gifford, 'Frances Willard', 117–34; *Report of the Seventh Convention of the World's Woman's Christian Temperance Union* (Evanston: Woman's Temperance Publishing Association, 1906), p. 174.
133   Bordin, *Woman and Temperance*, pp. 140–55; L. McGirr, *The War on Alcohol: Prohibition and the Rise of the American State* (New York: W. W. Norton & Company, 2016), pp. 5–11.
134   White, *The Republic*, pp. 17, 389; P. Young-Lee, 'The Temperance Temple and architectural representation in late nineteenth-century Chicago', *Gender & History*, 17:3 (2005), 793–825.
135   R. E. Bohlmann, '"Our 'house beautiful'": The Woman's Temple and the WCTU effort to establish place and identity in downtown Chicago, 1887–1898', *Journal of Women's*

History, 11:2 (1999), 110–34; White, *The Republic*, pp. 555, 825; Young-Lee, 'The Temperance Temple', 800.

136 Excerpts from the speech were reprinted in a leaflet beloved among Midwestern radicals, 'Francis Willard on socialism'. Buhle, *Women and American Socialism*, p. 108. See *Report of the National Woman's Christian Temperance Union at the Twenty-Fourth Annual Meeting* (Chicago: Woman's Temperance Publishing Association, 1897), pp. 113–21.

137 Bordin, *Woman and Temperance*, p. 140; *Report of the National Woman's Christian Temperance Union at the Twenty-Fifth Annual Meeting* (Chicago: Woman's Temperance Publishing Association, 1898), pp. 27, 47–53.

138 ATL, 79-057-08/03, Auckland WCTU Minute Book 1889–98, 13 April 1898; SLSA, SRG186/1/2, South Australian WCTU Minute Book 1895–1900, June 1899.

139 Willard's allusion to the subject in her 1893 speech was the exception that proved the rule. *Minutes of the Second Biennial Convention of the World's WCTU*, pp. 73–4; *The World's Woman's Christian Temperance Union* (Chicago: World's Woman's Christian Temperance Union, 1890), p. 15.

140 SLSA, SRG186/22, Elizabeth Waycroft to Mary Lockwood, 10 March 1907.

141 CM, ARC176.53/365, Anna Gordon to Sheppard, 21 August 1906.

142 *Our Federation*, 15 October 1900, pp. 158–61.

143 *Minutes of the Second Biennial Convention of the World's WCTU*, pp. 43, 73–4.

144 W. S. Bain, *The International Council of Women: The Berlin Congress* (Christchurch: Lyttelton Times Company, 1904), p. 6.

145 *Dundee Courier*, 26 February 1907, p. 1; *Scottish Women's Temperance News*, April 1913, p. 51; M. Smitley, *The Feminine Public Sphere: Middle-class Women in Civic Life in Scotland, c. 1870–1914* (Manchester: Manchester University Press, 2009), pp. 101–2.

146 *Minutes of the Second Biennial Convention of the World's WCTU*, p. 25.

147 Tyrrell, *Woman's Empire*, pp. 223–6, 235–9; L. Edwards, 'Chinese feminism in a transnational frame: Between internationalism and xenophobia', in M. Roces and L. Edwards (eds), *Women's Movements in Asia: Feminisms and Transnational Activism* (Oxford: Routledge, 2010), pp. 59–63.

148 J. van Voris, *Carrie Chapman Catt: A Public Life* (New York: The Feminist Press, 1987), pp. 12–17.

149 Tyrrell, *Woman's Empire*, p. 2; *Union Signal*, 16 October 1902, p. 3.

2

'My heart ... yearn[s] for a genuine voting Australian woman!': Australasian suffragists and the international suffrage movement

On 30 March 1906, Carrie Chapman Catt, president of the International Woman Suffrage Alliance (IWSA), wrote plaintively to Rose Scott, secretary of the Womanhood Suffrage League (WSL) of New South Wales, 'my heart ... yearn[s] for a genuine voting Australian woman'.[1] On its face, her plea appeared unusual. A few years earlier, the bond between the United States and Australia appeared to lie at the heart of the emerging international suffrage movement.[2] In February 1902, Scott's confidante, the Victorian suffragist Vida Goldstein, stood alongside Susan B. Anthony, Anna Howard Shaw, Alice Stone Blackwell, and a dozen more of Catt's contemporaries in the US Capitol. There, Goldstein urged the Senate Select Committee on Woman Suffrage to 'trust your women' and ratify a constitutional amendment allowing the female franchise.[3] A week earlier, in what she described as 'the great memory of my life', Goldstein represented Australia and New Zealand at the International Woman Suffrage Conference in Washington, DC. There, delegates from nine countries laid the foundations for the IWSA.[4] Although, unlike many of her compatriots, Goldstein could not yet vote, she nevertheless personified the spirit of a new nation 'pleased to the point of self-righteousness', as Clare Wright observes, with its perceived social and political superiority, encapsulated by its push towards gender equality.[5] Sustained by these certainties, Goldstein concluded her speech before the Washington conference with a promise to her peers: 'Woman suffrage is with us to stay, and that our success may hasten the day when you American women will stand before the world as the political equal of your men folk is the earnest desire of the countries which have sent me here.'[6]

On her return to Australia, Goldstein reiterated her message at a reception at the Sydney Mechanics' School of Arts: 'let us enter the new international alliance, and never rest until we have obtained for the women of other lands the same privileges which we enjoy in Australia'.[7]

Over the preceding decade, similar rhetoric had echoed across the Tasman as women first from New Zealand, and then a rash of Australian colonies, celebrated winning the vote with proclamations of solidarity with their disenfranchised sisters across the world.[8] To many observers it seemed clear that antipodean women, guided by such a clear sense of their historical significance, would play a vital role in the international campaign for women's enfranchisement, and particularly in its most formalised expression, the IWSA. Catt certainly thought so. A parting note scrawled in Goldstein's diary expressed her hope that their 'bond of sympathy and good fellowship' would connect 'the Australian Woman Suffrage movement and that in the U.S. ... [and] bind us continually closer until every woman in both our countries has gained the right to self-government'.[9] Yet, as Catt's letter to Scott four years later made clear, until the end of the First World War the two countries Goldstein represented at the 1902 conference had become more notable by their absence.

Goldstein's journey, and the impression she made in the United States, has captivated historians as much as it intrigued American progressives at the time. Yet, while feminists' interwar internationalism remains the subject of sustained historical interest – coinciding with a historiography characterising these years as an 'internationalist moment' – the matter of Australasian women's participation in international organisations before the First World War has attracted much less attention.[10] As it stands, the pre-war history of Australasian suffrage internationalism is largely considered through histories of women's travel and scattered among authorised chronicles produced by the National Councils of Women (NCW).[11] This treatment is contrasted by a surfeit of European and American analyses of the international women's movement that followed Leila Rupp's *Worlds of Women*.[12] There is ample room, then, to extend Marilyn Lake's call for historians to 'understand the conditions and contexts that both enabled and constrained women's exercise of [international] leadership' into the early twentieth century.[13]

In Australia, at least, scholars have historically justified their inattention to the years before 1914 on the grounds that women's internationalism was tepid. As Barbara Caine wrote in 1998, Australians 'had acknowledged, but rarely been involved in, pre-war ... organisations like the International Council of Women'.[14] However, women did not shun the international sphere. Explanations that cite the colonists' distance from Europe and inability to speak its languages as impediments to women's travel are partial, at best.[15] Rather, the records of the International Council of Women (ICW) and its contemporaries show that, in the anticipation and afterglow of enfranchisement, Australian women joined a wave of international organisations. However, their enthusiasm for these liberal initiatives – for, unlike their Northern Hemisphere contemporaries, Australasian women had little appetite for radical internationalism – was circumscribed by international leaders' insistence that 'self-governing nation states or federal states formed the ... foundation of any organisation'.[16] The transition from the transatlantic friendship networks of the mid-century, and organisations like the World's Woman's Christian Temperance Union (WCTU) that sought to transcend national boundaries, to a new, state-based international order reflected women's desire for legitimacy in an arena dominated by nation states, their faith in the progressive nature of state building, and members' fear that admitting sub-national groups would anger authoritarian European federal governments.[17] Nationalism, many historians agree, was not considered anathema to cross-border cooperation, but rather an essential prerequisite to true internationalism.[18] For Australian and New Zealand women seeking international solidarity, adhering to these new norms would require extensive domestic reorganisation, namely the formation of 'national' representative bodies, a centralising project that many activists – who preferred to organise along old colonial lines – stubbornly resisted.

Few of Vida Goldstein's contemporaries would have contested her declaration that they had a 'great obligation to those [suffragists] who blazed the tracks in England & other countries many years ago'.[19] Nevertheless, Australasian women appeared reluctant to join the IWSA. Despite their world-leading enfranchisement, the disintegration of New Zealand's women's organisations in the 1900s precluded formal internationalism. As a result, this chapter is more concerned with their neighbours across the Tasman. Indeed, in Australia debate raged over whether state or national organisations should serve as the platform for women's internationalism. The principle had urgent consequences for a splintering Europe. Hence, between 1899 and 1904, the ICW – a conglomerate of peak national women's organisations established in 1888 with the aim of becoming a 'permanent International Parliament of Women' – was more preoccupied by the question of how to accommodate Australia's five 'national' councils than any other piece of business.[20] In 1905, it reached a compromise that facilitated Australian women's international participation by preserving the states' autonomy behind a flimsy national façade that remained intact until 1931.[21] The IWSA, an organisation devoted to women's enfranchisement, took a more rigid stance on national organisation. To prevent the fragmentation of European suffrage movements along ethnic or factional lines, it restricted admission to a single representative body per country, enshrining national unity as a precondition of international cooperation.[22]

This chapter traces Australasian women's engagement with international women's suffrage organisations, from promising beginnings in the 1890s to marginality over the following decade. Expanding on efforts to fathom Australians' 'civic indolence', I argue that Australian women's lacklustre participation in the IWSA was a consequence of their unsettled position in an institution predicated on national representation.[23] As Vida Goldstein discovered on returning from the United States tasked with building a national auxiliary to the IWSA, 'there was as yet no imagined Australian community' among the suffragists.[24] While the rhetoric of 'maternal service' to the nation prevailed in domestic politics, most Australian women who entered the international sphere after 1901 mobilised under existing state organisations.[25] For some, like Goldstein, Federal enfranchisement prompted a profound identification with the Commonwealth, a sentiment that underpinned their international endeavours. For others, like Rose Scott, internationalism offered an opportunity to resist the existential threat of 'national singularity'.[26] Such persistent localism clashed with the IWSA's membership criteria. Although pre-war Australian feminists were enthusiastic travellers, a heady mix of organisational politics, unease with Federation, and personal disputes circumscribed their participation in international women's organisations during the high tide of international suffragism.

Beginning with a comprehensive picture of Australian women's participation in the pre-war international women's movement, this chapter also explains New Zealand women's absence from the international arena beyond the realm of the WCTU. It then turns to the problems that colonial and federated Australia posed for an international order predicated on the participation of nation states, assessing Goldstein's assertion that Australian women's ambivalence towards the IWSA was the result of parochialism. Finally, it illuminates the career of the Sydney suffragist Madge Donohoe, who, as one of the few antipodean women who consistently attended international conferences in the 1900s, enriches existing understandings of the mechanics and shortcomings of Australian feminists' overseas endeavours.

Australasia's feminist travellers: International women's conferences, 1893–1914

Like abolitionists, pacifists, socialists, and trade unionists, European and American women began organising across borders in the mid-nineteenth century. Initially, they forged personal ties, but as women gained experience in non-governmental organisations they built institutions to advance their emancipatory agenda. World's fairs and international conventions – the increasingly coincident nodes of steam-era transnationalism – attracted women's rights activists, who created an axis for collaboration based on the universalising belief that their common oppression necessitated collective action.[27] Early organisations like the Association Internationale des Femmes (1868–72) and the British, Continental, and General Federation for the Abolition of Government Regulation of Prostitution (1875) permitted individual and sub-national membership.[28] However, when the ICW, often considered the first important transnational women's organisation, was founded in 1888 it curtailed 'any internationalism not based exclusively on the national'. As articulated by its American de-facto president, May Wright Sewall, the ICW's governing 'Council Idea' restricted membership to National Councils of Women, composed of delegates from existing women's organisations.[29] The insistence on national affiliation was intended to grow a mass membership rapidly. It was also becoming typical of contemporary international associations, such as the World Methodist Council (1881) and the International Secretariat of National Trade Union Centres (1901). As Christine von Oertzen argues, the project was paradoxical, at once engendering 'an intimate connection between the development of the international network and the establishment of individual, national organisations with their own biases'.[30]

Despite its rigid constitution, the ICW's politics remained amorphous. The organisation's roots lay in a much-mythologised meeting in Liverpool. There in 1893, Susan B. Anthony and Elizabeth Cady Stanton proposed the formation of an 'International Woman Suffrage Association'.[31] Five years later, when the Council was established in Washington, DC, suffrage featured nowhere on its agenda. From the beginning, its leaders hoped to bridge religious, cultural, and political divides so that they could speak authoritatively on all issues that affected women. Yet, in prioritising unity, the Council's executive undermined their lofty ambitions. In 1899, the ICW's secretary, Teresa Wilson, stated that her colleagues' deliberate 'vagueness about both our methods and aims' meant that they found it difficult to explain 'who we are and what we want'. Though she feared such caution hindered the pursuit of immediate objectives, Wilson admitted that 'this very vagueness allows us to be all-embracing', paving the way for the Council's future endeavours, should they be agreed on.[32]

As tensions within the World's WCTU demonstrated, the preference for moral reform over thornier demands for political equality was not unique to the ICW. Its approach learnt from the demise of the Association

Internationale des Femmes, whose leaders' emphasis on women's enfranchisement had alienated potential members.[33] However, the Council's pursuit of a universally palatable agenda proved impossible. While its president, Lady Ishbel Aberdeen, tolerated the discussion of women's enfranchisement, she refused to accredit a suffrage symposium at its 1899 congress unless anti-suffragists could speak. In response, disgruntled members convened the International Woman Suffrage Committee in 1902.[34] Two years after laying plans for a federation of national woman suffrage associations, in 1904 the committee inaugurated the IWSA to 'secure the enfranchisement of the women of all nations, and to unite the friends of women suffrage throughout the world in organized co-operation and fraternal happiness'.[35] The emergence of a rival prompted the ICW to reconsider women's enfranchisement. However, to assuage members' fears that the new Committee on Suffrage and the Rights of Citizenship (1904) was 'radically progressive', its chair, Anna Howard Shaw, emphasised its voluntary basis. For the next decade, the committee was the Council's quietest. Its subsequent meeting, for example, was held outside the ICW's 1909 Toronto congress programme, a silence which reiterated the message that women like Vida Goldstein needed to work through the IWSA to further the cause of suffrage internationalism.[36]

As a rule, Australian participation in these organisations has been underestimated, a consequence of the archival deficits that plague historians of women's international institutions. Most NCWs retain detailed records, yet, until the 2010s, these collections had not been examined comparatively. Furthermore, extant personal papers only document distinguished individuals' networks, and few of the myriad records produced by the ICW and IWSA are held in Australasian repositories. Thus, in the 1990s, when both organisations' archives were inaccessible from the antipodes, historians believed Australian women remained aloof from international conferences after 1893.[37] Over the past decade, however, a flurry of digitisation has revolutionised access to the archives of the international women's movement. Read alongside the records of domestic women's organisations, these materials show that Australian women were, in fact, enthusiastic members of an international community.

Twenty-two Australian representatives attended the ICW's quinquennial congresses between 1893 and 1914. In the Council's first decade, delegations largely consisted of proxy representatives: either expatriates or foreign stand-ins. Mirroring the slow formation of state councils, most delegates hailed from the populous southeast.[38] By the 1910s, this trend had altered. With councils in every state, the number of proxy delegates fell, and larger parties travelled abroad. However, with

2.1 Australasian attendance at ICW congresses, 1893–1914

	NSW	NZ	QLD	SA	TAS	VIC	WA	States present (total delegates)
1893 Congress (Chicago)	Margaret Windeyer	n/a	n/a	n/a	n/a	n/a	n/a	33 (600)[1]
1899 Congress (London)	Dora Armitage, Emma Dixson	Kate McCosh Clarke, Maud Pember Reeves, Beatrice Webb	n/a	Sarah Cockburn, Mrs Gawler	Emily Dobson, Lady Theresa Hamilton	Lady Janet Clarke	Laura Wittenoom	29 (67)
1904 Congress (Berlin)	Emma Dixson, Isabel Dickson, Madge Donohoe	Isabel Napier, Wilhelmina Sherriff Bain	n/a	0	Emily Dobson	0	n/a	17 (100)
1909 Congress (Toronto)	0	n/a	0	0	Emily Dobson, Ada Stourton	Alice Baker, Evelyn Gough, Janet Grieg	n/a	14 (93)
1914 Congress (Rome)	Edith Fry, E. Vickery	n/a	Elizabeth Kingsbury, Nellie Smyth	0	Emily Dobson, Ada Stourton	Marie Bage, Gladys Marks	A. J. Bennett, E. L. Sutherland	20 (110)

[1] The 1893 congress had such a large attendance because it coincided with the World's Columbian Exposition.

Source: The published reports of the ICW's quinquennial conventions, 1893–1914.

Note: Proxy delegates in italics.

the exception of Tasmania's Emily Dobson, a life patron who attended eleven of the ICW's seventeen meetings between 1893 and 1914, few Australians could accrete the thick social and political networks their Northern Hemisphere peers enjoyed.[39]

Over the same period, Australians attended IWSA meetings in smaller numbers. Australian representatives travelled to six of the Alliance's first seven conferences, though not its inauguration in 1904. As with every woman who represented the colonies at ICW events, and reflecting the homogenous character of pre-war international women's meetings, all seven delegates were of European heritage.[40] Alliance meetings attracted European and North American suffrage grandees but its Australian delegates seldom boasted the equivalent domestic stature. Between Goldstein's homecoming in 1902 and the First World War, two women – Dobson and Lille Cowley – travelled to meetings from Australia; the rest lived abroad. European residents Margaret Hodge, Harriet Newcomb, and Madge Donohoe had all served on the WSL of

2.2 Australasian attendance at IWSA conferences, 1902–13

	Australian delegates	New Zealand delegates	States present (total delegates)
1902 Conference (Washington, DC)	Vida Goldstein (VIC)	0	9 (13)
1904 Conference (Berlin)	n/a	Isabel Napier, Wilhelmina Sherriff Bain	10 (47)
1906 Conference (Copenhagen)	Emily Dobson (TAS), *Madge Donohoe* (NSW)	0	15 (73)
1908 Conference (Amsterdam)	Emily Dobson (Commonwealth Govt.), *Madge Donohoe* (NSW)	Alice Steele	18 (107)
1909 Conference (London)	Lille Cowley (NSW), *Madge Donohoe* (NSW)	Isabella May	22 (147)
1911 Conference (Stockholm)	Margaret Hodge (UK), Harriet Newcomb (UK)	0	21 (195)
1913 Conference (Budapest)	Gertrude Spencer (VIC)	0	22 (331)

Source: The published reports of the IWSA's biennial conferences, 1902–13.
Note: Proxy delegates in italics.

New South Wales' executive, yet when they travelled their names were not immediately familiar to women across Australia or abroad.

Combined with the absence of Australia's handful of internationally recognised suffragists, the country's small delegations alarmed the IWSA. The Alliance's biennial conferences expanded from the thirteen women who gathered in 1902 to over 300 delegates by 1913, but featured few enfranchised women. As Carrie Chapman Catt explained to Rose Scott in a long letter – which also revealed her stadial conception of feminist awakening – urging Australians to attend international events,

> The value of the Alliance depends directly upon the connection of the enfranchised countries with it. The feeble organizations of those countries where women are just beginning to emerge from centuries-old conditions are strengthened by the contact with the broadminded women from the countries where larger opportunities have [been] obtained, and the knowledge they get of the benefit of the suffrage sends them home to work with faith and courage which they would never possess otherwise, and therefore the attendance upon International meetings of such enfranchised women is doing a far mightier work for the enfranchisement of the world than it is possible for those at a distance to conceive. How to secure this connection in the best way is the problem we are now considering.[41]

Despite Catt's complaints about Australians, New Zealanders were scarcer still. The colony's NCW, established in 1896, was among the first in the world, but it also endured a fractious relationship with the ICW. Conflict between moderates, led by Lady Anna Stout, the wife of a former premier, and radicals, like Kate Sheppard and Amey Daldy, over the pursuit of women's economic independence led to accusations that its leadership ostracised groups 'antagonistic to the political principles in [its] aims and objectives'. Rebuked for breaching the ICW's non-partisanship principle, the New Zealand council delayed its membership application until 1900.[42] In the meantime, its members' international endeavours reached a nadir when the English social researcher Beatrice Webb represented them at the ICW's London congress. Although she stood in for the Council's sole enfranchised affiliate in 1899, Webb, a known anti-suffragist, endorsed a motion prohibiting the discussion of 'New Woman ideas'.[43]

Back in New Zealand, the divisions that delayed the NCW's affiliation remained unresolved. Unlike in Australia, parochialism was not the primary reason behind the organisation's demise. Nevertheless, the abolition of provincial government in 1876 had not resulted in the immediate centralisation of New Zealand life, as a fierce dispute in 1897 over whether the NCW should meet in the North or South Island revealed.⁴⁴ More significant was the death or retirement of many of the Council's leaders soon after its inception. Without uniting figures, tensions between moderates and radicals over the Council's agenda resulted in the disaffiliation of member organisations. After several years of declining attendances, it ceased meeting in 1903 and three years later entered permanent recess, forcing New Zealand to withdraw from the ICW. In appointing Kate Sheppard as an honorary vice-president in 1910, the ICW hoped to retain ties with New Zealand. However, the gesture proved hollow. Sheppard expressed her 'deep regret' at seeing 'N.Z. left out' of the list of members on the ICW's letterhead, and Stout declared her embarrassment that 'New Zealand was the only civilised country which was unrepresented' at international women's conferences.⁴⁵ Yet without the political will from atomised women's associations, it took until 1918 for the NCW to reform. Between 1905 and 1919, no New Zealand woman attended an ICW meeting.

The colony's relationship with the IWSA was similarly troubled. The organisation commissioned pamphlets by Sheppard and Stout describing their experience under universal enfranchisement and invited New Zealand to affiliate or, at the very least, send delegates to its conferences throughout the 1900s.⁴⁶ However, as with the ICW, without a national organisation New Zealand women could not meet their requests. Three of the four delegates that attended its meetings as guests between 1904 and 1909 lived in Britain and retained little connection to local women's organisations. Further, and to Alliance members' chagrin, New Zealand disappeared from its meetings until 1926.⁴⁷

While New Zealanders' exile from the international women's movement was self-imposed, it is harder to reconcile Vida Goldstein's proclamations of Australian leadership with her countrywomen's indifference to the IWSA. Geographical barriers are often cited as the most significant obstacles to feminist internationalism.⁴⁸ These claims warrant scrutiny. The 14,000 miles separating Australia from the international women's movement's Euro-American powerbase undoubtedly circumscribed women's ability to attend meetings. Until the 1960s, European delegates spurned proposals to meet outside the North Atlantic on account of prohibitive travel costs. Emily Dobson skewered the ICW's hypocrisy in 1909, reminding its Toronto congress that 'the distance is exactly the same going out to Australia as it is coming [to the Northern Hemisphere]'. As she recognised, the policy deterred mass participation and curtailed the ambitions of Southern Hemisphere women.⁴⁹ For the affluent, the age of rail and steam revolutionised women's mobility. Late

2.3 Australasian attendance at World's WCTU conventions, 1891–1913

	NZ	NSW	QLD	SA	TAS	VIC	WA	WCTU of Australasia	States present (total delegates)
1891 Convention (Boston)	0	0	0	0	0	Mary Love	n/a	0	20 (40)
1893 Convention (Chicago)	Mrs Smith	0	0	0	0	Mary Love	0	Jessie Ackermann	8 (171)
1895 Convention (London)	Isabel Napier, Kate Sheppard	0	Susan Sagar	0	0	*Mrs Crouch*	0	Jessie Ackermann	23 (380)
1897 Convention (Toronto)	0	Lizzie Vincent	Ada Murcutt	0	Miss Ware	Marie Kirk	Emily Cummins	Louisa Ardill	18 (210)
1900 Convention (Edinburgh)	Mary Powell	Bessie Harrison Lee	T. A. Johnson, Margaret Murray	Mrs Drake	Mrs Barber	Mrs Howden, Margaret McLean	Mrs Hamilton	Ada Murcutt, Elizabeth Nicholls	28 (242)

Convention						Lucy Pettifer	Miss Hanlin, R. Hanlin	Bessie Harrison Lee	
1903 Convention (Geneva)	Marie Kirkland, Mary de Renzi Newton, Mrs Wright	o	A. Maria Cole	o	o				21 (184)
1906 Convention (Boston)	Miss Wallace	n/a	n/a	n/a	n/a	n/a	n/a	Mrs Thomson	32 (368)
1910 Convention (Glasgow)	Anderson Hughes, Miss E. Morice, Jane Roberts, Lady Anna Stout	n/a	n/a	n/a	n/a	n/a	n/a	Mrs Chapple, Emma Dixson, Mrs Hocking, Mrs Murray, Sara Nolan, Miss Thompson, Mrs Wills	14 (378)
1913 Convention (New York)	Anderson Hughes-Drew	n/a	n/a	n/a	n/a	n/a	n/a	Lady Julia Holder	32 (415)

Source: The published reports of the World's WCTU conventions, 1891–1913.
Notes: Proxy delegates in italics.

nineteenth-century travellers enjoyed improvements in shipping speeds, and cheap fares allowed 'ordinary' women a remarkable degree of mobility before the era of mass transportation. Nevertheless, comfortable (and respectable) cabin berths were beyond most women.[50] Until 1920, when the ICW instituted travel grants, its unofficial policy was to elect officers with 'large means' above worthier candidates who 'ha[d] not the money for travelling'.[51] Although the Australian NCWs recruited the wives of prominent politicians as figurehead presidents, few of the women who led their constituent societies possessed such means, making even one European sojourn a test of their financial and familial freedom. Dobson, who spent much of her life shipboard, travelling to Europe a staggering thirty-three times between 1842 and 1934, was an outlier.[52]

The sundering effects of the antipodes' distance from Europe can also be overstated, as women in other reform organisations demonstrated. Between 1891 and 1913, eleven New Zealanders and thirty-two Australians attended World's WCTU conventions. Hundreds more explored Asia and the Pacific as Christian missionaries.[53] As an organisation established to combat the transnational trade in intoxicants, travel was woven into the union's fabric. Unlike the ICW and IWSA, the WCTU did not employ proxy delegates, meaning that all representatives were both funded by and returned home to local branches, strengthening emotional ties between members and the World's union.

Allied with its peripatetic culture, the WCTU's structure further diminished the obstacles to travel. Until 1906, when the Australasian WCTU instituted unified delegations to overseas events, state unions cherished the 'privilege of direct affiliation' to the World's WCTU.[54] Members considered World's conventions an important expression of local and international identity as well as a forum for interstate competition. As a result, the triennial conventions entertained a more geographically diverse Australian presence than did ICW or IWSA meetings and constituted the only international forum that New Zealand women consistently attended before the 1920s. The World's WCTU also provided Australasian delegates with indirect assistance by appointing experienced organisers like Lizzie Vincent, Emily Cummins, Ada Murcutt, Anderson Hughes, and Bessie Lee Cowie as 'round-the-world' missionaries. Such positions were unsalaried, but those credentialed by the World's executive could embark on years-long journeys subsisting on members' charity.[55] Reporting in 1910, after travelling through the United Kingdom, the Middle East, and Australasia, Lee Cowie boasted that she had survived for three years at the cost of just £22 to the World's treasury.[56]

Australasian missionaries also benefited from sharing a common tongue with the WCTU's American progenitors. Since the emergence of the 'transnational activist' earlier in the century, the capacity for languages had been a considered a prerequisite for cultural and political intermediaries. As the *New York Tribune* reported in 1904, 'foreign languages' were 'part of the successful woman's equipment' in polyglot organisations like the ICW and IWSA.[57] The New Zealand peace activist Wilhelmina Sherriff Bain spoke from experience when she warned prospective delegates that the 'inability to comprehend any language save one's own proved a very real disqualification' at international meetings, and Kate Sheppard admitted that few of her compatriots could 'drop into French or German'.[58] However, nothing suggests these linguistic barriers discouraged their compatriots from travelling. Unlike the Socialist Women's International, whose insistence on German as a working language restricted its membership, the ICW and IWSA conducted business in English, French, and German, while English doubled as the primary language of publication. Martina Kramers, the Dutch editor of the IWSA's predominantly English-language newspaper *Jus Suffragii* (1906–24), grudgingly accepted the situation as an economic necessity: 'the poor monolingual Americans must also know what is going on'.[59] If Kramers' sentiments were widespread, they did not disadvantage travelling English speakers. When Madge Donohoe toured the Netherlands as a suffrage lecturer in 1908, her hosts supplied a translator, a courtesy seldom extended to non-speakers of the three official languages.[60] Language and travel were obstacles some women's organisations overcame, suggesting that deeper reasons lay behind Australian women's neglect of international suffrage conventions.

Inter/national politics in the International Council of Women and International Woman Suffrage Alliance[61]

Writing to IWSA president Carrie Chapman Catt in 1909, Vida Goldstein identified another cause for her countrywomen's lukewarm embrace of international suffragism. Australians, she told Catt 'over and over again', suffered an 'utter absence of national feeling'.[62] The statement contrasted with Goldstein's confident self-presentation as an Australian citizen abroad. Federation had laid the foundation for the Commonwealth Franchise Act 1902 and provided women with a platform to speak internationally on progressive issues. Yet colonial and imperial loyalties died hard. The Commonwealth eventually became the 'focus of intense nationalist identification on the part of (white) women', but in 1901 it had limited emotional resonance for its citizens. Politically active women continued to organise themselves along state lines and resisted ceding power to national bodies into the 1920s and beyond. Overlooked in the history of twentieth-century feminism, Goldstein's struggle to build a national women's political organisation to join the IWSA revealed a conflict between her vision of the Commonwealth as a 'sphere for patriotic action' and the prevalence of older colonial nationalisms that complicated women's participation in international organisations.[63]

Although she had little to show for it by the end of the decade, Goldstein envisaged Australia's admission to the IWSA as a model of national collaboration. Nominated as a delegate to the 1902 International Woman Suffrage Congress, she launched a nationwide fundraising appeal. Yet, aside from £30 donated by the New South Wales WSL, the bulk of the United Council for Woman Suffrage's 'American Delegates Fund' was collected from fellow Victorians.[64] Writing later, the South Australian Catherine Helen Spence believed Goldstein's supporters felt 'sore' that women in other states 'did so little towards sending Vida to America'.[65] As quickly became apparent, the ambivalent response to Goldstein's request foreshadowed her compatriots' indifference to the Alliance's work.

A louder warning of the difficulties Goldstein faced reverberated from Europe, where the ICW executive challenged Australia's sub-national affiliations to the Council. Seeking to demonstrate growth before the Council's showpiece London congress, in 1899 the departing executive committee bent its membership criteria and admitted the self-governing colonies of New South Wales and Tasmania as full members. Viewed from Australia, the ruling did not appear unusual. Colonial 'nationalisms' preceded and overlapped patriotic identification with the Commonwealth.[66] However, the ICW's incoming leadership – headed by May Wright Sewall – repudiated the decision, branding the colonies' admission a violation of the Council's 'fundamental ideal'. Reflecting on her presidency (1899–1904), Sewall identified the question of 'national autonomy' as the 'most serious problem' she had faced, a debate 'precipitated and made a practical issue by the federation of the Australian states'.[67] As Isabel Dickson, New South Wales' delegate to the ICW's 1904 Berlin congress, explained to her compatriots, the 'Australian question' was not merely a domestic dispute but had 'political application in Europe':

> If the federated states of the Commonwealth each have a national council, what is to prevent each federated state, say of the German Empire from making the same demand? That could be regarded by the German government as in direct opposition to the policy which has built up the powerful German Empire, & could only have one result,

the suppression of Women's National Councils as dangerous political societies.[68]

Staged in Paris, Copenhagen, and The Hague, the ICW's federation debates proceeded without Australian participation. In 1902, the executive vetoed a suggestion that its secretary travel to Australia to convince the state councils to amalgamate, hoping that they would do so of their own accord once 'political federation had become a settled reality'.[69] Yet Australia's 'transitional condition' was not easily resolved. The ICW's oversight became apparent in 1903, when the South Australian and Victorian NCWs sought to join as independent affiliates. Their applications instigated another round of debates over 'political and racial representation' on the Council, which transpired over several 'electric days' in 1904.[70] Worried that separate state membership would award Australia twelve votes at executive meetings, 'whilst the whole of America only had three', the US delegate, May Wood Smith, blocked the states' admission.[71]

Mutual misunderstanding prolonged the dispute. Wilhelmina Sherriff Bain, one of the few antipodean delegates in Berlin, was surprised by the 'superabundance of parochial sentiment' that animated the congress. Nevertheless, like her European counterparts, she satisfied herself that once apprised of the ICW's objections, 'Australia will probably arrange this for herself ere long'.[72] Yet, despite the rumblings from Berlin, the state councils remained opposed to the ICW's favoured solution, the formation of 'one great National Council' in Australia, 'as it is in the United States'.[73] Even after Federation, the state, rather than the continent, remained women's primary point of reference. Rose Scott's 1903 speech to the New South Wales Council encapsulated members' concerns:

> The difficulty here is scarcely realised by people who have never been in Australia, and that is, that our States are really so huge, so far apart, so sparsely populated, that it would be almost impossible for an Executive Council of an Australian National Council to meet in order to do business [...] I cannot personally agree with Mrs Sewall and Lady Aberdeen that our position is analogous to that of the 45 American States.[74]

Confronted by antipodean intransigence, the ICW yielded. Emily Dobson conceded that the American delegates had 'justly' opposed Australian 'over-representation' on the executive. Nevertheless, along with most of her colleagues she believed that the 'time was not yet ripe for actual federation'. Instead, in 1905 the Australian councils rejected unification in favour of a 'limited federation in matters such as finance and [international] representation'.⁷⁵ The ICW begrudgingly accepted their proposal three years later. In the short term, the separate recognition afforded to the state councils 'reinforce[d] provincialism over national interest'. While the councils' common ICW membership ensured their activism followed similar trajectories, like Federation itself, it did not diminish 'old colonial loyalties, but merely provide[d] ... new structures within which they could compete'.⁷⁶ Despite regular interstate meetings, the problems of distance and poor communication that Scott raised in 1903 delayed the formation of the NCW of Australia until 1931. Even then, some Western Australian members, inspired by the state's secession movement, decried the push for amalgamation as a form of 'sovietism'. Only in the aftermath of the Second World War did the unified NCW develop a truly national focus.⁷⁷ Clearly, the ICW's solution was imperfect, yet the bifurcation of state and national responsibilities encouraged international participation. As the IWSA discovered, there was little to be gained by insisting Australian women unite under a single banner.

As a member of Victoria's NCW, Vida Goldstein must have realised the scale of her task in 1902. In spite of her conviction that the Commonwealth was a beacon for progressives across the world, Goldstein reflected on the challenge ahead before she left America. 'The new Federated Australia', she told the *San Francisco Chronicle*, 'is so far, rather a doubtful venture. It has always appeared to me to be premature. We have not yet developed sufficient statesmanship to manage such a large concern.'⁷⁸ Goldstein was returning to a country that Alfred Deakin, its Attorney General and one of the architects of Federation, considered 'a loosely allied set of communities divided from each other by vast distances and preoccupied by parochial aims'.⁷⁹ Although she had long opposed Federation, Goldstein soon came to identify with the Commonwealth, even if only as a pragmatic response to the shifting locus of political power. In 1903, she led 700 women in dedicating a 'memorial of gratitude' to the Barton Ministry for making Australia 'the first nation to recognise that women are justly entitled to the inalienable right of self-government'.⁸⁰ However, as her attempt to form a Women's Federal Political Association (WFPA) proved, those further from the seat of federal government in Melbourne were less eager to enlist in continental endeavours.

From the outset, Goldstein struggled to balance her state commitments with the demands of national organisation. In 1902, she returned to the Victorian suffrage campaign and, early the following year, stood as the first female candidate for the Federal Senate. In the meantime, to recoup her outstanding travel expenses, Goldstein deferred her plans to create the WFPA, instead taking a magic lantern show, 'To America and

Back', on the speaking circuit.[81] Whereas the WCTU was a triumph of grassroots evangelism, Goldstein was forced to create her organisation from the top down. From her Melbourne apartment, she wrote to interstate women's leaders, describing her plans for a national body. Yet, without widespread appeal, the idea fell into obscurity.[82]

Two years after Goldstein's homecoming, Australia still lacked a national women's political organisation. Alone among the countries present in Washington, DC, it was not officially represented at the IWSA's inauguration in 1904. The setback drove Goldstein to revive the WFPA, a scheme she proposed to Rose Scott before visiting her in Sydney that year.[83] However, Goldstein's five-week stay gave her pause. There she was immersed in the rivalry between Scott's non-partisan Women's Political Educational League and the Labor-aligned Women's Progressive Association – a conflict that epitomised the complications her nationalist project faced. Annie Golding, president of the larger Association, already considered Goldstein's newspaper, *Australian Woman's Sphere*, 'an advertisement for Miss Scott'. So, when Goldstein stayed at Scott's Woollahra home, her neutrality came under further attack.[84] As she privately admitted, material considerations again disrupted her political ambitions; the trip was intended more to 'bring in some grist to the mill' than it was to lay the foundations for a national women's organisation. On both counts, her tour was a disaster. She sustained 'heavy financial loss[es]', and worse still, misreading the city's politics had jeopardised her international ambitions. Louisa Lawson, already outside Scott's camp, reported that Goldstein had 'totally ignore[d] me'.[85] Within a small community, such actions had serious repercussions. In future, Lawson, editor of Australia's best-circulated feminist newspaper, *Dawn*, would blacklist Goldstein's ventures.

Australia ultimately joined the IWSA in 1905 under the auspices of the National Australian Women's Political Association. Despite its name, the Association had no presence outside Victoria, the only state where white women remained disenfranchised. Goldstein confessed as much in 1909, admitting it was 'nothing but a paper organisation'.[86] IWSA president Carrie Chapman Catt knew the Association failed the Alliance's membership criteria, but the prospect of proceeding without representation from the countries that she believed had 'out-Americanized America' by taking 'the principles of democracy … furthest and nearest to their logical conclusion' compelled her to show leniency.[87] Catt's hope that membership would stimulate Australian interest in the IWSA was misplaced. Reporting to the Alliance in 1906, Goldstein lamented, 'most disappointing progress has been made in national organization, owing to the almost universal indifference of Australian people to international propaganda'. With the state campaigns largely concluded, women's enfranchisement proved an unpopular premise for a national organisation. Stung by her countrywomen's indifference, Goldstein counted herself among 'the handful of Australian women ... awake to the value of international propaganda and comradeship'. Elsewhere, she complained, enfranchised women had turned inwards, eschewing internationalism in pursuit of 'opportunities for obtaining social and domestic legislation'.[88]

Despite these admissions, Goldstein remained Australia's link to the IWSA for another thirteen years. In 1908, she discarded the charade of national unity altogether. Removing the words 'National Australian' from the Alliance's membership register, Goldstein made the Women's Political Association (WPA) of Victoria the vehicle for organised Australian suffrage internationalism. By then, a handful of women, including Scott and the South Australian Rosetta Birks (a member of the world committee of the Young Woman's Christian Association) had joined the Alliance as individual affiliates, which freed them from working through Goldstein. Undermined by state leaders, Goldstein abandoned her attempt to build an IWSA auxiliary.[89] Instead, she redoubled her pursuit of federal office, running twice for the House of Representatives and twice more for the Senate between 1910 and 1917, and fulfilled her sense of obligation to her suffragist foremothers by spending 1911 as a guest of the Women's Social and Political Union in Britain. Goldstein returned to Europe for three years in 1919 but, exhausted by her crusading wartime pacifism, disbanded the WPA before her departure and avoided Alliance meetings on the continent.[90] As scholarship on Alice Henry in the United States and Anna Stout, Nellie Martel, Muriel Matters, Dora Meeson Coates, Harriet Newcomb, and Margaret Hodge in the United Kingdom has shown, women of Goldstein's generation were receptive to her exhortations to assist suffragists overseas.[91] However, in the absence of a national women's organisation, they were usually permanent settlers and travelled and worked individually, relying on personal networks rather than working through the peak international body of suffragists.

'I think I am justified in describing myself as a veteran representative!' Madge Donohoe and the perils of representing Australia abroad, 1899–1909

The tension between state loyalties and new demands for Australian women to embrace their continental citizenship was encapsulated in Sydney schoolteacher Madge Donohoe's international career. Contemporaries thought her 'a charming and eloquent lecturer', yet as with many middle-ranking suffragists, she seldom features in Australian historiography. Donohoe's invisibility was compounded by her emigration to Britain in 1899, positioning her outside the state-based history of women's enfranchisement.[92] Nevertheless, her activism did not end when she left New South Wales. After settling in Bayswater, Donohoe became a conduit between suffragists in Sydney and London. Combined with her command of European languages, these connections made her an attractive candidate to represent the Commonwealth abroad. Ten years after departing Australia, Donohoe had attended seven international women's summits and considered herself a 'veteran representative' on the conference circuit.[93] Despite her achievements, exactly 'who' she represented remained open for debate. Could a New South Welshwoman who had never set foot in the Commonwealth speak for all Australian women? It was answered in 1909, when Donohoe's stint as an international suffragist ended abruptly, curtailed by the collision of state and national interests. An exceptional woman in her own right, Donohoe invites a re-examination of the Australian presence within the international suffrage movement and the internal struggles that paralysed Australian participation in the IWSA.

Born Margaret Tilley in Sydney in 1864, Donohoe would later claim to have been a suffragist from girlhood. An evangelical upbringing provided a perfect introduction to the WCTU, on whose state executive she sat between 1890 and 1894. Unusually for a WCTU member, she joined the WSL in 1892 and served on its executive for seven years, combining her duties as a teacher with work as a branch organiser. Soon after joining, Donohoe befriended Rose Scott and supported her through the league's leadership struggles. As a result, the pair maintained a lifelong correspondence.[94] Still, prominence in Sydney feminist circles did not translate into national recognition. When she left for London to marry the Irish-Australian war correspondent Martin Donohoe, few outside the colony would have identified her as a prominent suffragist.

Contrasting with previous émigrées like Dora Montefiore, the WSL's co-founder, who ended her association with the New South Wales suffrage campaign on returning to London in 1892, Donohoe left Sydney with a sense of unfinished business. At her final WSL meeting in July 1899, she promised to 'help our cause' in London.[95] An opportunity arose almost immediately. In March 1900, the National Union of Women's Suffrage Societies (NUWSS) invited 'Women's Suffrage Societies in the British Colonies to appoint a representative each to attend our meetings' where they would 'act as intermediaries [with] ... their respective societies'.[96] Together with journalist Mary Hirst Alexander, with whom she founded the Austral Club – a Mayfair hub for 'professional and creative [Australasian] women of independent means' – Donohoe began attending meetings in May.⁹⁷ Evidence of her value came in 1902, when the union retained her services after the WSL's dissolution, citing the need to satisfy Englishwomen's 'intense interest' in the fortunes of her enfranchised compatriots.⁹⁸ Three years with the NUWSS and intermittent work as a suffrage lecturer furnished Donohoe with impeccable connections. From 1903, she was a fixture in the *Englishwoman's Year Book*, the who's who of British feminism, and numbered among the forty-seven women profiled in Emilie Matters' 1913 book, *Australasians who Count in London*.⁹⁹ A gift for languages allowed Donohoe to build European networks. After moving to France in 1906, she joined the Conseil International Permanent des Femmes, travelled in the city's literary and artistic circles, and supported herself by writing 'Paris letters' for British and South African newspapers.¹⁰⁰

In 1904, Donohoe's friendship with Scott saw her appointed to represent New South Wales at the ICW's Berlin congress. Her nomination as an IWSA delegate two years later is undocumented. However, having declined multiple invitations to attend IWSA meetings, Scott likely recommended that Goldstein select Donohoe in her stead.¹⁰¹ Representation by proxy was an ineluctable fact of IWSA membership for Goldstein. She was not, as she made a virtue of in her electoral campaigns, 'a moneyed woman', and it would have been difficult to justify fundraising for another international trip while Victorian women remained disenfranchised.¹⁰² Elsewhere, the practice was widespread but discouraged by international organisers, as it undermined the ideal of the convention as a forum for women rooted in national work. The ICW's 1902 meeting, for example, descended into farce when stand-ins represented all thirteen voting members in Copenhagen. In response, May Wright Sewall urged affiliates to 'send as your proxy one of your active workers, who is entirely familiar with the condition of affairs in your own country, and within your council and who has some knowledge of the International Council, and is interested in it'.¹⁰³ Cosmopolitan, sociable, and married to 'a firm believer in the cause' who was 'quite willing to spare me', Madge Donohoe met most of Sewall's stipulations.¹⁰⁴ Although she knew little of Goldstein's domestic organisation, Donohoe could leave Paris at short notice, and her intimate understanding of the New South Wales and British suffrage campaigns left her well positioned to mediate between enfranchised Australian women and the international suffrage movement.

For a few years, Goldstein's arrangement with Donohoe flourished. Alongside the wealthy Tasmanian Emily Dobson, she represented

Australia at the IWSA's Copenhagen summit in 1906. Whereas Dobson (an odd choice of delegate, given her opposition to the universal franchise) conveyed Goldstein's regrets that Australians had not embraced the Alliance, Donohoe's address was uplifting. Her speech outlined the 'chief benefits' of women's enfranchisement. Hoping 'Australia's experience' would 'cast [critics] to the four winds of heaven', she recited an exhaustive list of social and economic reforms, all attributed to the transformative power of the female ballot.[105] The pair reprised their roles at the IWSA's Amsterdam conference in 1908. While Goldstein believed that the Alliance best served its members by facilitating the discussion of 'tactics' and 'election policy', matters most left to national discretion, Donohoe appreciated international conferences foremost as a source of solidarity. She relished the spectacle of Alliance meetings and contributed to the glamorous image of its conferences with her 'graceful panache'. Donohoe also threw herself into committee work and contributed to the creation of the Alliance's banner and song.[106] After several encounters, Carrie Chapman Catt praised her as 'a most creditable, conscientious, pleasing delegate to send to any International meeting ... we all admire and like her very much'.[107] As a subsequent lecture tour sponsored by the Dutch Woman Suffrage Association, and invitations to speak in Denmark and Belgium attested, Donohoe fulfilled her brief to inspire disenfranchised women and 'send ... them home to work with faith and courage which they never would possess otherwise'.[108]

Although she was beloved abroad, interstate jockeying undermined Donohoe's position on the international stage. Here, reading members' letters alongside the Alliance's sanitised records illuminates the tensions that beset their project. Rose Scott's correspondence with Catt reveals that she mistrusted Goldstein's leadership. The pair were friends, drawn to the international through their mutual alienation from domestic party politics. Nevertheless, they endured an uneasy political relationship. Scott's reservations first manifested on Goldstein's return from America in 1902. Contrasting mainstream newspapers' pride in Goldstein's exploits, which, they argued, demonstrated that the Commonwealth could hold its own overseas, Scott was disturbed by the Victorian's newfound nationalism.[109] Upon receiving the proceedings of the Washington conference, which the WSL's donation enabled Goldstein to attend, Scott was devastated to find it made no reference to her or to New South Wales. Despite Goldstein's protest that she had spoken 'frequently to Mrs Catt about you' and even 'showed her your photo, which I had with me', Scott's suspicions remained. Four years later, she questioned Catt about the omission.[110]

The issue was not only a matter of pride but, as Alan Atkinson contends, fortified Scott's conviction that her 'individuality was directly threatened by any scale of nationality beyond that which already existed' in the 1890s. As 'one of the angriest opponents of federation', Scott objected to the removal of power from citizens – especially women, whose politics were 'immersed in home and family' – to a 'faraway national parliament'.[111] Others in New South Wales echoed her concerns, and resentment at Melbourne's prominence as the national capital was widespread. Even Sydney's *Ladies' Own Paper*, which typically avoided political commentary, complained that 'the ignoring of New South Wales since ... Federation has been too flagrant to pass over without comment'.[112] Despite her peripatetic youth and unlike Goldstein, whose wanderlust increased as she aged, Scott seldom left New South Wales, let alone her 'native shores'. She would never reconcile herself to the Commonwealth.[113] When Goldstein first ran for the Senate, Scott recounted the split in the WSL, aggravated by her unwavering anti-federalism, telling *New Idea*, 'I broke my heart over federation'.[114] Five years later, Catherine Spence reported that her friend 'hated and feared everything the Commonwealth does or proposes to do'.[115]

Scott's disdain for the centralisation of power extended to women's organising. In 1906, she freed herself from working through Goldstein by enrolling as an associate member of the Alliance. Over the following two years Scott ignored barbed references to parochialism and 'self-centredness' in Goldstein's letters and Catt's overtures to 'throw your influence and best endeavor into the organisation of a national committee'. Instead,

2.1 Madge Donohoe (back row, sixth from left), billed as New South Wales' delegate to the International Council of Women's 1904 conference in Berlin. (*Der Tag*, 11 June 1904, n.p., ATL, MS-Papers-4331)

she campaigned to amend the Alliance's constitution, pursuing separate representation for New South Wales, along the lines that the states had brokered with the ICW.[116] Donohoe followed suit, her letters home emphasising her pride in travelling to European capitals 'to worthily represent N.S.W.'[117] By the decade's end, Goldstein accepted that her reliance on Scott had jeopardised her attempts to build a national association. In January 1909, she enumerated the fledging organisation's failings, including Scott's refusal to cooperate with political rivals. She defied Scott to 'undertake the work of organising [an] Australian body'. 'As the leading Australian pioneer' – that foremost of settler compliments – 'the privilege & honour should be yours.' There is no record of Scott's response, but she undoubtedly refused the offer.[118]

Differences over Federation and lingering suspicions about her loyalties curtailed Madge Donohoe's fledging career. Outwardly, she appeared to be the 'genuine voting Australian woman' Catt so wanted to grace Alliance meetings.[119] Yet, as her career demonstrated, the Commonwealth did not conform to the IWSA's notion of a nation state. Although Goldstein remained friendly with Donohoe, providing news from the Victorian suffrage campaign to enliven her overseas lectures, and even admitted that she was 'loved by the Alliance', in 1909 Goldstein moved to replace the Parisian expatriate with a 'delegate fresh from Australia'.[120] The conflict between her national ambition and Scott's localised vision of international participation had culminated the previous year. Scott denied that she was a 'provincialist' during New South Wales' fierce Federation debates, but after 1901 she nevertheless sought to put the state on an equal footing with the Commonwealth.[121] In advance of the IWSA's Amsterdam summit, she supplied Donohoe with a separate New South Wales report to read alongside her Australian notes and unsuccessfully demanded her separate accreditation as the state's international representative. Donohoe attended the IWSA's London conference in 1909, though her appointment went against Goldstein's better judgement. She lived in Europe for the rest of her life but never attended another Alliance meeting.[122] Instead, Goldstein ensured that she was succeeded by a string of London-based proxy representatives, seemingly united by their antipathy to Scott.[123] Despite Goldstein's earlier pronouncement, the IWSA would wait until 1920 to receive a 'delegate fresh from Australia'.

Read alongside Australian suffragists' personal papers, the IWSA's records reveal an ambivalent relationship between women and nation in the early Commonwealth. Whereas discontent with the Do-Everything policy had seen suffrage slip from the World's WCTU's agenda, the rise of specialist organisations like the IWSA held out the promise of Australian international leadership at the dawn of the twentieth century. For the suffragists to take part, they first had to unite under a single banner. To Vida Goldstein in 1902, the task appeared straightforward. Within two years, Federation and the passage of the Commonwealth Franchise Act had transformed white women into national citizens with unparalleled political freedom. Yet, while Goldstein embraced the Commonwealth as an arena in which to advance feminist ambitions, others viewed continental collaboration with suspicion. Although the value of international solidarity in the fight for enfranchisement seemed apparent to Victorian women, who lacked the state vote until 1908, it did not resonate elsewhere. State legislatures still governed the matters that most concerned women activists. Struggles for wage equality and reforms to marriage and divorce legislation were fought separately, limiting the necessity for a national organisation.[124] Instead, women like Rose Scott resisted the sway of the national and sought to share their state-situated experiences with women overseas. For all its flaws, the ICW reached a solution that melded these approaches: the state councils retained distinct identities but lost their voting rights. The IWSA, however, demanded unity, a policy that precluded the participation of Australian women.

The situation changed after the First World War, when international pressure for Australia to end the practice of state representation coincided with an emerging sense of national identity. Perhaps most important was the realisation that stronger interstate bonds were required before women could 'hope to exercise their influence in national or international affairs at full strength', as the journalist Stella Allen argued in 1932, on the occasion of the NCW of Australia's first anniversary.[125] In the meantime, new organisations like the conservative Australian Women's National League (1904–44) and the progressive Australian Federation of Women Voters (1921–82) had melded an 'All-Australia outlook' with a 'firm sense of belonging to nation, region, Empire', and, in the Federation's case, world. Such progress was hard won. That the United Associations of Women – the Federation's New South Wales affiliate – reminded members to behave 'as Australian women and not merely as State Units' in 1933, suggests the message had not yet been internalised.[126] Across the Tasman, where provincial barriers were less entrenched, the war also catalysed a resumption of national women's organising. After twelve years of dormancy, the NCW of New Zealand reconvened and resumed its affiliation with the ICW in 1920.[127]

Enabled by the resources drawn from these national organisations, a new generation of Australasian feminists became prominent contributors to a diversified international women's movement. Following the wave of European and North American women's enfranchisements clustered around the First World War and, revealing the limits of their sympathy for the ongoing suffrage struggles in Africa, Asia, and Latin America, from the late 1920s the ICW and IWSA increasingly focused on expanding women's legal and economic rights.[128] At the same time, a new crop of women's organisations based in Asia, the Americas, and the Pacific were formed to promote cross-cultural understanding as well as to pursue more traditional women's rights campaigns. Although Australasians were instrumental in the formation of regional organisations like the British Dominions Women's Suffrage Union (1914); its broader-based successor, the British Commonwealth League (1925); and the Pan-Pacific Women's Association (1930), they nevertheless remained committed to the ICW and IWSA. They also participated in new global forums like the Women's International League for Peace and Freedom (1915), Equal Rights International (1930), and the League of Nations (1920), whose assemblies Australian women attended as 'substitute delegates' from 1922, and New Zealanders from 1929.[129]

As we saw in the first two chapters of this book, the pursuit of formal organisational ties with the international women's movement appealed immensely to Australian and New Zealand feminist leaders, if not always to the 'rank and file' of the organisations they led. Yet, women like Donohoe and Goldstein largely worked in vain to use their enfranchisement as a platform to assist the struggle elsewhere in the world. Their difficulties in surmounting the bias against suffrage in the WCTU and ICW, as well as meeting the IWSA's strict membership criteria, serve as a reminder that for all its utopian trappings, the international women's movement also had conservative instincts. In each instance, the desire to preserve organisational unity marginalised progressive ideas. As the regional and international correspondence between turn-of-the-century suffragists further reveals, similar challenges arose for Australian and New Zealand women concerning the idea that an indivisible bond between friendship and politics unified the international women's movement.

Notes

1 SLNSW, A2272/980-2, Carrie Chapman Catt to Rose Scott, 30 March 1906.
2 Goldstein's trip came at a much-discussed moment when Australasian ideas played an influential role in the development of progressive politics across the world, particularly in the United States. Lake, *Progressive New World*, see Chapter 3 for an account of Goldstein's visit understood in these terms; Stevenson, 'Imagining women's suffrage', 638-66.

3 *Hearing before the Select Committee on Woman Suffrage, United States Senate* (Washington, DC: Government Printing Office, 1902), p. 34.
4 *Report, First International Woman Suffrage Conference* (New York: International Woman Suffrage Headquarters, 1902), p. 4; *AWS*, 10 April 1902, p. 165.
5 Wright, 'A splendid object lesson', 14.
6 *First International Woman Suffrage Conference*, p. 33.
7 *Woman's Journal*, 11 October 1902, p. 324.
8 *Prohibitionist*, 25 November 1893, p. 3; *SAR*, 10 April 1895, p. 7; *SMH*, 16 September 1902, p. 3.
9 SLNSW, M2309, Vida Goldstein autograph book January–June 1902, p. 37.
10 D. Gorman, *The Emergence of International Society in the 1920s* (Cambridge: Cambridge University Press, 2012); D. Lacqua (ed.), *Internationalism Reconfigured: Transnational Ideas and Movements between the World Wars* (London: I. B. Tauris, 2011). Among many other works, see Lake, 'Women's international leadership', pp. 71–90; Paisley, *Glamour in the Pacific*; E. Warne, 'Learning from the League: Supranational women's groups and the League of Nations', *Lilith*, 17–18 (2012), 54–67; A. Woollacott, 'Inventing Commonwealth and pan-Pacific feminisms: Australian women's internationalist activism in the 1920s–30s', *Gender & History*, 10:3 (1998), 425–48. Even a 2014 survey of Australian women's international activism omitted the years between 1902 and 1914. See Campo and Lake, 'International activism and organisations'.
11 R. Pesman, *Duty Free: Australian Women Abroad* (Melbourne: Oxford University Press, 1996), pp. 109–20. For a comprehensive list of the authorised histories, see M. Quartly and J. Smart, *Respectable Radicals: A History of the National Council of Women of Australia 1896-2006* (Melbourne: Monash University Publishing, 2015), pp. 477–87.
12 Rupp, *Worlds of Women*. For a summary of this work, see de Haan *et al.*, 'Introduction', 1–12.
13 Lake, 'Women's international leadership', p. 76.
14 Caine, 'International links', p. 164.
15 In particular, see Rupp, *Worlds of Women*, pp. 51–81.
16 Neither New Zealand nor Australia was represented at the International Socialist Women's Conferences (1907–15) or the International Federation of Working Women (1919–24). This absence was mirrored at the Second Socialist International (1889–1916), which welcomed one Australian delegate and no New Zealanders. More broadly, despite their shared commitment to universal enfranchisement, socialists' rejection of gender separatism and refusal to collaborate with bourgeois women were anathema to the largely middle-class leadership of the early twentieth-century Australasian women's movements, who resented their marginalisation in the party system and deemed gender barriers more divisive than class differences. Dora Montefiore, the founder of the WSL of New South Wales, was an exception. In 1893, she returned to Britain and joined the Social Democratic Federation. By the end of the decade she had attended the Second International and toured the world disseminating a brand of 'woman-focused socialism'. J. Damousi, *Women Come Rally: Socialism, Communism and Gender in Australia 1890-1955* (Melbourne: Oxford University

Press, 1994), pp. 89–91; D. Gaido and C. Frencia, '"A clean break": Clara Zetkin, the socialist women's movement, and feminism', *International Critical Thought*, 8:2 (2018), 277–303; K. Hunt, '"Whirl'd through the world": The role of travel in the making of Dora Montefiore, 1851–1933', *Österreichische Zeitschrift für Geschichtswissenschaft*, 22:1 (2011), 41–62.

17 S. Zimmermann, 'The challenge of multinational empire for the international women's movement: The Hapsburg monarchy and the development of feminist inter/national politics', *Journal of Women's History*, 17:2 (2005), 87.

18 G. Sluga, *Internationalism in the Age of Nationalism* (Philadelphia: University of Pennsylvania Press, 2013), pp. 150–6.

19 SLNSW, A2272/1019–20, Vida Goldstein to Rose Scott, 27 June 1909.

20 M. W. Sewall, *Genesis of the International Council of Women and the Story of Its Growth, 1888–1893* (Indianapolis: International Council of Women, 1914), p. 70.

21 *International Council of Women Report of Transactions during the Third Quinquennial Term Terminating with the Third Quinquennial Meeting, Volume I* (Boston: International Council of Women, 1909), pp. xviii–xix, 90, 242–3.

22 Zimmermann, 'Feminist inter/national politics', 90–2.

23 Holbrook, 'What sort of nation?', 1–10. See, for example, Atkinson, 'Against a single Australia', 262–79; A. Atkinson, *The Europeans in Australia, Volume 3: Nation* (Sydney: UNSW Press, 2014); M. Quartly and J. Smart, 'Making the National Councils of Women national: The formation of a nation-wide organisation in Australia 1896–1931', in I. Sulkunen et al. (eds), *Suffrage, Gender and Citizenship: International Perspectives on Parliamentary Reform* (Cambridge: Cambridge Scholars Press, 2009), pp. 339–57; M. Quartly and J. Smart, 'Mainstream women's organisations in Australia: The challenges of national and international co-operation after the Great War', *Women's History Review*, 21:1 (2012), 61–73.

24 Quartly and Smart, *Respectable Radicals*, p. 26.

25 Lake, 'Feminist history as national history', 157. See also M. Lake, 'Mission impossible: How men gave birth to the Australian nation – nationalism, gender, and other seminal acts', *Gender & History*, 4:3 (1992), 305–22; M. Lake, 'Women and nation in Australia: The politics of representation', *Australian Journal of Politics and History*, 43:1 (1997), 41–52.

26 Atkinson, 'Against a single Australia', 262–79.

27 N. Berkovitch, 'The emergence and transformation of the international women's movement', in J. Boli and G. M. Thomas (eds), *Constructing World Culture: International Nongovernmental Organisations Since 1875* (Stanford: Stanford University Press, 1999), pp. 100–26; K. Offen, *European Feminisms, 1700–1950: A Political History* (Stanford: Stanford University Press, 2000), pp. 144–81; T. J. Boisseau, 'Forging the transnational out of the international: Feminist internationalism at world's fairs and international exhibitions', in R. Rogers and M. Boussahba-Bravard (eds), *Women in International and Universal Exhibitions 1876–1937* (Oxford: Routledge, 2018), pp. 234–54.

28 *Fédération Britannique, Continentale et Générale Cinquième Congrès International* (Geneva: Secrétariat Général de la Fédération, 1890), pp. 6–7.

29 Zimmermann, 'Feminist inter/national politics', 89; K. Offen, 'Overcoming hierarchies through internationalism: May Wright Sewall's engagement with the International

Council of Women', in de Haan *et al.* (eds), *Women's Activism: Global Perspectives*, pp. 16–17.

30 L. Beers, 'Feminism, internationalism and the Women's International League for Peace and Freedom', *History & Policy*, www.historyandpolicy.org/dialogues/discussions/women-peace-and-transnational-activism-a-century-on (accessed 9 July 2018); C. von Oertzen, 'Whose world? Internationalism, nationalism and the struggle over the "language question" in the International Federation of University Women, 1919–1932', *Contemporary European History*, 25:2 (2016), 277.

31 In some accounts, the gathering was a formal meeting, while in others it was simply 'tea with one or two friends'. ATL, MS-Papers-4331, Wilhelmina Sherriff Bain notebook, 1904; *Fortnightly Review*, 1 July 1899, pp. 156–7; Sewall, *International Council of Women*, pp. 1–6.

32 Offen, 'Overcoming hierarchies through internationalism', pp. 16–17; *International Council of Women, Report of Transactions of the Second Quinquennial Meeting* (London: T. Fisher Unwin, 1900), p. 85.

33 Offen, *European Feminisms*, pp. 151–2.

34 Rupp, *Worlds of Women*, pp. 19–22.

35 *Report, Second and Third Conferences of the International Womanhood Suffrage Alliance* (Copenhagen: Bianco Luno, 1906), p. 116.

36 By the time the ICW's 1914 congress opened, however, it was 'impossible' to supress the discussion of suffrage any longer. DuBois, 'Woman suffrage around the world', p. 265; *International Council of Women, Report of Transactions of the Fourth Quinquennial Meeting* (London: Constable & Co., 1910), pp. 107, 199; U. Wikander, *Feminism, Familj och Medborgarskap: Debatter på Internationella Kongresser om Nattarbetsförbud för Kvinnor 1889–1919* (Gothenburg: Makadam, 2006), pp. 227, 315.

37 Quartly and Smart, *Respectable Radicals*; Quartly and Smart, 'Making the National Councils of Women national', pp. 339–57; Pesman, *Duty Free*, p. 113.

38 The NCW of New South Wales was formed in 1896, followed by councils in Tasmania (1899), South Australia (1902–9, 1920), Victoria (1902), Queensland (1905), and Western Australia (1911).

39 *International Council of Women, First Annual Report of the Fifth Quinquennial Period 1909–1910* (Berlin: Langenscheidtsche Buchdruckerei, 1910), p. 8.

40 Rupp, *Worlds of Women*, pp. 51–81.

41 SLNSW, A2272/998–1002, Catt to Scott, 16 December 1908.

42 ATL, MS-Papers-3969-1, NCW of New Zealand to Ishbel Aberdeen, 24 May 1899; Nicholls, *The Women's Parliament*, pp. 31–49.

43 Webb only publicly retracted her opposition to women's enfranchisement in 1906. B. Caine, 'Beatrice Webb and the "woman question"', *History Workshop Journal*, 14:1 (1982), 33–6; B. Holt, *Women in Council: A History of the National Council of Women of New Zealand* (Wellington: National Council of Women, 1980), p. 33.

44 *Evening Post*, 6 April 1897, p. 2. On the persistence of localism in New Zealand, see J. Cookson, 'How British? Local government in New Zealand to *c.* 1930', *New Zealand Journal of History*, 41:2 (2007), 143–60.

45 Nicholls, *The Women's Parliament*, pp. 50–80; *Evening Star*, 19 September 1914, p. 11; *ICW Report of Transactions of the Fourth Quinquennial Meeting*, pp. 61–2; ATL, MS-Papers-3969-1, Sheppard to Aberdeen, 2 November 1910; Archives New Zealand, Wellington, ACGO 8333, Box 1257/[21], Catt to the Premier of New Zealand, 21 January 1913.
46 Sheppard, *Woman Suffrage in New Zealand*; A. Stout, *Woman Suffrage in New Zealand* (London: The Woman's Press, 1911); ATL, MS-Papers-1376-01, Catt to Sheppard, 24 February 1908, 2 and 4 February 1909.
47 *Press*, 15 November 1913, p. 6.
48 Rupp, *Worlds of Women*, pp. 51–81; A. Summers, 'Liberty, equality, morality: The attempt to sustain an international campaign against state regulated prostitution 1875–1906', in E. Schöck-Quinteros *et al.* (eds), *Politische Netzwerkerinnen: Internationale Zusammenarbeit von Frauen 1830–1960* (Berlin: Trafo, 2007), pp. 298–301.
49 *ICW Report of Transactions of the Fourth Quinquennial Meeting*, p. 124; M. Sandell, 'Regional versus international: Women's activism and organisational spaces in the inter-war period', *The International History Review*, 33:4 (2011), 611.
50 E. Robinson-Tomsett, *Women, Travel and Identity: Journeys by Rail and Sea, 1870–1940* (Manchester: Manchester University Press, 2013), pp. 18–42.
51 CM, ARC176.53/327, Louisa Martindale to Kate Sheppard, 21 March 1904; CM, ARC176.53/329, Aberdeen to Sheppard, 9 April 1904; *International Council of Women, Report on the Quinquennial Meeting, Kristiania 1920* (Aberdeen: Rosemount Press, 1920), p. 32.
52 Quartly and Smart, *Respectable Radicals*, p. 10; *Mercury*, 6 June 1934, p. 9.
53 Piggin and Linder, *The Fountain of Public Prosperity*, pp. 549–52.
54 UMA, 101/85, Box 15/241/1, Sara Nolan and Alice Masterman to Elizabeth Webb Nicholls, 14 September 1899.
55 Tyrrell, 'International aspects of the woman's temperance movement', 300–1.
56 *Report to the Eighth Convention of the World's Woman's Christian Temperance Union* (London: John Heywood, 1910), pp. 103–4.
57 Berger and Scalmer, 'The transnational activist', pp. 5–12; *New York Tribune*, 29 August 1904, p. 5.
58 Bain, *The Berlin Congress*, pp. 1–2. CM, ARC1992.50/6, Sheppard to Aberdeen, 24 July 1906.
59 A. Towns, 'Global patterns and debates in the granting of women's suffrage', in Franceschet *et al.* (eds), *The Palgrave Handbook of Women's Political Rights*, pp. 10–11; New York Public Library, New York, MSSCol2703/A12, Martina Kramers to Rosika Schwimmer, 31 May 1907, cited in Rupp, *Worlds of Women*, p. 71.
60 *Het Nieuws van den Dag*, 21 November 1908, pp. 6–7.
61 The term 'inter/national' is from Zimmermann, 'Feminist inter/national politics', 89.
62 SLNSW, A2272/1017–18, Catt to Scott, 18 May 1909.
63 Lake, 'Women and nation', 41.
64 *AWS*, December 1901, p. 128; January 1902, p. 136; February 1902, pp. 144–5.
65 SLSA, PRG88/7/10, Catherine Helen Spence to Alice Henry, 19 March 1902.

66 International Council of Women Executive Committee Minutes 1897–1900, *Women and Social Movements, International*, http://wasi.alexanderstreet.com.ezproxy2.libr ary.usyd.edu.au/view/1654707 (accessed 17 September 2018); A. Coote, 'Out from the legend's shadow: Re-thinking national feeling in colonial Australia', *Journal of Australian Colonial History*, 10:2 (2008), 103–22.
67 *ICW Report of Transactions during the Third Term*, pp. xviii, 91.
68 SLNSW, MLMSS38/46/87, Isabel Dickson, 'Report on the International Council of Women', 1904.
69 *ICW Report of Transactions during the Third Term*, pp. 56, 92; *Memorandum on the Meeting of the Executive Committee of the International Council of Women* (London: Reform Press, 1901), p. 16.
70 ATL, MS-Papers-4331, Bain notebook, 1904.
71 SLNSW, MLMSS3739, National Council of Women of New South Wales (NCW of NSW) Minutes 1895–1905, pp. 172–4; *ICW Report of Transactions during the Third Term*, pp. 117, 129; SLNSW, A2274/191–4, May Wood Swift to Scott, 8 April 1904.
72 ATL, MS-Papers-4331, Bain notebook, 1904.
73 *ICW Report of Transactions during the Third Term*, p. 6.
74 SLNSW, MLMSS38/49/97–123, Rose Scott, 'Speech to the National Council of Women', 26 May 1903. Emily Dobson, then president of the Tasmanian NCW, made an identical argument in 1904. *Mercury*, 12 February 1904, p. 6.
75 SLNSW, MLMSS3739, NCW of NSW Minutes 1904–10, pp. 13–17; *National Council of Women: Report of the Interstate Conference* (Melbourne: A. H. Macdonald, 1905).
76 Quartly and Smart, *Respectable Radicals*, pp. 33–4; J. Rickard, *Australia: A Cultural History* (Melbourne: Monash University Press, 3rd edn, 2017), pp. 107–8. For example, the states advocated for separate representation at the ICW's meetings and reported individually to its standing committees. See SLNSW, MLMSS3739, NCW of NSW Minutes 1910–17, p. 70.
77 Quartly and Smart, *Respectable Radicals*, p. 133; SLNSW, MLMSS38/46/273–7, Emily Dobson, 'Report of quinquennial meetings, Toronto', June 1909.
78 *San Francisco Chronicle*, 20 July 1902, p. 2.
79 *Morning Post*, 10 February 1903, n.p.
80 SLNSW, A2272/393, Goldstein to Scott, 14 July 1899; Lake, 'Women and nation', 44–5.
81 J. M. Bomford, *Vida Goldstein: That Dangerous and Persuasive Woman* (Melbourne: Melbourne University Press, 1993), pp. 47–50; V. Goldstein, *To America and Back: January–June 1902* (Sydney: Australian History Museum, 2002).
82 SLNSW, A2272/791, 806–7, Goldstein to Scott, 13 and 21 January 1903; *AWS*, 10 October 1903, p. 363.
83 SLNSW, A2272/969, 974, Goldstein to Scott, 11 August and 24 September 1904.
84 SLNSW, A2272/791, Goldstein to Scott, 9 March 1903.
85 Bomford, *Vida Goldstein*, pp. 76–7; SLNSW, A2272/974, Goldstein to Scott, 22 August 1904; SLNSW, MLMSS364/10/107–9, Goldstein to Franklin, 16 November 1904.
86 SLNSW, A2272/1019–20, Goldstein to Scott, 27 June 1909; *Report, Second and Third Conferences of the IWSA*, p. 60.

87 SLNSW, A2272/980-2, Catt to Scott, 16 December 1908; I. H. Harper (ed.), *The History of Woman Suffrage, Volume 5 1900-1920* (New York: National American Woman Suffrage Association, 1922), p. 144; *New York Times*, 16 February 1902, p. 2.
88 *Second and Third Conferences of the IWSA*, pp. 60-1.
89 SLNSW, A2272/980-2, Catt to Scott, 16 December 1908; SLNSW, A2272/989, Goldstein to Scott, 5 November 1906; *The International Woman Suffrage Alliance Report of Fourth Conference* (Amsterdam: F. van Rossen, 1908), p. 3.
90 K. Laing, 'World war and worldly women: The Great War and the formation of the Women's International League for Peace and Freedom in Australia', *La Trobe Journal*, 96 (2015), 129-33. Goldstein's variety of uncompromising pacifism was also met with hostility within the post-war IWSA. See D. Wernitznig, 'Out of her time? Rosika Schwimmer's transnational activism after the First World War', *Women's History Review*, 26:2 (2017), 262-79.
91 Caine, 'Goldstein and the English militant campaign', 363-76; D. Kirkby, *Alice Henry, The Power of Pen and Voice: The Life of an Australian-American Labor Reformer* (Melbourne: Cambridge University Press, 1991), pp. 68-206; Nugent, 'Nellie Alma Martel', 142-59; M. Scott, *How Australia Led the Way: Dora Meeson Coates and British Suffrage* (Melbourne: Arcadia, 2018); Trethewey and Whitehead, 'Transnationalism in two teacher/suffragettes' work', 547-59; M. R. Webb, 'Anna Patterson Stout: Portrait of a New Zealand lady' (MA thesis, Massey University, 2015), pp. 68-84; Wright, *You Daughters of Freedom*.
92 *Lady's Realm*, May-October 1902, pp. 510-11. On the exclusion of antipodean 'exiles' from a state- and nation-based historical canon, see H. Bones, *The Expatriate Myth: New Zealand Writers and the Colonial World* (Dunedin: Otago University Press, 2018).
93 SLNSW, A2274/381, Madge Donohoe to Scott, 16 October 1908.
94 *Rotterdamsch Nieuwsblad*, 18 November 1908, p. 5; *Evolutie: Veertiendaagsch Blad voor de Vrouw*, 18 November 1909, p. 134; SLNSW, MLMSS186/14/109-17, 125, Scott to Lady Mary Windeyer, 15 and 22 August 1893.
95 Montefiore returned to Sydney between 1910 and 1912, yet unlike Donohoe, there is no evidence that she remained in communication with her former colleagues in the intervening years. SLNSW, MLMSS38/33/2, Womanhood Suffrage League of New South Wales Minute Book 1899-1902, p. 20.
96 The Women's Library, London School of Economics, London (hereafter WL), 2NWS/A/01, National Union of Women's Suffrage Societies Executive Committee Minutes 1899-1903, 11 January 1900.
97 Mrs L. W. [Emilie] Matters, *Australasians Who Count in London and Who Counts in Western Australia* (London: Jas. Truscott & Son, 1913), pp. 42-3; WL, 2NWS/A/01, NUWSS Minutes 1899-1903, 1 March 1900.
98 SLNSW, A2272/787, Donohoe to Scott, 2 January 1903; SLNSW, MLMSS38/33/2, WSL of NSW Minute Book 1899-1902, pp. 258, 284.
99 Matters, *Australasians Who Count*, pp. 42-3. Donohoe's name appeared between 1903 and 1908. See, for example, *Englishwoman's Year Book 1903* (London: Adam & Charles Black, 1903), p. 327.

100 Matters, *Australasians Who Count*, pp. 42–4; *Figaro*, 2 March 1906, p. 3; *International Woman Suffrage Alliance, Report of the Fifth Conference and First Quinquennial* (London: Samuel Sidders & Co., 1909), p. 32.
101 SLNSW, MLMSS3739, NCW of NSW Minutes 1895–1905, pp. 172–4; SLNSW, A2272/806–7, 913, Goldstein to Scott, 21 January 1903 and 8 February 1904.
102 *Argus*, 14 November 1903, p. 16.
103 *ICW Report of Transactions during the Third Term*, pp. 63–4; SLNSW, A2274/168–70, May Wright Sewall to Scott, 13 June 1903.
104 The pair met when Martin Donohoe reported on a WSL meeting. SLNSW, A2274/381, Donohoe to Scott, 16 October 1908; *Rotterdamsch Nieuwsblad*, 18 November 1908, p. 5.
105 *Report, Second and Third Conferences of the IWSA*, pp. 12, 60–8.
106 *De Telegraaf*, 16 November 1908, p. 5; *IWSA Report of Fourth Conference*, pp. 8, 10, 16, 29, 44–5, 82–4. On the spectacle of international women's conferences as well as the importance of symbols of collective identity, see Paisley, *Glamour in the Pacific*, pp. 112–13, 218–22; L. J. Rupp and V. Taylor, 'Forging feminist identity in an international movement: A collective identity approach to twentieth-century feminism', *Signs*, 24:2 (1999), 370–1.
107 SLNSW, A2272/998–1002, Catt to Scott, 16 December 1908.
108 SLNSW, A2274/381, Donohoe to Scott, 16 October 1908; *De Telegraaf*, 14 November 1908, p. 2; *Jus Suffragii*, 15 November 1908, p. 17.
109 *Telegraph* [QLD], 18 January 1902, p. 5; *Daily Telegraph*, 20 August 1902, p. 9.
110 Goldstein was probably telling the truth. For example, a photograph of Scott that can only have been supplied by Goldstein illustrates a feature that the *San Francisco Chronicle* published before she departed for Australia. *San Francisco Chronicle*, 20 July 1902, p. 2; *First International Woman Suffrage Conference*, pp. 27–33; SLNSW, A2272/791, Goldstein to Scott, 13 January 1903; SLNSW, A2272/976–8, Catt to Scott, 11 November 1906.
111 Atkinson, 'Against a single Australia', 268; Lake, 'Feminist history as national history', 164–5.
112 *Ladies' Own Paper*, 1 May 1904, p. 2.
113 Reflecting on Scott's life in 1938, the novelist Miles Franklin speculated on 'what effect a deep acquaintance with life in other countries' would have had on her friend's politics. M. Franklin, 'Rose Scott: Some elements of her personality and work', in Eldershaw (ed.), *The Peaceful Army*, p. 104; J. McIntyre and J. Conway, 'Intimate, imperial, intergenerational: Settler women's mobilities and gender politics in Newcastle and the Hunter Valley', *Journal of Australian Colonial History*, 19 (2017), 171–84.
114 *New Idea*, 1 January 1903, p. 430.
115 SLSA, PRG88/7/95, Spence to Henry, 11 May 1908.
116 *Second and Third Conferences of the IWSA*, p. 60; SLNSW, Catt to Scott, A2272/998–1002, 1017–18, 16 December 1908 and 18 May 1909.
117 SLNSW, A2274/268, 376, Donohoe to Scott, 14 July 1906, 7 August and 14 August 1908.
118 SLNSW, A2272/1019–20, Goldstein to Scott, 27 June 1909. On the 'pioneer' trope among progressives in settler societies, see Lake, *Progressive New World*, p. 77.

119 SLNSW, A2272/980–2, Catt to Scott, 30 March 1906.
120 SLNSW, M2309/2, Vida Goldstein 1908 diary, 19 August 1908; SLNSW, A2272/1019–20, Goldstein to Scott, 27 June 1909.
121 SLNSW, MLMSS38/27/31–185, Rose Scott, 'Federation speech notes', c. 1899.
122 *Table Talk*, 5 February 1914, p. 33; SLNSW, A2272/998–1002, Catt to Scott, 16 December 1908; SLNSW, A2272/1019–20, Goldstein to Scott, 27 June 1909; *IWSA Report of the Fourth Conference*, p. 11.
123 Margaret Hodge and Harriet Newcomb, Australia's delegates to the IWSA's 1911 conference, ended their long association with Scott in 1909, after she accused them of faking illness to avoid representing New South Wales at the ICW's Toronto congress. SLNSW, A2274/413–15, 18, Harriet Newcomb to Scott, 15 May 1909; Margaret Hodge to Scott, 22 May and 29 July 1909.
124 H. Irving, 'A gendered constitution? Women, federation and heads of power', in H. Irving (ed.), *A Woman's Constitution? Gender and History in the Australian Commonwealth* (Sydney: Hale & Iremonger, 1996), p. 106.
125 Quartly and Smart, *Respectable Radicals*, pp. 25–105; *Argus*, 30 November 1932, p. 13.
126 Z. Simic, 'A hall of selective mirrors: Feminism, history and identity 1919–1969' (PhD thesis, University of Sydney, 2003), pp. 31–70; SLNSW, MLMSS2160 ADD-ON 1317/1, United Associations Annual Report 1933, p. 8. On the Australian Women's National League's efforts to 'rouse the dormant patriotism' of Australian women, see Crozier-De Rosa, *Shame and the Anti-Feminist Backlash*, pp. 95–107.
127 Nicholls, *The Women's Parliament*, pp. 96–113.
128 Towns, 'Global patterns and debates', pp. 4–10.
129 Lake, 'Women's international leadership', pp. 73–86; Page, 'Women and nationality', pp. 157–75; Paisley, *Glamour in the Pacific*; F. Paisley, *Loving Protection? Australian Feminism and Aboriginal Women's Rights 1919–1939* (Melbourne: Melbourne University Press, 2000), pp. 10–69; Woollacott, 'Australian women's metropolitan activism', pp. 207–23.

3

The business of correspondence: Politics, friendship, and intimacy in suffragists' letters

In March 1902, Margaret Sievwright, president of the National Council of Women (NCW) of New Zealand, expressed her frustration with the unfulfilled promise of correspondence. Writing to Rose Scott, she professed, 'how I wish we Inter-colonial people could see more of each other! Writing, at best, is unsatisfactory; & intercourse (personal) so strengthening, encouraging and helpful in every way.'[1] Over the following year, Sievwright attempted to bridge this gap. Her letters emphasised the pair's shared acquaintances, sympathised with Scott's antipathy toward the Australian Commonwealth and, at the behest of British suffragist Elizabeth Wolstenholme Elmy, attempted to recruit her as a contributor to a French encyclopaedia of women's achievements. Displaying her attention to New South Wales politics, Sievwright advised Scott to demand female parliamentary representation as well as the vote. Avoiding the subject 'was the mistake in N.Z.'[2] Despite her professed dissatisfaction with the 'intimacy of the envelope', Sievwright enjoyed their exchanges. 'Sharing the hopes & fears, successes and disappointments of those travelling parallel paths in other lands', she later told Scott, helped 'one over one's own rough places.'[3]

At first glance, Sievwright's letters do not seem unusual. In 1902, they numbered among the three million that left New Zealand annually.[4] Advances in shipping and the mid-century institution of international communications agreements saw the advent of cheap, reliable postage and, until the arrival of inexpensive international telephony in the second half of the twentieth century, letters remained the primary means of sharing information and maintaining relationships across long distances. Together, these developments allowed Sievwright to amass connections across the globe. When the trailblazing American suffragist Elizabeth Cady Stanton died in 1902, Sievwright quickly proffered condolences to her friends and associates. During her term as president of the International Council of Women (ICW) (1899–1904), May Wright

Sewall counted Sievwright among her 'most energetic correspondents', while her exchanges with Wolstenholme Elmy were rich enough for the Englishwoman to compose a heartfelt obituary for her 'dear friend' in 1905.[5] Through the post, a woman living on New Zealand's remote east coast found her place in a worldwide movement. Her efforts accord with the notion that the British Empire and, by extension, the English-speaking world was 'inherently relational': individuals occupied multiple positions in relation to other parts of the empire.[6] Women like Sievwright and Scott were geographically marginal but inhabited the centre of their own complex networks, cultivated through assiduous correspondence and intellectual exchange.

Confronted with Sievwright's warm prose, it is tempting to view her international networks through the lens of friendship. Since the 1970s, feminist historians have used letters to trace the 'intimate social, emotional and intellectual fabric of personal relations'. In this enterprise, they have not only considered letters as a 'window into the intimate, and usually feminine, self', but examined how women used them as vectors for political organisation.[7] For nineteenth-century women, letters connected the public and private spheres, allowing them to participate in wholehearted political debates, build networks, and disseminate information, all under the guise of a 'sanctioned, "lady-like" form'.[8] Correspondence was clearly central to the Australian and New Zealand suffrage campaigns. However, while the place of writing and preserving letters in settler and indigenous women's lives has been recognised, the shape and rhythm of antipodean suffragists' epistolary networks have received little attention.[9]

Mirroring imperial historiography, for the past twenty years internationally minded suffrage historians have pieced together the intimate networks that sustained cross-border organising.[10] As ever, Anglo-American relations have received particular emphasis. From the emergence of a republic of letters among a coterie of Euro-American women in the 1820s to the Pankhursts' tours of the United States in the 1910s, the study of epistolary networks has enriched histories of suffrage.[11] Beyond the Anglophone world, Mineke Bosch and Annemarie Kloostermann's research on correspondence between the leaders of the International Woman Suffrage Alliance (IWSA) revealed a set of long-distance friendships that shaped international feminist activism in the early twentieth century. Their conclusions that women's rights campaigners of the fin-de-siècle blurred distinctions between their personal lives and their political correspondence and, further, that 'within the movement ... friendships were indispensable' have proved influential, spawning an explosion of research on nodal individuals whose letters connected one another and drew activists across the Western world into a 'global' suffrage movement.[12]

Nevertheless, looking exclusively for friendship in the papers of suffrage activists can obscure as well as illuminate the past. Sievwright's letters are among the most effusive of the thousands Scott preserved, even though the pair were barely acquainted. Spanning six letters over sixteen months, their correspondence did not form part of an open-ended conversation like those that would have connected friends or family sundered by the Tasman Sea. For Scott, a self-described 'writing machine' who scrawled 'over 50 letters a day', correspondence was largely functional. Like most of her letters, Scott's responses to Sievwright were not intended as a private dialogue. They are better understood as a 'collective voice': dictated by and read aloud to the organisations she worked for.[13] Having secured her object, Sievwright's support for reforms to the ICW, Scott's replies were brief. Within a year, the pair fell out of touch, as many correspondents did when the exchange ceased to be mutually expedient.

Friendships of the kind discussed by scholars of Atlantic suffrage movements are not analogous to Sievwright's relationship with Scott. However, the New Zealander drew unabashedly on a 'rhetoric of intimacy' to elicit a reply. Whether calculated or genuine, Sievwright's earnest overtures were commonplace in late nineteenth-century associational culture. Drawing on an intimate lexicon helped individuals to consider themselves members of communities that extended across space and time.[14] Whatever her intentions, Sievwright's paean to the power of correspondence to bring strangers into the same imagined world did not obviously resonate with Scott. Nonetheless, it is worth examining how antipodean suffragists employed and transgressed codes of intimacy in their relations with the international suffrage movement. Their correspondence reveals the more nebulous set of connections that suffragists built during their struggles for colonial, national, and international enfranchisement.

Focusing on correspondence prompts a reconsideration of Caroline Daley and Melanie Nolan's call for scholars to acknowledge that 'New World suffragists ... were engaged in a dialogue with their Old World sisters'.[15] In the intervening years, suffrage historians have adopted the language of connection, yet the content and quality of this dialogue has not always been scrutinised. Intimate epistolary practices are not always obvious. Even if they leave tidy records, intimacies function as codes that unacquainted readers must decipher.[16] Nevertheless, the concept of intimacy – rather than friendship – provides a more useful framework for examining relationships between internationally minded antipodean feminists at the dawn of the twentieth century. Starting from the premise that suffragists' letters demand greater scrutiny than providing vignettes to enliven campaign histories, this chapter begins by examining the functions of their correspondence. Focusing on the papers of Kate Sheppard and Rose Scott, two of the most prominent figures in the New Zealand and New South Wales women's suffrage movements, it investigates how and why suffragists corresponded within and across colonial borders, and examines letters as both vectors for transmitting information between activists and residues of otherwise ephemeral political networks. In exploring these interactions, I test the limits of nodal connections in contemporary reform networks. Rather than build epistolary friendships, Australasian suffragists sought to write themselves 'in' to the metro-centric history of women's rights activism through their letters with renowned British and American feminists.

And yet, letters were as much a force for disruption as cooperation. By the turn of the century, the advent of the Imperial Penny Post and widespread female literacy had profoundly democratised letter writing.[17] With pen and paper alone, activists marginalised in colonial women's movements forged bonds with their counterparts overseas and leveraged these connections to shape the course of national and international feminist debates. Focusing on Mary Steadman Aldis, a British expatriate social purity campaigner whose postal activism inflamed a trans-imperial scandal concerning New Zealand's Contagious Diseases Act, this chapter elucidates the tensions that existed between metropolitan women's rights activists and those at the colonial periphery.

Correspondence and campaigning in the colonies

For geographically isolated women like Margaret Sievwright, letter writing proved vital in co-ordinating political campaigns. Organisers wrote to schedule meetings, request and share intelligence, plan lecture tours, and address the public through the press. In New Zealand, where suffragists were not concentrated in a capital city but scattered throughout a colony with poor terrestrial transport links, letters were the only consistent means of communication.[18] The suffrage petitions held under the auspices of the Women's Christian Temperance Union (WCTU) in 1891–93 were, for the most part, masterminded by Kate Sheppard in Christchurch but implemented by lieutenants across the colony.[19] Each year, she dispatched hundreds of printed petition papers to community organisers and pasted returned sheets into 'monster' rolls. These she posted to Sir John Hall, the former Premier (1879–82) and chief parliamentary advocate of women's enfranchisement, who theatrically unrolled them while the House of Representatives debated suffrage bills.[20]

In common with much nineteenth-century correspondence, suffragists' letters straddled the boundary between public and private writing. Although exchanges ostensibly occurred between individuals, suffragists considered letters public documents, to be shared and read aloud. For instance, in 1891 the South Australian WCTU articulated its expectation that letter reading was a communal activity. Upon discovering that their president, Elizabeth Webb Nicholls, had maintained a private correspondence parallel to her official communication with Australasian president Jessie Ackermann, the executive reprimanded her for 'insult[ing]' the membership.[21] Letters were not only shared with those who attended meetings; extracts were often transcribed or originals sent to new readers. Unable to read aloud to her diffuse membership, Sheppard instead published letters from overseas activists in her popular newspaper column.[22] As well as reinforcing social bonds, letters formed part of suffragists' organisational memory. Like most Victorian organisations, the WCTU and local suffrage leagues preserved important communications in minute books, a practice that made past decisions available for future consultation and displayed their awareness of posterity.[23]

However, the fusion of personal and organisational relationships did not always benefit the cause. In 1893, the Womanhood Suffrage League (WSL) of New South Wales was riven by a constitutional dispute, with its president, Lady Mary Windeyer, and secretary, Rose Scott, on opposing sides. Rather than plunge League meetings into acrimony, the pair conducted their dispute by post. Windeyer believed that her protégé's push to devolve power to the league's branches undermined her presidency. Scott insisted that the two had written past one another, conjuring a 'network of misunderstanding', but Windeyer suspected a plot against her and resigned as president.[24] In addition to losing Windeyer's social capital – she was married to William Windeyer, a justice of the Supreme Court of New South Wales – the dispute fractured the WSL's intercolonial networks. Mary Lee, secretary of South Australia's Women's Suffrage League, ceased writing to Scott in solidarity with Windeyer, ending communication between the organisations.[25] Since the WSL's formation, Windeyer had relied on Lee's counsel. The pair regularly swapped suffrage literature, speeches, and annual reports, and her rift with Scott deprived the WSL of an experienced advisor.

Still, the fleeting relationship between the WSL and its South Australian counterpart was unusual. During the New Zealand campaign, Kate Sheppard seldom wrote to Australian women. Of the twenty-nine letters she received from across the Tasman in the 1890s, two came from outside the southeastern colonies. Until 1899, when Scott began an enduring friendship with the Victorian suffragist Vida Goldstein, which the pair sustained by post – their letters alternating political and organisational news with quips, personal confessions, and arguments – her correspondence was similarly circumscribed. Instead, Sheppard's most fruitful intercolonial relationship developed with John Vale, secretary of the Victorian Alliance, the colony's peak temperance organisation. After reading about the defeat of a New Zealand suffrage bill in 1891, Vale introduced himself to Sheppard by sending a 'packet of our Womanhood suffrage literature'.[26] Over the following months, Sheppard posted suffrage pamphlets to Melbourne in exchange for transcripts of Victorian parliamentary debates. At Vale's suggestion, they swapped subscriptions and contributions to their respective newspapers, *Alliance Record* and *Prohibitionist*.[27] Born out of necessity at a moment when both colonies appeared to be on the verge of women's enfranchisement, their relationship petered out soon after the New Zealand victory. In the following years, Sheppard wrote periodically to Vale, but her refusal to deliver a public lecture when she visited Melbourne in 1895 marked the end of their correspondence.[28]

As with Sheppard's letters, Sir John Hall's correspondence suggests that the webs linking suffrage activists were partial, and that nodal individuals did not always facilitate cross-border cooperation. A self-conscious member of the colonial elite, Hall was possessed by the need to leave 'materials for history'. His admittedly 'excessive' record-keeping, which stretched to binding copies of his correspondence, permits a closer examination of how Tasman correspondence networks operated.[29] After a stalled bureaucratic career in Britain, Hall emigrated to New Zealand with his two brothers in 1852. The family amassed an estate on the Canterbury Plains, freeing John to pursue his political ambitions. Three years after his arrival, he entered parliament and gained a reputation as its pre-eminent conservative voice. His support for women's enfranchisement stemmed from these principles; from 1878, he advocated the reform as a bulwark against radicalism.[30] Still, like Sheppard and Scott, he considered the women's movement a transnational enterprise. In 1886, Hall joined the Primrose League, a British Conservative Party organisation with suffragist sympathies. Soon after, he strengthened these bonds and boosted his profile by paying women's organisations across the British Empire to disseminate transcripts of his parliamentary speeches.[31] After the narrow defeat of a suffrage bill in 1892, Hall received praise for his efforts from British suffragists and accepted honorary memberships to the London-based Women's Progressive Society and International Women's Union.³² Hall's British ties were matched by his Australian connections. He visited New South Wales in 1889 and 1894, where he discussed suffrage with Sir Henry Parkes, another former colonial Premier whose consistent support for women's enfranchisement had seen him branded 'king of the petticoats'. Hall also corresponded with Mary Lee and exchanged at least a dozen letters with Rose Scott. When he retired from parliament in 1893, Scott lauded Hall's career: 'the women of Australia ... will hold up your name in grateful remembrance as it is due to you that they have gained the first step in Political Liberty & Equality.'³³

For all his personal connections, Hall did not become a central node deepening connections within the Tasman suffrage world. True, Scott found their correspondence productive. She pored over Hall's speeches, disseminated them in Sydney, and recycled choice phrases in her writing.³⁴ By contrast, nothing in Hall's public rhetoric or private archive suggests that he derived similar benefits. He made no reference to the Australian colonies when parliament debated women's enfranchisement and appeared flustered when anti-suffragists deployed Australian examples.³⁵ Hall occasionally forwarded to Sheppard letters from acquaintances like Mary Lee or Lady Rosalind Carlisle of the British Women's Liberal Federation, but he did not mention his longer, more candid exchanges with Scott and Parkes. Nor did he introduce his British or Australian correspondents to New Zealand activists. Despite their decade-long association with Hall, Sheppard and Scott did not begin writing to one another until 1899.³⁶

Organisational ties, rather than personal connections, provided a more reliable platform for spreading information. The WCTU, as an Adelaide member explained, was a 'world-wide organisation for moral and social improvement [which] has the gratification of knowing that the complex machinery of its crusade is kept in splendid working order'.³⁷ Like all global missionary organisations, mass print was central to its operations. By 1892 the Woman's Temperance Publishing Association published 235 million pages a year.³⁸ An important precursor to the New Zealand suffrage campaign came in 1885, when Kate Sheppard received a parcel of American 'franchise pamphlets' on behalf of the Christchurch WCTU.³⁹ Alongside the stream of literature emanating from Chicago, these channels encouraged the exchange of ideas between branches. Rather than continue importing propaganda, Sheppard began publishing her own. Her 1891 polemic *Sixteen Reasons for Supporting Woman's Suffrage* proved more successful than she could ever have realised. Published first in the New Zealand WCTU's newspaper, *White Ribbon*, through the union it drew readers across Australasia, where it became

3.1 An autographed portrait sent by Sir John Hall to Rose Scott in 1894. Despite the pair's frequent correspondence, Hall did not furnish Scott with introductions to his acquaintances in the New Zealand women's movement. (SLNSW, PXA1023/102)

'integral ... [to] the suffrage movement's intellectual rationale'.[40] Her 1892 tract, *Is it Right?*, enjoyed even wider distribution. Within a year, the text featured in the South Australian, Victorian, Tasmanian, and Coloradoan suffrage campaigns and was reprinted by Boston's *Woman's Journal*.[41]

The dissemination of Sheppard's writing had little to do with her personal international connections, which were few in the early 1890s.

Instead, it testified to her tracts' suitability for reproduction – they were, pithy and geographically non-specific – and the WCTU's efficacy as a distributive network. *Sixteen Reasons* first appeared in the *Prohibitionist*, which the Christchurch WCTU swapped with Sydney's *Woman's Suffrage Journal* and Melbourne's *Alliance Record*. It was also included in the 'packet[s] of literature' that the branch sent to WCTU franchise superintendents across Australia.[42] Soon after receiving a copy from Sheppard, the union's South Australian president, Elizabeth Nicholls, had it reprinted in South Australia and Western Australia.[43] The distribution of *Is it Right?* followed a similar pattern, with samples circulated by the New Zealand union then reprinted by their recipients. From their initial transmission between WCTU branches, Sheppard's writings entered the imperial commons, a 'zone of textual production' that existed outside copyright, free for other writers to copy and reuse.[44] Thus, as Ian Tyrrell argues, many British and American suffrage tracts written from the mid-1890s followed Sheppard's 'structure and rhetorical style', if not her radical egalitarian message. Over the next fifteen years, iterations of *Sixteen Reasons* resurfaced all over the world. As was common for authors of such 'viral texts', Sheppard was oblivious to her success: reprints seldom included authorial bylines, and when they did, it would have required unusually attentive readers to bring them to her attention.[45]

In contrast with this organisational pattern, by 1900 personal connections between Australasian suffragists remained inchoate. Within the colonial suffrage campaigns, correspondence bound dispersed activists, co-ordinated parliamentary politics with public activism, and engendered organisational solidarity. Although powerful individuals like Sir John Hall corresponded with suffragists across the English-speaking world, there is little evidence that he became a vital link in a chain connecting New Zealand women with like-minded activists across the world. The WCTU proved a more effective instrument for disseminating propaganda. Like most evangelicals, its members were united by their thirst for the printed word, and the union's organisational structure facilitated interchange between branches, enabling Sheppard's tracts to transcend their antipodean origins and enter a global vernacular. Just as an examination of Tasman suffrage networks revealed the limits of focusing on nodal figures and the corresponding importance of organisational ties in the diffusion of suffrage literature, it also challenges the notion that politics and friendship were always intertwined in suffragists' international networks. Despite the vagaries of individual epistolary connections, the surviving letters sent between metropolitan and colonial feminists offer fresh perspectives on how intimacy operated within the international women's movement, and uncover the motives that lay behind antipodean suffragists' international endeavours.

Intimacy and history in international suffrage correspondence

In October 1893, Kate Sheppard received a letter congratulating her on the 'attainment of our object – the "Female Franchise". I say our, for I have desired it earnestly for 50 years, and I have secretly worked for it since 1860'.[46] Its author, then unknown to Sheppard, was seventy-three-year-old Mary Ann Müller, New Zealand's first female advocate of women's enfranchisement. To escape an abusive marriage in London, Müller emigrated to New Zealand, settling in Nelson in 1850. Soon after, she began studying the British and American women's rights movements. Adopting the pseudonym 'Fémmina', Müller distilled her findings into a pamphlet, *An Appeal to the Men of New Zealand* (1869), which demanded women's enfranchisement as a matter of democratic principle. The tract soon slipped from public consciousness, leaving the succeeding generation of suffragists ignorant of their intellectual lineage. 'In proof' of her endeavours, Müller sent Sheppard a copy in 1893. Enclosed within was an 1870 letter from John Stuart Mill, praising her work as 'an excellent beginning' and encouraging her to join the London Society for Women's Suffrage.[47] Müller's writing had briefly stoked debates about women's rights in New Zealand, yet Sheppard was oblivious to its existence. Surprised by Müller's letter, she exposed her identity in the *Prohibitionist*, thanking her interlocutor 'and doubtless to many others who, like her, worked quietly ... educating the public mind for the political change that has only now taken place'.[48]

Müller's is not merely a heart-warming story of a germinal suffragist receiving belated recognition in her twilight years. Rather, it illustrates the degree to which Australian and New Zealand women's rights activists were unaware of their colonial predecessors. Since the institution of responsible government in the 1850s, white women had contested the masculine political citizenship conferred on the Australasian colonists.[49] However, without the preservation of their writing, or organisations to burnish their legacies, Müller and others' voices went unheard by their successors. Alienated from their forebears, Australasian suffragists traced their lineage directly to the United States and Britain. As avid consumers of imported tracts, colonial suffragists sought to correspond with the luminaries of the British and American women's rights movements. Yet, rather than asking advice on political activism, their letters attempted to write the antipodes into the already metro-centric history of women's struggle for freedom. In this respect, Sheppard and Scott's correspondence exemplifies women's impulses to showcase their achievements abroad and their use of intimate documents as tangible signifiers of internationalism. Whereas such personal ties were often ephemeral, it is in the routine, unglamorous, and often impersonal work of transnational organisational correspondence that we find a more durable internationalism.

Like most social reformers in late nineteenth-century Australasia, feminists drew on a joint Anglo-American intellectual tradition. John Stuart and Harriet Taylor Mill's ideas on women's rights found immediate currency in the colonies, and early activists like Müller, Mary Ann Colclough in Auckland, and Henrietta Dugdale in Melbourne drew particular inspiration from John Stuart's 1869 essay, *On the Subjection of Women*.[50] From the 1880s, women's literary societies considered 'the major theoretical works of turn-of-the-century feminism', while WCTU branches discussed the latest American reform literature.[51] Furthermore, the feminist newspapers that emerged alongside the suffrage movements encouraged their readers to study political tracts. Sydney's *Woman's Voice* published lists of 'Books that Everybody Should Read', which spanned feminist texts by Mary Wollstonecraft, Millicent Garrett Fawcett, and Frances Power Cobbe to offerings from Eleanor Marx, August Bebel, and Henry David Thoreau. Such books were readily available in the colonies' numerous libraries and radical bookshops, which had advertised 'works of special interest to women' since the 1860s.[52]

Colonial women devoured texts that concerned the 'woman question' but seldom interacted with their authors. During the New Zealand suffrage campaign, for example, Kate Sheppard exchanged a dozen letters with women beyond the Tasman littoral. The figure appears low, especially when compared to Elizabeth Wolstenholme Elmy's network of 5,000 correspondents, yet Sheppard enjoyed more frequent exchanges with British and American women during the 1890s than did contemporaries like Scott and Elizabeth Nicholls.[53] The infrequency of communication between antipodean and metropolitan feminists suggests that personal international connections were less important to Australasian women during the suffrage campaigns than has been suggested.[54] This challenge to the 'seemingly indestructible thesis of "British world networks"' resonates with John Griffiths' research on early twentieth-century municipal officials in the British Empire. Mirroring the suffragists, these men were typically British-born and subscribed to agenda-setting London publications. Instead, localised Tasman networks predominated, as bureaucrats sought solutions to their problems close to home. As Sheppard and Scott's papers also indicate, communications with British municipalities were infrequent, and letters to America rarer still.[55] Yet, while direct contact with Northern Hemisphere women was uncommon, interest in their activities was high. As I explore further in Chapter 5, suffragists who had travelled to Britain and America found themselves in demand as public speakers and often turned to the lecture circuit to defray their travel expenses or appease their sponsors.

When Australasian suffragists entered prolonged correspondence with their British counterparts, they sought, above all, to insert themselves into the metro-centric narrative of nineteenth-century suffrage history. Kate Sheppard's letters to Millicent Garrett Fawcett, a pre-eminent figure in the British suffrage movement, exemplify this impulse. Sheppard encountered Fawcett's ideas in 1890, when she read her introduction to a centenary edition of Wollstonecraft's *A Vindication of the Rights of Woman*.[56] Their correspondence began soon after, when Sheppard asked Fawcett to send her a parcel of suffrage leaflets. Her overture assumed a degree of intimacy with the Briton. In thanking Fawcett, she acknowledged their shared experience as suffrage campaigners and, in Wollstonecraft, a mutual source of inspiration for a 'womanly' mode of activism.[57] Nevertheless, neither woman sought a lasting friendship. After professing her indebtedness for 'the manner in which you have steered the question', Sheppard devoted her letters to explaining the New Zealand campaign's origins, methods, and prospects. Fawcett who, like many of her contemporaries, believed Britain was the 'storm-centre' of the international suffrage movement, gave perfunctory replies. Although her tone remained deferential, Sheppard had embarked on a mission to demonstrate that the colony was home to a credible women's movement whose experiences could benefit Britain. After all, as she archly told Fawcett after New Zealand instituted the universal franchise, women in the 'old country' faced a more arduous struggle to overcome the 'ancient barriers' impeding progress.[58]

Sheppard wrote to Helen Blackburn, editor of the influential *Englishwoman's Review*, for similar reasons. Like her contemporaries, Sheppard read the *Review* avidly and promised to forward Blackburn 'items of interest in connection with "woman's suffrage" in New Zealand'.[59] Mirroring her relationship with Fawcett, theirs was not an earnest correspondence. Unlike the IWSA's grandees or those in the World's WCTU's inner circle, Sheppard and her correspondents did not use diminutives or fond sign-offs, 'the protestations of intimacy' that, to Bosch and Kloostermann, emphasised the indivisibility of feminist politics and friendship.⁶⁰ Rather, the pair's letters were brief, functional documents that served both women's interests. Blackburn gathered news for the *Review* and, in turn, Sheppard's achievements featured prominently in the magazine's 'colonial intelligence' columns.⁶¹

After New Zealand women's enfranchisement in 1893, the *Review*'s interest in the colony waned. Nevertheless, Sheppard continued to disseminate the colonial suffrage story overseas. In 1900, she commissioned *White Ribbon*'s publisher, William Sidney Smith, to write a series of articles explaining the history of New Zealand's suffrage campaign. Originally intended for a colonial audience, the articles were republished as *Outlines of the Women's Franchise Movement in New Zealand* (1905). Sheppard, seeking to combat the gift narrative propagated by 'men who should know better', chief among them William Pember Reeves, sent copies to prominent British and American suffragists.⁶² She was not alone in her desire to showcase colonial women's accomplishments abroad. Members of the Auckland and Dunedin Women's Franchise Leagues also wrote to Fawcett, while the *Review*'s popularity in Australia allowed Blackburn to amass a series of correspondents whose letters she condensed into suffrage digests.⁶³ As well as exchanging ideas with Blackburn, the *Review*'s contributors communicated with future generations. Correspondents like Sheppard and Mary Lee ensured the Australasian colonies featured more in the *Review*'s suffrage pages during the 1890s, and Blackburn's 1902 history of the Victorian suffrage movement, than anywhere else outside the British Isles.⁶⁴

Letter writing not only constituted a dutiful attempt to inscribe colonial women into the nascent history of the suffrage movement but also signified individuals' commitment to internationalism. As well as helping isolated activists to view themselves as actors in a world movement, possessing letters with exotic postmarks enhanced the recipient's prestige. Thus, when Elizabeth Nicholls printed Jessie Ackermann's correspondence from Siam and China in Adelaide's *Alliance and Temperance News*, she made sure to include the American's asides to 'my dear Mrs Nicholls'. Kate Sheppard used the *Prohibitionist* in a similar fashion, publishing letters from prominent suffragists that had little news value but nevertheless displayed her proximity to the leading lights of the international women's movement.⁶⁵

The exchange of portrait photographs served as a more potent signifier of women's international connections. By the late nineteenth century, the carte-de-visite craze had swept the globe, and the practice of swapping, signing, and collecting miniature portraits of one's friends and relatives was a firmament of middle-class life. It also extended to international women's conferences, where delegates acquired personalised souvenirs to share at home.[66] Importantly, portrait collecting prevailed among women who had never met, allowing them to strengthen cross-border relationships. As ICW secretary Maria Ogilvie Gordon explained to Sheppard in 1906, 'I felt I ought to send it [her photograph] to you as it is a real help in correspondence to know what the other person is like'.[67] The practice was one of 'mutual obligation', as illustrated by the relationship between Sheppard and Dutch suffragist Aletta Jacobs. After first exchanging letters in 1898, Sheppard requested a photograph of the Dutchwoman. Jacobs agreed, asking the New Zealander 'to send me yours in return, which I will give a place in my collection of ardent and devoted friends for our holy sake'.[68] Rose Scott had a similar habit, enclosing signed photographs in her letters to kindred activists and filling an album with personally dedicated portraits of her correspondents. Unlike traditional family albums, which – the odd celebrity carte aside – were filled with images of friends and family, Scott's collection was more eclectic: juxtaposing images of lifelong friends like Louisa Macdonald, principal of the University of Sydney's Women's College with distant luminaries like the American suffragist Anna Howard Shaw and the IWSA's British treasurer Adela Coit.[69]

Like the letters in which they were enclosed, photographs combined public and private functions. Jacobs and Sheppard were barely acquainted, so at first glance the Dutchwoman's enthusiasm appears exaggerated. Yet, scrapbooks like Jacobs' were not merely aides for the 'private recollection of past experiences', but were intended to be shown and discussed. In this way, the webs of association that constituted an international movement were domesticated and conveyed to viewers. Such collections emphasised that cartes-de-visite were inherently serial, intended to be viewed 'as part of a set or series rather than as unique objects'.[70] These were imaginatively curated archives that allowed women to re-contextualise individual portraits and thus articulate their place in otherwise abstract global networks. In preparation for the 1906 New Zealand International Exhibition, Sheppard solicited dozens of photographs from 'the world's most prominent pioneers' to illustrate an exhibit on the history of women's suffrage. At her instruction, portraits of famous women and group shots of women's organisations flanked the crowning achievement of her political career, the 1893 suffrage petition. The display, a masterpiece of self-representation, was described by *White Ribbon* as 'the most cosmopolitan Bay in the Exhibition', providing fairgoers tangible evidence of New Zealand women's place in a continuing transnational struggle and the breadth of Sheppard's personal connections.[71]

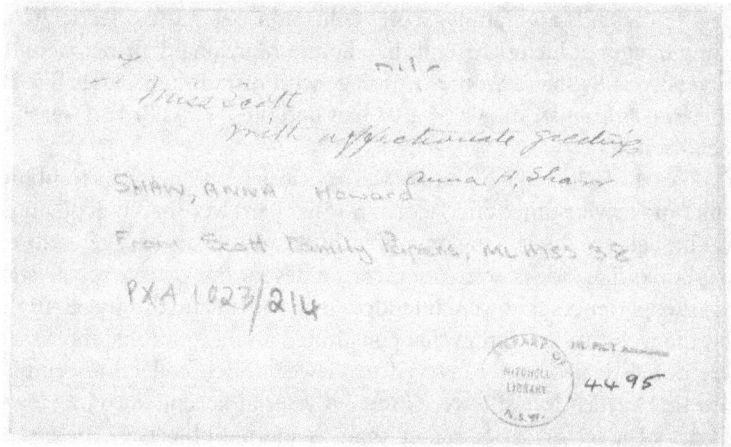

3.2 and 3.3 Although they were infrequent correspondents, Rose Scott's signed portrait of Anna Howard Shaw (c. 1910), accompanied by the American's 'affectionate greetings', was a potent signifier of her personal connection to the international suffrage movement. (SLNSW, PXA1023/214)

Australasian suffragists may have featured in the albums of their overseas counterparts, but they remained outside the Euro-American cadre at the heart of the international women's movement. Although there was never a unidirectional current of ideas from British suffragists to women at the edges of empire, it is hard to consider Sheppard and others' exchanges as freewheeling conversations about women, citizenship, and political activism. Instead, their correspondence was fragmentary, focused

3.4 Kate Sheppard's photo collection on display in the WCTU booth at the New Zealand International Exhibition, Christchurch 1906. (CM, ARC2008.144.43)

on discrete issues, and rarely blossomed into friendship. Most of the relationships Sheppard formed during her 1894–95 stay in Britain withered on her return to New Zealand. Even her most vibrant correspondence, an extended exchange with the 'Bright circle' of Quaker radicals as they investigated the civil rights activist Ida B. Wells' accusations of systematic racism within the American WCTU, petered out soon after her departure. Similarly, while her erstwhile correspondents Helen Blackburn and Millicent Garrett Fawcett vowed to keep Sheppard abreast of 'our doing here', neither wrote after she left Britain.[72] Sheppard's correspondence with overseas activists peaked again during tours of Britain and North America in 1903–4 and 1908 when she reconnected with old acquaintances but dwindled when she returned to Christchurch. These fluctuations in her archive constitute a reminder that 'living connections' undergirded long-term personal correspondence.[73] In the afterglow of New Zealand women's enfranchisement, Sheppard had been a useful ally in Britain. Yet, without guarantee of her return, the 1895 professions of 'friendship' proved hollow.

If Sheppard's fleeting connections with women she met on her travels represented one version of antipodean epistolary internationalism,

Rose Scott's decades of service at the margins of international feminist communities offer another. Scott emerged as a leader in the New South Wales suffrage campaign at the same time as Sheppard but, except for Sir John Hall, she refrained from writing to overseas activists. Only after the formation of the NCW of New South Wales in 1896 did she begin to expand her horizons. As her time in the WSL exemplified, Scott was a dedicated organiser and took her responsibilities as the NCW's international secretary seriously.[74] Over the next twenty years, she diligently upheld New South Wales' commitments to the ICW: reporting to its committees, responding to requests for information, and co-ordinating the state's presence at overseas meetings.

Scott's interest in international politics heightened as her domestic fortunes waned. Marginalised in New South Wales after her suffrage coalition collapsed in 1902, Scott was able through international correspondence to maintain a modicum of her former influence. Yet her letters offer little evidence of an indivisible mesh between 'politics and friendship' in the international suffrage movement. Although Scott corresponded with women like Olga von Beschwitz, convenor of the ICW's Committee on Laws, and Carrie Chapman Catt, president of the IWSA, for almost twenty years, the collegiality that connected women discussing a common enterprise never blossomed into friendship. Unlike the scribbled letters she traded with Vida Goldstein, affectionate gestures were absent from the typewritten communiqués Scott received on official letterhead. Terms of endearment and nicknames – more rudimentary traces of the 'intense affective ties' that bound the IWSA's leaders, for example – were few and far between. Instead, reserve ruled. Throughout her tenure as international secretary, ICW officials wrote interchangeably to Scott and her colleague, the New South Wales corresponding secretary Mary Booth.[75]

Rather than an extension of her 'personal' life, Scott's roles with the ICW and IWSA are better understood as work: labour she enjoyed, but also an arduous, impersonal, and occasionally unrequited practice of internationalism. Indeed, Scott maintained a formal register, eschewing all unnecessary pleasantries. Although, by the 1900s, she had no dependents and means well in excess of the 'five hundred pounds a year' that Virginia Woolf considered a benchmark for maintaining financial and bodily autonomy, Scott spurned repeated invitations to visit Europe so Alliance delegates might deepen the relationship they had begun by post.[76] Rather than camaraderie, a sense of duty to the international project sustained her. Belying her efficient prose, Scott was a passionate advocate of the ICW's work. In 1903, she explained that her diligent reporting ensured that women the world over could 'joyfully indicate

Precedent' – as she had when deploying Hall's speeches or the successful extension of the franchise in Wyoming to rebut the claims of anti-suffragists – when arguing for reform. For this reason, Scott argued, 'constant correspondence kept up with all other National Councils … is of the utmost importance'.[77]

Even before their organised campaigns, individual suffragists in New Zealand and Australia felt compelled to correspond with like-minded activists overseas. Yet, despite what has been written of their British and American counterparts, international friendships between suffrage activists were rare. Most letters had more prosaic purposes, such as ensuring that colonial women's exploits featured in metropolitan feminists' papers of record. Sheppard's haphazard dialogue with British feminists and Scott's dutiful reportage to the ICW and IWSA did not presage epistolary friendships. Nevertheless, their letters reveal the role of intimate practices in international organisations.[78] The exchange of letters and photographs between strangers was not necessarily intended as a prelude to friendship but signified an individual's commitment to internationalism. Such items, displayed on mantels, pasted into scrapbooks, or published in magazines, served as symbols of solidarity. However, the world of feminist correspondence was not solely one of mannered sociability in the interest of cross-border cooperation. Letter writing also had subversive potential, allowing those marginalised in colonial feminist circles to mobilise metropolitan opinion and alter the course of domestic political debates.

'From time to time I try to help in keeping the question before the public': Mary Steadman Aldis' postal activism, 1894–96

By the late nineteenth century, anyone able to read and write could communicate along the same channels, allowing otherwise peripheral figures to upset hierarchies in the women's movement. Seizing on the possibilities offered by the WCTU's global reach, disgruntled members used its American newspaper *Union Signal* to air local grievances to an international audience. Outside the union, women like the Auckland social purity activist Mary Steadman Aldis circumvented local organisations altogether, and instead harnessed metropolitan outrage to prompt colonial reform. Together, these examples show how previously marginalised women used correspondence to disseminate and amplify their critiques of domestic organisations as well as mobilise external support to sway colonial political debates.

Soon after Mary Clement Leavitt landed in Australasia to preach the temperance gospel, women began to appreciate the amplifying power of the WCTU's international networks. In 1893, for example, New Zealand members Ellen Hewett and Helen Snow played a pivotal role in the downfall of celebrated British missionary Kate Marsden. Ten years earlier, Marsden immigrated to New Zealand, where she enjoyed an apparently unremarkable nursing career before returning to Britain in 1886. Within a few years, however, she had risen to fame by virtue of her 1890–91 expedition to deliver aid to 'outcast Siberian lepers'. Yet Marsden's celebrity was fleeting. After publishing an account of her exploits, she became ensnared in a web of gossip stretching from Wellington to London, via New York.[79] Accused of embezzlement by the American journalist Isabel Hapgood, Marsden withdrew from public life. Hapgood fortified her case with affidavits from Hewett and Snow, alleging Marsden had lied about curing leprosy patients and had pursued 'impure relationships' with women in New Zealand. Hewett and Snow did not spread their allegations through the WCTU, but their familiarity with the tone and pattern of its networks had turned them into skilled communicators who understood how such testimony would be received abroad.[80] At home, the press hailed their 'instrumental' role in Marsden's downfall, a sentiment shared by the union's membership. In 1894, delegates to the union's annual convention took the unusual step of commenting on foreign affairs by recording their 'indignation at the conduct of Miss Kate Marsden'.[81]

Disgruntled WCTU members used postal networks not only to police missionaries' behaviour but also to intervene in internal disputes. By 1891, *Union Signal* circulated up to 200,000 copies and provided stories for fifty union mastheads across the world.[82] Combined with its global readership, a permissive editorial policy made the *Signal* a lively forum for women seeking to highlight injustices ignored by their local leaders. One such instance occurred in February 1894, when Serena Lake, the South Australian WCTU's disaffected former suffrage superintendent, addressed an explosive letter to the paper. Describing her marginalisation, she labelled the South Australian president, Elizabeth Nicholls, the ringleader of 'a new party [which] elbowed its way to the helm of the movement'. Under Lake, the union relied on sympathetic politicians to persuade their colleagues to extend the franchise, and she contended that Nicholls' insistence on mass petitioning had condemned the 1893 suffrage bill to failure. As intended, Lake's intervention embarrassed her former colleagues and prompted a mass resignation from the executive.[83] So alarmed was the South Australian WCTU by the possibility of further 'communications being sent to … other lands with the intention of doing injury' that they elevated the issue to the Australasian WCTU, which recommended that branches 'authenticate' submissions to the *Signal*.[84] A similar incident that year scandalised the New Zealand union. Rather than appoint censors, the union published an editorial entitled 'Thou Shalt Not Bear False Witness' in the *Prohibitionist*, seeking to shame would-be critics into silence.[85]

In South Australia and New Zealand, WCTU leaders re-established their authority by preventing dissenters from amplifying their complaints through the union's transnational communication channels. However, non-members adopted similar methods without fear of censure. Between 1888 and 1897, an Auckland couple, William and Mary Steadman Aldis, wrote to metropolitan reformers advocating causes that they believed New Zealanders ignored. Although the pair were liminal figures in colonial activist circles, they drew on deep connections with British social reformers to stimulate metropolitan interest in the repeal of New Zealand's 1869 Contagious Diseases Act. During their decade in the colony, the Aldises depicted a society bent on eroding liberty and uninterested in ending the scourge of state-regulated vice. Although their early repeal efforts fell flat, these laid the groundwork for future success. In 1895, the pair amplified a minor scandal into a flashpoint in the imperial struggle against regulated prostitution, turning British minds to the supposed inaction of the colony's newly enfranchised women.

William and Mary Steadman Aldis emigrated from Britain to New Zealand in 1884 for William to take the chair of mathematics at Auckland University College. The pair had married twenty years earlier and, on William's graduation from Cambridge, moved to Newcastle. There, they joined numerous reform movements, including the campaigns for women's enfranchisement and against the Contagious Diseases Acts. Seeking a fresh start, the pair resolved to take 'two years of vowed abstinence … from public work' when they departed for New Zealand.[86] Within a few months, however, their vow was forgotten. In 1885, William joined the Auckland Education Board and, alongside Mary, became a vociferous advocate for the repeal of the Contagious Diseases Act. Like the swathe of regulations implemented across the British Empire, the New Zealand act empowered police to incarcerate and forcibly treat suspected prostitutes for venereal disease. Although the act emulated the infamous British model, it exceeded the original by making the regulations universally enforceable, rather than limited to the vicinity of military garrisons.[87] Despite its framers' zeal, the legislation was never enthusiastically enforced. With the costs of detention incumbent on those provincial governments that implemented the act, it was only applied in Canterbury. When the provincial system was abolished in 1876, municipal authorities assumed responsibility for enforcement. In Canterbury the act operated between 1872 and 1885, while the Auckland City Council implemented it between 1882 and its repeal in 1910. However, reflecting public displeasure with the cost of running a lock hospital, enforcement ceased in 1886. Neither jurisdiction recorded many convictions, but the Contagious Diseases Act's extension to Auckland energised the repeal campaign.[88] Without a colonial network to support them, the city's repealers sought advice from British allies and established chapters of metropolitan organisations, notably Auckland's Association for the Abolition of the State Regulation of Vice.[89]

Mary Steadman Aldis lay at the heart of these efforts. Echoing British repealers, she argued that the act amounted to state sanctioned immorality, violated women's bodily integrity, entrenched a moral double standard and, crucially, failed as a public health measure. At her insistence, the Auckland WCTU joined the campaign in 1886, months after delegates at the union's colonial convention first demanded repeal. The campaign lost momentum when retrenchment at the City Council prompted the closure of the Auckland lock hospital, but Aldis was undeterred.[90] However efficacious her methods appeared, the Auckland women's movement never embraced the Briton. As members of the Personal Rights Association, the Aldises adhered to a radical brand of libertarianism. Although their crusade against immorality appeared suited to a colony eager to shed its frontier past, they abhorred New Zealanders' 'disposition ... to set up the State as a kind of earthly Providence'. For this reason, and Mary's persistent ill-health, which further isolated her from Auckland's reform circles, the pair found themselves at odds with the collectivist society they encountered in New Zealand.[91]

Within a few years of their arrival, the Aldises had become notorious for their caustic contributions to the Auckland press. William railed against 'State Despotism in the Antipodes', while Mary – determined 'to tell the truth about New Zealand' – discouraged potential British settlers from emigration, decried 'useless' defence expenditure, and denounced the WCTU's anti-barmaid campaign. Both loathed 'rabid teetollers [sic]'.[92] The WCTU might have otherwise overlooked their candour but could not countenance Mary's public 'opposition to temperance principles'. Although local unions continued to support small repeal petitions, the WCTU turned its collective attention to the vote. Careful to avoid tainting the suffrage campaign by association with the 'social evil', the Auckland executive declined Mary's request to dedicate itself to the act's repeal in 1889.[93]

Alienated from Auckland society, Mary Steadman Aldis instead pursued local causes through transnational channels. In 1893 she experimented with postal activism after William was controversially dismissed by Auckland University, orchestrating an unsuccessful Anglo-New Zealand press campaign seeking his reinstatement.[94] However, the Contagious Diseases Act remained her enduring concern. As a veteran of the campaign to end regulated prostitution in India, Mary understood the power of metropolitan opinion to force colonial reform. Thus, from 1888, she worked assiduously to generate sufficient pressure among British activists to force the act's repeal. Although white settler women were far from the 'degraded' Indian woman imagined by British feminists, Mary maintained that they needed metropolitan guidance.[95] Resuming her relationship with the Ladies' National Association for the Repeal of the Contagious Diseases Acts (LNA) and its sister organisation, the British Committee of the British, Continental and General Federation for the Abolition of State Regulation of Vice, Aldis detailed the shortcomings of the repeal movement. Rather than complaining privately, from the outset she wrote for the abolitionist press. After describing thwarted repeal bills in 1887 and 1888, Aldis asked readers of Josephine Butler's newspaper, *Dawn*, 'ought not [we] … to have strong support from England?' and demanded they 'take the matter up' in New Zealand.[96] Her letters followed this pattern over the next four years, lamenting 'feeble' local repeal efforts and the indifference of the colonial establishment.[97]

Aldis' appeals resonated with British social purity campaigners' sense of imperial duty, but had little immediate effect in New Zealand. At Butler's behest, *Dawn*'s readers 'sen[t] out some literature gratis' to the 'abolitionists at the antipodes', but Aldis received no further support. Until 1894 the British Committee refused to interfere in settler colonial politics.[98] However, women's enfranchisement had transformed New Zealand into an object lesson for metropolitan reformers. The moment coincided with a decline in the repeal movement's fortunes: officials in the Crown colonies refused to extirpate regulated prostitution, while Butler's European allies had begun to abandon abolitionism.[99] For British feminists, repeal and suffrage activism were intertwined, making New Zealand an emblematic frontier where enfranchised women could display their strength and reinvigorate the flagging imperial campaign.

In 1894, Aldis realised the time had come to press her case. Although women's organisations had broached repeal before the 1893 general election, mass protest remained a distant prospect. She suggested direct action, asking that the British Committee write 'to the women of New Zealand, pointing out to them that since they have the suffrage it will be a disgrace to them not to use it to sweep away the C.D. Act'.[100] Josephine Butler agreed and published a trenchant pamphlet explaining her expectations of New Zealanders. Following Aldis' prompt, Butler argued that as the 'only women in the British Empire' with the parliamentary franchise, they had a 'great responsibility to demand the repeal of a law which is an insult to womanhood'. 'It would be a bitter grief to us', she continued, 'and a subject of self-abasement as women if it could be said ... that the first group of Anglo-Saxon women who possessed the vote had failed to use it in this great purifying purpose.'[101]

Although Aldis found Butler and the British Committee willing allies, her vision of a trans-imperial repeal campaign lacked a local scandal around which to coalesce. Her opportunity came in June 1895 when the recently established Auckland Women's Liberal League (AWLL) demanded the Contagious Diseases Act's 'rigorous' enforcement, provided it was 'made applicable for men and women alike'.[102] Within days, women across the colony pressed the League to reconsider its position. Regulated prostitution, the Women's Franchise League and WCTU reiterated, needed to be 'swept from the statute book'.[103] Nevertheless, fearing such responses would not be parlayed into a concerted repeal campaign, Mary and William Steadman Aldis sent monthly reports to the British Committee. After a decade in the colony, they knew that the AWLL occupied a marginal place in the women's movement. However, reflecting their immersion in the radical evangelical tradition that had nurtured Josephine Butler, the pair were adroit at manipulating 'earthly fact by appealing to a divine reality'. Whatever the 'facts' of the case, what mattered to the Aldises was the colonists' indifference to legally sanctioned immorality.[104] Butler, in turn, relayed the news to her repeal network, and New Zealand women's organisations soon began receiving corrective letters from their British counterparts. Again, she memorialised the episode in pamphlet form, describing the AWLL's resolution, in her millennialist fashion, as evidence of women's 'defection' from the abolitionist cause.[105] By late 1895, the Aldises were circulating Butler's *Letter of Earnest Appeal and Warning* and had placed another open letter, urging women voters to force the act's repeal, in the Auckland press.[106]

At the same time, *Dawn*'s sister publication, *Sentinel*, used the episode to spread rumours intended to rouse abolitionist sentiment across Australasia. Warning of an 'approaching crisis', the paper made the baseless argument that, emboldened by the AWLL's proclamation, the Australasian Medical Congress would press for 'the energetic enforcement of the C.D. Acts' throughout the region. In response, Elizabeth Nicholls wrote to its editor, Alfred Dyer, scotching his sensational claims: 'the news of any intention to countenance this iniquity on the part of the approaching Medical Congress comes to us as a surprise.'[107] Nevertheless, such rhetoric appealed to British readers. Urged by Dyer, fifteen branches of the Women's National Liberal Association wrote 'letter[s] of remonstrance' to the AWLL, which the Aldises published in pamphlet form in 1896.[108]

Many members of the WCTU-led coalition that won the female franchise in New Zealand felt compelled by Butler to publicly rededicate themselves to the repeal cause. Yet, while the Dunedin Women's Franchise League apologised for the AWLL, and reaffirmed their commitment to repeal, others criticised British activists' intervention.[109] In October 1895, the influential feminist newspaper *Woman's Signal* claimed the AWLL had undermined women's reputation as political citizens. 'They have Woman's Suffrage on trial in the eyes of the English-speaking world, and deep will be the mischief ... if they now disgrace it.' Then in London, Kate Sheppard persuaded the *Signal* to issue a correction, clarifying that the AWLL was a 'recently formed' splinter group, whose actions had been repudiated.[110] Others were less sanguine. The Auckland WCTU 'deplored the need for a second appeal' and expressed their indignation that the British Committee had framed the AWLL as representative of the women's movement. Writing in *White Ribbon*, Lucy Smith of the Christchurch WCTU criticised uninformed metropolitans meddling in New Zealand politics in more forthright terms. Dismissing Butler's 'pathetic pamphlet', she concluded that 'a little enquiry would have made the matter clear'.[111]

The zenith of Butler and the Aldises' choreographed intervention in New Zealand politics arrived in 1896, when the Premier, Richard Seddon, tabled a repeal bill. The Legislative Council had vetoed an attempt in 1895, before metropolitan activists could muster a response. As earlier, Aldis anticipated that British criticism would galvanise the colonial parliament, and she worked to mobilise metropolitan pens rather than rally local activists. Announcing his agenda to the House, Seddon drew attention to those 'outside the colony watching their conduct with regard to this measure'. After the Legislative Council dismissed his first bill, Seddon made the extraordinary decision to introduce an identical measure in the same session, attributing his haste to the 'large number of communications' he had received 'from societies in the Mother-country, whose object was to get reform in the direction undertaken in this Bill'.[112] Pre-empting the second debate, the British Committee shipped 10,000 leaflets to New Zealand, prompting parliamentarians to complain that their 'pigeonholes had been stuffed full of pamphlets' from the act's opponents.[113] Despite the intense scrutiny Butler and Aldis brought to the bill, and the Premier's personal commitment, the upper house again rejected it.

Without the backing of a robust local repeal campaign, Mary Steadman Aldis' efforts were futile. Despite the skill with which she used her postal networks to engender British sympathy for her cause, the parachute activism she orchestrated with Josephine Butler ultimately hindered the abolitionist movement. Lingering anti-feminist sentiment contributed to the bills' failure, which heralded a backlash against women exercising their newfound political power, especially when they tried to 'curb men's sexual liberties'.[114] With repeal thwarted three times in two years, Seddon abandoned the cause. Liberal backbenchers tabled another four repeal bills, but the Ministry never included them in its legislative agenda. Before long, British observers lost interest in New Zealand. While the LNA branded New Zealand one of its 'two great battlegrounds' in 1896, within months the reinstatement of regulated prostitution in India ended its focus on the colony.[115] By then, Mary's illness forced the Aldises to return to Britain. She died soon after, and although William sat on the British Committee's executive until 1900, he said nothing further about New Zealand.[116] The New Zealand NCW passed resolutions demanding repeal from 1896 until it ceased meeting in 1903, and the WCTU periodically campaigned on the issue, but neither group generated sufficient momentum to force repeal. Instead, the Contagious Diseases Act remained on New Zealand's statute books until 1910, when fears about venereal disease undermining national vitality, rather than feminist criticism, prompted its replacement.[117]

Mary Steadman Aldis' activism revealed the subversive power of correspondence and the asymmetries in the relationship between metropolitan and colonial feminists. Before departing Britain, her apprenticeship in the social purity movement had imparted an acute awareness of how abolitionists harnessed sensational reportage to force change on intransigent colonial officials. Bedridden and alienated from the New Zealand women's movement, Aldis could nevertheless write. Rather than drawing on personal connections, she laid the groundwork in the British reform press for a decade, so when news leaked that the AWLL had 'endorsed' New Zealand's contagious diseases regime, she knew it would rouse Josephine Butler's reform network. Fearful of losing further ground in the global campaign against regulated prostitution, Butler and the British Committee broke their silence on the self-governing colonies and orchestrated a lobbying effort that saw Richard Seddon take the unprecedented step of attempting to repeal an act twice in the same parliamentary session. Although it temporarily accelerated the progress of a desired law reform, the outpouring of opprobrium from Butler and her British associates angered many New Zealand women, who felt they had wilfully appropriated the AWLL scandal. Behind the deferential apologies lay notes of defiance and disappointment that their voices were seldom heard and often misrepresented in metropolitan debates about women, feminism, and social reform.

Despite her importance to the New Zealand women's movement, few records of Margaret Sievwright's life have survived. As attested in this chapter, she was an energetic correspondent, but it is hard to tell whether her effusive letters to Rose Scott were typical. Viewed in isolation, they appear to conform to Charlotte Macdonald's description of the 'intimacy of the envelope' and the mid-nineteenth-century New Zealand settler Mary Taylor's conception of the letter as a medium which allowed her to dwell 'in 2 places at once'.[118] However, read against the epistolary relationships maintained by the European and North American women at the heart of the IWSA, and the more intense emotional ties forged by members of the Pan-Pacific Women's Association amid the geopolitical turbulence of the 1930s, the letters sent by prolific writers like Kate Sheppard and Rose Scott reveal an alternate, and overlooked, mode of political communication.[119] Earnest friendships conducted through the post were rare, and nodal individuals, whose extensive personal networks reshaped domestic and international feminist activism, were rarer still. Rather than writing to build or maintain friendships, Sheppard wrote to suffragists overseas to ensure that New Zealand women's 'pioneer' achievements were instilled in metropolitan minds, both as a point of pride and from a sense of duty to suffragists in the 'old country'. The channels she used swelled and shrank according to necessity and opportunity, reflecting her movement between Britain and New Zealand. Rose Scott, by personality more than design, also eschewed the intimacies of the international sphere. Above friendship, she considered the exchange of information the highest goal of feminist internationalism – a task she laboured at for twenty years.

However, while Sievwright and others' correspondence emphasises that the link between politics and friendship was not always at the heart of the international women's movement, their letters also divulge the role of intimate practices in cross-border organising. Possessing missives from distant activists, however perfunctory their contents, signified an individual's commitment to the international cause. Such connections were made manifest when women inserted letters and cartes-de-visite into scrapbooks, propped them on mantelpieces, or exhibited them at World's Fairs. Yet, the democratic nature of letter writing meant that correspondence constituted a weapon in the hands of those ostracised in domestic feminist circles. With pen and paper alone, Serena Lake and

Mary Steadman Aldis harnessed metropolitan opinion to remedy their grievances with the direction of colonial women's movements. In return, Josephine Butler used open letters to communicate with the Australasian public. While Lake's mutinous contribution to *Union Signal* was embarrassing for the WCTU, Aldis' letter-writing campaign testified to the influence women wielded through the post and challenges the progressive narrative of epistolary intimacy that dominates accounts of the early international women's movement. Turning from personal correspondence to mass communication, the following chapter considers the rise and fall of a women's advocacy press in the 1890s as another vector for suffrage internationalism, tracing the circulation of printed – rather than handwritten – texts to reveal the contours of Australasian suffragists' mental world of women's activism.

Notes

1 SLNSW, A2274/156, Margaret Sievwright to Rose Scott, 21 March 1902.
2 SLNSW, A2272/705, Sievwright to Scott, 25 July 1902; A2274/184, Sievwright to Scott, 8 January 1903.
3 C. Macdonald, 'Intimacy of the envelope: Fiction, commerce, and empire in the correspondence of friends Mary Taylor and Charlotte Brontë, c. 1845–55', in T. Ballantyne and A. Burton (eds), *Moving Subjects: Gender, Mobility, and Intimacy in an Age of Global Empire* (Chicago: University of Illinois Press, 2009), pp. 89–109; SLNSW, A2274/184, Sievwright to Scott, 8 January 1903.
4 'Post and Telegraph Department (report of the) for the year 1902', *Appendix to the Journals of the House of Representatives* [New Zealand] 1903, F-01, p. 24.
5 'Margaret Sievwright and Christina Henderson to Susan B. Anthony, 22 December 1902', in A. D. Gordon (ed.), *The Selected Papers of Elizabeth Cady Stanton and Susan B. Anthony: Volume VI, An Awful Hush, 1895 to 1906* (New Brunswick: Rutgers University Press, 2013), p. 461; *ICW Report of Transactions During the Third Quinquennial Term*, Vol. I, p. 179. Sievwright and Wolstenholme Elmy had worked together during the British campaign against the Contagious Diseases Acts, and the pair evidently remained in contact after Sievwright left Edinburgh for New Zealand in the mid-1870s. British Library, London, Add.MS47454/fol.109, Elizabeth Wolstenholme Elmy to Harriet McIlquham, 26 April 1905; *Ethical World*, 29 April 1905, pp. 133–4.
6 T. Ballantyne, *Orientalism and Race: Aryanism in the British Empire* (New York: Palgrave, 2002), pp. 13–17.
7 C. Macdonald, 'Introduction', in C. Macdonald (ed.), *Women Writing Home, 1700–1920, Female Correspondence across the British Empire, Volume 5: New Zealand* (London: Pickering & Chatto, 2006), pp. xix–xx; M. A. Favret, *Romantic Correspondence: Women, Politics, and the Fiction of Letters* (Cambridge: Cambridge University Press, 1993), p. 10. See especially C. Smith-Rosenberg, 'The female world

of love and ritual: Relations between women in nineteenth-century America', *Signs*, 1:1 (1975), 1–29.

8 J. Rendall, 'Friendship and politics: Barbara Leigh Smith Bodichon (1827–91) and Bessie Rayner Parkes (1829–1925)', in S. Mendus and J. Rendall (eds), *Sexuality and Subordination: Interdisciplinary Studies of Gender in the Nineteenth Century* (London and New York: Routledge, 1989), pp. 136–70; L. M. Gring-Pemble, 'Writing themselves into consciousness: Creating a rhetorical bridge between the public and private spheres', *Quarterly Journal of Speech*, 84:1 (1998), 41–61.

9 D. Coleman (ed.), *Women Writing Home, 1700–1920, Volume 2: Australia* (London: Pickering & Chatto, 2006); J. Garner and K. Foster (eds), *Letters to Grace: Writing Home from Colonial New Zealand* (Christchurch: Canterbury University Press, 2011); Macdonald (ed.), *Women Writing Home, Volume 5: New Zealand*; Patterson and Wanhalla, *He Reo Wāhine*; F. Porter et al. (eds), *My Hand Will Write What My Heart Dictates: The Unsettled Lives of Women in Nineteenth-Century New Zealand as Revealed to Sisters, Family and Friends* (Auckland: Auckland University Press, 1996).

10 J. Sangster, 'Crossing boundaries: Women's organizing in Europe and the Americas, 1880s–1940s', in P. Jonsson et al. (eds), *Crossing Boundaries: Women's Organizing in Europe and the Americas, 1880s–1940s* (Uppsala: Uppsala University Press, 2007), p. 11. See also T. Ballantyne and A. Burton, 'Introduction: The politics of intimacy in an age of empire', in Ballantyne and Burton (eds), *Moving Subjects*, p. 1.

11 See, for example, McFadden, *Golden Cables of Sympathy*; P. Harrison, *Connecting Links: The British and American Woman Suffrage Movements, 1900–1914* (Westport: Greenwood Press, 2000); Offen, 'Overcoming hierarchies through internationalism', pp. 15–27.

12 Bosch with Kloostermann (eds), *Politics and Friendship*, p. 26. See, for example, H. Dampier, '"Going on with our little movement in the hum drum-way which alone is possible in a land like this": Olive Schreiner and suffrage networks in Britain and South Africa, 1905–1913', *Women's History Review*, 25:4 (2016), 536–50; K. M. Marino, 'Transnational Pan-American feminism: The friendship of Bertha Lutz and Mary Wilhelmine Williams, 1926–1944', *Journal of Women's History*, 26:2 (2014), 63–87; Rupp, *Worlds of Women*; C. Sato, '"A picture of peace": Friendship in interwar Pacific women's internationalism', *Qui Parle*, 27:2 (2018), 475–510; V. Taylor and L. J. Rupp, 'Loving internationalism: The emotion culture of transnational women's organizations, 1888–1945', *Mobilization: An International Journal*, 7:2 (2002), 141–58.

13 SLNSW, MLMSS364/8, Scott to Miles Franklin, 15 December 1902; Allen, *Rose Scott*, p. viii; Patterson and Wanhalla, *He Reo Wāhine*, p. 12.

14 A. R. Gere, *Intimate Practices: Literary and Cultural Work in US Women's Clubs, 1880–1920* (Chicago: University of Illinois Press, 1997), pp. 1–13.

15 Nolan and Daley, 'International feminist perspectives on suffrage', p. 6.

16 M. Lyons, 'Love letters and writing practices: On *ecritures intimes* in the nineteenth century', *Journal of Family History*, 24:2 (1999), 232–9.

17 Favret, *Romantic Correspondence*, pp. 7–10. By 1901, 81 per cent of women in Australasia could read and write. Imperial Penny Post was introduced in 1898, but New Zealand (1901) and Australia (1910) delayed its adoption for fear of losing

postal revenue. 'Census: 1871–1916', *Statistics New Zealand*, www.stats.govt.nz/br owse_for_stats/snapshots-of-nz/digitised-collections/census-collection (accessed 5 May 2019); 'Historical and colonial census data archive', *Australian Data Archive Dataverse*, https://dataverse.ada.edu.au/dataset.xhtml?persistentId=doi:10.26193/M P6WRS (accessed 12 April 2020); R. M. Pike, 'National interest and imperial yearnings: Empire communications and Canada's role in establishing the Imperial Penny Post', *Journal of Imperial and Commonwealth History*, 26:1 (1998), 36.

18 E. Pawson, 'Time-space convergence in New Zealand: 1850s to 1990s', *New Zealand Journal of Geography*, 94:1 (1992), 14–16. During the suffrage campaign, no more than three of the WCTU's fifteen regional franchise superintendents gathered at the union's annual conventions.

19 The impetus for the largest of New Zealand's suffrage petitions, in 1893, came from Helen Nicol and the Dunedin Women's Franchise League, who convinced Hall and Sheppard – against the latter's wishes – to persist with the strategy after the defeat of the 1892 Electoral Bill. ATL, MSX-0914/403, Sir John Hall to Sheppard, 4 November 1892; ATL, MS-Papers-1784-91/11, Sheppard to Hall, 7 November 1892; ATL, MSX-0917/5-7, Hall to Sheppard, 6 December 1892; J. Tolerton, 'Nicol key to women's suffrage', *Otago Daily Times*, www.odt.co.nz/lifestyle/magazine/nicol-key-wo mens-suffrage (accessed 23 September 2019).

20 ATL, MS-Papers-1784-177/36, Sheppard to Hall, 20 June 1891; *Bay of Plenty Times*, 19 August 1891, p. 4; *Auckland Star*, 13 July 1893, p. 3.

21 SLSA, SRG186/1/1, South Australian WCTU Minute Book 1889–95, 14 July 1891.

22 See, for example, *Prohibitionist*, 22 October 1892, p. 3; 29 July 1893, p. 3.

23 E. G. Garvey, *Writing with Scissors: American Scrapbooks from the Civil War to the Harlem Renaissance* (New York: Oxford University Press, 2013), pp. 173–207.

24 Allen, *Rose Scott*, pp. 128–30; SLNSW, MLMSS186/13/59–63, 125–7, Scott to Mary Windeyer, 16 July and 22 August 1893.

25 SLNSW, MLMSS186/14/275, Mary Lee to Mary Windeyer, 4 January 1894.

26 *Prohibitionist*, 10 October 1891, p. 3.

27 CM, ARC176.53/70, 73, 226, 229, John Vale to Sheppard, 27 October 1891, 1 February 1892, 23 December 1893, and 19 January 1894.

28 CM, ARC176.50/278, Vale to Sheppard, 5 August 1895.

29 J. Garner, *By His Own Merits: Sir John Hall – Pioneer, Pastoralist & Premier* (Hororata: Dryden Press, 1995), p. 12.

30 J. McAloon, *No Idle Rich: The Wealthy in Canterbury & Otago 1840–1914* (Dunedin: University of Otago Press, 2002), pp. 35–6, 41, 177.

31 Garner, *Sir John Hall*, pp. 213, 263; CM, ARC176.53/24, Hall to Sheppard, 15 August 1890.

32 ATL, fMS-Papers-4923-1, Hall to Rosalind Carlisle, 16 January 1893; ATL, MS-Papers-1784-190/19–20, Helen Blackburn to Hall, 6 October 1892; ATL, MSX-0914/439, Hall to Sheppard, 17 November 1892; ATL, MSX-0918/427, Hall to Sheppard, 18 December 1893.

33 See, for example, *Bulletin*, 16 July 1892, p. 7; *Star*, 17 August 1891, p. 3. Rose Scott described Hall and Parkes's 'interesting correspondence … on the subject of W. Suffrage' in 1894, but their letters on the subject have not survived. ATL,

MS-Papers-1784-202/30, Scott to Hall, 6 January 1894; CM, ARC176.53/123, Hall to Sheppard, 24 October 1892.
34 ATL, MS-Papers-1784-189/39, Scott to Hall, 15 September 1892; SLNSW, MLMSS38/34/3, WSL of New South Wales Record Book *c.* 1892. Scott's annotated copies of Hall's speeches can be found at SLNSW, Z396.3/S.
35 See, for example, *New Zealand Parliamentary Debates* (*NZPD*), 1891, Vol. 73, pp. 497–503, 549–50.
36 CM, ARC176.53/123, 132, Hall to Sheppard, 24 October 1892 and 17 January 1893; SLNSW, A2274/127–9, Sheppard to Scott, 26 June and 1 September 1899.
37 *Advertiser*, 31 March 1900, p. 6.
38 J. L. McKeever, 'The Woman's Temperance Publishing Association', *The Library Quarterly*, 55:4 (1985), 374.
39 Devaliant, *Kate Sheppard*, p. 21.
40 Tyrrell, *Woman's World*, p. 224. Although Sheppard's pamphlet, and its precursor, *Ten Reasons Why the Women of New Zealand Should Get the Vote*, followed the format of a British tract, *Sixteen Reasons for Women's Suffrage* (*c.* 1870), she did not mimic its rhetoric. *Ten Reasons Why the Women of New Zealand Should Get the Vote* (Christchurch: n.p., 1888); *Sixteen Reasons for Supporting Woman's Suffrage* (Christchurch: Smith, Anthony, Sellars & Co., 1891).
41 *Is It Right?* (Christchurch: Smith, Anthony, Sellars & Co., 1892); *Hawke's Bay Herald*, 18 November 1893, p. 5; *Prohibitionist*, 13 January 1894, p. 3; *Mercury* supplement, 8 April 1893, p. 2; *Woman's Journal*, 18 November 1893, p. 362.
42 CM, ARC176.53/70, Vale to Sheppard, 27 October 1891; CM, ARC176.53/74, 'The Editor, W.S.J.' to Sheppard, 9 March 1892; *Prohibitionist*, 7 November 1891, p. 3; 12 November 1892, p. 3; 6 May 1893, p. 3.
43 *Sixteen Reasons for Supporting Woman's Suffrage* (Adelaide: Holden & Strutton, 1892); J. R. Henderson, *The Strength of White Ribbon: A Year-by-Year Record of the Centennial History of the Woman's Christian Temperance Union of Western Australia* (Perth: The Union, 1992), p. 4.
44 A. Burton and I. Hofmeyr, 'The spine of empire? Books and the imperial commons', in A. Burton and I. Hofmeyr (eds), *Ten Books that Shaped the British Empire: Creating an Imperial Commons* (Durham: Duke University Press, 2014), p. 2.
45 Tyrrell, *Woman's World*, pp. 224–32; R. Cordell, 'Reprinting, circulation and the network author in antebellum newspapers', *American Literary History*, 27:3 (2015), 417–18, 423–9. See, for example, *Woman's Herald*, 25 May 1893, p. 224; *Woman's Signal*, 14 June 1894, p. 416; *Woman Suffrage Leaflet*, March 1904, n.p.; *Englishwoman's Review*, 15 April 1904, pp. 99–100; *Woman's Tribune*, 26 May 1906, p. 43; *Fourteen Reasons for Supporting Women's Suffrage* (London: National Union of Women's Suffrage Societies, *c.* 1913).
46 CM, ARC176.53/215, Mary Ann Müller to Sheppard, 5 October 1893.
47 Fémmina, *An Appeal to the Men of New Zealand* (Nelson: J. Hounsell, 1869). Müller's claim that her writing was published by 'divers other papers in the Colony' has generally been taken at face value, but I have found no evidence to support her assertion, or even that the pamphlet was widely discussed in the contemporary press. CM, ARC176.53/215–16, 310, Müller to Sheppard, 5 and 18 October 1893, 18 August

1898; R. Dalziel, 'Müller, Mary Anne', *Te Ara: The Encyclopedia of New Zealand*, www.TeAra.govt.nz/en/biographies/1m59/muller-mary-anne (accessed 11 February 2019).
48 *Prohibitionist*, 4 November 1893, p. 3.
49 J. E. Malone, 'What's wrong with Emma? The feminist debate in colonial Auckland', in B. Brookes *et al.* (eds), *Women in History*, pp. 69–85; Woollacott, *Settler Society in the Australian Colonies*, pp. 124–51.
50 *Daily Southern Cross*, 27 June 1871, p. 2; M. Sawer and M. Simms, *A Woman's Place: Women and Politics in Australia* (Sydney: Allen and Unwin, 2nd edn, 1993), pp. 1–4.
51 Magarey, *Passions of the First Wave*, p. 40; SLNSW, MLB693, Women's Literary Society Minute Book 1892–93; ATL, 79-057-08/03, Auckland WCTU Minute Book 1889–98, 23 May, 28 June, and 12 July 1900.
52 *Woman's Voice*, 27 July 1895, p. 306; Brookes, *A History of New Zealand Women*, p. 81; Scates, *A New Australia*, pp. 48–56.
53 Nicholls' papers contain only eight letters from outside Australia during the South Australian suffrage campaign. Similarly, Rose Scott's correspondence with women outside Australia only began in earnest late in the decade, when she became the National Council of Women of New South Wales' international secretary. M. Wright, '"An impudent intrusion?" Assessing the life of Elizabeth Wolstenholme Elmy, first-wave feminist and social reformer (1833–1918)', *Women's History Review*, 18:2 (2009), 257–8.
54 See Devaliant, *Kate Sheppard*, pp. 54–5, 72, 125–6; Grimshaw, *Women's Suffrage in New Zealand*, pp. 37, 53–4, 111–13.
55 J. Griffiths, 'Were there municipal networks in the British World *c.* 1890–1939?', *Journal of Imperial and Commonwealth History*, 37:4 (2009), 577–87.
56 M. Fawcett, 'Introduction to the new edition', in M. Wollstonecraft, *A Vindication of the Rights of Woman* (New York: Scribner and Welford, 1890), pp. 1–30.
57 E. H. Botting *et al.*, 'Wollstonecraft as international feminist meme', *Journal of Women's History*, 26:2 (2014), 13–38.
58 Carrie Chapman Catt coined the phrase 'storm-centre' in 1908, but it accurately characterises the attitudes of the previous decade. Manchester Libraries, Information and Archives, Manchester (hereafter MLIA), GB127.M50/2/1, Sheppard to Fawcett, 22 April 1891, 3 April and 4 October 1893; CM, ARC176.53/33, 219, Fawcett to Sheppard, 30 May 1891 and 11 November 1893; *Prohibitionist*, 12 August 1893, p. 3; A. Burton, *Burdens of History: British Feminists, Indian Women, and Imperial Culture, 1865–1915* (Chapel Hill: University of North Carolina Press, 1994), pp. 200–1.
59 MLIA, GB127.M50/2/1, Sheppard to Fawcett, 22 April 1891.
60 Bosch with Kloostermann (eds), *Politics and Friendship*, p. 34; Tyrrell, *Woman's World*, pp. 117–18.
61 CM, ARC176.53/214, 241, Blackburn to Sheppard, 5 October 1893 and 27 July 1894; Girton College Library, Cambridge, P396.3/8, Sheppard to Blackburn, 13 October 1892. See, for example, *Englishwoman's Review*, 15 April 1892, p. 94; 15 January 1893, pp. 24–6; 16 July 1894, pp. 171–3.
62 Smith, *Outlines of the Women's Franchise Movement*; CM, ARC176.53/350–1, 366, Isabella Ford to Sheppard, 20 January 1906; Louisa Martindale to Sheppard, 13 February 1906; Lucy E. Anthony to Sheppard, 28 September 1906.

63 MLIA, GB127.M50/2/1, Amey Daldy to Fawcett, 28 December 1892; Marion Hatton to Fawcett, 3 January and 25 April 1893.
64 H. Blackburn, *Women's Suffrage: A Record of the Women's Suffrage Movement in the British Isles* (London: Williams & Norgate, 1902), pp. 229–44; J. H. Murray and A. K. Clark, *The Englishwoman's Review of Social and Industrial Questions: An Index* (New York: Garland Publishing, 1985), pp. 243–63; *Englishwoman's Review*, 15 April 1892, p. 95; 15 October 1893, pp. 245–7; 15 April 1893, pp. 92–3; 15 October 1894, pp. 236–7; SLNSW, MLMSS38/33/1, WSL of NSW Minute Book 1891–96.
65 *Alliance and Temperance News*, 1 March 1890, p. 5; 1 April 1890, p. 5; *Prohibitionist*, 26 March 1892, p. 3; 12 August 1893, p. 3.
66 Sato, 'A picture of peace', 487–8.
67 CM, ARC176.53/367, Maria M. Ogilvie Gordon to Sheppard, 8 November 1906.
68 M. Jolly, 'Delicious moments: The photograph album in nineteenth-century Australia', in J. Annear (ed.), *The Photograph and Australia* (Sydney: Art Gallery of New South Wales, 2015), p. 234; CM, ARC176.53/312, Aletta Jacobs to Sheppard, 5 November 1899.
69 ATL, MS-Papers-1784-202/30, Scott to Hall, 6 January 1894; SLNSW, MLA2274/159, Annie Watson Lister to Scott, 12 August 1902; SLNSW, PXA1023, Scott Family Collection of Studio Portrait Photographs. For example, 93 per cent of the nearly 5,000 images in the Toitū Otago Settlers Museum's collection of late-nineteenth-century photograph albums are 'studio portraits of people identified as family and friends'. J. Haley, 'Otago's albums: Photographs, community and identity', *New Zealand Journal of History*, 52:1 (2018), 29–37.
70 Sato, 'A picture of peace', 482; L. Perry, 'The carte de visite in the 1860s and the serial dynamic of photographic likeness', *Art History*, 36:4 (2012), 747.
71 SLSA, SRG186/1/4, South Australian WCTU Minute Book 1904–8, 26 June 1906; ATL, MS-Papers-3969-1, Sheppard to Ishbel Aberdeen, 10 April and 24 July 1906; CM, ARC176.53/14, Lucy E. Anthony to Sheppard, 28 September 1906; CM, ARC176.53/14, Catt to Sheppard, 3 December 1906; *White Ribbon*, 15 August 1906, p. 8; 15 December 1906, p. 9.
72 CM, ARC176.53/292, Blackburn to Sheppard, 28 November 1895; CM, ARC176.53/293, Fawcett to Sheppard, 28 November 1895.
73 Porter et al., *My Hand Will Write*, p. 2. Likewise, there is little to suggest that Vida Goldstein remained imbricated in webs of correspondence with the activists she lived among in the United States after she returned home in 1902. The American suffragist Maud Wood Park's reciprocal visit to Australia in 1909 seems to be an exception, rather than the rule here. See Lake, *Progressive New World*, pp. 160–8.
74 The NCW named Scott their 'international correspondent' in 1906, but she had performed the role since the late 1890s. SLNSW, MLMSS3739, NCW of NSW Minutes 1904–10, p. 21.
75 Taylor and Rupp, 'Loving internationalism', 147–51. This paragraph draws on my reading of the NCW of New South Wales' papers. See especially SLNSW, MSS3739, NCW of NSW Minutes 1895–1905 & 1904–10; and the letters collected in SLNSW, boxes A2272 and A2274.
76 Scott inherited an allowance of £500 per annum upon her father's death in 1879, and a further £5,000 in 1907 when her cousin, David Scott Mitchell, died. Allen, *Rose*

Scott, pp. 64–5, 138; SLNSW, A2272/980-2, 998–1002, Carrie Chapman Catt to Scott, 20 March 1906 and 16 December 1908; V. Woolf, *A Room of One's Own* (London: Hogarth Press, rev. edn, 1935), pp. 56–7.

77 SLNSW, MLMSS38/49/105-9, Rose Scott, 'Speech to the National Council of Women', 26 May 1903. See, for example, SLNSW, MLMSS38/38/1-63, Rose Scott, 'Speech on womanhood suffrage', March 1892; *Newcastle Herald and Miners' Advocate*, 26 November 1894, p. 6.

78 The phrase 'intimate practices' is borrowed from A. R. Gere's *Intimate Practices*.

79 K. Marsden, *On Sledge and Horseback to Outcast Siberian Lepers* (London: Record Press, 1892).

80 H. Chapman, 'The New Zealand campaign against Kate Marsden, traveller to Siberia', *New Zealand Slavonic Journal*, 34 (2000), 130–6.

81 *Wanganui Chronicle*, 12 October 1894, p. 2; *Minutes of the New Zealand Woman's Christian Temperance Union at the Ninth Annual Meeting* (Invercargill: Ward, Wilson and Co., 1894), p. 8.

82 Tyrrell, *Woman's World*, pp. 36–7.

83 *Union Signal*, 1 February 1894, p. 5; SLSA, SRG186/1/1, South Australian WCTU Minute Book 1889–95, 5 March 1894 and 21 June 1894.

84 See UMA, 241/1, Box 15, WCTU of Australasia Executive Council Minutes 1891–1909, pp. 14–15.

85 *Union Signal*, 15 March 1894, p. 15; *Prohibitionist*, 19 May 1894, p. 3.

86 Auckland Public Library, Auckland, 920 ALD, A. L. Aldis, 'William Steadman Aldis: A brief biography', 1940.

87 P. Levine, *Prostitution, Race & Politics: Policing Venereal Disease in the British Empire* (London: Routledge, 2003), pp. 1, 46–51, 323.

88 *Contagious Diseases Act 1869* [New Zealand], s. 4; C. Macdonald, 'The "social evil": Prostitution and the passage of the Contagious Diseases Act (1869)', in Brookes *et al.* (eds), *Women in History*, pp. 23–5; S. Eldred-Grigg, *Pleasures of the Flesh: Sex and Drugs in Colonial New Zealand 1840–1915* (Wellington: A. H. & A. W. Reed, 1984), p. 35; *Oamaru Mail*, 6 March 1885, p. 4; *Press*, 2 June 1885, p. 2.

89 *Auckland Star*, 4 May 1896, p. 4; J. Coleman, 'Apprehending possibilities: Tracing the emergence of feminist consciousness in nineteenth-century New Zealand', *Women's Studies International Forum*, 31:5 (2008), 471–2.

90 *NZH*, 23 September 1885, p. 6; *Auckland Star*, 4 June 1886, p. 2; 3 September 1886, p. 4; *Minutes of the New Zealand WCTU at the First Annual Meeting*, p. 14.

91 MLIA, GB127.M50/2/1, Mary Steadman Aldis to Fawcett, 29 November 1892; M. Wright, '"The perfect equality of all persons before the law": The Personal Rights Association and the discourse of civil rights in Britain, 1871–1885', *Women's History Review*, 24:1 (2014), 72–95; *Personal Rights Journal*, February 1889, p. 7.

92 See, for example, *NZH*, 17 May 1887, p. 3; 10 February 1888, p. 3; *Englishwoman's Review*, 15 October 1888, pp. 448–50; MLIA, GB127.M50/2/1, Aldis to Fawcett, 29 November 1892; *Personal Rights Journal*, October 1889, pp. 74–5.

93 Hocken Collections, AG613/020, Diary 1890, 30 May 1890; ATL, 79-057-08/03, Auckland WCTU Minute Book 1889–98, 26 June and 10 July 1889.

94 K. Sinclair, *A History of the University of Auckland 1883–1983* (Auckland: Auckland University Press, 1983), pp. 50–8.
95 Burton, *Burdens of History*, pp. 1–12.
96 *Dawn* [UK], 1 August 1888, p. 9.
97 See, for example, *Dawn* [UK], 1 November 1888, n.p.; 1 May 1889, pp. 5–8.
98 *Dawn* [UK], 1 October 1890, pp. 13–14; 1 July 1891, p. 10; WL, 3BGF/C/1, Box FL076, British Committee of the Continental and General Federation for Abolition of Government Regulation of Prostitution Records (BC) Minute Book 1893–97, 26 January 1894.
99 J. Jordan, *Josephine Butler* (London: John Murray, 2001), pp. 279–80; Levine, *Prostitution, Race & Politics*, pp. 112–18.
100 MLIA, GB127.M50/2/1, Aldis to Fawcett, 29 November 1892; WL, 3BGF/C/1, Box FL076, BC Minute Book 1893–97, 7 December 1894.
101 *A Second Letter of Appeal and Warning from Josephine E. Butler to Members of the British, Continental, and General Federation for the Abolition of the State Regulation of Prostitution* (London: Pewtress & Co., 1895), p. 4.
102 *Press*, 13 June 1895, p. 5.
103 ATL, 79-057-08/03, Auckland WCTU Minute Book 1889–98, 26 June 1895; *Auckland Star*, 27 June 1895, p. 2; *NZH*, 18 June 1895, p. 5; *Otago Daily Times*, 2 July 1895, p. 4.
104 WL, 3JBL/34/39, Josephine Butler to Mary Priestman, 26 July 1895; WL, 3BGF/C/1, Box FL076, BC Minute Book 1893–97, 16 October 1895, 11 November 1895, 10 February 1896, 20 February 1896, 16 April 1896, 26 June 1896, 22 July 1896; L. Matthews-Jones, '"Granny thinking what she is going to write in her book": Religion, politics and the Pontefract by-election of 1872 in Josephine Butler's *Personal Reminiscences of a Great Crusade* (1896)', *Women's History Review*, 26:6 (2017), 947.
105 ATL, 79-057-08/03, Auckland WCTU Minute Book 1889–98, 25 September 1895; CM, ARC176.53/287, F. Forsaith to Sheppard, 17 October 1895.
106 *A Letter of Earnest Appeal and Warning from Josephine E. Butler to the Members of the British, Continental and General Federation for the Abolition of the State Regulation of Prostitution* (London: Pewtress & Co., 1895), p. 3; WL, 3JBL/34/39, Butler to Priestman, 10 August 1895; *Auckland Star*, 26 October 1895 supplement, p. 4.
107 *Sentinel*, September 1895, pp. 127–8; October 1895, pp. 143–5; January 1896, pp. 7, 12; February 1896, pp. 23; May 1896, p. 56.
108 *English Opinion Evoked by the Recent Resolution of the Auckland Women's Liberal League* (Auckland: H. Brett, 1896).
109 *Otago Daily Times*, 29 June 1895, p. 8; *Press*, 11 October 1895, p. 4.
110 *Woman's Signal*, 17 October 1895, p. 249; 2 December 1895, p. 378; CM, ARC176.53/294, Helen Hood to Sheppard, 28 November 1895. A group of Auckland women made this argument in *Dawn* [UK], April 1896, p. 8.
111 ATL, 79-057-08/03, Auckland WCTU Minute Book 1889–98, 23 October 1895; *White Ribbon*, 1 October 1895, p. 4.
112 *NZPD*, Vol. 93, 1896, p. 465.
113 *NZPD*, Vol. 94, 1896, pp. 527–32; WL, 3BGF/C/1, Box FL076, BC Minute Book 1893–97, 10 February 1896.

114 B. Brookes, 'A weakness for strong subjects: The women's movement and sexuality', *New Zealand Journal of History*, 27:2 (1993), 143–8.
115 *Twenty-Fourth Annual Report of the Ladies National Association for the Abolition of Government Regulation of Vice for the Years 1894 and 1895* (London: J. W. Arrowsmith, 1896), p. 72.
116 *Auckland Star*, 2 September 1897, p. 8; WL, 3BGF/C/1, Box FL076, BC Minute Book 1897–1912.
117 See, for example, ATL, MS-Group-0225, 91-176-22/8, National Council of Women of New Zealand Register of Resolutions 1896–1990; *White Ribbon*, 1 October 1900, p. 7; 1 April 1902, p. 3; 1 October 1902, p. 7; 21 April 1909, p. 4; B. Dalley, 'Lolly shops "of the red-light kind" and "soldiers of the King": Suppressing one-woman brothels in New Zealand, 1908–1916', *New Zealand Journal of History*, 30:1 (1996), 3–23.
118 Macdonald, 'Intimacy of the envelope', pp. 14–15.
119 Sato, 'A picture of peace', 475–510.

4

Shaking hands across the seas: The Australasian women's advocacy press

On 3 April 1900 Elizabeth Webb Nicholls, president of the Australasian Woman's Christian Temperance Union (WCTU) and editor of its journal, *Our Federation*, presented the paper's accounts to the union's triennial convention. Having established the organ in 1898 on the proviso that Nicholls would 'make it pay', those gathered listened with dismay as Nicholls explained the 'hindrances to financial success' that left *Our Federation* £200 in debt. The moment was galling, as Nicholls believed members' parochial refusal to embrace the venture had muted a necessary national voice for the WCTU. Beyond distressing the union's leadership, *Our Federation*'s parlous finances had, Nicholls disclosed, limited the number of newspaper subscriptions she held. As a result, its pages ran 'a little behind the time', an admission that revealed much about readers' expectations. Despite these difficulties, Nicholls insisted that 'the literary part of the undertaking' remained 'a labour of love'.[1] Over her six years in charge, she filled her columns with the work of an intercolonial community of writers and, assisted by sympathetic editors across the world, drew on a pool of foreign news, opinion, and fiction large enough to publish seventy-two editions between 1898 and 1903.

In reflecting on *Our Federation*'s beginnings, Nicholls described what historian Christopher Bayly termed 'a print network that transected national boundaries'.[2] To fill pages that did not contain branch news, she built an exchange network with fifty-five papers in nine countries. Each issue juxtaposed stories submitted by branches across Australia with clippings derived from a 'global paper empire' that Nicholls both fed and relied on. Historians of communication have expounded in detail on the role of newspapers as agents that aggregated information from across the world, bound distant communities, and moulded national and imperial identities.[3] Their project, as Tony Ballantyne outlines, demands that newspapers be considered as 'assemblages' of 'materials, skills, technologies, financial arrangements, and cultural conventions' that were consumed within specific reading cultures. The focus on newspapers as objects read and repurposed by readers, rather than as unsophisticated 'vehicles for ideological transmission', offers as productive a challenge to histories of the Australasian women's advocacy press as the mainstream newspapers at the heart of Ballantyne's critique.[4]

In this chapter, I document the emergence of a regional women's advocacy press and trace its operation as a network that connected readers and editors with one another and an international publishing community. Turn-of-the-century Australasian women's movements offer an important opportunity to examine how news was produced and transmitted beneath the 'imperial press system' that supplied London with news and relayed it across the world.[5] Unlike their Canadian and South African counterparts, who produced few dedicated newspapers, Australasian women enjoyed a proliferation of politicised journals. Across the region, campaigns for women's enfranchisement coincided with the expansion of the reading public.[6] Amid a newspaper boom, a vibrant women's press emerged. Between 1880 and 1910, thirty-seven women's newspapers were launched in Australia and New Zealand. Owing to the prescience of their publishers, who used their enterprise to historicise the women's movement as well as to inform its participants, and the diligence of organisational archivists, most of these titles survive in public repositories.

Alongside newspapers' longevity, women's marginalisation in non-fiction book publishing has made journalism a vital source for historians of suffrage-era feminism in Australasia. Yet, rather than addressing the interchange between readers, writers, and publications, most scholarship focuses on individual mastheads.[7] Biographers of editors like Maybanke Wolstenholme and Vida Goldstein detail their subjects' motivation to join the newspaper boom, their struggles to remain solvent, and, finally, the 'monotonous regularity' of their publications' failure.[8] Beyond their editors' ambitions, as the largest repository of the suffragists' writing, newspapers have long been scrutinised to understand the ideologies of the women's movement. The historiography concerning the most studied of these titles, Sydney's *Dawn* (1888–1905), exemplifies the layered meanings that historians have found in their pages. In 1975, Anne Summers cast *Dawn* as an 'abrasively feminist' weapon wielded by its editor, Louisa Lawson. A decade later, scholars found 'bourgeois' reformism where Summers saw crusading radicalism. Latterly, historians have explored the paper's fiction, fashion, and household offerings, looking beyond the editorial pages to assess Lawson's vision of gender relations.[9]

Such careful re-reading of an iconic newspaper has exposed the intricacies of suffrage-era feminism. Nevertheless, understanding suffrage print cultures requires historians to situate individual mastheads within the complex networks of production and circulation that linked readers, writers, and organisations.

For all the allure of these texts, it is important to recognise that past reading practices are largely opaque. Without readers' recollections, it is impossible to know exactly who read the women's advocacy press or measure the influence of editorial decisions. Furthermore, as Maria DiCenzo, Lucy Delap, and Leila Ryan note, historians have typically considered suffrage media as 'a separate press that spoke for and to women'. Their reminder that feminist periodicals targeted male readers bears consideration, but it is less apt in the Australasian context.[10] Prominent British and American publications were viable businesses that boasted healthy circulation figures, boosted by street sales. However, their subscription-only Australasian counterparts were limited to small print runs, restricting their readership to those already interested in the movement: for the most part, white, middle-class women.

This chapter begins with the origins of the women's advocacy press in Australia and New Zealand. Rather than imposing national distinctions, it details the conditions that allowed for the brief efflorescence of a thriving trans-Tasman market in women's newspapers. The intercolonial trade was small, but it encouraged solidarity of sentiment among its participants and, as the third section examines, shaped the news disseminated to ordinary readers. These exchanges constituted a microcosm of the 'imperial commons', an unregulated space that allowed publishers to freely repurpose printed matter for new audiences.[11] Finally, a content analysis of seven newspapers between 1894 and 1902 examines how editors presented the news to readers. Illuminating the worlds that women's newspapers described to their readers qualifies previous assertions of these titles' exuberant internationalism and provides a clearer picture of Australians' and New Zealanders' knowledge of women's movements across the globe.

'My sisters, read! Read!! Read!!!': The women's advocacy press, 1888–1905

My letter on woman suffrage in todays paper. Oh how lovely to be able to speak even a few of ones thoughts to the world! To sow a few seeds of what one believes will develop into the flowers of reform & progress. It is to be one with the gods! A newspaper! Now some scorn the idea, it is so common a thing, to write in it is vulgar & common – oh despise not the day of small things. Are not newspapers more widely read by humanity than anything else. Can we not reach their ears & hearts more in this way than any other?[12]

Rose Scott, c. January 1891.

Mass-market women's newspapers appeared in the Northern Hemisphere in the eighteenth century. Produced by commercial publishers, these papers considered fashion, femininity, and etiquette but avoided the 'woman question'.[13] Although, as Barbara Caine contends of nineteenth-century Britain, debates over gender relations were mainstays of the periodical press, activists like Josephine Butler believed that 'a conspiracy of silence' surrounding the 'woman question' behoved politically engaged women 'to create a literature of our own'.[14] Fuelled by such convictions, European and American women began publishing political newspapers in the 1840s, though few had any longevity. The advent of organised suffrage movements invigorated the genre. In Britain and America, long-running newspapers lay at the heart of the nineteenth-century women's rights campaigns: London's *Englishwoman's Review* (1866–1910) and Boston's *Woman's Journal* (1870–1931). They were supplemented by a host of sister publications as feminists sought to advertise their activities, document their achievements, and memorialise their forebears. Amid a publishing boom, the number of women's advocacy periodicals exploded after 1870. In Britain, seventy-one titles appeared before 1900, compared to twenty-nine in France and thirty-three in America.[15]

The transatlantic efflorescence of women's political publications had no Australasian parallel. Women avidly consumed imported periodicals and occasionally read local offerings. Yet, while papers like Sydney's *Spectator* (1858–59) contributed women's perspectives to debates about gender roles, stable alternatives did not arise for another thirty years.[16] Mainstream newspapers published women's pages from the 1850s onwards, but it took decades for a standard model to emerge. Intermittent articles on 'serious topics' were offset by domestic advice, society news, and fashion features.[17] Early iterations were compiled from overseas clippings, but in the 1890s women's pages began employing local writers. One consequence of their expansion was the ghettoisation of women's journalism. From the 1870s, Stella Allan, Mary Ann Colclough, and Catherine Helen Spence published weighty articles in the mainstream press, yet the succeeding generation of female journalists were often confined to the ladies' columns, a professional marginalisation that lingered into the 1970s.[18]

From 1880, local magazines supplemented the women's pages. Yet, publications like Melbourne's *Australian Woman's Magazine and Domestic Journal* (1882–84) and Sydney's *Parthenon* (1889–92) disavowed the emerging women's movement. Such enterprises hoped to capitalise on the popularity of British and American magazines but made little headway against polished metropolitan offerings.[19] With the exception of the flourishing *New Zealand Graphic and Ladies' Journal* (1890–1908), which also targeted male readers, none survived for more than a few years. Although these aspirant mass-market magazines 'reinforced dominant prescriptions regarding women's ... role in social organisation', Jenny Coleman argues they also prompted readers to 'reflect critically on their place in society'.[20] Thus, when Louisa Lawson launched *Dawn* in 1888, she positioned it not as a counterpoint to the 'masculinist' press – a category that included her previous venture, the nationalist *Republican* (1887–88) – but against 'society magazines'. Kate Sheppard made a similar distinction between her journalism and 'ladies' columns' after launching the New Zealand WCTU newspaper *White Ribbon* in 1895.[21] Despite her critique of women's magazines, Lawson understood that publishing a paper dedicated to women's voices challenged male authority in the newspaper industry. In 1889 she purchased a printery and, following the policy of *Englishwoman's Review*, hired only female staff. Her acquisition ensured *Dawn's* self-sufficiency but incensed the New South Wales Typographical Association, which orchestrated a boycott of her premises. Emboldened by messages of support from as far afield as Boston, Lawson weathered the union's threats, and although it officially ended in 1899, the boycott soon ceased to have any practical effect.[22]

As Figure 4.1 shows, *Dawn* was a vanguard for the myriad newspapers concerned with women's emancipation that blossomed in the 1890s. As occurred in the United States and Britain, a feminist press developed alongside the colonial suffrage campaigns, binding activists into a coherent movement.[23] After experimenting with petitions and rallies, suffragists realised that to convert sympathetic politicians into reliable allies, they needed to demonstrate mass support for the reform. As Scott attested, the belief that expanding an activist organisation beyond its urban base required a newspaper was widespread. In their own pages, women could control their representation, explain their 'common' oppression, persuade readers that they could transform society, and shape them into a coherent group by disseminating the movement's accomplishments and aspirations – in short, enmeshing them within an 'imagined community'.[24]

For the suffragists, many of whom were politicised in the women's literary societies that emerged across Australasia in the 1880s, newspapers

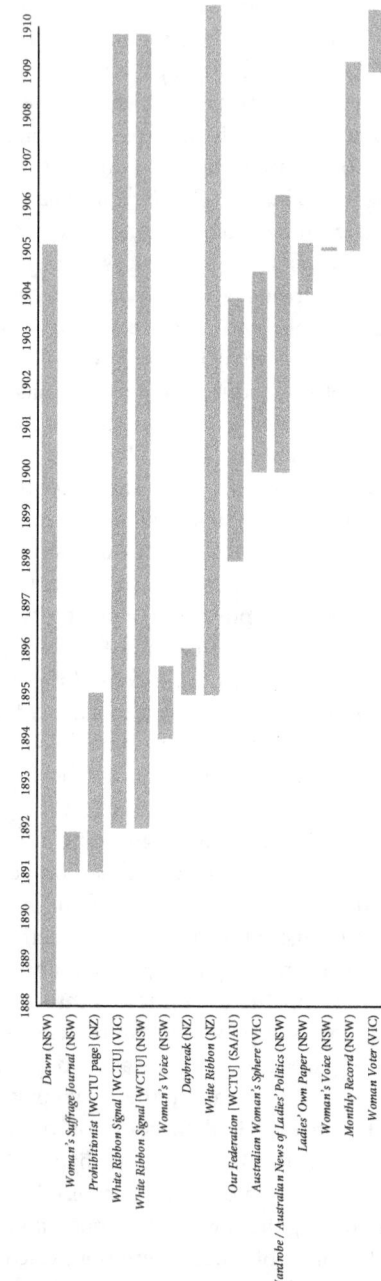

4.1 Print runs of Australasian women's advocacy newspapers, 1888–1910

provided the perfect medium. Whereas public lectures were transitory and required the goodwill of mainstream publications to reach more than a handful of listeners, newspapers were popular, portable, and inexpensive. Newsprint invited clipping and postage to friends or insertion in scrapbooks, 'flexible archives' that informed future writing.[25] Disseminating text in this fashion created communities that stretched far beyond readers' social circles. Driven by rising literacy rates after the institution of compulsory education in the 1870s and fragile local book cultures, which lent periodicals a more important public role than their British and European contemporaries, colonial newspaper production soared. In 1882, Australia and New Zealand boasted one newspaper for every 7,400 people, compared to one for every 18,000 Britons.[26] In Australia, a vibrant radical press emerged at the turn of the century, providing the labour movement with a sense of identity, as well as disseminating information and shaping policy debates. It is little wonder, then, that Lawson likened *Dawn* to a 'phonograph' whose pages would 'wind out audibly the whispers, pleadings and demands of the Sisterhood'.[27]

Sydney, already a hothouse for literary and radical publishing, became the locus of women's journalism. Following in *Dawn*'s wake, in 1891, J. H. Theobald and J. A. Simpson launched the *Woman's Suffrage Journal* in association with the Womanhood Suffrage League (WSL) of New South Wales. The *Journal*, Australia's only single-issue suffrage periodical, survived for little over a year. In 1894, the league's president, Maybanke Wolstenholme, established a fortnightly paper, *Woman's Voice* (1894–95). Frustrated with the *Journal*'s scope, Wolstenholme addressed controversial subjects, like marital rape. This tendency alienated subscribers and hastened the paper's demise.[28] That year, in a testament to the Sydney market's vibrancy, the *Australian Woman*, a hoax publication designed to discredit the WSL, attracted a small but significant readership.[29] As a rule, Sydney's domestic journals did not indulge in political commentary, yet after 1902 titles like *Home Queen* (1903–4) and a new *Australian Woman* (1900–4) began catering to their newly enfranchised audience by reporting on the city's plethora of women's political meetings.[30]

Outside Sydney, few cities could support a women's advocacy newspaper. Crippled by the long depression, Melbourne, the centre of women's publishing in the 1880s, lacked a feminist periodical until 1900, when Vida Goldstein established the ironically titled *Australian Woman's Sphere*. During its five years in print, the paper documented the Victorian state suffrage struggle, condemned the moral double standard, investigated women's economic disadvantages, and lamented the constraints of marriage. Five years earlier, Louisa Adams launched *Daybreak* (1895–96) in Wellington. Despite Adams' promise to produce a paper 'written by women for women about women' and its posthumous reputation as a progressive publication, *Daybreak* was not a reliable 'forum for feminist opinions'. Instead, Adams' overriding contrarianism saw *Daybreak* ridicule enfranchised women's concerns: dress reform, female parliamentary representation, and raising the age of consent.[31]

WCTU and temperance newspapers, excluded from most Australian studies of the women's press, offered activists another outlet to spread their ideas.[32] The union's American president, Frances Willard, was 'first and foremost [a] journalist' who considered newspapers the perfect tool to unite dispersed communities of women. As she explained in 1895, print held an unparalleled cultural authority: 'When you have got a thought into "cold type," it is there "for keeps." There is no magician in this age like the clear-headed, far-sighted man or woman who impresses the thoughts that he believes are winged with God's truth, upon the printed page.' Under Willard's stewardship, *Union Signal* became the world's most popular women's advocacy newspaper, reaching hundreds of thousands of readers.[33] As explored in Chapter 1, branch headquarters doubled as reading rooms where members could peruse back editions and titles from the Woman's Temperance Publishing Association's extensive catalogue.

The WCTU's colonial membership shared Willard's faith in the power of print. Yet they also grew frustrated with the *Signal*'s focus on 'matters not of interest to the average Australasian white-ribboner', prompting branches to join forces with sympathetic local publications.[34] Such agreements, as brokered with Adelaide's *Alliance and Temperance News* in 1889, and Christchurch's *Prohibitionist* in 1891, were contingent on branches leasing column inches.[35] As the WCTU grew, members demanded more editorial space. In 1892, the New South Wales and Victorian unions began printing separate newspapers, both entitled *White Ribbon Signal*. In 1895, Kate Sheppard resigned as editor of the WCTU's page in the *Prohibitionist* to establish *White Ribbon*, a monthly concerned with 'the many phases of the "Woman Question"'.[36] Three years later, the Australasian union inaugurated *Our Federation*. In contrast to its New Zealand counterpart, the paper defined its mission in evangelical terms, seeking to 'deepen our hatred of the closely allied evils of gambling, impurity, war, cruelty, and injustice'.[37]

Within a few years, the women's advocacy press had blossomed into a vibrant sector of the Australasian periodical market. In 1895, Sydney journalist Annie Bright praised *Dawn* and *Woman's Voice* for demonstrating that 'papers can be successfully edited by women'.[38] By then, the market appeared buoyant enough for entrepreneurs to pursue commercial opportunities. Inspired by the wildly successful American *Ladies' Home Journal*, Edward Wright launched the *Australian Home Journal* in 1894. In an era when a periodical needed 2,000 subscribers to break even, Wright boasted 7,000.[39] Suitably encouraged, other publishers looked to collaborate with women's organisations. In the 1890s, the New South Wales WSL received several proposals from businesses seeking to produce a suffrage journal, yet its members refused to 'give their name to [a] newspaper without having full control'.[40] For this reason, the National Council of Women (NCW) of New South Wales rebuffed a proposal to collaborate with a publisher in 1905.[41] These attempts emphasised the existence of distinct branches of the press, profit-driven publications, and advocacy newspapers that existed to share information and raise consciousness among religious and ethnic communities and activist organisations.[42]

Even without a profit motive, newspapers required considerable expenditure to stay afloat. Failure was encoded in the DNA of the colonial press. Audiences were small and competition fierce. Only half of the almost 600 Australian periodicals launched between 1822 and 1922 survived their first year.[43] Furthermore, antipodean women's difficulty in accessing capital prevented editors from adopting the joint-stock model that underpinned successful British and American ventures. Instead, as J. H. Theobald of the *Woman's Suffrage Journal* explained, they relied on subscribers and advertisers. In 1892, he believed a suffrage newspaper could survive with 600 subscribers, so long as it drew healthy advertising revenues.[44] Most publications fell between his yardstick and the benchmark for commercial success. *Dawn* fluctuated between 1,000 and 2,000 subscribers in the 1890s, and *Australian Woman's Sphere* mustered just 764 in 1902.[45] WCTU newspapers' readerships varied considerably. New Zealand's *White Ribbon* began with just 222 subscribers in 1895 but reached 1,500 by 1907. Victoria's *White Ribbon Signal* enjoyed steady growth, increasing its circulation from 2,000 to 3,000 copies in the 1890s, matching *Our Federation*, which – thanks to the WCTU practice of encouraging members to take overseas papers – reached small audiences in Britain and the United States. Its New South Wales namesake was less popular, but maintained a steady circulation of 1,500 copies.[46]

With few subscribers, debt menaced newspaper proprietors. Unlike their British counterparts, Australasian women's advocacy newspapers seldom paid contributors. Production costs alone hobbled most publications. Enquiring about the annual cost of printing a monthly paper in 1897, Elizabeth Nicholls received quotes ranging from £114 to £250, to be covered by subscriptions and advertising revenues.[47] However, the business model promoted by Nicholls' publishers and Theobald was flawed. To break even, mainstream newspapers dedicated half of each issue to advertisements.[48] As Table 4.1 shows, the figure fell to between 5 per cent and 15 per cent in most advocacy periodicals. In the American context, Anne Ruggles Gere provides similar figures to argue that women's newspapers subverted the capitalist model of publication.[49] Her thesis makes less sense in Australia and New Zealand. Although advocacy newspapers rejected alcohol, pharmaceutical, and tobacco advertisements, similar restrictions did not diminish the *Australian Home Journal*'s profits.[50] Low advertising rates were not the result of editorial rectitude, but reflected businesses' lack of faith in advocacy papers' ability to attract readers. Writing from experience in 1895, the New South Wales WCTU president Sara Nolan warned that 'a penny paper cannot really pay and folks are not anxious to advertise, unless the circulation is large'.[51]

Operating on the fringes of the market truncated the lifespan of women's newspapers. Sydney's *Woman's Suffrage Journal* and *Woman's Voice* were esteemed in suffrage circles, yet they collapsed before their second anniversaries. In Melbourne, Vida Goldstein debuted *Australian Woman's Sphere* with a grant from an anonymous benefactor and the assistance of her brother-in-law, the journalist and publisher Henry Hyde Champion. Even still, the paper operated at a 'dead loss'. Donors kept the *Sphere* alive until 1905 when, exhausted by the enterprise, Goldstein ceased publication.[52] *Daybreak* suffered more dramatic losses. Four months after its launch, the paper owed creditors £95, and when a fanciful £500 share offer failed it went bankrupt within a year of its launch.[53]

4.1 Composition of Australasian women's advocacy newspapers, 1901–02

	Australian Woman's Sphere (%)	*Dawn* (%)	*Our Federation* (%)	*White Ribbon* (%)
Advertising	14.4	41.7	4.7	12.9
Correspondence	4.1	2.7	4.9	4.0
Editorial	18.5	5.2	7.5	21.2
Entertainment	6.4	38.9	24.8	12.3
Miscellaneous	19.2	7.4	8.3	9.1
News	37.4	4.1	49.8	40.5

Source: Data from a random sample of twelve copies of each newspaper. A description of my sampling methods can be found on p. 151–2, 167.

Newspapers backed by institutions fared slightly better than their owner-editor counterparts. Recognising the risks inherent in publishing, WCTUs limited their exposure by refusing to underwrite their papers' deficits. In 1898, the Australasian union launched *Our Federation* 'without capital'. Failure to meet its ambitious target of 5,000 subscribers left the paper £123 in debt to its publishers by 1899.[54] Over time, the paper's finances stabilised, but it never generated sufficient revenue to repay its debts, which amounted to £173 (twice the union's annual income) when it folded in 1903.[55] Only those editors who resisted the 'cash nexus of printing' could ensure their papers' longevity. New Zealand's *White Ribbon* waited fourteen years to break even, kept alive by a printer with family ties to its editors, while *Dawn*'s integration with Louisa Lawson's printery reduced the pressure for the paper to turn a profit.[56]

Publishing economies alone do not explain *Dawn*'s longevity. Lawson was a gifted self-promoter who understood readers' desires. Although *Dawn* is remembered for its political agenda, Lawson marketed it as 'the best family journal in Australia'.[57] As Table 4.1 shows, she ensured that entertainment outweighed instruction, devoting only 10 per cent of each issue to news and editorial (compared with over 50 per cent among her competitors). Instead, readers could expect four times as much household advice, fashion news, and fiction – from her own poetry to stories by acclaimed writers like Olive Schreiner. By contrast, when new owners renamed the successful Sydney periodical *Wardrobe* as *Australian News of Ladies' Politics* in 1905, and replaced all 'unimportant feminine frippery' with 'serious' news, its audience evaporated within a year.[58]

Above all, Lawson incorporated readers within her enterprise. Rather than seeking charity, she used the tools of 'new journalism' to entice an expanding lower-middle-class readership that were at once activists and consumers. In 1892, *Dawn* featured a reader satisfaction survey, while an arrangement with a haberdashery saw the paper double as a 'shopping catalogue' and provided prizes for reader competitions. By encouraging her readers to share their quotidian experiences in her correspondence columns, to which she always appended pithy rejoinders, Lawson forged an intimate communal enterprise.[59] Other newspapers attempted to follow suit, but none insinuated itself as closely into readers' lives as *Dawn*. Uniquely of her counterparts, when Lawson ended *Dawn* in 1905, the decision was precipitated not by financial hardship but by her ill health.[60]

Alongside the demise of *Dawn* and *Australian Woman's Sphere*, the abortive launch of a new *Woman's Voice* in 1905 marked the end of an era. Instigated by Sydney's City Publishing Company in conjunction with the New South Wales NCW, the *Voice* ostensibly concerned itself with the 'higher and broader education and advancement of women'. Its first issue advocated for enhanced child protection legislation and the reform of the moral double standard, both touchstones of the post-suffrage women's movement. Despite its apparent bona fides, the paper's conservative overtones, anachronistic features – exemplified by a column explaining 'why women should have the franchise' – and unwitting decision to pair profiles of bitter rivals Rose Scott and Annie Golding doomed the project to failure. Stranded between the suffrage campaigns and the age of the 'woman citizen', the *Voice* quietly disappeared.[61] Within a year, Sydney's *Australian News of Ladies' Politics* and *Ladies' Own Paper* and Melbourne's *Women's News* all collapsed. Although a new crop of political journals emerged in the 1910s, notably Goldstein's *Woman Voter* (1911–19), most, like the WCTU's publications, the Women's Service Guilds' *Dawn* (1919–67), and the conservative Australian Women's National League's *Woman* (1907–34) were not generalist publications, but aligned to organisations.[62] Without the binding power of the suffrage campaigns, the heyday of the owner-editor magazine had ended. It took another fifty years and the 'cultural renaissance' enabled by the coincidence of the mimeograph revolution and Women's Liberation to surpass the range of feminist periodicals produced during the suffrage campaigns.[63]

Sinews: A Tasman suffrage 'mediasphere'?

Although women's political newspapers developed simultaneously on either side of the Tasman, historians have not considered their emergence as a regional phenomenon. Studies of individual publications have illuminated suffrage-era feminists' concerns but remain restricted by colonial fields of vision. Yet, newsprint travelled far from its point of origin, forming part of the cultural traffic that bound nineteenth-century empires. Suffrage newspapers were no different. If anything, their exclusion from the 'industrialization of the press', a process that began with the advent of the telegraph and submarine cables in the mid-nineteenth century, and was accelerated by the formation of news cartels, pushed them into closer relations with their overseas counterparts.[64] Historians have marvelled that *Dawn* reached readers in locations as far-flung as Berlin, Boston, and Suva, yet a wider story of intercolonial competition and collaboration in the production and distribution of newspapers remains to be told.[65]

Print historians have embraced the story of a turn-of-the-century Tasman cultural marketplace. Journalists were 'inky wayfarers' who inhabited a Tasman 'mediasphere' animated by the flow of letters, newspapers, books, and writers.[66] However, if it existed, the Tasman mediasphere's contours need closer definition. As described by the region's bestselling weekly, the *Bulletin*, it centred on Melbourne and Sydney, with an imagined readership that encompassed 'the bushman of the Far North, the stockman of Central Australia, the pearl-sheller of Torres Straits, and the digger in the New Zealand Ranges'.[67] Certainly, New Zealanders had an appetite for Australian news. Between 1881 and 1906, the volume of newspapers shipped east across the Tasman tripled, surpassing two million issues annually. Australians reciprocated New Zealanders' interest. Although newspapers travelled west in lower volumes, reaching a ratio of two to five by 1906, the return traffic was high for a colony with 20 per cent of Australia's population.[68] Nevertheless, anecdotal evidence suggests that New Zealanders felt ignored by Australian publications. Visiting Sydney in 1901, Premier Richard Seddon complained that the press contained 'meagre and sparse news' from his homeland.[69]

If Australian dailies sometimes neglected New Zealand news, the continent's periodicals – reflecting their longer shelf life – cultivated a regional audience. True to its claim to be 'the first journal in Australasia to organise the Australasian sentiment', the *Bulletin* sold well in New Zealand and, between 1888 and 1908, published stories from the colony more frequently than anywhere outside New South Wales and Victoria.[70] Trade publications, literary magazines, and illustrated weeklies all courted Australasian audiences and published substantial New Zealand content. So too did self-improvement organisations like the Australasian Home Reading Union. At its peak, the union boasted 341 New Zealand members, the second largest bloc in the region.[71] According to Helen Bones, these literary, educational, and commercial connections meant that colonial readers and writers 'saw themselves as being part of an Australasian world'.[72]

Despite the existence of a pan-colonial print market, scant attention has been paid to the trade in women's newspapers. While it was nowhere near as extensive as the print-cultural exchanges that animated contemporary Atlantic feminist movements, from the outset editors built Australasian distribution networks.[73] In the 1890s, Sheppard and J. H. Theobald developed a collegial relationship. Upon discovering the *Woman's Suffrage Journal*, Sheppard began sending copies to friends. During its short lifespan she collected 'between thirty & forty' New Zealand subscriptions for the *Journal*, amounting to 5 per cent of its readership.[74] Without published circulation figures, the New Zealand audience of the *Journal*'s successors is impossible to determine. Nevertheless, *Woman's Voice* and *Australian Woman's Sphere* clearly targeted New Zealand readers. Following the *Australian Home Journal*, each listed two subscription prices: one for readers in their home colony and another for the rest of Australasia. *Woman's Voice* branded itself as an 'Australasian' women's reform magazine, working alongside 'our sisters (the Dawn in Sydney, and Daybreak in New Zealand)'.[75] Encouraged by her tenure as secretary of the Australasian Home Reading Union, Maybanke Wolstenholme built her largest network of agents outside New South Wales in New Zealand. On its launch, she sent samples across the Tasman, where enthusiastic reviews and the endorsement of the Canterbury Women's Institute boosted the magazine's profile and saw its stories frequently republished in the mainstream press.[76]

Dawn did not advertise its agents' details or subscription figures, yet its correspondence columns played home to an enthusiastic community of New Zealand readers. Between 1892 and 1903, the paper featured letters from two dozen New Zealanders, more than anywhere but New South Wales and Queensland. Some, like Auckland's Emmeline Edmonds, were long-term subscribers who fostered local reading communities. From 1894, Edmonds was among *Dawn's* foremost correspondents. Within months of her first letter, a second woman from her suburb began writing to the paper. Lawson's practice of rewarding readers for enlisting subscribers paid dividends in New Zealand. In 1896 Edmonds gifted a subscription to another friend, Mrs Cowdell, who maintained her subscription into the twentieth century. Another cluster of correspondents centred on Christchurch, stimulated by Mrs Rutherford's recruitment of five subscribers in 1899, for which Lawson sent her a silk sunshade.[77] Without these readers' testimony, it is hard to verify *Dawn's* correspondence columns. Nevertheless, they reveal as much about how Lawson imagined and advertised her community of readers. In any case, by the 1900s, *Dawn's* New Zealand correspondents disappeared, perhaps a symptom of enfranchised women's indifference to the Australian movement. *Australian Woman's Sphere* faced a similar problem. Two years after its launch in 1900, just nine of the paper's 764 subscribers hailed from New Zealand.[78]

As with the general circulation press, less evidence exists of Australian demand for New Zealand publications. Nevertheless, *Daybreak* and *White Ribbon* found their way across the Tasman. In 1895, *Woman's Voice* publicised *Daybreak's* inauguration, 'hail[ing] with a feeling of kinship another paper written by women for women'. It is unclear whether many *Voice* readers took up subscriptions to 'our new sister'.[79] Although *Daybreak* featured letters from Australian readers and employed a Hobart correspondent, Louisa Adams never employed overseas agents, indicating that she did not seriously cultivate her trans-Tasman audience. *White Ribbon* took a direct approach, advertising for subscribers in *Our Federation* between 1900 and 1903.[80] The strategy appears to have been ineffective: during its first decade, the *Ribbon* published just two letters from Australian readers.

While correspondence columns and subscription records show a higher degree of trans-Tasman circulation than previously documented, the intercolonial trade constituted a fraction of newspaper sales. Editors targeted local readers, enabled by local advertisers. In 1901–2, 18 per cent of *Australian Woman's Sphere*'s subscribers lived outside Victoria or New South Wales. Accounting for the American readership Goldstein attracted during her tour of the United States, just 10 per cent of the *Sphere*'s readers came from the other five colonies.[81] *Dawn*'s correspondence columns paint a similar picture. Between 1890 and 1905, 92 per cent of the 2,442 letters it published came from New South Wales, a figure that matches the distribution of readers from the paper's extant subscription list.[82]

Low intercolonial subscription rates were the product of parochial sympathies and bureaucratic borders. Until Federation, most colonies provided for the free carriage of registered newspapers, but cross-border postage attracted tariffs. The excess was small, around three and thirteen pence per annum for subscribers, but likely deterred price-sensitive consumers.[83] Although *Union Signal* circulated throughout Australia, parochialism prevented *Our Federation* from performing the same function. While popular in South Australia and Queensland, the paper struggled in New South Wales and Victoria, where members deemed it 'disloyal to the colonial paper to take an Australian paper'. Nicholls' appeals to New Zealand readers were even less successful. Perhaps for similar reasons, the New Zealand WCTU ignored her request to appoint a permanent correspondent, and by 1903 the paper reached just twenty trans-Tasman subscribers.[84]

By the 1890s, interested readers could access an array of Australasian periodicals without trouble. Papers like *Dawn* and *Woman's Suffrage Journal* cultivated audiences outside their home colonies, aided by local agents and enthusiastic subscribers. As well-read women testified, the experience encouraged solidarity of sentiment and a sense of collective belonging. In 1896, Alice Masterman, secretary of the New South Wales WCTU, remarked, 'we seem to shake hands across the seas ... [and] have a more exact knowledge of our doings throughout Australasia than we ever had, through the medium of our respective papers'.[85] For all her optimism, the intercolonial market in women's advocacy newspapers was small. Nevertheless, in a press system predicated on the free exchange and cannibalisation of newspapers, connections between a cadre of editors could influence much wider reading communities. To investigate the extent to which editors' cosmopolitan reading habits were distilled to ordinary women, the following section documents the mechanics of intercolonial newsgathering, then uses a content analysis to flesh out the world women's advocacy periodicals presented to Australasian readers.

Qualifying internationalism in the women's advocacy press

Cross-border connections in the women's advocacy press cannot be measured by circulation data alone. Instead, historians must consider the circumstances of newspapers' production and the reading cultures that sustained them.[86] The arrival of the All-Red telegraph network and international press cartels in the 1870s revolutionised the daily press. Within a few decades, ad-hoc 'scissors and paste' journalism was superseded by standardised news bulletins. Excluded from journalism's industrial era by the cartels' prohibitive fees, monopolistic business practices, and the fact that mainstream journalists overlooked the daily realities of women's activism in favour of reporting on spectacular events or – as with the British Edwardian suffrage campaign – supressed news of their activities altogether, women's newspapers relied on informal newsgathering networks. Pre-telegraphic journalistic practices are well documented in the mainstream press, yet less is known about collaborative newsgathering in the Australasian women's press.[87] Furthermore, questions about how editors assembled overseas copy alongside local reportage, and the degree to which they educated readers about women's movements in other jurisdictions remain unanswered. This section fills these gaps by documenting cross-border cooperation and competition in the creation of women's advocacy newspapers, then conducting a comparative content analysis on seven prominent Australasian titles across two print runs: 1894–95 and 1901–2.

As with other 'special interest' publications, the connection of Australia (1871) and New Zealand (1876) to the transcontinental telegraph line had little effect on women's advocacy publications. Instead, the 'free list' system remained the primary means of disseminating news. In essence, it saw editors swap newspapers – for the purpose of circulating their stories and aggregating news – with like-minded colleagues across the world. The practice offered an inexpensive means of extending a newspaper's influence beyond its subscribers, while simultaneously sharing the burden of providing readers with fresh stories. Yet, drawing on what Isabel Hofmeyr and Antoinette Burton call the 'imperial commons', a textual empire of information that existed beyond the realm of copyright had another purpose. By pairing local stories with international clippings, editors both signalled the extent of their newsgathering networks and sought to convince readers that they played an important role in a global endeavour, despite their geographic isolation.[88] Likewise, readers seeing their exploits memorialised in print could be sure that this news would read by distant women.

As the only women's advocacy paper with extant editorial archives, *Our Federation* offers rare insight into the exchange system. Heeding Frances Willard's exhortations for her adherents to swap newspapers, Elizabeth Nicholls launched *Our Federation* with a drive to build a network of sympathetic editors. She soon discovered that 'free lists' were governed by a status system. As her British counterparts had discovered, Nicholls found that few mainstream periodicals acquiesced to her requests.[89] However, over time she integrated the paper into a global publishing community. By 1903, *Our Federation* exchanged copies with fifty-five temperance, religious, and women's newspapers. Nicholls' reading was, unsurprisingly, dominated by WCTU publications. Yet, rather than uniformity, the union's geographical spread ensured that her sources stretched beyond familiar British fare, with women's advocacy and social reform titles coming from across Australasia, Canada, the United States, and the union's missions in India and Southeast Asia.[90]

Where exchanges could not be brokered, editors called on readers to fill gaps in their makeshift newsgathering system. Mainstream titles like *Englishwoman's Review*, *Woman's Signal*, and *Woman's Journal* found wide audiences through informal reading networks and the colonies' 'extraordinary proliferation' of public libraries and reading rooms.[91] Kate Sheppard read the *Review* at the Christchurch Public Library, while Sydney WSL members browsed the latest editions of the *Review* and *Woman's Journal* at the Women's Literary Society clubrooms. Louisa Macdonald, the founding principal of the University of Sydney's Women's College, received the *Signal* and *Woman's Herald*, which she displayed 'in the Common Room for the girls to see'.[92] While these papers' subscription lists have not survived, anecdotal evidence suggests that they were well read. In 1902, the *Signal*'s former editor Florence Fenwick Miller fondly recalled the 'many letters' she received from Australian 'Signallites'.[93] While their popularity meant that such titles were often attributed in the Australasian women's press, most newspapers cited a richer patchwork of sources. In 1892 alone, the New Zealand WCTU page in the *Prohibitionist* attributed stories to twenty-one overseas publications, from the London *Graphic* to the *National Bulletin*, an obscure American suffrage pamphlet. The breadth of Sheppard's sources suggests she did not stumble on them all but received stories from her readers. Louisa Lawson acknowledged the practice in *Dawn*, while Elizabeth Nicholls hinted that *Our Federation* 'would be more interesting' if subscribers posted clippings to her Adelaide headquarters.[94]

While 'free lists', particularly those as extensive as Nicholls', were impersonal, the exchange of newspapers occasionally led to closer editorial partnerships. Sheppard and Theobald's correspondence began in 1892, when she purchased the *Woman's Suffrage Journal*'s printing block of Sydney artist Benjamin Minns' iconic cartoon *Just Out of Reach*, intending to republish the image (Figure 4.2) in the *Prohibitionist*. The pair's correspondence proved mutually beneficial. That April, a transcript of Sheppard's annual 'Franchise Report' adorned the *Journal*'s cover under the headline 'Progress in New Zealand'.[95] A similar arrangement with John Vale, editor of Melbourne's *Alliance Record*, saw Sheppard act as the paper's correspondent on New Zealand women's enfranchisement.[96] Sheppard and Theobald's relationship extended beyond sharing copy. Disheartened by the *Journal*'s collapse in May 1892, Sheppard investigated the possibility of publishing her own 'suffrage journal'. Asked for advice, Theobald posted Sheppard the *Journal*'s accounts along with '4 parcels of back numbers' and a promise to 'do all I could here to obtain subscribers for you in N.S.W.'.[97]

4.2 The trans-Tasman exchange of woman's advocacy newspapers saw Sydney artist Benjamin Minns' cartoon 'Just out of Reach' (1891) widely circulated in New Zealand. (SLNSW, SV/80)

Sheppard and Theobald's collaborative ethos was not universally shared. Although advocacy newspapers recommended political texts from across the world to their readers, they could also treat other publications as rivals. When *Woman's Voice* launched from an office several hundred metres from *Dawn*'s Sydney premises in 1895, Lawson did not emulate the British practice of promoting kindred publications. Instead she curtly 'wish[ed] the new venture the success it deserves', then ignored the paper for its entire print run.[98] Competition extended beyond colonial borders, suggesting that editors had motives beyond commercial rivalry. *Australian Woman's Sphere* launched in 1900, but Lawson only brought it to her readers' attention in 1904. Commenting on the *Sphere's* 'impoverished condition', Lawson revealed the source of her irritation: by positioning her paper as the 'first and only journal written in the interests ... of the woman movement', Vida Goldstein had ignored her debt to *Dawn*. Reporting on the *Sphere's* reduction from eight to four pages in 1905, Lawson bemoaned the loss of an outlet for women's voices, but not without a jibe about *Dawn's* diminished 'chance of a notice' in its Melbourne cousin.[99]

Lawson's disdain for Goldstein's demands on readers' purses reflected her pride in building a viable magazine. Yet she too relied on the collegiality of the publishing community, depending on the arrival of exchange newspapers to fill her pages. Previous histories of women's advocacy newspapers have eschewed analysis of news in favour of reading opinion columns and, as a result, attribute a broadminded internationalism to their editors.[100] Such work has been invaluable for understanding feminist politics, but it is necessary to read beyond the editorial page to evaluate the extent to which news of distant women's movements reached Australasian readers. To determine which parts of the 'imperial commons' editors drew on, what issues they presented to their readers, and where they remained silent, this chapter concludes with a content analysis of the women's advocacy press.

To span the variety of published newspapers, whose print runs seldom overlapped, as well as cover flashpoints in the Australasian suffrage campaigns, the content analysis is divided into two periods, 1894–95 and 1901–2. For each period, I analysed four newspapers, based on a random sample of twelve issues, six from each year. The first spans the aftermath of New Zealand's first general election under universal suffrage and the enfranchisement of South Australian women. The papers under consideration reflect the geographical concentration of the publishing community, comprising Sydney's *Dawn* and *Woman's Voice*, and the New Zealand WCTU's page in *Prohibitionist* (1894), whose editors decamped to produce the full-length *White Ribbon* in 1895.[101] The second period, 1901–2, encompasses women's enfranchisement in the Commonwealth and New South Wales. Mirroring the diversification of the women's press, my analysis continues with *Dawn* and *White Ribbon* and expands its geographical spread by including *Our Federation*, the Australasian WCTU's Adelaide-based newspaper, and Melbourne's *Australian Woman's Sphere*.[102]

Sorting news by location reveals that women's advocacy newspapers conformed to the 'village and globe' model that predominated in the mainstream press. Local items formed the bulk of each edition, augmented by 'the globalising work of the [editor's] scissors', whose tastes favoured Australasia, the United Kingdom, and the United States.[103] New Zealand papers were especially parochial. In 1894, over 60 per cent of the stories published in the WCTU's page in the *Prohibitionist* concerned New Zealand. Belying the union's boast that the paper was 'read from one end of the Colony to the other', most of these came from Christchurch, where its editorial staff lived. Unease with the paper's localism prompted the establishment of *White Ribbon* as a 'national' alternative in 1895.[104] Expanding from one to eight pages allowed the *Ribbon* to include several pages of news submitted from branches across New Zealand, but it published proportionally fewer stories from the outside world. By 1901–2, colonial stories accounted for 75 per cent of its news and editorial content.

Colonial news also predominated in Australian newspapers, yet all five titles maintained a more even balance between local reportage and intercolonial and international affairs. With *Dawn* the only publication that spanned the colonial and federal eras, it is difficult to gauge the impact of Federation on the women's press. In 1894–95, 48.5 per cent of the news published in *Woman's Voice* came from New South Wales, slightly higher than the 43.5 per cent of in-state news printed by *Australian Woman's Sphere* in 1901–2, suggesting that the creation of the Commonwealth had no immediate effect. These figures match historians' conclusions about the mainstream press, which published little interstate news until the 1920s.[105] Perhaps because of the ferocity with which New South Wales suffragists contested Federation, Louisa Lawson, despite publishing the children's newspaper *Young Australia* concurrently with *Dawn*, kept quiet on the issue.[106] None of the stories in the 1901–2 sample contained 'national' news. Similarly, as Table 4.3 shows, Commonwealth affairs occupied a small portion of *Australian Woman's Sphere*. Only *Our Federation*, a newspaper explicitly committed to national integration, provided consistent coverage of Commonwealth issues, devoting just over 12 per cent of its editorial space to these each month.

Our Federation was unique not only among the women's advocacy newspapers but in the Australian periodical press, for its explicit positioning as a 'national' publication. Seeking to overcome regionalism within the WCTU, Nicholls provided readers with a wider variety of interstate news than any other of the newspapers surveyed. None of the six colonies fell below 6 per cent of the paper's editorial space. Unusually for a contemporary women's newspaper, Queensland was the primary source of news in *Our Federation*, accounting for a quarter of the stories published during 1901-2. The anomaly was a consequence of Nicholls' extensive reportage from a five-month tour of the state in 1901.[107] Although *Dawn*, *Woman's Voice*, and *Australian Woman's Sphere* all featured substantial intercolonial news coverage, their stories overwhelmingly concerned the southeastern mainland, and occasionally New Zealand. Without their own newspapers to supply the exchange system, women in Tasmania, Queensland, and Western Australia were ignored. When news from Australia's north and west reached editors, they treated it perfunctorily. For example, nine months after Western Australia became the second Australian colony to enfranchise women, *Dawn's* cursory report focused on its implications for New South Wales.[108] In New Zealand, the Tasman bias was more pronounced. As depicted in Tables 4.2 and 4.3, just 0.1 per cent

4.2 Geographical location of news and editorial in Australasian women's advocacy newspapers, 1894-95

	Dawn (%)	*Prohibitionist/White Ribbon* (%)	*Woman's Voice* (%)
Asia	0.2	1.4	1.5
Europe	5.5	2.6	3.4
New South Wales	46.1	1.0	48.5
New Zealand	11.2	69.0	8.0
Other	0.8	0.0	1.5
Queensland	1.1	0.0	0.9
South Australia	1.5	0.5	2.8
Tasmania	0.5	0.0	0.3
United Kingdom	24.2	19.2	15.6
United States of America	5.6	4.4	9.5
Victoria	3.2	1.9	8.0
Western Australia	0.1	0.0	0.0

Source: Data from a random sample of twelve copies of each newspaper between 1894 and 1895.

4.3 Geographical location of news and editorial in Australasian women's advocacy newspapers, 1901–02

	Australian Woman's Sphere (%)	Dawn (%)	Our Federation (%)	White Ribbon (%)
Asia	0.8	5.5	0.3	0.0
Australian Commonwealth	6.4	0.0	12.6	0.0
Europe	6.6	10.4	0.2	7.3
New South Wales	7.5	55.0	9.7	0.5
New Zealand	4.0	0.0	0.5	76.7
Other	0.2	0.0	0.3	0.0
Queensland	2.8	0.0	27.0	0.0
South Australia	6.4	0.0	11.4	0.8
Tasmania	1.6	0.0	8.2	0.1
United Kingdom	6.5	16.4	3.9	8.8
United States of America	13.9	12.7	11.1	5.4
Victoria	43.2	0.0	6.9	0.4
Western Australia	0.1	0.0	7.9	0.0

Source: Data from a random sample of twelve copies of each newspaper between 1901 and 1902.

of the news coverage in the *Prohibitionist* and *White Ribbon* concerned Tasmania, and neither paper published stories from Queensland or Western Australia.

As their neglect of Australia's peripheries indicated, newspapers adopted a metro-centric editorial policy. Replicating the biases in the exchange system, the United Kingdom was the second most common source of news for five of the seven newspapers across each sample period, followed by the United States. While Western Australian women's enfranchisement was barely acknowledged, landmark overseas events received blanket coverage. When the American suffragist Elizabeth Cady Stanton died in October 1902, she was eulogised by women's newspapers across the world, including Australasia.[109] Although British women's newspapers reported on settler women in Canada and the Cape Colony, their Australasian equivalents did not. As with Australasia's peripheries, the lack of editorial affinity with white women in other parts of empire resulted from the absence of comparable women's journals from which to excise content.[110] By contrast, European stories constituted between 2 per cent and ten per cent of the news coverage in most periodicals. As Elizabeth Nicholls admitted in 1901, they would have featured more prominently but for the problem of translation. Eager to publish the 'good news' from the Norwegian temperance newspaper *Det Hvite Bånd*, she canvassed her readers to find a 'friend who can read "Norsk," and so let us into the mystery of this little paper'. Her request went unheeded, and while *Det Hvite Bånd* republished stories from *Our Federation*, the Australian paper gave no further news of its Scandinavian subscribers. A similar language barrier prevented Kate Sheppard recycling excerpts from *Centralblatt des Bundes Deutscher Frauenvereine* and *Unione Femminile*, the German and Italian newspapers with whom she shared copies of *White Ribbon*.[111]

Although editors like Louisa Lawson viewed their enterprise as a conduit for 'women, all over the world' to 'hold out helping hands to one another', their newspapers presented a less cosmopolitan worldview than has been suggested by contemporaries and historians alike.[112] Reflecting editors' reading habits, news from the Anglophone world predominated in a hierarchy with local reportage at the top, followed by stories from Britain and America. Qualifying generous descriptions of the 'Tasman writing world', the 1894–95 and 1901–2 samples show that, while a flow of information linked women in New Zealand, New South Wales, South Australia, and Victoria, news from beyond Australia's southeast was absent from the women's advocacy press, as it was from other British settler colonies. Yet, while the world these newspapers presented to readers was uniform, the range of subjects explored in the press varied considerably by masthead and over time.

As Tables 4.4 and 4.5 display, independent newspapers were the most catholic in their interests. Both samples confirm that the single-issue suffrage journal disappeared with the *Women's Suffrage Journal*'s collapse in 1892. In future, editors published a broad array of stories concerning women's emancipation, including education, employment, marriage and divorce, temperance, and the sexual double standard. Given Louisa Lawson's lifelong pursuit of economic independence, *Dawn* focused on stories about work, taking care to publicise women's achievements in previously male spheres.[113] Lawson left the WSL under acrimonious circumstances in 1893 but remained committed to the suffrage cause, devoting almost a fifth of *Dawn*'s editorial space to reports of suffrage activism at home and abroad over both sample periods.[114] Stories about women's struggle for economic independence were also staples of *Australian Woman's Sphere*, which, reflecting Vida Goldstein's role as general secretary of the United Council for Woman Suffrage, allocated half of its editorial space to news of the struggle for the vote. Similarly,

4.4 Subject matter of news and editorial in Australasian women's advocacy newspapers, 1894–95

	Dawn (%)	Prohibitionist/White Ribbon (%)	Woman's Voice (%)
Economic rights	28.1	3.4	11.9
Education	4.9	4.0	3.9
Organisational reports	3.0	47.5	5.2
Other legislative reform	10.6	8.7	28.5
Other	35.8	15.4	26.1
Suffrage	17.7	4.8	20.9
Temperance	0.4	16.1	3.5

Source: Data from a random sample of twelve copies of each newspaper between 1894 and 1895.

4.5 Subject matter of news and editorial in Australasian women's advocacy newspapers, 1901–02

	Australian Woman's Sphere (%)	Dawn (%)	Our Federation (%)	White Ribbon (%)
Economic rights	20.1	21.7	0.2	9.1
Education	3.8	7.0	1.3	2.0
Organisational reports	9.6	5.9	69.9	45.8
Other legislative reform	8.7	1.2	3.2	4.2
Other	8.5	36.9	0.6	9.5
Suffrage	43.2	24.5	2.6	9.4
Temperance	6.1	2.8	22.2	20.0

Source: Data from a random sample of twelve copies of each newspaper between 1901 and 1902.

Woman's Voice, edited by Maybanke Wolstenholme, then president of the Womanhood Suffrage League, followed the New South Wales campaign closely. However, from Table 4.4, it is also clear that the paper devoted 'more space to sex than to suffrage' as Wolstenholme demanded divorce law reform and, controversially, an end to 'compulsory motherhood' in marriage.[115]

Contrasting with their owner-editor counterparts, neither WCTU newspaper addressed the 'woman question' in all its complexity.

Established to build solidarity and set goals for the union's disparate membership, the bulk of these publications – almost 60 per cent of *White Ribbon* and 70 per cent of *Our Federation* – were given over to reports from local, colonial, and national union meetings. Most of each paper's remaining space was apportioned to temperance news. In New Zealand, the deficiency of suffrage stories in the union's newspapers in 1894–95 indicates a turn away from the suffrage internationalism that their absent editor, Kate Sheppard, preached after winning the vote in 1893.[116] The dearth of suffrage reportage in *Our Federation* is more surprising, given the state unions' prominent role in Australia's suffrage campaigns and Elizabeth Nicholls' continued suffrage advocacy on her intercolonial tours. As the bulk of each issue was filled with contributions from local and state unions, it suggests that either Nicholls screened such items, or members did not consider them fit to print. In either case, it upholds the conclusion that the Australasian union was an ambivalent participant in the suffrage campaigns.

While the content analysis shows similarities in the interests and geographical biases of the Australasian women's advocacy press, particularly the WCTU's mastheads, a closer look at coverage of indigenous women reveals sharper differences between New Zealand and Australia. As Patricia Grimshaw has identified, Aboriginal people were seldom discussed during the Australian suffrage campaigns. When they were, as the crudely drawn racial stereotypes on the cover of *Australian Woman's Sphere* in October 1900 exemplified, it was to draw parallels between disenfranchised white women and 'undesirable' electors, specifically 'blackfellows' and naturalised Chinese migrants.[117] In this climate, *Dawn's* November 1897 editorial was a rare exception. Building on her prior claim that 'the colony of New South Wales was stolen from the blacks', Louisa Lawson reminded missionaries bound for Asia that Aboriginal women deserved the 'first claim upon our beneficence'. Despite her insistence that white women had a duty to 'honor … their womanhood as we honor our own', Lawson did not seek interracial solidarity. Instead, drawing on a worn settler trope, she asked her readers to show 'kindness to these poor remnants of a dying race'. *Dawn* did not mention Indigenous women again until 1900, when Lawson offered a prize to whoever submitted the 'best droll saying by an Australian Aboriginal'.[118]

By contrast, the more inclusive franchise New Zealand's Parliament instituted in 1893 altered Pākehā relations with Māori women. Although demands for female political representation in the Māori Parliament were influenced by the WCTU-led campaign for women's suffrage, there was little crossover between the movements.[119] Yet, as explored in Chapter

1, from the mid-1890s the New Zealand union sought to mobilise this new portion of the electorate. Alongside its travelling 'Maori organisers' – typically bilingual Pākehā – *White Ribbon* constituted an important instrument in the union's outreach. The paper initially published reports from missionaries seeking donations for their 'Maori work'. However, the *Ribbon*'s late-1890s inclusion of Māori-language stories occurred at a moment when independent niupepa (Māori-language newspapers) began to proliferate, providing women new avenues for public speech. Soon the paper began juxtaposing romanticised accounts of 'tribal' life with articles and meeting reports written by Māori members, mirroring its offerings to Pākehā readers.[120] Despite these overtures, the union's Māori membership declined from its peak in 1899. To maintain its foothold in Māori communities, in 1911 the union inaugurated Māori conventions, and *White Ribbon* debuted monthly 'Ripoata Maori' (Māori-language reports), seeking to persuade Māori that the paper – and by extension the union – was for them, rather than about them.[121]

Another issue overlooked by quantitative analysis is the fact that, however thoroughly editors scoured overseas publications, they covered foreign news in a desultory fashion. The fragmented style of international news columns not only was designed to match the reading habits of busy consumers, as Jennifer Scanlon argues, but reflected the circumstances of their production.[122] Reportage required overseas correspondents, an unimaginable luxury for Australasian newspapers. Editors reliant on snippets could not elaborate on stories, leaving readers with a vague sense of women's movements in other countries. Fixating on the proportion of overseas news in Australasian publications distorts these stories' value to readers. *Dawn*'s 'From Far and Near' page of January 1901 was typical of the genre, entitled 'Chit Chat' in *Woman's Voice* and 'Mild and Bitter' in *Daybreak*. The page crammed in seventeen items – all, betraying the genre's didactic intent, optimistic in nature – ranging from a report on the achievements of 'women physicians' in Russia to news of an unnamed Javanese state 'which is entirely controlled by women'.[123] Such 'morsels', as Ellen Gruber Garvey explains, were easily digestible, and the format encouraged their clipping, preservation, and reassembly by readers.[124] Nevertheless, these deracinated fragments cannot have given them more than the barest sense of the women's movement outside Australasia. Although, as Catherine Spence remarked after attending a National Society for Women's Suffrage meeting in 1894, 'the names' of leading British activists 'were nearly all familiar to Suffragists at the Antipodes', few of her contemporaries could have said much about the organisation's past or prospects. Instead, the New Zealand journalist Jessie Mackay's

1913 complaint that 'those who have to rely on the cablegrams alone have a hazy idea that Suffrage in England is mainly a matter of hatchets and hysteria' could have been made of the women's newspapers she wrote for a decade earlier.[125] Louisa Lawson and her contemporaries were eager to document the progress of women's movements across the English-speaking world and, in doing so, to show readers that Australasian women fitted within an international movement. While their efforts to realise the latter goal can be considered a qualified success, women's newspapers lacked the wherewithal to explain why overseas movements succeeded or how readers might emulate their success at home.

In Sydney, another kind of publication, not considered alongside subscription press, achieved the depth of coverage Lawson had perhaps imagined when she described newspapers as a vehicle for internationalism. Melding the stability of the WCTU's newspapers with a sharper editorial voice, the *Annual Report of the Womanhood Suffrage League of New South Wales* (1892–1901) drew on a newspaper tradition and, in its scope and single-column layout, resembled the *Englishwoman's Review*. Like the *Review*, it took great interest in the international prospects of women's enfranchisement. Officially, the report existed to document the WSL's activities, but under Rose Scott's editorship it became a global digest of women's political advancement. Whereas commercial titles sacrificed news for features that would attract subscribers, Scott had the freedom to focus on suffrage. Although she read the same sources as subscription newspapers, without the burden of monthly publication she transcended the scissors and paste model. Instead of recycling clippings she published her own analysis, commentating on the previous year in suffrage activism.

Over time, Scott's writing mapped the Australasian suffrage movement's shifting fortunes. Initially, news from New Zealand and South Australia predominated, but their success turned her focus south, to Victoria and Tasmania. As enfranchised women realised their political ambitions, Scott revisited the sites of past victories. Like the periodical press, news from Britain and 'those dear shining examples, our sisters in America' dominated Scott's international précis.[126] However, she also drew attention to women's emancipatory struggles in Eastern Europe, the Middle East, and Asia. Each edition ended with a didactic coda, which fell between emphasising the universality of the suffrage struggle and arguing that New South Wales had a unique responsibility to 'clear a path for those who follow us'.[127]

League members did not unequivocally welcome Scott's transformation of their annual report into a suffrage almanac. In 1895, the executive voted to preserve a record 'solely of the doings of this League'. Scott had the decision reversed, but it nevertheless revealed tensions between her expansive vision and her contemporaries' domestic ambitions.[128] Subsequent editions show that Scott won out. She enlarged the publication from twelve pages to twenty-eight, expanding her digests on New Zealand, Britain, and America into essays, in which she contextualised suffragists' victories and explained their failures. Stressing the report's collaborative origins while showing off her wide reading, Scott attributed an eclectic array of sources. Since the 1880s she had amassed an archive featuring thousands of clippings on women's activism from sources as diverse as London's *Lady Cricketers' Gazette* and Stockholm's *Aftonbladet*, and she put it to use in the WSL's reports.[129] Although they were not sold publicly, Scott often sent copies to non-members and exchanged them with overseas newspapers.[130] Despite her long estrangement from Scott, when Maybanke Wolstenholme reminisced about the New South Wales suffrage campaign in 1925, she identified Scott's journalism as her signal contribution to the women's movement. Recalling her old colleague's 'passion for acquiring and recording knowledge of women in other lands', Wolstenholme argued that her annual reports 'may yet be very valuable as authentic history'.[131]

The *Annual Reports of the Womanhood Suffrage League* occupied a niche in the women's publishing community. Freed from market pressures, Scott produced a wide-ranging survey of women's suffrage movements across the world. Crucially, her writing existed in the context of Sydney's vibrant women's publishing scene, which drew on and fed a wider Tasman world of women's advocacy newspapers. These connections were decidedly uneven. News from New Zealand and South Australia, the sites of early suffrage victories, and the populous eastern colonies, Victoria and New South Wales, predominated. Developments elsewhere went unnoticed. Furthermore, advertising, correspondence, and subscription records show that, despite courting intercolonial audiences, these newspapers were primarily produced for, and consumed by, women in their home colonies. While readers of *Dawn* and *Daybreak* learnt about women from all parts of the globe, such stories were presented without analysis. British and American news dominated the international offerings, while women's movements in Britain's white settler colonies, to say nothing of Africa, Asia, and Latin America, were overlooked. This idiosyncratic and, at times, hollow internationalism was necessarily the product of the vast, unregulated information commons that connected readers across the English-speaking world.

Whether or not the qualified suffrage internationalism found in the pages of women's advocacy newspapers persuaded readers to consider themselves part of a worldwide movement is difficult to determine. Few individuals subscribed to several advocacy newspapers, yet communal reading practices, discussed in Chapter 1, and the mechanics of the exchange system allowed news to reach much larger audiences. Although they knew their chances of surviving were slender, suffrage organisations and enterprising journalists across Australasia felt strongly enough to take on the risky enterprise of a late nineteenth-century newspaper. Their efforts testify to the suffragists' belief in the power of print and the untold hours that editorial staff spent reading, writing, and building international networks sufficient to fill each issue with fresh news. Among their number were women like Kate Sheppard, Catherine Spence, and Elizabeth Nicholls, who combined their duties as journalists and editors with itinerant suffrage activism. The relationship between the press and these women's political tourism lies at the heart of Chapter 5, which considers the successes and failures of their intercolonial and international campaigns alongside their efforts to communicate their endeavours to audiences at 'home'.

Notes

1 *Woman's Christian Temperance Union of Australasia, Minutes of the Fourth Triennial Convention* (Adelaide: Hussey & Gillingham, 1900), pp. 67–9.
2 C. A. Bayly, 'Informing empire and nation: Publicity, propaganda and the press 1880–1920', in H. Morgan (ed.), *Information, Media and Power through the Ages* (Dublin: University College Dublin Press, 2001), p. 179.
3 Burton and Hofmeyr, 'The spine of empire', p. 2. See, for example, S. J. Potter, *News and the British World: The Emergence of an Imperial Press System, 1876–1922* (Oxford: Oxford University Press, 2003); P. Putnis *et al.* (eds), *International Communication and Global News Networks* (New York: Hampton Press, 2011).
4 T. Ballantyne, 'Reading the newspaper in colonial Otago', *Journal of New Zealand Studies*, 12 (2011), 49–50.
5 Potter, *News and the British World*, pp. 27–35.
6 Docker, *Nervous Nineties*, p. 233; L. Wevers, 'Reading and literacy', in P. Griffith *et al.* (eds), *Book & Print in New Zealand: A Guide to Print Culture in Aotearoa* (Wellington: Victoria University Press, 1997), pp. 212–20.
7 S. Sheridan, *Along the Faultlines: Sex, Race and Nation in Australian Women's Writing 1880s–1930s* (Sydney: Allen and Unwin, 1995), p. xiii. For examples of this relational approach to women's newspapers, see M. M. Solomon (ed.), *A Voice of their Own: The Woman Suffrage Press, 1840–1910* (Tuscaloosa: University of Alabama Press, 1991); M. DiCenzo *et al.*, *Feminist Media History: Suffrage, Periodicals and the Public Sphere* (London: Palgrave Macmillan, 2011); M. E. Tusan, *Women Making*

News: Gender and Journalism in Modern Britain (Chicago: University of Illinois Press, 2005).
8 Bomford, Vida Goldstein, pp. 26–31, 74–9; J. Roberts, Maybanke Anderson: Sex, Suffrage & Social Reform (Sydney: Hale & Iremonger, 1993), pp. 72–8.
9 Summers, Damned Whores and Gods Police, p. 350; P. Johnson, 'Nineteenth-century feminism: A study of "the Dawn"', Australia 1888 Bulletin, 13 (1984), 71–81; S. Pearce, Shameless Scribblers: Australian Women's Journalism (Rockhampton: Central Queensland University Press, 1998), pp. 21–9; S. Cousins, 'Drunken, selfish "boors?" Images of masculinity in the Dawn', Hecate, 25:2 (1999), 85–96; K. Hansord, 'The literary Dawn: Re-reading Louisa Lawson's poetry and politics', Hecate, 39:1 (2014), 188–201; G. E. Sykes, 'The new woman in the new world: Fin-de-siècle writing and feminism in Australia' (PhD thesis, University of Sydney, 2002), pp. 97–109.
10 DiCenzo et al., Feminist Media History, pp. 3, 56, 83.
11 Burton and Hofmeyr, 'The spine of empire', pp. 4–5.
12 SLNSW, MLMSS7312, Rose Scott Journal 1889–93, p. 143 (errors in original).
13 S. Sheridan, 'Women's magazines', in M. Spongberg et al. (eds), Companion to Women's Historical Writing (New York: Palgrave Macmillan, 2005), p. 607.
14 B. Caine, 'Feminism, journalism, and public debate', in J. Shattock (ed.), Women and Literature in Britain 1800–1900 (Cambridge: Cambridge University Press, 2001), p. 102; J. E. Butler, Personal Reminiscences of a Great Crusade (London: Horace Marshall & Son, 1896), p. 402.
15 E. C. Jerry, 'The role of newspapers in the nineteenth-century woman's movement', in Solomon (ed.), A Voice of their Own, pp. 16–24; Tusan, Women Making News, pp. 246–52; P. Langlois, 'The feminine press in England and France: 1875–1900' (PhD thesis, University of Massachusetts, 1979), pp. 442–7.
16 Woollacott, Settler Society in the Australian Colonies, pp. 123, 143–4. For more on the Spectator and its entrepreneurial proprietor, Cora Anna Weekes, see C. Bishop, Minding her own Business: Colonial Businesswomen in Sydney (Sydney: NewSouth, 2015), pp. 251—5.
17 Ballantyne, 'Reading the newspaper', 51; P. Clarke, Pen Portraits: Women Writers and Journalists in Nineteenth Century Australia (Sydney: Allen and Unwin, 1988), pp. 203–24.
18 J. Baker, 'Australian women journalists and the "pretence of equality"', Labour History, 108 (2015), 9–15; Coleman, Polly Plum, pp. 39–79; J. Lloyd, 'Women's pages in Australian print media from the 1850s', Media International Australia, 150 (2014), 61–3.
19 M. V. Tucker, 'The emergence and character of women's magazines in Australia 1880–1914' (PhD thesis, University of Melbourne, 1975), pp. 18, 26–8, 80, 90, 143.
20 Coleman, 'Apprehending possibilities', 470.
21 Dawn, 5 May 1890, p. 5; White Ribbon, 1 June 1896, p. 8. For the debate over the influence of the 'masculinist' press, see M. Lake, 'The politics of respectability: Identifying the masculinist context', Historical Studies, 22:86 (1986), 116–31; J. Docker, 'The feminist legend: A new historicism?', in Magarey et al. (eds), Debutante Nation, pp. 16–26.
22 Magarey, Passions of the First Wave, pp. 127–8; Woman's Journal, 21 September 1889, p. 297.

23 D. Kirkby, '"Those knights of the pen and pencil": Women journalists and cultural leadership of the women's movement in Australia and the United States', *Labour History*, 104 (2013), 82–5.
24 B. Anderson, *Imagined Communities: Reflections on the Origins and Spread of Nationalism* (London: Verso, rev. edn, 2006); M. M. Solomon, 'The role of the suffrage press in the woman's rights movement', in Solomon (ed.), *A Voice of their Own*, p. 13.
25 Ballantyne, 'Reading the newspaper', 59. For examples of such 'flexible archives', see CM, ARC176.53/491, K. W. Sheppard 'Franchise Scraps', 1888–93; SLNSW, M2309/2, Vida Goldstein 1908 diary; SLNSW, M2309/5, Vida Goldstein album of letters, autographs, and photographs, 1911.
26 In 1871, 62 per cent of Australasian women could 'read and write', compared with 81 per cent in 1901. Figures from 'Census: 1871–1916', *Statistics New Zealand*, www.stats.govt.nz/browse_for_stats/snapshots-of-nz/digitised-collections/census-collection (accessed 5 May 2018); 'Historical and colonial census data archive', *Australian Data Archive Dataverse*, https://dataverse.ada.edu.au/dataset.xhtml?persistentId=doi:10.26193/MP6WRS (accessed 12 April 2020); J. A. Reid, *The Australian Reader: Selections from Leading Journals on Memorable Historic Events* (Melbourne: J. Whitelaw and Son, 1882), pp. 9–10; J. E. Traue, 'But why Mulgan, Marris and Schroder? The mutation of the local newspaper in New Zealand's colonial print culture', *Bulletin*, 21:2 (1997), p. 115; Tucker, 'Women's magazines in Australia', pp. 23–4.
27 Scates, *A New Australia*, pp. 57–64; *Dawn*, 15 May 1888, pp. 1–2. For these reasons, the failure to establish a dedicated newspaper haunted organised labour in late nineteenth-century New Zealand. See J. Keating, 'Manufacturing consensus? New Zealand press attitudes toward the labour movement in 1890' (MA thesis, Victoria University of Wellington, 2011).
28 J. Donovan, 'The intellectual traditions of Australian feminism: Women's clubs and societies, 1890–1920' (PhD thesis, University of Sydney, 2004), pp. 105–7.
29 S. Sheridan, 'Transvestite feminism: The politics of the *Australian Woman*, 1894', *Women's History Review*, 2:3 (1993), 349–61.
30 *Australian Woman*, 1 October 1901, p. 21; 1 December 1901, pp. 21–2; 1 September 1902, pp. 3–4; *Home Queen*, 18 November 1903, p. 7.
31 C. Macdonald, *The Vote, the Pill and the Demon Drink: A History of Feminist Writing in New Zealand, 1869–1993* (Wellington: Bridget Williams Books, 1993), p. 33. See, for example, *Daybreak*, 9 February 1895, p. 3; 20 July 1895, p. 1; 17 August 1895, pp. 2–3.
32 Maria DiCenzo, Lucy Delap, and Leila Ryan criticise such 'reductive attitudes' toward the 'official organ', noting that such publications are routinely misread by scholars who suspect they fulfilled a 'propagandist function or that they represented little more than newsletters for league activities'. In Australia, the neglect of WCTU newspapers dates from 1975, when Maya Tucker omitted them from her PhD thesis because they 'appealed to a much smaller audience' than independent titles. The circulation figures discussed in this chapter indicate that the opposite was true. DiCenzo et al., *Feminist Media History*, pp. 78, 118; Tucker, 'Women's magazines in Australia', p. iii.
33 Tyrrell, *Woman's World*, p. 50; Willard, *Do Everything*, p. 72.

34 *Woman's Christian Temperance Union of Australasia, Minutes of the Third Triennial Convention* (Adelaide: Shawyer & Co., 1897), p. 47.
35 SLSA, SRG186/435/2, Adelaide WCTU Minute Book 1887-91, 4 October 1889; *Press*, 10 April 1891, p. 3.
36 *White Ribbon*, 1 July 1895, p. 1.
37 *Our Federation*, 15 January 1898, p. 9.
38 *Cosmos*, 31 May 1895, p. 480.
39 Tucker, 'Women's magazines in Australia', pp. 289-90. By contrast, in 1904 the *Ladies' Home Journal* surpassed a million subscribers. J. Scanlon, *Inarticulate Longings: The Ladies' Home Journal, Gender, and the Promises of Consumer Culture* (New York: Routledge, 1995), p. 4.
40 SLNSW, MLMSS38/34/1, 'The Woman' to Scott, 8 July 1892; SLNSW, MSS38/33/1, WSL of NSW Minute Book 1891-96, pp. 15, 103, 106, 177.
41 SLNSW, MLMSS3739, NCW of NSW Minutes 1904-10, 31 August 1905.
42 Tusan, *Women Making News*, p. 12. Philippa Levine elaborates on this division in '"The humanising influences of five o'clock tea": Victorian feminist periodicals', *Victorian Studies*, 33:2 (1990), 293-306.
43 J. E. Traue, *New Zealand Studies: A Guide to Bibliographic Resources* (Wellington: Victoria University Press, 1985), p. 12; L. Stuart, *Australian Periodicals with Literary Content, 1821-1925: An Annotated Bibliography* (Melbourne: Australian Scholarly Publishing, 2003), p. ix.
44 H. Studdert, 'Women's magazines', in M. Lyons and J. Arnold (eds), *A History of the Book in Australia, 1891-1945: A National Culture in a Colonised Market* (Brisbane: University of Queensland Press, 2001), pp. 277-8; CM, ARC176.53/80, J. H. Theobald to Kate Sheppard, 7 June 1892.
45 *AWS* subscription figures were taken from paper's 'subscriptions received' columns, published between September 1901 and September 1902. O. Lawson, *The First Voice of Australian Feminism: Excerpts from Louisa Lawson's The Dawn 1888-1895* (Sydney: Simon and Schuster, 1990), pp. 17-20; SLNSW, A893, Vol. 23, p. 318, Louisa Lawson to Sir Henry Parkes, 21 November 1890.
46 M. Lovell-Smith, *Plain Living High Thinking: The Family Story of Jennie and Will Lovell-Smith* (Christchurch: Pedmore Press, 1995), p. 76; *Australasian WCTU Minutes of the Second Triennial Convention*, pp. 65-8; *Australasian WCTU Minutes of the Third Triennial Convention*, p. 18; *Australasian WCTU Minutes of the Fourth Triennial Convention*, pp. 58, 68; *Australasian Woman's Christian Temperance Union, Minutes of the 5th Triennial Convention* (Melbourne: Green & Fargher, 1903), pp. 44, 61.
47 Levine, 'Victorian feminist periodicals', p. 297; SLSA, SRG186/55, Shawyer & Co. to Elizabeth Webb Nicholls, 23 August 1897; George Hassell & Son to Nicholls, 27 August 1897; Hussey & Gillingham to Nicholls, 2 December 1897.
48 H. Mayer, *The Press in Australia* (Melbourne: Lansdowne, 1964), p. 12.
49 Gere, *Intimate Practices*, p. 252.
50 The consensus on advertising bans was maintained until the interwar years, when middle-class women began demanding equal access to tobacco, if not always alcohol. In 1940, for example, the United Associations, Sydney's most prominent feminist organisation, installed a cigarette machine in its rooms for 'the convenience of

members'. *Standard*, 15 April 1940, p. 7; I. Tyrrell, *Deadly Enemies: Tobacco and Its Opponents in Australia* (Sydney: UNSW Press, 1999), pp. 26–8, 114, 133.

51 Elizabeth Nicholls envisaged a sixty-forty split between editorial content and advertising before *Our Federation* launched. SLSA, SRG186/889, Sara Nolan to Flora B. Harris, 12 December 1895; Tucker, 'Women's magazines in Australia', pp. 165, 276.

52 Bomford, *Vida Goldstein*, pp. 27, 74–9; SLNSW, A2277/232, Vida Goldstein to Rose Scott, 30 March 1900.

53 ATL, PER DAY, *Daybreak* Vol. 1 March–July 1895, Prospectus of the Daybreak Newspaper Company, 1895.

54 SLSA, SRG186/55, Nicholls to the Australasian WCTU, 24 August 1896; *Australasian WCTU Minutes of the Fourth Triennial Convention*, pp. 53, 61, 68, 127.

55 *Australasian WCTU Minutes of the 5th Triennial Convention*, pp. 59–62; UMA, 101/85, Box 15/241/1, WCTU of Australasia Executive Council Minutes 1891–1909, 19 October 1903; *Australasian WCTU Minutes of the 6th Triennial Convention*, p. 51.

56 Gere, *Intimate Practices*, p. 104; Lovell-Smith, *Plain Living*, pp. 65–77.

57 *Dawn*, 1 February 1894, p. 2.

58 *Australian News of Ladies' Politics*, March 1906, pp. 13–14.

59 Atkinson, *The Europeans in Australia*, p. 307; B. Green, 'Complaints of everyday life: Feminist periodical culture and correspondence columns in *The Woman Worker*, *Women Folk*, and *The Freewoman*', *Modernism/modernity*, 19:3 (2012), 461–85; B. Griffin-Foley, 'From *Tit-Bits* to *Big Brother*: A century of audience participation in the media', *Media, Culture & Society*, 26:4 (2004), 534–7; Tucker, 'Women's magazines in Australia', p. 22.

60 *Dawn*, 1 July 1905, pp. 5–6.

61 SLNSW, AW44, 'Prospectus relating to the monthly journal, the *Woman's Voice*', 1905; *Woman's Voice*, May 1905, pp. 1–34; Donovan, 'The intellectual traditions of Australian feminism', p. 107; M. Lake, 'A history of feminism in Australia', in Caine et al. (eds), *Australian Feminism*, pp. 137–9.

62 In 1931, the Victorian and New South Wales editions of *White Ribbon Signal* were amalgamated into a national newspaper, which remains in print under the title *WRS*. New Zealand's *White Ribbon* appeared in print under various guises until 2011, when it was replaced by an electronic newsletter.

63 At least thirty such publications existed in Australia between 1971 and 1988. S. Magarey, 'Feminism as cultural renaissance', *Hecate*, 30:1 (2004), 231–46.

64 S. J. Potter, 'Webs, networks, and systems: Globalization and the mass media in the nineteenth- and twentieth-century British Empire', *Journal of British Studies*, 46:3 (2007), 629–33.

65 Lawson, *The First Voice of Australian Feminism*, p. 13; Magarey, *Passions of the First Wave*, p. 58.

66 A. Oosterman, 'Inky wayfarers: New Zealand journalism and the Australian connection in the early 20th century', *Australian Journalism Review*, 27:1 (2005), 77–91; I. Morrison, 'Cook's choice: Reflections on trans-Tasman literary culture', in J. Thomson (ed.), *Books and Bibliography: Essays in Commemoration of Don McKenzie* (Wellington: Victoria University Press, 2002), pp. 160–3.

67 *Bulletin*, 30 August 1890, p. 19.
68 R. Arnold, 'Some Australasian aspects of New Zealand life, 1890–1913', *New Zealand Journal of History*, 4:1 (1970), 60; J. Sanders, *Dateline-NZPA: The New Zealand Press Association: 1880–1980* (Auckland: Wilson and Horton, 1979), pp. 24, 39.
69 *Sunday Times* [Sydney], 10 February 1901, p. 6.
70 J. O. C. Phillips, 'Musings in Maoriland – or was there a *Bulletin* school in New Zealand?', *Historical Studies*, 20:81 (1983), 521–3.
71 Arnold, 'The Australasian peoples', p. 62. *Argus*, 27 January 1893, p. 7; Donovan, 'The intellectual traditions of Australian feminism', pp. 170–3.
72 Bones, *The Expatriate Myth*, pp. 73–94.
73 See L. Delap, *The Feminist Avant-Garde: Transatlantic Encounters of the Early Twentieth Century* (Cambridge: Cambridge University Press, 2007).
74 ATL, MS-Copy-Micro-0694-58/36, Sheppard to Sir John Hall, 20 April 1892.
75 *Woman's Voice*, 18 May 1895, p. 239; 27 July 1895, pp. 299–300; *AWS*, May 1901, p. 69; *Australian Home Journal*, 1 November 1902, p. 6.
76 *Evening Post*, 20 October 1894, p. 1; *NZH*, 27 August 1894, p. 4; *Star*, 14 February 1895, p. 4; 28 May 1895, p. 4. For examples of *Woman's Voice* stories reprinted in New Zealand, see *NZH*, 20 August 1895, p. 5; *Star*, 13 December 1894, p. 1; 11 February 1895, p. 4; 2 March 1895, p. 3.
77 *Dawn*, 1 September 1894, p. 32; 1 July 1895, p. 34; 1 September 1895, p. 40; 1 June 1896, p. 35; 1 April 1898, p. 32; 1 April 1899, p. 33; 1 July 1899, p. 28; Lawson, *The First Voice of Australian Feminism*, p. 17.
78 Griffin-Foley, '*Tit-Bits* to Big Brother', 540. Only three of the twenty-six letters *Dawn* published from New Zealand readers appeared after 1900. See also the 'subscriptions received' column in *AWS* between September 1901 and September 1902.
79 *Woman's Voice*, 23 March 1895, p. 199.
80 *Daybreak*, 1 June 1895, pp. 5–6; 13 July 1895, p. 1; 20 July 1895, p. 3; 24 August 1895, p. 7. See, for example, *Our Federation*, 15 December 1899, p. ii.
81 Figures from the 'subscriptions received' column in *AWS* between September 1901 and September 1902.
82 Author's calculations from *Dawn*, 1888–1905; Lawson, *The First Voice of Australian Feminism*, pp. 17–20.
83 Mayer, *The Press in Australia*, p. 18; *AWS*, May 1901, p. 69; *Woman's Voice*, 18 May 1895, p. 239. See also L. Delap, 'The *Freewoman*, periodical communities, and the feminist reading public', *Princeton University Library Chronicle*, 61:2 (2000), 245.
84 *Australasian WCTU Minutes of the Fourth Triennial Convention*, pp. 53, 65–7, 82–3, 127; SLSA, SRG186/54, List of subscribers to *Our Federation*, 1903; SLSA, SRG186/748, Sheppard to Nicholls, 18 October 1898.
85 *Women's Christian Temperance Union of New South Wales Annual Report of the Fourteenth Convention* (Bathurst: National Advocate, 1896), p. 54.
86 Ballantyne, 'Reading the newspaper', 49–58.
87 Potter, *News and the British World*, pp. 12–16, 30–3; R. Arnold, *New Zealand's Burning: The Settlers' World in the Mid 1880s* (Wellington: Victoria University Press, 1994), pp. 229–34; R. Harvey, 'Bringing the news to New Zealand: The supply and control of overseas news in the nineteenth century', *Media History*, 8:1 (2002), 26–32.

88 Burton and Hofmeyr, 'The spine of empire', pp. 4–5; Garvey, *Writing with Scissors*, pp. 21–31; H. McNamara, 'The *New Zealand Tablet* and the Irish Catholic press worldwide, 1898–1923', *New Zealand Journal of History*, 37:2 (2003), 160–5.
89 *Australasian WCTU Minutes of the Fourth Triennial Convention*, p. 69; SLSA, SRG186/55, Paul Chipsham to Mary Lockwood, 1 June 1899; Frank Catford to Nicholls, 22 August 1899; *Our Federation*, 15 May 1901, pp. 71, 77; Delap, 'The Freewoman', 250–2.
90 SLSA, SRG186/54, List of subscribers to *Our Federation*, 1903.
91 J. E. Traue, 'The public library explosion in colonial New Zealand', *Libraries & the Cultural Record*, 42:2 (2007), 151–64.
92 MLIA, GB127.M50/2/1, Sheppard to Millicent Garrett Fawcett, 22 April 1891; SLNSW, MSS38/33/1, WSL of NSW Minute Book 1891–96, pp. 109, 112; Women's College Archive, University of Sydney, SC Box 1, Item 1, 20/01/2, Louisa Macdonald to Eleanor Grove, 4 November 1893, 4 August, 30 September, and 24 November 1894.
93 SLNSW, A2272/731a, Florence Fenwick Miller to Scott, 30 August 1902.
94 *Australasian WCTU Minutes of the Fourth Triennial Convention*, p. 69; *Dawn*, 1 December 1894, p. 301.
95 CM, ARC176.53/74, Theobald to Sheppard, 9 March 1892; *Prohibitionist*, 13 February 1892, pp. 2–3; *Woman's Suffrage Journal*, 16 April 1892, p. 1.
96 CM, ARC176.53/229, John Vale to Sheppard, 19 January 1894; *Alliance Record*, 15 January 1894, p. 9; 15 February 1894, p. 21.
97 ATL, MS-Copy-Micro-0694-58/36, Sheppard to Hall, 20 April 1892; CM, ARC176.53/80, Theobald to Sheppard, 7 June 1892.
98 DiCenzo et al., *Feminist Media History*, pp. 94–8; *Dawn*, September 1894, p. 23. See, for example, the friendly reviews of *White Ribbon* in British journal *Shafts*. October 1896, p. 135; October 1897, p. 273.
99 *Dawn*, 1 June 1904, p. 6; 1 March 1905, p. 6.
100 See, for example, Docker, *Nervous Nineties*, pp. 4–6; Grimshaw, *Women's Suffrage in New Zealand*, pp. 53–4; Roberts, *Maybanke Anderson*, pp. 72–7.
101 Although the New South Wales and Victorian WCTUs' respective editions of *White Ribbon Signal* overlap the sample period, few copies printed before 1903 survive.
102 For each two-year sample period, twelve issues were selected using a random number generator. The data in each table is expressed as a percentage of total column space (measured to the millimetre) in each newspaper and averaged across the sample period. The data in Table 4.1 shows the amount of column space each newspaper devoted to advertising, reader correspondence, editorial content, entertainment, news, and miscellaneous items. Tables 4.2 and 4.3 provide a breakdown of the 'news' and 'editorial' sections of each newspaper by geographical location. Tables 4.4 and 4.5 divide the same data into seven subject matter categories – economic rights, education, organisational news and reports, other legislative reform (covering issues from marriage and divorce law reform to child protection legislation), women's suffrage, temperance, and other – spanning the central concerns of the suffrage-era women's movements in Australasia.
103 The term, used by Rollo Arnold to describe the late nineteenth-century New Zealand press, matches Henry Mayer's observations of contemporary Australian newspapers. Arnold, *New Zealand's Burning*, pp. 220–34; Mayer, *The Press in Australia*, pp. 12–13.

104 *Prohibitionist*, 5 November 1892, p. 3; *Lyttelton Times*, 14 February 1895, p. 2.
105 Mayer, *The Press in Australia*, p. 13; Griffin-Foley, 'Tit-Bits to Big Brother', 537.
106 H. Irving, 'Fair federalists and founding mothers', in Irving (ed.), *A Woman's Constitution?*, pp. 7–14.
107 Australasian WCTU *Minutes of the Fourth Triennial Convention*, p. 70.
108 *Dawn*, 1 April 1900, p. 8.
109 AWS, 10 December 1902, pp. 238–9; 10 January 1903, p. 253; *Our Federation*, December 1902, p. 7; *White Ribbon*, 1 January 1903, pp. 1–3.
110 Murray and Clark, *The Englishwoman's Review*, pp. 245–7. On Canada's historical marginality to the international suffrage movement, see J. Sangster, 'Exporting suffrage: British influences on the Canadian suffrage movement', *Women's History Review*, 28:4 (2019), 566–9.
111 *Our Federation*, 15 May 1901, pp. 71, 77; CM, ARC176.53/319, Ersila Majno Bronzini to Sheppard, 16 April 1902; *White Ribbon*, 1 October 1902, p. 9.
112 *Dawn*, 1 May 1894, pp. 8–9.
113 Docker, *Nervous Nineties*, p. 12.
114 Magarey, *Passions of the First Wave*, p. 52.
115 Roberts, *Maybanke Anderson*, pp. 74–5.
116 See, for example, *Prohibitionist*, 23 September 1893, p. 3; 25 November 1893, p. 3; 9 December 1893, p. 3.
117 Grimshaw, 'Colonising motherhood', 329–49; AWS, October 1900, cover. See also *Evening News*, 16 July 1895, p. 6; 5 March 1898, p. 5; *SMH*, 11 September 1901, p. 5.
118 *Republican*, 7 January 1888, p. 1; *Dawn*, 1 November 1897, p. 9; 1 January 1900, p. 30. See also R. McGregor, *Imagined Destinies: Aboriginal Australians and the Doomed Race Theory, 1880–1939* (Melbourne: Melbourne University Press, 1997).
119 Charlotte Macdonald argues that the two campaigns ought to be considered in unison. However, as Miranda Johnson contends, Māori women's arguments for rights in 'their own political domain' followed a very different path to their Pākehā counterparts. To date, just nine Māori women have been identified from the 25,520 names presented before parliament in 1893. Macdonald, 'People of the land, voting citizens in the nation, subjects of the Crown: Historical perspectives on gender and law in nineteenth-century New Zealand', *Law & History*, 2 (2015), 45–8; Johnson, 'Chiefly women', pp. 228–45; He tohu rangatira – Māori women & the 1893 suffrage petition,' *Archives New Zealand*, https://archives.govt.nz/discover-our-stories/he-tohu-rangatira-maori-women-and-the-1893-suffrage-petition (accessed 13 March 2020).
120 *White Ribbon*, 1 December 1896, p. 9; 1 May 1900, p. 7. Macdonald, 'Gender and law', 55–7; Patterson and Wanhalla, *He Reo Wāhine*, pp. 186–9, 320.
121 C. Brooks and G. Simpkin, *A Bibliography of Articles Published in the White Ribbon, the Official Organ of the New Zealand Women's Christian Temperance Union 1895–1919* (Wellington: National Library of New Zealand, 1975), pp. 47–9.
122 Scanlon, *Inarticulate Longings*, p. 8.
123 *Dawn*, 1 January 1901, p. 8.
124 Garvey, *Writing with Scissors*, p. 7.
125 *Minutes of Fifth Annual Convention of the WCTU of South Australia*, p. 38; *Otago Daily Times*, 26 March 1913, p. 2.

126 *Womanhood Suffrage League of New South Wales, Seventh Annual Report and Balance Sheet for the Year ending June 1st, 1898* (Sydney: Christian World Printing and Publishing House, 1898), p. 17.
127 *Womanhood Suffrage League of New South Wales, Ninth Annual Report and Balance Sheet for the Year ending June 1st, 1900* (Sydney: John Sands Printer, 1900), p. 19.
128 SLNSW, MLMSS38/33/1, WSL of NSW Minute Book 1891–96, pp. 286–8.
129 See, for example, *Womanhood Suffrage League of New South Wales, Tenth Annual Report and Balance Sheet for the Year ending June 1st, 1901* (Sydney: S. D. Townsend & Co. Printers, 1901), p. 27. Scott's clippings are scattered throughout the SLNSW's holdings, but see especially MLMSS38/35/4-6, Newspaper Cuttings re Women Suffrage; MLMSS38/61/3–5, Newspaper Cuttings re Women's Issues 1890–1911.
130 SLNSW, MSS38/33/1, WSL of NSW Minute Book 1891–96, pp. 166, 301; *WSL of NSW Seventh Annual Report*, p. 17.
131 *SMH*, 2 May 1925, p. 9.

5

Suffragists on tour: Exporting and narrating the female franchise

Intercolonial and transnational suffrage networks were not only constituted through the press and the post but were built and sustained by travel. Alongside seasoned nomads like Madge Donohoe, who were fixtures at international conventions, many Australasian suffragists embarked on extended speaking tours. This chapter considers the 'political tourism' of three women who, in the anticipation and aftermath of colonial enfranchisement, travelled to the United States, to Great Britain, and within Australia. Between 1893 and 1903, the South Australian journalist Catherine Helen Spence, the New Zealand suffragist Kate Sheppard, and the Australasian Woman's Christian Temperance Union (WCTU) president Elizabeth Webb Nicholls joined the late nineteenth-century legion of peripatetic propagandists. All three were united by their desire to use their political experience to inspire women in distant places, as well as their attempts to leverage their exposure to foreign cultures to further domestic causes. This chapter examines the material bases of women's travel, the personal and political changes wrought by their journeys, how and why they narrated their encounters at home and abroad, and their negotiation of the challenges that their mobility presented to accepted standards of female behaviour within and beyond the women's movement.

Following trends in imperial and post-colonial studies, suffrage historians have begun to consider how and why travelling activists moved and forged connections across borders. In this pursuit, biography has been revived as a means of escaping national teleology in favour of attempts to understand the worlds in which mobile subjects lived.[1] Karen Hunt and Joan Sangster have written extensively on political tourism, using case studies to classify women's international endeavours and examine how travelling women fought for voting rights. Political tourism, they suggest, was 'as much about how ... foreign experiences were deployed by the political traveller as it was about the experiences themselves'.[2] The importance of political travel for those at 'home' is evident in the plethora of travel narratives published by itinerant suffragists. Following the example of her American predecessor Jessie Ackermann, Elizabeth Nicholls documented six years of missionary travel in the Australasian WCTU's newspaper, *Our Federation*.[3] Likewise, Sheppard, Spence, and many other suffrage-era feminists felt compelled to memorialise their journeys in print, a 'cultural duty' that converted private tourism into a public practice, to be lauded and scrutinised by their scattered audiences.[4] Despite their efforts, we lack understanding about the influence of travel on their politics or what they hoped to convey to audiences at home. Instead, recent suffrage histories focus on women – like Vida Goldstein, Muriel Matters, and Anna Stout – who lived overseas for extended periods and found fame as members of British and American reform organisations.[5]

Men and women, as feminist geographers have emphasised, pass differently through the same spaces. Thus, any exploration of the processes of travel alongside the sites created by travelling ideas, people, and products must not only consider 'women's differential mobility', but discern how suffragists felt these differences and the meanings they ascribed to their journeys.[6] Scholars of nineteenth-century women's interactions with new modes of transport – the steamship, the railway, and the automobile – have provided insight into how travellers networked, entered new public spaces, and found personal empowerment and transformation.[7] Such analytical tools offer rich insights into how Spence, Sheppard, and Nicholls used travel to advance their politics and explain the shifts in their identities as they moved across the world. Furthermore, while the outlines of each woman's journeys are more or less known in Australasia, they offer an important contribution to the wider history of women's travel. Existing studies of suffragists' mobility dwell on Euro-American elites, whether they enjoyed the rarefied air of international conferences, undertook study tours in other Western nations, or travelled to 'educate' colonised women in Asia and Africa.[8] Enfranchised antipodean women disrupt these categories.

With this in mind, 'Suffragists on tour' begins with contrasting journeys: Catherine Spence's 1893–94 visit to the United States and Kate Sheppard's 1894–95 return to Great Britain. Spence and Sheppard derived authority from their domestic achievements and used them as a platform to teach women overseas. Yet, they travelled not to deliver salvation to 'benighted' subjects but to share their success among equals. The reception of these interventions from the periphery revealed as much about their audiences as it did each woman's personal qualities. Spence's enthusiasm resonated with Americans, who saw her not as an upstart but a counterpart, whereas Sheppard's anxiety marked her as a colonial, heightening metropolitan suspicions that New Zealand women had not truly fought for the vote. Despite her setbacks, Sheppard's orchestration of a whispering campaign to discredit Emma Packe, a New Zealand critic of women's enfranchisement, exposed her belief in the potency of political travel and the colony's significance to the metropolitan struggle.

While the burgeoning scholarship on imperial mobility and political tourism provides a robust framework with which to consider Australasian suffragists' travels, the focus on international crossings tends to reify borders. In Australia, suffrage historians have worked within colonial demarcations, focusing on largely sedentary urban women rather than those who travelled to aid campaigns in other colonies.[9] The campaign for Commonwealth enfranchisement did not feature the spectacular rail and automobile journeys undertaken by American suffragists, yet intercolonial activism remains an underappreciated part of the Australian story. For Elizabeth Nicholls, travel constituted a multi-faceted project that used the WCTU's model of missionary internationalism in service of her colonial, national, and international objectives. During her decade as Australasian WCTU president, she relentlessly toured the continent. Unlike other union organisers, Nicholls lectured on women's enfranchisement as well as prohibition and entertained visions of building a woman-centred Commonwealth. More so than Spence or Sheppard, Nicholls understood the radical connotations of her position as a lone female traveller and her transition from Adelaide's private halls to the coach stop, steamship, and railway carriage. Using her newspaper columns to emphasise the ease of travel and the generosity of WCTU members, which allowed her to cross Australia without entering a hotel, Nicholls pre-empted rumours about her respectability. At the same time, her public recitation of the material practices of her journeys was calculated to show her mastery over the Australian continent and stake a claim to the Commonwealth as an arena for white women as well as white men.

'Australian answers to American problems': Catherine Helen Spence in North America, 1893–94

Although she spent most of her adult life in Adelaide, Catherine Spence was the quintessential political tourist. After thirty years of promoting proportional representation in South Australia, in 1889 she was invited speak on the subject in the United States. Spence left on a lecture tour in 1893, her arrival coinciding with the surge of progressive interest in Australasian social experiments.[10] After landing in San Francisco, she traversed North America, returning to Adelaide via Britain in December 1894, a week before South Australian women won the vote. Throughout, Spence worked tirelessly as a lecturer and journalist. She was driven by her conviction that travel provided an unparalleled education, which behoved her to render her experiences as 'object lessons' for American and Australian audiences.[11] Motivated by financial necessity, Spence also spoke on women's enfranchisement, a subject she had self-consciously neglected at home.[12] On her return to Adelaide, Spence used her travels as fodder for her writing and encouraged others to follow suit. Her correspondence with the journalist Alice Henry – which spanned the latter's departure from Melbourne in 1905 and her long career at the Women's Trade Union League's Chicago headquarters – reads as a primer to the art of political travel: the business of making a life, and a living, using 'our two weapons – and our two tools ... Pen and Voice'.[13]

Catherine Spence's career with 'pen and voice' began in earnest when she reached middle age. Born in the Scottish Borders in 1825, she immigrated with her family to South Australia in 1839. In her late teens, Spence began work as a governess and, alongside teaching, wrote pseudonymous newspaper columns and serialised fiction, including 'Adelaide's first novel', *Clara Morrison*, in 1854. After decades of anonymity, she entered public life in the 1870s as a member of the city's philanthropic class and built a reputation as a social commentator, joining the *South Australian Register* under her own byline in 1878. Tired of earning a pittance writing fiction, she devoted her energies to journalism and political campaigning in 1889.[14] Despite her profile, Spence seldom spoke in public before she reached her sixties. Her reticence was not uncommon. Until the advent of the suffrage movement, Australasia had few female orators. Exceptions existed in non-conformist circles, including the Unitarian congregation she first preached to in 1878, but most churches resisted the erosion of male prerogatives. Nevertheless, Spence was one of a small group who made female platform-speakers familiar, if not popular, figures on the cultural landscape.[15] She took proportional representation as her subject, specifically the adoption of the single transferable vote. Terming her system 'effective voting', in 1892 Spence toured the colony advocating its implementation. Her efforts had little short-term success, they but raised her profile and emboldened her to accept an invitation from Alfred Cridge – described by his friends as 'the world's foremost advocate of proportional representation' – to 'teach us [Americans] how to vote'.[16]

Spence departed Adelaide claiming to know 'only two human beings in America'.[17] In reality, months of networking preceded her departure. She aired her travel plans in 1892, triggering an avalanche of introductory letters from colonial worthies to American reformers. Before leaving, Spence also secured appointments to represent reform organisations overseas, most notably the State Children's Council at the International Conference of Charities, Correction and Philanthropy, held at Chicago's World's Columbian Exposition in 1893.[18] After arriving in America, she spent several weeks lecturing in California. However, she was soon drawn east. Spence spent four months at the World's Fair, boasting that 'no individual took as large a part in so many Congresses in Chicago as I did'. As she told Henry, these months brought no immediate reward but 'prepared the way for earning'.[19] The mock elections Spence staged to showcase proportional representation were well received and attracted the notice of eminent feminists like Jane Addams and Susan B. Anthony. When the exposition closed, Spence departed for the East Coast with 'the prospects of lecturing engagements for some time before me'.[20]

For the next six months, Spence 'lived the strenuous life to the utmost'.[21] The variety and scale of her enterprise upsets neat typologies of women's travel. Tracing the career of the Anglo-Australian suffragist Dora Montefiore, Karen Hunt devised categories to classify women's transnational activism: passive political tourism, purposeful 'fact-finding' missions, propaganda tours, and travel as a means of networking.[22] Motivated by financial imperatives as well as the knowledge that, at sixty-eight, she was unlikely to return to America, Spence did all four at once. Beyond proselytising effective voting, she secured sponsors by framing her trip as a study tour, on which she would investigate subjects as diverse as child welfare and currency reform. Like her contemporaries, Spence saw no contradiction between her advocacy and her journalism, through which she communicated pithy lessons for readers. To justify her provision of 'Australian answers to American problems', Spence argued that the similarities between Britain's former colonies of settlement facilitated policy transfer. Australia, she informed *Harper*'s readers, was 'more nearly of kin to America than even England'. In Australia, she reversed the formula, stressing that her compatriots had much to learn from a country 'honeycombed with new ideas as to land, as to railroads and telegraphs, [and] as to labour rights and wrongs'.[23]

Journalism allowed Spence to deploy her touristic observations in political debates, but freelancing paid poorly. Since taking her first teaching position, Spence had been proud of her financial independence.[24] Reflecting these beginnings, as well as the precarity of itinerant life, anxieties about money litter her diaries. Six months without 'earn[ing] a cent' in America tested her commitment to proportional representation.[25] Although Spence considered effective voting the *sine qua non* of political reform and detested the single-mindedness she detected among suffragists, pragmatism trumped ideological purity. While the lucrative lyceum circuit was in decline when she arrived in the United States, paying women to speak at suffrage rallies – unprecedented in Australia – remained commonplace. For talented orators, as Lisa Tetrault argues, presenting oneself as a suffragist was still a pathway to financial security.[26] Spence discovered as much in 1893. After speaking on electoral reform 'at a great many places without payment', she capitalised on women's organisations' desire to meet the Women's Suffrage League of South Australia's vice-president, and styled herself as a suffrage lecturer. Fees from fourteen speeches on 'equal suffrage' between November 1893 and March 1894 – many more than she had given in South Australia – constituted the bulk of Spence's American income. Earning up to $50 per appearance, Spence could prolong her journey and advance her beloved cause by remitting money to Chicago's ailing *Proportional Representation Review*.[27]

As with many reformers, travel refigured Spence's politics. Her return to Britain in 1865–66 preceded her entry into Adelaide's philanthropic circles and shaped her thinking on public education and electoral reform. The 1893–94 journey was no less transformative. During her unsuccessful bid for election as a delegate to the 1897 Federal Convention, Spence's campaign was based not on her status as Australia's first female political candidate but on the experience she had accrued 'in her travels'. As her manifesto informed voters, Spence 'had studied [the] … Federal Constitutions … of the United States, Canada, and Switzerland' and consequently understood which precedents Australia should adopt.[28] As well as enlarging her political ambitions, travel reinforced Spence's conviction that Australia occupied an important place on the 'social horizon' that compelled her to share antipodean innovations overseas. Commissioned to write a pamphlet on the State Children's Council in 1906, Spence exceeded her brief, producing an expansive manuscript comparing Australia's state welfare systems with American 'private benevolence'.[29] Before publication, she announced her intention to distribute the book 'all over the world' and, over the next two years, shipped dozens of copies to America. Having exhausted its Australian print run, Spence – adamant that her ideas deserved a wider audience – wrote a revised American edition, but she died in 1910 before securing a publisher.[30]

Spence's success offered a blueprint for a generation of like-minded women to follow in her footsteps. Long before American-trained professionals began encouraging Australian women to seek their fortune across the Pacific, Spence exhorted her contemporaries to forgo the pilgrimage to Britain in favour of the United States.[31] Those in middle age, like

Rose Scott and Caroline Clark, resisted her blandishments, but she had better luck with younger women. Spence contributed to the travel expenses of Elizabeth Nicholls, Vida Goldstein, and Alice Henry and furnished the latter two with social introductions and advice on how to navigate the speaking circuit.[32] Reflecting her background as a teacher, Spence's instructional letters to Henry expose the financial underpinnings of itinerant feminist activism. Living on the road, she told Henry, required 'precious hard work every day and all day long'. In this spirit, her missives were crammed with advice. She recommended cheap hotels, like the Manhattan Young Women's Christian Association's Margaret Louisa Home, 'of course also highly respectable'; introduced Henry and her companion, the novelist Miles Franklin, to editors and organisers; and told them where to expect paying audiences.[33] Spence also emphasised the importance of freelancing as a source of income outside the lecturing season. Although she complained about newspapers' rates, contracts with Australian dailies, boosted by several well-paid American magazine features, accounted for over half of the £140 she earned in the United States. As a working journalist with ambitions of shaping popular discourse, writing unpaid for women's newspapers, as Sheppard and Nicholls did, was unthinkable. Keeping abreast of colonial affairs, Spence reminded Henry, was also vital for remaining 'up to date on … the matters which make the stuff for treatment by pen and voice you want for Americans'. Without fresh intelligence from Australia, she warned, Henry's value as a commentator would soon diminish.[34]

Because of Spence's adaptability, her North American tour was a triumph. She arrived at a moment when American progressives, seeking to remedy the excesses of capitalism, were intrigued by Australasian 'social experiments'. From the moment she landed in San Francisco, Spence found that hailing from 'Australia, the home of the secret ballot' acted as a 'passport to the hearts of reformers all over America'.[35] When she left for Scotland in 1894, Spence had delivered over a hundred lectures. While the United States was no closer to adopting proportional representation, she departed in good spirits, telling her brother, 'I am really a personage [here].' However, the 'animal magnetism' to which she attributed her success faded during the Atlantic crossing.[36] Whereas she felt at ease with the 'homeliness' which characterised middle-class American life, like many settlers who travelled 'home', Spence felt herself an outsider in Britain. Reflecting on her fortunes, Spence worried that London rendered her 'strangely stupid' and admitted to experiencing 'more hesitation in speaking in England than I did in America'. When she departed for Adelaide, it was with a confession to her readers: 'I have done very little public work in my native land'. Whatever motivated her reticence, Spence understood that it was bad for business, warning Alice Henry that 'I earned nothing in England or Scotland at all'.[37] While the democratisation of the suffrage movement in the late 1900s made room for a new wave of Australasian activists, Spence's contemporaries were similarly disheartened by the 'introverted focus of the British movement'. Ten years later, Henry left London for the United States, disillusioned with 'the English lack of interest in Australia and its experimental legislation', while the New Zealander Jessie Mackay joked that being 'talked at or talked down to' was a rite of passage for professional women 'go[ing] home'. By then, such status anxiety had become a trope in antipodean literature and remained a common experience for expatriate Australasians until well into the twentieth century.[38]

Although Spence arrived in America at a propitious moment, her success was not a matter of circumstance. Rather than being a hindrance, her age and decision not to marry liberated Spence from the strictures that inhibited many female travellers. Her experience of travel undoubtedly differed from her male counterparts', yet nowhere did she hint that she faced opprobrium for spending two years travelling alone. Spence also married her intellect with charm. She was an assiduous networker, a skill that helped her find audiences and allowed her to spend half of her ten months in the United States lodging 'with friends' – both invaluable for a woman to whom activism constituted a livelihood.[39] Her experience as a journalist was crucial in translating her observations into lessons for the masses. Most nineteenth-century women's travel writing focused on domestic details as authors advertised their 'properly feminine interests'.[40] Yet such fare was unsuitable for the mainstream press. Rather than describe the minutiae of her personal encounters, Spence addressed the public at large. By comparison, the New Zealand peace activist Wilhelmina Sherriff Bain discovered the perils of reporting on 'women's issues'. Contracted by a newspaper consortium to write from Europe and North America, Bain's descriptions of the 1904 Berlin conference of the International Council of Women (ICW) infuriated her editors. Told that her 'work was interesting but not popular', she was refused payment and was unable to promote her causes in the New Zealand press for the remainder of her five years abroad.[41]

Catherine Spence's final novel, *A Week in the Future* (1888–89), reads as a precursor to her American adventure. While convalescing from a heart attack in Adelaide, her narrator, Emily Bethel, is transported to London in 1988, from whence she describes a society free from pollution, overcrowding, and the drudgery of domestic labour. As the text evinced, Spence was a utopian and constantly pursued social, political, and moral improvement. Her quest for 'pure democracy' can be seen in this light.[42] Although her electoral experiments gained little traction, Spence's achievement lay in the fact that, like the characters in her fiction, she had made a living with 'pen and voice' in America. Unlike wealthy Dora Montefiore, Spence embraced her overlapping roles as a researcher, journalist, and propagandist, suggesting that these categories were hybrid and, for working women at least, could not be inhabited in isolation. Exhilarated by her travels, on returning to Adelaide, Spence insisted that younger women cross the Pacific, where 'so much grand work [remained] to be done'.[43] For Spence, travel and politics were indivisible. Her activism allowed her to cross the globe, and the knowledge she accrued overseas invigorated her Australian work. Yet, political travel was seldom as free from friction, or as productive. Kate Sheppard appeared to share Spence's commitment to promoting Antipodean social experiments aboard. However, her unhappy stint as a travelling activist diminished her desire to present an uplifting suffrage narrative overseas. Over the course of fifteen years spent between Britain and New Zealand, she abandoned the project in favour of the escapism of conventional tourism.

'Scarcely anything ... does more good to woman suffrage in England than seeing those who can speak from personal experience': Kate Sheppard in Great Britain, 1894–95

On 11 July 1894, Spence, Sheppard, and the New South Wales suffragist Margaret Windeyer met for the only time at a suffrage rally in Westminster.[44] Of the three, Sheppard had the surest platform to succeed in Britain, having arrived as one of the leaders of the first successful campaign for women's enfranchisement in the British Empire. Conscious that New Zealand had drawn international attention, in 1893 Sheppard urged her compatriots to demonstrate the virtues of women's suffrage for the 'benefit of women in other countries'. Thus, when she announced plans to make an extended return 'home', colleagues believed that Sheppard would 'aid British women in their struggle for freedom'.[45] Despite their optimism, her 1894–95 journey – sometimes mislabelled a 'triumphal tour' – and subsequent trips in 1903, 1908, and 1913 were unsuccessful.[46] While Sheppard strove to control how New Zealand's experience under universal suffrage was portrayed and silence those who spread 'misleading' propaganda, she proved unable to embed a credible counternarrative. Beyond her personal distress, Sheppard's public breakdowns reveal much about the value of political speech and remind us that, whatever its utopian trappings, international suffragism 'did not always lead to respect, equality, or common agreement'.[47] Behind the façade of the political tourist, Sheppard's unease with the pressures of embodying enfranchised womanhood saw her withdraw from the role of travelling propagandist and become a wistful observer at the margins of the international women's movement.

From the beginning of the New Zealand women's suffrage campaign, Sheppard impressed upon her compatriots that they belonged to a wider world of women's activism. Her rhetoric borrowed from British and American suffrage tracts, as well as her correspondence with suffragists in both countries. In July 1893, at a reception for the Anglo-American singer and temperance campaigner Antoinette Sterling, she explained the 'special interest' that New Zealand women took in their English and American 'sisters' and their corresponding desire 'to prove that the women of our Colony are not behind their sisters in other parts'. Between women's enfranchisement in September 1893 and the December general election, Sheppard reminded WCTU members that the world was watching New Zealand, 'to see whether Women's Suffrage is to be for good or evil'.[48] Motivated by this conviction, from the comfort of her Christchurch home Sheppard crafted a narrative that emphasised the virtues of women's enfranchisement to the rest of the world.

Despite her public statements, Sheppard's correspondence suggests that she was uncertain about her intentions when she left New Zealand. Among the congratulations she received in 1893 came requests to lecture in Australia. Whereas Catherine Spence cultivated such invitations before her departure, Sheppard declined them. She also avoided the opportunities for political persuasion that characterised her contemporaries' shipboard experiences. Spence perfected her pitch aboard the *Monowai* in 1893, 'enlivening' the trans-Pacific voyage with 'talks on effective voting'. Seven years later, en route to Britain, Elizabeth Nicholls lectured on the *Cuzco*'s third-class deck and visited WCTU branches in Colombo and Port Said while the ship refuelled.[49] Although Sheppard took a similar route north, she refused to speak in public during layovers, demurring that she was enjoying a 'pleasure trip to the old country'.[50]

Sheppard's silence might have been explained by the presence of her husband and son on the voyage but for the fact that such reticence characterised her stay in Britain. Despite her biographer's claim that Sheppard found herself 'in constant demand', she gave fewer than ten speeches over the next eighteen months.[51] Her first important public outing occurred on 9 July, when she and Sir John Hall, the parliamentary sponsor of the New Zealand suffrage campaign, addressed a Westminster suffrage rally alongside Frances Willard and the World's WCTU's vice-president, Lady Henry Somerset. Together, Sheppard and Hall explained 'the struggle of fourteen years' in the hope that 'ere long England will share the privileges with us'. *Woman's Signal* praised Sheppard, but she was visibly intimidated by the vast Queen's Hall. Observers reported that her nerves were apparent and her voice 'scarcely audible'.[52] She had neither the financial incentives that compelled Spence to speak, nor the connections that later primed her compatriot, Lady Anna Stout, the wife of a former New Zealand premier, to succeed as a suffrage lecturer in Britain. Instead, Sheppard retreated from London. She spent the next year between Scotland and the southwest. Both areas were temperance strongholds, but divisions over suffrage in the British Women's Temperance Association (BWTA) prevented Sheppard from broaching the subject.[53] She returned to London to address the World's WCTU convention in June 1895, yet her second appearance before a large audience was more disastrous than her first. During her speech, Sheppard 'broke down from nervousness' and required the 'gallant' assistance of an acquaintance, the 'long-haired apostle of temperance', Tennyson Smith, to recover her composure. Embarrassed by the incident, she withdrew from the public eye – preferring, as one observer noted, to work 'quietly' – and returned to New Zealand having said little about the campaign that made her name across the world.[54]

Although numerous prominent New Zealand suffragists toured Britain describing their efforts in 1894, within a few years it was believed that the Liberal government had unexpectedly bestowed the vote on women. Sheppard's withdrawal from the lecture circuit crippled her attempt to entrench a counter-narrative. From the beginning, she faced an uphill struggle. For Britons inured to the parliamentary gridlock that had stymied their attempts to introduce a successful suffrage bill, New Zealand's embryonic party system, the lack of entrenched opposition to women's enfranchisement, and Māori women's enfranchisement in 1893 together affronted their notions of metropolitan and racial superiority and meant that the colony's politics had limited educational value.[55] For others, the taint of colonial naïveté diminished its salience. Such prejudices were even held by women like Helen Blackburn, editor of the *Englishwoman's Review*, whose correspondence with Sheppard was discussed in Chapter 3. When, for example, Sheppard criticised British women willing to accept partial suffrage, Blackburn accused her of political immaturity.[56] Finally, in an era before suffrage campaigners had access to all the instruments of mass communication, the 'unmediated voice' remained a vital tool of persuasion. Sheppard's halting delivery compounded perceptions of her inexperience. Although she charmed her acquaintances, those who learnt of Sheppard's breakdowns were unlikely to have been reassured that New Zealand women had struggled to win the vote, a suspicion that lingered in the minds of many British suffragists.[57]

Perhaps because of her inability to deliver an uplifting suffrage narrative to London audiences, Sheppard was acutely aware of the power that travellers had to frame the colonial campaign. Despite her shortcomings as an orator, she remained a fixture on the drawing-room circuit. Unable to contest dissenting voices from the stage, Sheppard conspired to prevent anti-suffragist critics from attracting audiences in Britain. Worried by news that Emma Packe, the New Zealand WCTU's disaffected former president, had arrived in Britain, Sheppard wrote to Lady Henry Somerset in 1894, warning that Packe would speak 'against Woman's Suffrage while she is over here'. To avert the possibility, Sheppard suggested that Packe be blacklisted from BWTA and WCTU events.[58]

Since its inception, the New Zealand WCTU had been riven by factionalism. Whereas Sheppard and her allies envisaged the union as a broad church for reform-minded women, conservatives like Packe cherished the union's Christian character. In 1885, as president of the Christchurch union, Packe vetoed Sheppard's request to consult the Premier, Robert Stout, on their anti-barmaid campaign because he was a freethinker. Their conflict resumed in 1891, when Packe agitated to abandon the union's pragmatic non-denominationalism in favour of a constitutional amendment that would have alienated all but the most pious evangelicals. The issue was voted on at the union's 1892 convention. Defeated, the hardliners resigned from the union.[59] After two years' absence, Packe reappeared in the *Union Signal* of March 1894, offering as 'an actor in the scene some account of the first general election in which enfranchised British women had a share'. Contradicting Sheppard, Packe argued that suffrage had changed nothing, because women 'had no clear idea of measures for governing the country'. In their ignorance, she argued, women had elected 'men disloyal to Christ'.[60] When the edition reached New Zealand in May, Packe had already left for Britain, but her compatriots were incensed. The colonial WCTU condemned *Union Signal* for publishing the letter, while local members questioned her 'uncalled for ... allusion made to the enfranchisement of Woman', which, they argued, had been exercised 'on the side of righteousness & truth'.[61]

Even before Sheppard had landed, the New Zealand WCTU defended its reputation and, by extension, its claims about women's suffrage. Afraid that Packe would impart an 'incorrect impression of affairs in

New Zealand', the union's president, Annie Schnackenberg, worked to discredit her in Britain. Like Sheppard, Schnackenberg asked the BWTA to bar Packe from appearing as 'an accredited White Ribbon woman from New Zealand, while thus misrepresenting the work in this Colony'. Thus, before Packe met Lady Somerset, the Briton was convinced that she was an 'old-fashioned worker ... [who] may do harm here'.[62] More than reports submitted to British periodicals by disgruntled male anti-suffragists, the New Zealand WCTU leadership feared Packe's testimony would resonate overseas. Although they could not prohibit Packe from socialising in British reform circles, Sheppard and Schnackenberg prevented her from expanding on her explosive letter before the World's WCTU convention in 1895.[63] The episode not only revealed Sheppard and her colleagues' belief in the potency of public speech, but showed the limits of their ability to control the dissemination of news about women's suffrage, or stop women overseas from appropriating New Zealand's example for their own ends. In September 1894, Frances Willard, the World's WCTU president and *Union Signal*'s editor-in-chief, refused to indulge the New Zealanders' plea to 'give as great publicity to this refutation as ... to the slander'. Instead, she legitimised Packe's claims by apologising for publishing a 'private' letter, an impertinence she justified by stating that its 'valuable contents' and its author's 'offhand style' made it 'too good to keep'.[64]

Despite these traumatic episodes, Sheppard lingered on the margins of the international women's movement throughout her life. Although gossip about antipodeans abroad was relished in the colonies, the press traded in success stories, and little news of either breakdown reached New Zealand. Thus, like many colonials who returned when metropolitan accomplishments eluded them, Sheppard's standing at home was undiminished.[65] Nevertheless, while she continued the fight to expand the limited citizenship women had won in 1893, Sheppard did not recycle her touristic observations as propaganda, the experience too painful to either publicly acknowledge or recast, however tenuously, as a success. Without the financial pressures that impelled Spence to write, or the need to account for donated funds, she avoided making her travel the subject of further scrutiny. Instead, her public discussion of her time in Britain was limited to a series of anodyne sketches of prominent feminists for *White Ribbon*.[66] After seven years in New Zealand, Sheppard agreed to lecture on the fruits of women's enfranchisement at the ICW's 1904 congress. Despite her best intentions, Sheppard's anxieties returned. Upon landing in London, she rebuffed all speaking invitations and, explaining that she feared 'straining' her voice, cancelled her appearance in Berlin. By then, Sheppard's condition was discussed discreetly by contemporaries at home and in Europe, with the consensus that it was unfortunate for the cause but that her reasons were unimpeachable.[67] Thus, for the remainder of her visit, and when she returned to Britain in 1908 and 1912, she preferred to 'quietly assist the movement' as a donor, a pamphleteer, and a spectator at suffrage rallies. However, as the radical suffragist Mary Priestman reminded Sheppard in 1895, her hosts wanted to hear enfranchised women 'speak from personal experience' rather than receive lessons in the discreet managerialism that had defined her career.[68]

Kate Sheppard's unhappy stint as a travelling suffragist reminds us that 'transnational political connections and attempts to create internationalist organizations and sentiments were always a double-edged sword'.[69] For one versed in the history of feminism, visiting its metropoles, London and New York, held enormous appeal. Furthermore, as her muzzling of Emma Packe showed, Sheppard recognised the power of 'speak[ing] from personal experience' and silenced those who contradicted her tale of struggle and success. However, Sheppard could not fill the void with her own speech, and the distress caused by her breakdowns haunted her career. She never spoke in public outside New Zealand again and, unlike most suffrage travellers, seldom relayed her observations to audiences at home. While Spence's and Sheppard's careers provide contrasting tales of how antipodean women wielded international influence, it is important to remember that activists crossed colonial as well as national borders. Elizabeth Nicholls' largely forgotten journeys exemplify how intercolonial travel was used to advance the interlinked causes of temperance and women's enfranchisement and validate local reformers' work. As Nicholls' fruitful decade as Australasian WCTU president reveals, the boundary between domestic and international travel was porous, and her emphasis on travel as a means of intensifying national feeling in Australia was not antithetical to international cooperation.

'I have been ever on the move in the interests of the W.C.T.U.': Elizabeth Webb Nicholls in Australia, 1893–1903

On 17 October 1893, Elizabeth Nicholls stood before a crowd in Bunbury, a port town in remote southwestern Australia. Almost 3,000 kilometres from Adelaide, she told those gathered within the Masonic Hall that she had 'never [before] been away from home for more than three weeks at a time'.[70] Despite her professed inexperience, Nicholls had embarked on a two-month organising tour of Western Australia. Within the WCTU, an organisation that mythologised its missionary origins, the journey proved her making. Soon after returning home, Nicholls was elected the union's Australasian president and, enabled by the thousands of WCTU members spread across the continent, she spent much of the next decade on the move. Her tours were intended to 'deepen the feeling of unity' within the union, but also advanced her political ambitions.[71] Alongside temperance work, Nicholls contributed to all six colonial suffrage campaigns and argued for Federation across Australia. Throughout her presidency, Nicholls used *Our Federation* to disseminate comprehensive accounts of her travels. Her columns not only served as a form of moral and financial accountability to her diffuse membership but constituted an assertion of women's place in, and dominion over, the incipient Commonwealth of Australia. Setting Nicholls' formative Australian journeys against Spence's and Sheppard's overseas endeavours offers vital perspective on feminist travel as an act of political imagination and how travelling suffragists negotiated the gendered politics of mobility and respectability.

After a childhood spent between Britain and South Australia, Elizabeth Blackwell settled in Adelaide and married Alfred Nicholls, a warehouse clerk, in 1870. Although she had little education and spent the next twenty years raising seven children, Nicholls found opportunities for self-improvement and social advancement in the Methodist Church. In 1885, she entered public life as a speaker at a Wesleyan women's conference and joined the Adelaide WCTU soon after. In a testament to the temperance movement's democratic spirit, within three years she was elected colonial president, an office she used to persuade members to join the campaign for women's enfranchisement, won in 1894.[72] Seeking to emulate Jessie Ackermann, the Australasian WCTU's peripatetic founding president, Nicholls began raising her profile outside South Australia. Her tour of Western Australia replicated Ackermann's 1892 journey. When the Californian announced her departure for southern Africa in 1894, Nicholls capitalised on members' fear that the union would falter in the American's absence. Though she lacked Ackermann's 'wonderful magnetic power', Nicholls' demonstrated commitment to evangelism at the union's peripheries established her bona fides to its members.[73]

The Australasian WCTU elected Nicholls president in April 1894, a success she celebrated by embarking on a mission to Tasmania. In 1897, encouraged by Alfred, she resigned the South Australian presidency and devoted the next five years to touring the continent.[74] Between 1893 and 1901, Nicholls traversed each colony except South Australia twice and, between 1897 and 1901, spent half of each year on the road. Each tour lasted between three and five months, taking Nicholls beyond the union's suburban strongholds to new audiences in provincial towns, funded

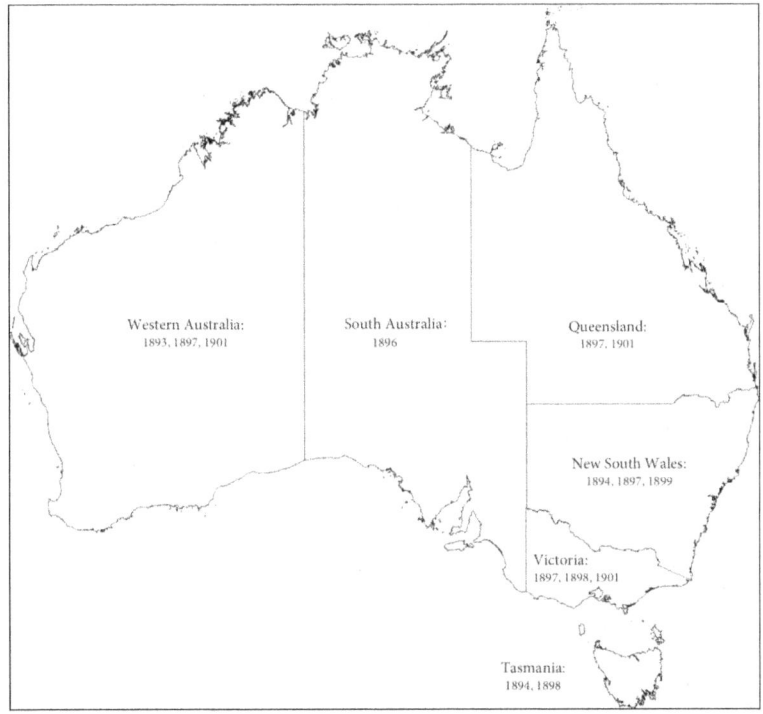

5.1 Elizabeth Nicholls' organising tours for the WCTU of Australasia, 1893–1901

entirely from the collection plate. During her Queensland mission of 1901, for example, Nicholls travelled 8,400 kilometres by rail, steamer, and coach, visiting '25 localities' between Toowoomba and Townsville and giving 136 speeches. Although Ackermann's 'circumnavigation' of Australia over three whirlwind visits between 1889 and 1894 inspired Nicholls, the scale of her subsequent tours was unprecedented.[75] By comparison, the National Council of Women (NCW) of Australia did not inaugurate a travel fund that enabled its presidents to visit each state during their term until 1939, a feat Nicholls accomplished several times before the interwar extension of transcontinental railway travel or the proliferation of the automobile.[76]

Nicholls' tours were primarily intended to grow the WCTU's membership. However, she gained renown across Australia as a suffrage activist. When her presidency ended in 1903, she was the first, and only, woman to stage suffrage rallies in all six states. The achievement reflected her belief that suffrage advocacy constituted a pillar of the union's mission. At each destination, she followed a well-rehearsed script. She gave three addresses: one on temperance, another recruiting new members, and a third on women's enfranchisement. Her speeches were didactic, drawing on her experiences and the testimonies of correspondents who were familiar with 'the working of the Women's Franchise in parts of the United States, South Australia, and New Zealand'.[77] Nicholls' willingness to collaborate with non-members, a feature of the South Australian campaign, allowed her to reach new audiences. In New South Wales, for example, she alleviated the enmity between the WCTU and Womanhood Suffrage League enough to lead joint suffrage rallies in 1899, prompting Rose Scott to make special notice of New South Wales women's immense 'debt of gratitude' to the South Australian on the eve of their enfranchisement.[78]

Crucially, Nicholls' travels took place in Australia's federal decade. Her staunch advocacy for Federation drew on a vision of 'Christianity in action, on a continental scale' that drove clergy of all denominations to endorse the project but also served her purpose of forging a woman-centred Commonwealth. Yet, despite efforts to recover Australia's 'founding mothers', Nicholls' role as Australia's foremost female exponent of Federation remains opaque.[79] At the Australasian WCTU's inaugural convention, she labelled the union a 'federation of our womanhood's forces for the overthrow of the strongest foe of intercolonial life … the provincial spirit which so narrows and hinders all real progress'. Upon accepting the presidency, Nicholls reiterated her belief that the WCTU was an instrument for 'cultivating a national spirit in these Australian colonies'. Federation would, in her estimation, hasten prohibition and provide women with a platform for international cooperation. Thus, she urged union members, as the representatives of 'the organised motherhood and sisterhood of these large territories', to consider themselves 'nation builders'.[80]

Nicholls was an effective speaker, yet journalism was more important to her activism. Like most evangelical organisations, 'travellers' tales' were integral to the WCTU's culture. Nicholls attempted the genre in 1893, describing her West Australian tour for an Adelaide newspaper.[81] The experiment was not repeated, but the idea of projecting her presence to members stuck with Nicholls. At the Australasian WCTU's 1897 convention, her promise to 'visit each of the colonies' was intertwined with the launch of *Our Federation*. As she outlined in her proposal for the paper, Nicholls intended it as a forum for discussing women's interests 'from an Australasian standpoint', helping to 'prepare the way for

... political federation'.[82] She envisaged that her accounts of travelling Australia's 'magnificent distances' would lie at the heart of her enterprise, the thread that bound the publication and the WCTU. Over the next six years she pursued her task with vigour, combining her presidential duties with her work as the *Federation*'s editor and roving reporter. Together, as the paper's title and logo (a map of Australia without colonial demarcations) implied, Nicholls' travel and writing not only sought to unify the WCTU but served her grander ambition of building a Commonwealth that 'every Christian mother' could claim as their own – *our* Federation.[83]

Serialised travel writing was a well-worn genre by the 1890s, yet Nicholls' style distinguished her from her contemporaries. Rather than mimicking *Union Signal*'s breathless tone or reprinting stump speeches, as editor-activists like Sheppard and Vida Goldstein had, Nicholls described the material experience of travel. By focusing on her everyday activities and the rhythms of branch life, Nicholls not only provided readers enough information to repeat her journeys but emphasised the commonalities that connected women across the continent. In contrast to most published missionary and women's travel writing, in which describing brushes with danger – or at least discomfort – was a trope designed to pique readers' interest, she stressed the ease and safety of intercolonial travel.[84] Although, as she later admitted, Nicholls had endured 'all the trials and difficulties, the mistakes and annoyances' that beset long-distance travellers, she considered it 'undesirable to record' such hardships. Rather than portray the countryside as exotic or awe-inspiring – as had American suffragists when imagining frontierswomen's freedoms – Nicholls domesticated it, seeking to assuage her readers' fears about the bush. Whether she steamed up the Clarence River in New South Wales or gazed upon the 'Golden West', the landscapes she passed through were uniformly 'pretty' and 'pleasant'. In the six years she edited *Our Federation*, her only complaint was that Australia took so long to cross, preventing her from reaching yet more listeners.[85] For subscribers, the cumulative effect of Nicholls' commentary was an assertion of womanly mastery over an 'empty' continent and the technologies that allowed her to traverse it.

Nicholls' evocation of a friendly continent bound by rail and steam rested upon her interpretation of the WCTU's ideology of sisterhood. The union's expansion was premised on the existence of a 'sisterly consciousness' that assumed women shared universal interests. Such a sisterhood was, understandably, felt most keenly in 'isolated parts of the WCTU's far-flung empire'.[86] Nicholls was committed to international solidarity; in 1900, she described arriving at the World's WCTU convention in Edinburgh as 'coming home'. Yet, befitting a proponent of Australian federation, her internationalism coexisted with a nationalist sensibility. When recounting her passage to Europe, Nicholls delighted in recounting the 'cries of "coo-ee"' that passed between Australian steamers on the Suez Canal. Likewise, when travelling in Australia, whether she had arrived in an unfamiliar town or disembarked at Adelaide after a spell on the road, Nicholls described the women who greeted her as 'pleasant little crowd[s] of sisters'.[87]

These professions of sisterhood were not merely rhetorical but reflected her lived experience. Nicholls' office was unsalaried, and Alfred's means limited. As a result, she declared, it was 'out of the question' for her 'to incur the necessary expense' of travelling.[88] Consequently, she depended on members' largesse to continue her journeys. Wherever possible she lodged in the union's urban headquarters or country members' homes. Unlike Spence, Nicholls refused to charge speaking fees, but she nevertheless honed a method of touring that maximised her 'financial results'. Wherever she spoke, Nicholls asked that 'collections be taken'. The eighteen months she spent touring Australia between 1897 and 1900 were entirely community-funded, and what remained of the £137 she raised was paid into the union's coffers.[89] Overseas trips were bankrolled by wealthy benefactors. Before Nicholls left for the World's WCTU's Edinburgh convention, Julia Holder, the wife of a former South Australian premier, presented her with a steamer ticket, 'a purse containing £34/10 in gold', and the promise of 'further remittances'.[90] As much as new technologies enabled Nicholls' extraordinary journeys, so did the tangible bonds of sisterhood, which permitted a woman of modest means to travel and live among WCTU members for over a decade.

Nicholls' articulation of a continental sisterhood had a hidden racial architecture. Nowhere in *Our Federation* did she display the fixation with racial integrity that led her male federalist counterparts to draw what Alfred Deakin, Australia's second Prime Minister, called 'a deep colour line of demarcation between Caucasians and all other races'. Neither did she complain about Indigenous men's putative eligibility to vote while white women remained disenfranchised, as had her contemporaries in New South Wales and Victoria.[91] Nevertheless, Nicholls shared a tacit understanding with her readers that the sisterhood she evoked was lily-white. Her position was not without contradictions. Since Mary Clement Leavitt, its first round-the-world missionary, departed for Hawai'i in 1883, the WCTU had been a critic and beneficiary of empire. Its evangelists thrived within the British world and, in the Crown colonies, the union's growth was predicated on co-opting local women into the fight against what it considered the excesses of colonialism, chiefly the trade in intoxicants.[92] While Deakin, like many Australian liberals, engaged in a global project to entrench the white monopoly on power in settler societies, Nicholls celebrated the World's WCTU's cosmopolitanism. Overlooking the union's monocultural leadership and – especially in Australia – its lack of interest in racial equality, in 1893 she argued that its rise 'proved conclusively ... that women of all colours and languages could be got to unite and work together'. Putting her principles into action, Nicholls maintained correspondence with the Indian WCTU leader, Manoramabai, after her 1903 tour of Australia.[93] Despite her pride in such interracial connections, Nicholls adhered more closely to a Deakinite vision of Australia than she cared to admit. During her tenure as editor, the WCTU forged alliances with Chinese communities in the anti-opium crusade and took tentative steps toward 'improving' the material lives of mission-based Aboriginal women, yet precious little evidence of such work – or the activities of any other non-white women in Australia – reached *Our Federation*'s readers.[94]

Considered alongside her contemporaries, such occlusions in Nicholls' writing were not unusual. As noted in Chapter 4, British settler suffragists maintained a 'wall of silence' about the plight of indigenous populations under colonial rule. In Australia, at least, it was only in the 1920s that feminists began to 'acknowledge themselves as colonisers' and to criticise the treatment of Aboriginal people.[95] This blind spot was cast into relief by turn-of-the-century travellers' reactions to the United States. Vida Goldstein and Wilhelmina Sherriff Bain returned home sympathetic to the civil rights struggle, while the effect of meeting the African American social reformers Frederick Douglass and Frances Harper in Chicago, then staying as a guest of the abolitionist William Lloyd Garrison in Boston, left Spence feeling 'ashamed of being so narrow in my views of the coloured question'.[96] Upon reading the black journalist Ida B. Wells' descriptions of racism within the American WCTU, Sheppard took up her cause. In advance of the 1895 World's convention, she infuriated its leaders with a flurry of letters questioning the existence of segregated branches in the South – charges serious enough for Frances Willard to offer a personal explanation.[97] Even Nicholls, who never set foot in America, proudly reported that 'Mrs Joseph, a coloured delegate from Louisania [sic], was my comrade and fellow speaker' during a tour of Glasgow's slums.[98] Yet, interracial contact could also reinforce prejudices. In 1909, Anglo-Australian suffragists Harriet Newcomb and Margaret Hodge reported from Washington, DC: 'the chief thing that we dislike is the host of black servants ... many of the negroes we have seen elsewhere have been extremely insolent, or rather showed that they could be so. Anyway we are more than ever devoted to the policy of a white Australia.'[99]

Whatever the effects of their encounters with black Americans, none of these women returned home less secure in their identity as white settler colonists, as interwar travellers would later report. Alongside Newcomb and Hodge, Vida Goldstein repeatedly endorsed the White Australia Policy and, in common with most of her contemporaries, remained indifferent to racial injustices at home. Before the extension of the railways across the outback, such a disjuncture was to be expected from city-dwellers who had seldom seen Aboriginal people. Even then, as Mark Twain reported with chagrin in 1895, the cumulative effect of the Protection Acts, which corralled Indigenous peoples on to reserves, made it possible to traverse the continent without encountering an Aboriginal person.[100] However, Nicholls' unusually extensive travel in country Queensland, New South Wales, South Australia, and Western Australia meant her mileage easily surpassed Twain's. All had significant Indigenous populations, as her mentor, Ackermann, documented after her return in 1910–11.[101] Of course, it is impossible to know whom Nicholls encountered. Nevertheless, her depiction of an empty country accorded with settler colonial strategies to refigure Indigenous lands as 'absent landscapes' and, in the process of exploring them, 'becoming-native-through-movement'.[102] Nicholls said nothing directly about these processes in *Our Federation*, but her whitewashed vision of the continent likely resulted from omissions that, at their most benign, suggest she considered Indigenous people among the dangers of the road that she concealed from her readers. Above all, it must be considered in light of the racially exclusive womanhood franchise that the Commonwealth adopted in 1902, celebrated unreservedly in *Our Federation* as the birth of the woman-centred Commonwealth that Nicholls had long dreamed about.[103]

Despite the seemingly untrammelled mobility she enjoyed by dint of her race, Nicholls remained conscious that her travel tested the limits of accepted gender conventions. The anxiety that inhabiting new public spaces, like the coach stop and railway station, threatened the respectability on which her enterprise depended permeated Nicholls' columns. Across the industrialised world, women's entrance into masculine domains like the steamship and railway carriage corresponded with heightened concerns about their safety. The discourses of sexual danger attached to technologies of motion constrained women and eroded the credibility of itinerant activists.[104] Thus, in addition to increasing her visibility, Nicholls' columns pre-empted readers' prying minds. After weathering the disapproval of the Australasian WCTU's executive, which urged her to travel first class, Nicholls explained that she travelled 'second saloon' out of respect for the union's 'ways and means'. Having made the economic imperative clear, she shielded herself from any suggestion of impropriety. Whenever she embarked on overnight journeys, Nicholls conspicuously assured readers that she had 'the fortune' to 'secure a cabin to myself', where she could seclude herself from the ship's dangers 'in sleep'. Similarly, her frequent references to members' pleasant homes forestalled the suggestion that she frequented hotels – doubly unsuitable for a lone female temperance advocate.[105]

Nicholls' circumspection was motivated, in part, by the challenge that her mobility presented to traditional ideas of marriage, which unsettled her critics and allies alike. As reactions to her mission demonstrated, the acceptability of a woman's travel varied by audience and her personal circumstances. For working-class women, 'onward mobility' was a well-trodden path to respectability.[106] Up the social scale, few qualms were raised about the peripatetic life led by Emily Dobson, the wealthy president of the Tasmanian NCW. Similarly, the tours of the United States by unmarried contemporaries such as Goldstein and Spence attracted little opprobrium. Nicholls also travelled alone but, as a married woman in the socially conservative WCTU, she was held to a different standard. Determining the Nicholls family's class position is difficult. Unusually for a Victorian marriage, it is Alfred, rather than Elizabeth, who barely features in the public record. Beyond his service as a Methodist lay preacher, and almost sixty years' employment as a merchant's clerk, little of his life is recoverable.[107] Although Elizabeth Nicholls' father and uncle briefly served in the South Australian legislature, Alfred's vocation and Elizabeth's admission that the costs of travelling lay beyond their means suggest that she belonged within the devout lower-middle class milieu that dominated the union's membership – to which the mantra of 'home protection' as the primary justification for political activism proved so appealing.[108]

Therefore, while nothing suggested that Elizabeth and Alfred enjoyed anything but a companionate marriage of the type the WCTU idealised, the juxtaposition between her wanderlust and his domesticity dogged her career. In 1897, her South Australian colleagues remarked on the unusual freedom Elizabeth enjoyed when they thanked Alfred for her service: 'No other man in the colony would have given up his wife like he had during the past eight years.' A year later, a crowd at one of Nicholls' rallies reacted with 'merriment' when informed that she 'had a husband in Adelaide'.[109] For critics, Nicholls' apparent liberation from the home constituted a portent of suffragists' ultimate agenda. The Adelaide satirical weekly *Quiz and the Lantern* addressed its 'Letters to Public Men' column to Nicholls in 1898, explaining, 'you are the person who wears the —— in your household'. Its anonymous author considered Nicholls' travel proof that she had both emasculated her husband and rejected femininity and family life altogether. Nicholls' inattention to her domestic duties, he continued, meant that 'Mutterings of discontent may not reach your ears. In fact you must be thoroughly sick of your wanderings, and the strains of "Home, sweet Home" must readily bring the tears to your eyes. That is just where the cruelty of public life comes in for a woman.'[110]

Such gossip aggravated Nicholls. Like many women, she strove to mitigate the perceived threat of her politics by cloaking herself in the respectability of marriage and motherhood. Rather than dignify her critics with a direct response, Nicholls retorted obliquely, publishing a glossy full-page photocollage of her and Alfred surrounded by their offspring in *Our Federation* (figure 5.2). With her adult children scattered across Australia, the picture was necessarily a composite. More closely resembling a theatrical bill than a family portrait, it perhaps lent credence to her critics' claims.[111] Nevertheless, as one of the few images of herself that Nicholls published, it revealed her desire to balance the peripatetic persona of her columns with an image of herself as a wife and mother.

Over the long term, *Quiz*'s line of attack resonated within the WCTU. Despite the union's lionisation of travelling missionaries, members prized stability above rootlessness. Their discomfort with women who had been too long on the move was a symptom of what Tony Ballantyne calls the 'contradiction at the heart of colonisation: that "settlers" were typically unsettled'. Such restlessness, and its attendant anxieties, was projected on to illegitimate mobile subjects: indigenous people, non-white colonists, and white Europeans 'who travelled without "good cause"' – hawkers, vagrants, and, it seems, itinerant female activists.[112] During their 'round-the-world' tours, Leavitt and Ackermann were as beloved as Frances Willard. However, neither woman was embraced by the World's leadership, and both died estranged from their former colleagues.[113] Although Ackermann combined her duties as Australasian WCTU president with those of a travelling organiser, she departed before the membership could sour on her. After a decade of Nicholls' rootless presidency, members' patience wore thin. In 1903, she stood for re-election but, to her surprise, was defeated by the union's Tasmanian secretary, Jessie Rooke. In stark contrast with Nicholls, Rooke 'declined to accept [the presidency] until she heard from her husband'. Hours later, delegates were read a telegram bearing his consent, 'on the condition that no travelling would be required'.

5.2 Like many of her contemporaries, Elizabeth Nicholls publicly emphasised her roles as a wife and mother to counteract negative perceptions of her political activity. (*Our Federation*, 15 November 1898, n.p.)

After some protest, a majority ruled that 'travelling was not a necessary part of the President's duties'.[114] Nicholls' replacement would be immobile and, living outside mainland Australia, almost entirely invisible.

Unlike Catherine Spence and Kate Sheppard, who drew on their domestic reform campaigns to assist progressive causes overseas, Elizabeth Nicholls' ambitions were predominantly national. Nevertheless, given the expanse of the Australian continent, travel was more central to her political life than either of her contemporaries, whose foremost achievements came in their home colonies. Sandwiched between fifty years of activism in Adelaide, Nicholls spent a decade touring Australia, documenting the minutiae of her journeys in *Our Federation*. Together, her travel and writing constituted a concerted effort to invigorate local temperance work and stitch together a Commonwealth 'federated in the interests of women as well as men'. Although she lacked formal education, Nicholls was a shrewd communicator who understood the necessity of performing 'rituals to constitute a nation' and reframed the WCTU's universalist ideology of sisterhood as a rhetorical tool in support of Federation.[115] As well as pre-empting questions about her respectability, Nicholls' articulation of the material practices of her travel – notably absent from her male counterparts' writing – emphasised her public mobility, encouraging readers to imagine the Commonwealth as an arena for women as well as men.

By 1903, her campaigns had achieved remarkable results. Although national prohibition remained a distant prospect, Federation had been realised and suffrage won everywhere but Tasmania and Victoria. Nevertheless, Nicholls' travel, and the spotlight it placed on her unconventional marriage, unsettled the WCTU. Her transgression was not campaigning for women's rights but the subtle and symbolic politics of her mobility, which threatened conventions regarding a married woman's place and the source of her moral power, the home. With the vote won, the union sought a return to its founding preoccupation with hearth and home, and replaced her with a woman forbidden to travel. Yet the sedentary life was not for Nicholls. She resumed the South Australian WCTU's presidency between 1906 and 1927, and in 1920 she made her international swansong as a member of Australia's delegation to the International Woman Suffrage Alliance's Geneva congress. Perhaps because Alfred died soon after she returned, or because the journey lacked the underlying sense of purpose that motivated her to traverse Australia twenty years earlier, Nicholls wrote little about her trip – a silence that underscored the singularity of her extended intercolonial travel narratives twenty years earlier.[116]

Catherine Spence, Kate Sheppard, and Elizabeth Nicholls believed in the importance of political travel, both to progress their respective causes in new territories and, through their writing, to encourage women's activism in their homelands. Whether it provided a career, an escape from domesticity, or the catalyst for new forms of organising, travel liberated all three. Together, their journeys not only reveal the limits of neat typologies of political travel but undermine them altogether. Personal knowledge of successful colonial campaigns – for women's enfranchisement or demonstrating the viability of proportional representation – served as a common currency on the road. However, their reception was contingent on the political cultures of their destinations, as well as their personal compatibility with those they encountered on their journeys.

Spence thrived among progressives in the United States and found their zeal infectious. For the rest of her life, she sought to persuade Australians to emulate the best aspects of American life. Reinvigorated by American interest in her ideas, she helped other women to follow in her footsteps. Nevertheless, like many colonials, Spence found Britain a tougher market to crack, as did Sheppard, despite the advantages bestowed by her status as the leader of the first successful national women's suffrage movement. Her 1894–95 tour exposed her deficiencies as an orator and, crucially, the divergent expectations of a suffrage activist in New Zealand and the United Kingdom. Notwithstanding her inability to 'speak from personal experience' and spread the news of New Zealand women's 'pioneer' victory from the stage, Sheppard's efforts to silence her adversary, Emma Packe, emphasised her belief in the potency of public speech. Of the three, Nicholls' travel was perhaps the most layered. On the surface, her journeys were intended to encourage temperance advocates and suffragists across Australia, serving the WCTU's global mission through her domestic activism. However, they also formed part of a wider project to stitch together a nation federated in the interests of white women as well as white men. Such grand ambitions contrasted with the subtler politics of her mobility, which she worked constantly to domesticate – to signal her respectability and to encourage others to follow in her wake. Nicholls never disclosed whether the Commonwealth met her expectations, but her replacement as WCTU president by a candidate who pledged to remain 'at home' underscored the precarity of her enterprise and the distance that women still had to travel to realise her expansive vision.

Notes

1 A. L. Stoler, 'Tense and tender ties: The politics of comparison in North American history and post (colonial) studies', *Journal of American History*, 88:3 (2001), 862; A. Curthoys and M. Lake, 'Introduction', in Curthoys and Lake (eds), *Connected Worlds*,

pp. 5–20; D. Deacon et al., 'Introduction', in Deacon et al. (eds), *Transnational Lives*, p. 5; D. Lambert and A. Lester, 'Introduction: Imperial space, imperial subjects', in D. Lambert and A. Lester (eds), *Colonial Lives Across the British Empire: Imperial Careering in the Long Nineteenth Century* (Cambridge: Cambridge University Press, 2006), pp. 1–32.

2 K. Hunt, 'Transnationalism in practice: The effect of Dora Montefiore's international travel on women's politics in Britain before World War I', in Jonsson et al. (eds), *Crossing Boundaries*, pp. 73–94; Hunt, 'Whirl'd through the World', 41–62; J. Sangster, 'Political tourism, writing, and communication: Transnational connections of women on the left, 1920s–1940s', in Jonsson et al. (eds), *Crossing Boundaries*, pp. 95–116.

3 See J. A. Ackermann, *The World through a Woman's Eyes* (Chicago: Woman's Temperance Publishing Association, 1896).

4 L. Wevers, *Country of Writing: Travel Writing and New Zealand, 1809–1900* (Auckland: Auckland University Press, 2002), p. 5.

5 See, for example, Scott, *How Australia Led the Way*; R. Wainwright, *Miss Muriel Matters* (Sydney: HarperCollins, 2017); Webb, 'Anna Paterson Stout'; Wright, *You Daughters of Freedom*.

6 G. Clarsen, 'Gender and mobility: Historicizing the terms', in G. Mom et al. (eds), *Mobility in History: The State of the Art in the History of Transport, Traffic and Mobility* (Neuchatel: Editions Alphil, 2009), p. 239; L. McDowell, *Gender, Identity and Place: Understanding Feminist Geographies* (Cambridge: Polity Press, 1999), pp. 1–23.

7 See, for example, T. Cresswell, 'Mobilising the movement: The role of mobility in the suffrage politics of Florence Luscomb and Margaret Foley, 1911–1915', *Gender, Place & Culture*, 12:4 (2005), 447–61; G. Clarsen, *Eat My Dust: Early Women Motorists* (Baltimore: Johns Hopkins University Press, 2008), pp. 86–103; F. Steel, *Oceania under Steam: Sea Transport and the Cultures of Colonialism, c. 1870–1914* (Manchester: Manchester University Press, 2011), pp. 126–48.

8 M. Sandell, *The Rise of Women's Transnational Activism: Identity and Sisterhood Between the World Wars* (London: I. B. Tauris, 2015), p. 148. See, for example, M. Bosch, 'Colonial dimensions of Dutch women's suffrage: Aletta Jacobs' travel letters from Africa and Asia, 1911–1912', *Journal of Women's History*, 11:2 (1999), 8–34; Burton, *Burdens of History*; Mukherjee, *Indian Suffragettes*; Rupp, *Worlds of Women*. Exceptions here include Trethewey and Whitehead, 'Beyond centre and periphery', 547–59, and Mukherjee, *Indian Suffragettes*.

9 Audrey Oldfield's *Woman Suffrage in Australia* exemplifies this approach. Although Oldfield argues that the suffragists shared a common tactical arsenal, she makes little reference to the travelling activists and artefacts that enabled the transmission of this political vocabulary. Even Australian histories of women's travel are limited to 'women abroad', while journeys within colonial Australia remain a byway in travel writing anthologies. See, for example, Pesman, *Duty Free*; R. Pesman et al. (eds), *The Oxford Book of Australian Travel Writing* (Melbourne: Oxford University Press, 1996); R. Lucas and C. Forster (eds), *Wilder Shores: Women's Travel Stories of Australia and Beyond* (Brisbane: University of Queensland Press, 1993). An important exception is J. Horne, *The Pursuit of Wonder: How Australia's Landscape was Explored, Nature Discovered and Tourism Unleashed* (Melbourne: Miegunyah Press, 2005).

10 Much has been written on this subject. On Australia, see especially Lake, *Progressive New World*; and for New Zealand, P. J. Coleman, *The Antipodean Connection: New Zealand Liberalism and American Progressivism* (Lawrence: University Press of Kansas, 1987).
11 *Daily Telegraph*, 26 December 1893, p. 6.
12 Although some historians argue that Spence was integral to the South Australian suffrage movement, Spence admitted that she had waited until 1891 to join the campaign and never considered women's enfranchisement more important than electoral reform. *South Australian Register (SAR)*, 17 May 1894, p. 6.
13 SLSA, PRG88/7/73, Catherine Helen Spence to Alice Henry, 12 October 1906.
14 Spence earned £100 from her first three novels, *Clara Morrison* (1854), *Tender and True* (1856), and *Mr Hogarth's Will* (1865), compared with an annual income of £300 as a journalist. P. Butterss, 'Building literary Adelaide, 1836–1860', *Journal of Australian Studies*, 39:3 (2015), 358; S. Magarey, *Unbridling the Tongues of Women: A Biography of Catherine Helen Spence* (Adelaide: University of Adelaide Press, rev. edn, 2010), pp. 27–120.
15 The Liverpudlian evangelist Margaret Hampson's 1883 tour of Australasia is considered a turning point, helping temperance women to reconcile public speaking with their understanding of biblically proscribed gender roles. M. Lake, *The Bible in Australia: A Cultural History* (Sydney: NewSouth, 2018), pp. 204–5; S. Swain, 'In these days of female evangelists and hallelujah lasses: Women preachers and the redefinition of gender roles in the churches', *Journal of Religious History*, 26:1 (2002), 65–77.
16 C. H. Spence, *An Autobiography* (Adelaide: W. K. Thomas & Co., 1910), pp. 67–9; Lake, *Progressive New World*, p. 74.
17 *SAR*, 16 June 1894, p. 6.
18 *Border Watch*, 10 December 1892, p. 2; *SAR*, 4 April 1893, p. 5; *Daily Telegraph*, 17 April 1893, p. 4; Magarey, *Catherine Helen Spence*, p. 135. Many of the forty invitations 'to stay or enjoy a family's hospitality' in the United States likely stemmed from Spence's preparations in 1892. Lake, *Progressive New World*, p. 18.
19 *Daily Telegraph*, 27 December 1893, p. 6; SLSA, PRG88/7/78, Spence to Henry, 16 February 1907.
20 *SAR*, 22 March 1894, p. 6; Spence, *Autobiography*, p. 71.
21 The phrase, borrowed from Theodore Roosevelt's eponymous 1899 lecture, was a favourite of Spence's. Variations appear throughout the *Autobiography*, suggesting her affinity with the ethos of the Progressive Era. See, for example, Spence, *Autobiography*, p. 74.
22 Hunt, 'Transnationalism in practice', 41–62.
23 *Boston Post*, 9 December 1893, p. 4; *Harper's New Monthly Magazine*, July 1894, p. 244; *Daily Telegraph*, 26 May 1894, p. 10.
24 Spence, *Autobiography*, p. 17.
25 SLSA, PRG88/7/8, 52, Spence to Henry, 16 September 1901 and 3 January 1905. For more detail on Spence's advocacy of proportional representation in the United States, see Lake, *Progressive New World*, pp. 75–105.
26 L. Tetrault, 'The incorporation of American feminism: Suffragists and the postbellum lyceum', *Journal of American History*, 96:4 (2010), 1033–48.

27 SLSA, PRG88/7/8, Spence to Henry, 16 September 1901; S. Magarey et al. (eds), *Ever Yours, C. H. Spence: Catherine Helen Spence's An Autobiography (1825–1910), Diary (1894), and Some Correspondence (1894–1910)* (Adelaide: Wakefield Press, 2005), p. 233.
28 *Advertiser*, 4 March 1897, p. 5.
29 SLSA, PRG88/7/68, Spence to Henry, 18 May 1906; C. Spence, *State Children in Australia: A History of Boarding Out and Its Developments* (Adelaide: Vardon and Sons, 1907), pp. 4–5.
30 SLSA, PRG88/7/79, 90, 93, 96, 99, 121, Spence to Henry, 8 March 1907, 18 December 1907, 11 March 1908, 5 June 1908, 2 August 1908, 24 March 1909, and 11 February 1910.
31 A. Rees, 'Bursting with new ideas: Australian women professionals and American study tours, 1930–1960', *History Australia*, 13:3 (2016), 387.
32 SLNSW, A2278/81, Spence to Rose Scott, 20 September 1902; SLSA, PRG88/7/3, 8, 51, Spence to Henry, 6 March 1901, 16 September 1901, and 9 December 1904; *Australian Woman's Sphere* (AWS), January 1902, p. 136; *WCTU of Australasia Minutes of the Fourth Triennial Convention*, p. 20.
33 Magarey et al. (eds), *Ever Yours*, p. 230; SLSA, PRG88/7/8, 63, 67–9, 78–9, Spence to Henry, 16 September 1901, 23 February 1906, 27 April 1906, 18 May 1906, 9 June 1906, 10 February 1907, and 8 March 1907.
34 SLSA, PRG88/7/8, 78–9, Spence to Henry, 16 September 1901, 16 February 1907, 8 March 1907.
35 I. Tyrrell, *Transnational Nation: United States History in Global Perspective since 1789* (New York: Palgrave Macmillan, 2007), pp. 123–4; Spence, *Autobiography*, p. 70.
36 Magarey, *Catherine Helen Spence*, p. 169; Spence, *Autobiography*, pp. 74–8.
37 Magarey et al. (eds), *Ever Yours*, p. 279; *Report of Meeting on 'Proportional Representation,' or Effective Voting, held at River House, Chelsea* (London: John Bale & Sons, 1894), p. 6; *SAR*, 6 November 1894, p. 6; Spence, *Autobiography*, p. 70; SLSA, PRG88/7/8, Spence to Henry, 16 September 1901.
38 Kirkby, *Alice Henry*, p. 59; Mukherjee, *Indian Suffragettes*, p. 30; *Time and Tide*, 15 July 1921, p. 679; Woollacott, *To Try Her Fortune in London*, pp. 19–46, 146, 151–5. A turning point can be seen in the 1930s. When, for example, the Melbourne born and New Zealand raised artist Dora Meeson Coates was asked if she felt that 'the inferiority complex amongst Australians here [in London]' remained intact, she replied, 'I honestly have never come across anything of the kind!' SLNSW, MLMSS2109/2/4, Dora Meeson Coates to Mary Booth, 20 August 1933.
39 SLSA, PRG88/7/8, Spence to Henry, 16 September 1901.
40 S. Smith, *Moving Lives: Twentieth Century Women's Travel Writing* (Minneapolis: University of Minnesota Press, 2001), pp. 18–19.
41 Auckland War Memorial Museum, Auckland (hereafter AWMM), MS94, Wilhelmina Sherriff Bain to Amey Daldy, 14 April 1905.
42 C. Spence, *A Week in the Future* (Sydney: Hale & Iremonger, 1987); C. Spence, *A Plea for Pure Democracy: Mr Hare's Reform Bill Applied to South Australia* (Adelaide: W. C. Rigby, 1861).
43 SLSA, PRG88/7/80, Spence to Henry, 9 April 1907.

44 Magarey *et al.* (eds), *Ever Yours*, p. 283. Like Spence, Windeyer – an inaugural member of the WSL of New South Wales – had attended the 1893 World's Columbian Exposition, where she had spoken on the vote. See J. Keating, 'International activism after the fair: New South Wales, Utah, and the 1893 World's Columbian Exposition', in R. Rogers and M. Boussahba-Bravard (eds), *Women in International and Universal Exhibitions 1876-1937* (Oxford: Routledge, 2017), pp. 192-212.
45 *Prohibitionist*, 9 December 1893, p. 3; 11 August 1894, p. 3.
46 Adams, *Women and the Vote*, p. 119.
47 Sangster, 'Crossing boundaries', pp. 18-19.
48 *Prohibitionist*, 15 July 1893, p. 3; 25 November 1893, p. 3.
49 Spence, *Autobiography*, p. 69; *Our Federation*, 15 June 1900, p. 88; 15 January 1901, p. 211; *West Australian*, 17 December 1900, p. 6.
50 CM, ARC176.53/277-8, 280, Elizabeth Webb Nicholls to Sheppard, 20 July 1895; John Vale to Sheppard, 5 August 1895; M. E. Kirk to Sheppard, 13 August 1895; *Evening Journal*, 3 April 1894, p. 2.
51 Devaliant, *Kate Sheppard*, pp. 135-9.
52 *Woman's Signal*, June 1894 supplement, pp. 421-4; 21 June 1894, p. 432; *Evening Star*, 24 July 1894, p. 4.
53 Barrow, 'Teetotal feminists', pp. 75-7.
54 *Evening Star*, 8 August 1895, p. 4; *Shafts*, October 1896, p. 135; CM, ARC176.53/294, 421, Leonard M. Isitt to Sheppard, *c.* 1895; Helen Hood to Sheppard, 28 November 1895.
55 Dalziel, 'Presenting the enfranchisement of New Zealand women abroad', pp. 43-50, 57-8; S. Mukherjee, 'Locating race in suffrage: Discourses and encounters with race and empire in the British suffrage movement', in E. van der Meulen (ed.), *From Suffragette to Homesteader: Exploring British and Canadian Colonial Histories and Women's Politics through Memoir* (Halifax: Fernwood Publishing, 2018), pp. 99-104.
56 CM, ARC176.53/247, Helen Blackburn to Sheppard, 27 July 1894.
57 In Britain, for example, Women's Social and Political Union recruits received oratorical training. K. Cowman, *Women of the Right Spirit: Paid Organisers of the Women's Social and Political Union 1904-18* (Manchester: Manchester University Press, 2007), p. 32; J. Damousi, 'An absence of anything masculine: Vida Goldstein and women's public speech', *Victorian Historical Journal*, 72:2 (2008), 252-3. On British suspicions that New Zealand women had neither truly fought for the vote nor appreciated its value, see J. Keating, '"The defection of women": The New Zealand Contagious Diseases Act repeal campaign and transnational feminist dialogue in the late nineteenth century', *Women's History Review*, 25:2 (2016), 187-206.
58 CM, ARC176.53/242, Isabella Somerset to Sheppard, 28 June 1894.
59 J. Stenhouse, 'Religion and society', in Byrnes (ed.), *The New Oxford History of New Zealand*, p. 349.
60 *Union Signal*, 15 March 1894, p. 5.
61 *Prohibitionist*, 19 May 1894, p. 3; 16 June 1894, p. 3; ATL, 79-057-08/03, Auckland WCTU Minute Book 1889-98, 23 May and 13 June 1894.
62 *Prohibitionist*, 14 July 1894, p. 3; CM, ARC176.53/242, Somerset to Sheppard, 28 June 1894.

63 *Dawn* [UK], 1 August 1894, p. 1; CM, ARC176.53/288, Hood to Sheppard, 4 November 1895. See also R. H. Bakewell, 'New Zealand under female franchise', *Nineteenth Century*, 35 (February 1894), 268–75; N. Young, 'The truth about female suffrage in New Zealand', *Westminster Review*, 142 (December 1894), 666–72.
64 *Prohibitionist*, 19 May 1894, p. 3; *Union Signal*, 6 September 1894, p. 4.
65 F. Barnes, *New Zealand's London: A Colony and Its Metropolis* (Auckland: Auckland University Press, 2012), pp. 115–16.
66 *White Ribbon*, 1 February 1896, pp. 2–3; 1 March 1896, pp. 2–3; 1 April 1896, pp. 3–4; 1 June 1896, pp. 1–3.
67 Bain, *The International Council of Women*, p. 3; AWMM, MS94, Margaret Sievwright to Daldy, 26 April 1904; British Library, London, Add MS47454/fol.284, Elizabeth Wolstenholme Elmy to Harriet McIlquham, 23 May 1904; CM, ARC176.53/325, 329, 331, Olga von Beschwitz to Sheppard, 18 March 1904; Ishbel Aberdeen to Sheppard, 9 April 1904; May Wright Sewall to Sheppard, 19 April 1904; *WR*, 15 April 1904, p. 10; 16 May 1904, p. 8.
68 Lovell-Smith, *Plain Living High Thinking*, pp. 101–2; CM, ARC176.53/265, 379, Mary Priestman to Sheppard, 2 February 1895; Margery Corbett to Sheppard, 27 May 1908; British Library, Add MS47454/fol.329, Elmy to McIlquham, 23 August 1904; Sheppard, *Woman Suffrage in New Zealand*.
69 Sangster, 'Crossing boundaries', p. 18.
70 *Southern Times*, 19 October 1893, p. 3.
71 *Australasian WCTU Minutes of the Third Triennial Convention*, p. 54.
72 H. Edwards, 'Our Australian chieftain', in I. McCorkindale (ed.), *Torchbearers: The Woman's Christian Temperance Union of South Australia 1886–1948* (Adelaide: Woman's Christian Temperance Union of South Australia, 1949), pp. 5–9.
73 *West Australian*, 17 August 1892, p. 3; 25 November 1893, p. 7; *Southern Times*, 19 October 1893, p. 3; *Union Signal*, 16 August 1888, p. 5.
74 Edwards, 'Our Australian chieftain', p. 8.
75 *SAR*, 14 October 1901, p. 8; *Australasian WCTU Minutes of the Second Triennial Convention*, pp. 60–1.
76 Quartly and Smart, *Respectable Radicals*, p. 139.
77 SLSA, SRG186/889, Sheppard to Nicholls, 20 May 1896; SLSA, SRG186/74, Sheppard to Nicholls, 18 October 1898; SLSA, SRG186/107, 'Methods of conducting unions', c. 1899.
78 *WSL of New South Wales Ninth Annual Report*, p. 9.
79 Atkinson, *The Europeans in Australia*, pp. 293–8; Irving, 'Fair federalists and founding mothers', pp. 1–20; H. Irving, *To Constitute a Nation: A Cultural History of Australia's Constitution* (Melbourne: Cambridge University Press, 1997), pp. 173–202.
80 *WCTU of South Australia Minutes of Eleventh Annual Convention*, p. 10; *Mercury*, 18 April 1894, p. 3; *Brisbane Courier*, 27 April 1897, p. 6; *Our Federation*, 15 September 1900, p. 142.
81 Tyrrell, *Woman's World*, p. 90; *Alliance & Temperance News*, 1 November 1893, p. 4.
82 UMA, 101/85, Box 77/231/2, Nicholls to the Australasian WCTU, 24 August 1896.
83 *WCTU of Australasia Minutes of the Third Triennial Convention*, p. 34; *Brisbane Courier*, 28 April 1897, p. 4; *Our Federation*, 15 January 1898, p. 9.

84 Horne, *The Pursuit of Wonder*, pp. 88–97; Lake, *The Bible in Australia*, pp. 125–6.
85 *Our Federation*, 15 August 1898, p. 131; 15 October 1898, p. 155; 15 September 1899, p. 135; 15 July 1901, p. 103; 15 November 1901, pp. 165–9. See also Stevenson, 'Imagining women's suffrage', 644–53.
86 Tyrrell, *Woman's World*, pp. 114–21.
87 *Our Federation*, 15 March 1899, p. 40; 15 June 1899, p. 88; 15 July 1900, p. 102; 15 September 1900, p. 142.
88 *WCTU of Australasia Minutes of the Fourth Triennial Convention*, p. 20.
89 Ibid., p. 70; SLSA, SRG186/107, 'Methods of conducting unions', c. 1899.
90 *Advertiser*, 2 May 1900, p. 9.
91 A. Deakin, *Federated Australia: Selections from Letters to the Morning Post 1900–1910*, ed. J. A. La Nauze (Melbourne: Melbourne University Press, 1968), p. 184; *Evening News*, 16 July 1895, p. 6; 5 March 1898, p. 5; *AWS*, October 1900, p. 9.
92 This project was rooted in the union's racialisation of the alcohol question, a world-view that drew on and validated the racial hierarches that underpinned European colonialism. Tyrrell, *Woman's World*, pp. 146–69; Valverde, 'Racial poison', pp. 33–50.
93 *Southern Times*, 19 October 1893, p. 3; *WCTU of Australasia Minutes of the Third Triennial Convention*, pp. 18–21; UMA, 101/85, Box 77/231/2, Manoramabai to Nicholls, 24 January 1904. See also M. Lake and H. Reynolds, *Drawing the Global Colour Line: White Men's Countries and the International Challenge of Racial Equality* (Cambridge: Cambridge University Press, 2008).
94 Warne, *Agitate, Educate, Organise, Legislate*, pp. 13–44; P. Grimshaw, 'Gender, citizenship and race in the Woman's Christian Temperance Union of Australia, 1890 to the 1930s', *Australian Feminist Studies*, 13:28 (1998), 199–208.
95 P. Grimshaw, 'Reading the silences: Suffrage activists and race in nineteenth century settler societies', in P. Grimshaw *et al.* (eds), *Women's Rights and Human Rights: International Historical Perspectives* (Basingstoke: Palgrave, 2001), pp. 1–48; Paisley, *Loving Protection*.
96 AWMM, MS94, Bain to Daldy, 14 April 1905; Goldstein, *To America and Back*, pp. 29–30; Lake, *Progressive New World*, pp. 80, 95–6, 100–1; Spence, *Autobiography*, pp. 72–3.
97 CM, ARC176/53/266a, 267, 272, 425, Hood to Sheppard, 21 February 1895; Kate Bushnell to Sheppard, c. February 1895; Priestman to Sheppard, 3 March 1895; Helen Bright Clark to Sheppard, 27 May 1895. For the substance of Wells' allegations, see *Woman's Signal*, 17 May 1894, p. 170.
98 *SAR*, 21 August 1900, p. 6.
99 SLNSW, A2274/411, Harriet Newcomb to Scott, 21 April 1909. Perhaps reflecting a change of heart or, more likely, the racial hierarchies that pervaded contemporary feminist thought, Newcomb's prejudices against black Americans did not prevent her from lobbying British Prime Minister Lloyd George to support the enfranchisement of Indian women in 1919. See Mukherjee, *Indian Suffragettes*, pp. 101–2.
100 W. Anderson, 'Liberal intellectuals as Pacific supercargo: White Australian masculinity and racial thought on the boarder-lands', *Australian Historical Studies*, 46:3 (2015), 425–39; K. Laing, '"The White Australia nettle": Women's internationalism, peace, and the White Australia Policy in the interwar years', *History Australia*, 14:2 (2017),

218–36; F. Paisley, 'No back streets in the bush: 1920s and 1930s pro-Aboriginal white women's activism and the trans-Australia railway', *Australian Feminist Studies*, 12:27 (1997), 119–37; M. Twain, *Following the Equator: A Journey around the World* (Hartford: American Publishing Company, 1897), p. 221; R. White, 'British travellers and the invisibility of Australia's past, 1868–1910', in M. Farr and X. Guégan (eds), *The British Abroad Since the Eighteenth Century, Volume 1: Travellers and Tourists* (New York: Palgrave Macmillan, 2013), pp. 152–3.

101 Ackermann, *Australia from a Woman's Point of View*, pp. 115–23.

102 G. Clarsen, 'Revisiting "Driving While Black": Racialized automobilities in a settler colonial context', *Mobility in History*, 8:1 (2017), 52; J. Hore, 'Capturing terra incognita: Alfred Burton, "Maoridom" and wilderness in the King Country', *Australian Historical Studies*, 50:2 (2019), 191–5.

103 *Our Federation*, 15 June 1902, p. 62.

104 R. J. Barrow, 'Rape on the railway: Women, safety, and moral panic in Victorian newspapers', *Journal of Victorian Culture*, 20:3 (2015), 341–66; Steel, *Oceania under Steam*, pp. 126–48.

105 SLSA, SRG186/748, Carvosso to Nicholls, 23 May 1901; *Our Federation*, 15 February 1898, p. 29; 15 October 1898, p. 156; 15 March 1899, p. 40. Such strategies were commonplace for nineteenth-century Australian women 'travelling without gentlemen escorts'. Horne, *The Pursuit of Wonder*, pp. 82–8.

106 Bishop, 'Women on the move', 38–59.

107 *Australian Christian Commonwealth*, 17 December 1920, p. 12.

108 A. Hyslop, 'Temperance, Christianity and feminism: The Woman's Christian Temperance Union of Victoria, 1887–97', *Historical Studies*, 17:66 (1976), 34.

109 *SAR*, 15 September 1897, p. 3; *Our Federation*, 15 September 1898, p. 140.

110 *Quiz and the Lantern*, 15 December 1898, p. 8. Images of women 'wearing the trousers' were a regular part of anti-suffragists' arsenal in the 1890s. See, for example, *Bulletin*, 8 August 1891, p. 7; 1 September 1894, p. 7.

111 Despite its awkward composition, the picture was not as incongruous as it first appears. Rather, it attests to Susan Sontag's observation that for the middle classes in the industrialising West, 'photography came along to memorialize, to restate symbolically, the imperilled continuity and vanishing extendedness of family life'. S. Sontag, *On Photography* (Harmondsworth: Penguin Books, 1979), pp. 8–9.

112 T. Ballantyne, 'Mobility, empire, colonisation', *History Australia*, 11:2 (2014), 27–36; C. Coleborne, 'Mobility stopped in its tracks: Institutional narratives and the mobile in the Australian and New Zealand colonial world, 1870s–1900s', *Transfers*, 5:3 (2015), 89–96.

113 Tyrrell, *Woman's World*, p. 112.

114 *Australasian WCTU Minutes of the 5th Triennial Convention*, pp. 15–18.

115 *Australasian WCTU Minutes of the Third Triennial Convention*, p. 34; Irving, *To Constitute a Nation*, p. 119.

116 M. Mune, 'Nicholls, Elizabeth Webb (1850–1943)', *Australian Dictionary of Biography*, http://adb.anu.edu.au/biography/nicholls-elizabeth-webb-7839 (accessed 20 September 2018).

Conclusion

On resettling in Sydney in 1924, after seventeen years of living abroad, the celebrated novelist Miles Franklin expressed her disappointment with the fruits of women's enfranchisement. Writing to Margaret Drier Robins, her long-time superior at the Chicago-based Women's Trade Union League, a forum where she had often extolled the virtues of 'advanced Australia', Franklin complained that her homeland, 'which took a wonderful lurch ahead in all progressive laws & woman's enfranchisement about 20 yrs ago [has] stagnated ever since'.[1] She was hardly the first to notice the disjuncture between Australasian women's early achievement of voting rights and their struggle to realise the visions of economic and sexual equality that the more radical among them had long desired. In 1920, channelling a deeper disillusionment with the fruits of Australasia's age of experiments, her mentor, Vida Goldstein, exhausted by four attempts to become Australia's first female Federal parliamentarian (the milestone was not reached until 1943, ten years after New Zealand), wrote as much in the influential British weekly review *Time and Tide*. European and Americans, she admitted, 'outdistance[d] their Australian sisters in every department of social and political life'.[2] Echoing Goldstein's analysis of Australia's 'spineless' women's movement, the New Zealander Jessie Mackay made her 'début' in the magazine 'under the ban of apology'. Like Goldstein, Mackay's regrets were heightened by her interactions with battle-hardened Northern Hemisphere suffragists. While she believed decades of struggle had equipped them with the tools to transform society, Mackay bemoaned the fact that twenty-seven years after obtaining voting rights, 'the New Zealand woman is not only politically unorganised, but she is not politically alive'. A lifelong internationalist – as a teenager in rural Canterbury, she had written poetry on the 'Armenian question' – it was to Mackay's chagrin that 'every visiting feminist' threw women's lack of 'sex consciousness … in her teeth' when they toured the Dominion.[3]

By the 1920s, Franklin, Goldstein, and Mackay's sense of frustration, and the ease with which they tapped into transnational communication channels, was common in feminist circles. Their complaints were exaggerated for effect and exposed a political consciousness tethered to the English-speaking world. After all, until 1928 women in Britain were only partially enfranchised and, with few exceptions outside Europe and the Americas, would not enjoy national voting rights until after 1945. By the same token, Indigenous Australians' voting rights would remain opaque until 1965. Nevertheless, the interwar feminists felt a shared disappointment, born from the conviction that the proclamations of international leadership made on their behalf by Goldstein and Kate Sheppard two decades earlier heralded an era of Australasian influence on the world stage. Beginning with the rise of the organised suffrage campaigns in the mid-1880s, and ending before the first international women's movement's enforced hiatus at the outbreak of the First World War, this book has explained and qualified this sense of failure by detailing the limits, as well as the possibilities, of Australasian suffrage internationalism.

To do this, *Distant Sisters* has explored the relationships among women and organisations at the local, intercolonial, and international level. By examining the networks that allowed white Australasian women to envisage a future of international leadership after winning the vote, and eventually led them to issue heartfelt apologies in globally circulated publications, it has cast off the national fetters that have bound suffrage histories. Suffrage was unique among the global reform movements of the fin-de-siècle in that, unlike campaigns to promote peace and international arbitration, prohibit the trade in intoxicants, or halt sex trafficking, its demands were not inherently transnational. Instead, they were formulated and fought for in colonial and national jurisdictions. Nevertheless, as we have seen, women in the Australasian colonies saw themselves as united by their common disenfranchisement and built networks to expedite their path toward citizenship. These connections were both informal, as mid-nineteenth century activists like Mary Ann Müller sought assistance and recognition from British suffragists, and formal, as antipodean women joined mass-membership organisations that pursued global goals and aided members in their local struggles. As I have argued throughout, and as becomes apparent when considering suffrage history through multi-tiered organisations like the World's Woman's Christian Temperance Union (WCTU) and International Woman Suffrage Alliance (IWSA), a sense of scale is vital in unpicking the knot of suffragists' connections. In the fight for voting rights, as in most turn-of-the-century reform movements, local, national, and international struggles were imbricated and must be understood in unison. While this book is unlikely to dislodge the centrality of 'pioneering' women's enfranchisement to New Zealand and Australia's national mythologies, it nonetheless aims to encourage thinking below and beyond the level of the nation, as the suffragists did so readily over a century ago.[4]

International networks have by no means been absent from histories of women's enfranchisement in Australia and New Zealand. However, the scholarship occasioned by centenary celebrations between 1993 and 2008 tended to gesture at the importance of such connections, rather than investigating them in detail. These histories are products of their time, influenced by history's transnational turn but lacking the archival basis to trace networks beyond national borders. Reading personal papers and suffrage periodicals alongside the archives of mass-membership organisations with local, intercolonial, and international 'layers', this book has substantiated the range and significance of the Australasian suffragists' transnational connections and encounters. Still, the suffragists' paths to internationalism resist easy categorisation. For example, the arrival of the WCTU in Australia and New Zealand legitimised suffrage activism among middle-class women, and its rapid spread allowed for the easy exchange of literature and personnel between branches and across borders. Yet, while Australasian members came closest to fulfilling Frances Willard's sprawling Christian socialist vision, struggles over suffrage elsewhere in her 'woman's empire' prevented them from using the World's WCTU to share the secrets of their success. By the same token, the longstanding epistolary connections between Australasian suffragists and their British and American counterparts were seldom the products of the type of robust friendship thought to underpin the international women's movement.

Much of *Distant Sisters* concentrates on a cadre of settler activists. Yet, retreating from national histories need not elide the experiences of all but a few globetrotting elites. Tracing life stories remains an invaluable method of examining the filaments that linked Australasian feminists with their counterparts across the world. By working across state and national archives, this book has added new figures to a familiar pantheon: women like Madge Donohoe, Hannah Main, Emma Packe, and Mary Steadman Aldis, whose mobile activism meant their work was underestimated in both their homelands and their expatriate communities. More importantly, mobility and circulation were not the sole preserve of the privileged. Rather, such forces shaped the lives of everyone involved in the suffrage campaigns, whether or not they left their hometowns.[5] Peeling back the layers of a transnational organisation like the WCTU reveals a flow of texts, objects, and personnel that connected branch members to like-minded women across the world. Similar networks allowed the efflorescence of a vibrant press intimately linked to the suffrage campaigns. Despite the limits of women's advocacy publications as vectors for news about feminist activism outside Australasia, readers were still given the unmistakable impression that they constituted an important part of a worldwide women's movement.

Cross-border connections, then, were pervasive in the Australasian suffrage campaigns. However, while it is important to affirm their existence, we must not lose sight of their fragility. It has become a truism that women, marginalised in domestic politics, entered the international stage in search of solidarity, a sense of importance, and the chance to exercise leadership.[6] Many of the stories told in this book support that conclusion, yet they also emphasise that participation in the international arena was neither without friction nor an uncomplicated source of political and emotional solace. Maintaining international ties from the antipodes was, in Catherine Helen Spence's parlance, 'precious hard work'.[7] Belying the scope of her ambition, Sheppard found herself unsuited to the role of embodying enfranchised womanhood that was thrust on her in the United Kingdom. Unlike the more illustrious New Zealander, the Sydney schoolteacher Madge Donohoe thrived on the public stage and proved an assiduous networker. For all her sterling qualities, parochial infighting cut short her stint as a 'veteran representative' on the international circuit, severing Australia's strongest link with the IWSA.[8] Furthermore, as Mary Steadman Aldis' letter-writing campaign denouncing New Zealanders' complacency regarding the Contagious Diseases Act revealed, white women marginalised in colonial feminist circles advanced competing agendas through international networks, sowing the seeds of discord in the process.

Transnational and feminist historians alike have not often considered these messy stories, preferring to write 'success histories'. However, reckoning with the history of internationalism requires us to consider 'why some networks proved stronger than others' rather than 'taking the success of certain traditions for granted'.[9] Internationalism was, and remains, a process of becoming, and the forces impeding its development deserve as much attention as those facilitating its spread. As white, English-speaking, and predominantly Protestant 'neo-Europeans' who nevertheless lived far from the North Atlantic, Australian and New Zealand feminists occupied a liminal space in the international women's movement.[10] Unlike the indigenous women they (often obliviously) lived alongside and, indeed, most women outside feminism's Atlantic nexus, they were encouraged to join formal international endeavours such as the WCTU, IWSA, and International Council of Women (ICW). Yet, despite their similarities with the Euro-American elites that constituted these organisations, in the aftermath of enfranchisement, antipodean women never fulfilled the leading role that women like Sheppard and Goldstein had envisaged for them.

Australasian women's marginalisation from the international women's suffrage movement was as much a product of the structures that undergirded cross-border organising as individual idiosyncrasies. In an era when a new internationalism predicated on the nation state replaced the fuzzy idealism of mid-nineteenth-century friendship networks, feminists' inability to form national coalitions prevented them from making effective use of the ICW and IWSA. In New Zealand, this disorganisation was primarily a product of the colony's challenging geography and scattered population. Despite Goldstein and Elizabeth Webb Nicholls' hopes that Federation would elevate white women's status in domestic and international politics, Australian feminists were crippled by disunity. Although few women repudiated Federation with Rose Scott's furious intensity, still fewer built national organisations. Australian feminists were not alone in their ambivalent relationship with the Commonwealth. The parochialism that Goldstein believed had undermined Australia's status as a worldwide beacon for progressives, and which prevailed in the women's movement into the 1930s, demands a reassessment of national sentiment and the prevalence of provincial feeling across the country.[11] At the personal level, problems of distance and expense did not preclude Australasian women from appearing on the international stage, but they did mean every journey had to count. However much the IWSA's strict membership criteria or the World's WCTU's conservatism diminished antipodean women's global influence, the story might have been different, for example, had Sheppard thrilled London crowds and accepted offers to assume the World's suffrage superintendency, or had Nicholls returned to the international conference circuit before her seventieth birthday.

Acknowledging Australian and New Zealand feminists' difficult relationship with the international suffrage movement should not diminish their achievements. Although major women's international organisations met exclusively in the Northern Hemisphere until the Pan-Pacific Women's Association held its 1952 conference in Christchurch, Australasian women were often present at their pre-war gatherings, contributing in myriad ways to the development of each organisation's culture and politics. For WCTU members, the expression of their cross-border connections through quotidian acts like the communal reading of *Union Signal*, singing the temperance doxology, or observing the noontide prayer hour cemented their identities as internationalists. Furthermore, exchanges of instructional literature, news, and personnel, both at the branch level and centrally coordinated by the World's WCTU, built its antipodean chapters into formidable activist machines. Not for nothing was the union central to the fight for suffrage in all seven colonies, and it would take New Zealand to the brink of prohibition in 1919. While flaring only fleetingly, the Australasian women's advocacy press burnt bright: it was certainly more polyglot and longer lived than its Canadian and South African counterparts. These attributes ensured that, through the exchange system, antipodean stories briefly dominated the foreign columns in popular British and American women's periodicals. Individuals like Spence also forged careers as transnational activists, paving the way for a new generation of women like Franklin, Alice Henry, and May Manning to forgo the traditional pilgrimage to Britain in favour of new horizons in the United States.[12] Many more New Zealanders crossed the Tasman and settled in WCTU branches in the Australian colonies, bringing with them the experience of a successful suffrage campaign. Although they never met in person and rarely exchanged anything more than the necessary pleasantries, Sheppard remained a lifelong correspondent of ICW president Lady Ishbel Aberdeen, while Goldstein and Scott performed a similar service for Carrie Chapman Catt and the IWSA. Judged on whether they forged close friendships with overseas feminist leaders, antipodean women fell short, but as this book has argued, using friendship as a barometer of international connection elides the range of contributions the suffragists made to pre-war women's organisations.

As tensions within mass-membership organisations like the ICW and WCTU had long suggested, suffrage ultimately proved an unstable concept around which to organise a durable international movement. Even the specialist IWSA only thrived for a decade before the outbreak of war in 1914 ended 'the international first wave'.[13] When the Alliance reconvened in 1920, the enfranchisement of most British and American women severed the 'bond of political powerlessness' that once united its members and saw the organisation pivot toward the pursuit of equal citizenship.[14] This new focus on pay equality, married women's nationality rights, and peace activism appealed to Australasians' self-interest. Alongside their increased participation in established international women's organisations and new intergovernmental organisations like the League of Nations, Australians and New Zealanders drove the creation of regional bodies, which offered to those women able to travel genuine leadership opportunities and a chance to develop both their own voices and a new internationalist agenda.[15] Elsie Andrews, Amy Kane, Mary Seaton, and, significantly, the Māori leader Victoria Te Amohau Bennett in New Zealand, and Mary Bennett, Constance Cooke, Eleanor Moore, Bessie Rischbieth, Linda Littlejohn, and Jessie Street in Australia – all comfortable speaking on behalf of the nation – occupied the role Goldstein had envisaged for herself thirty years earlier. These interwar activists rose from the embers of the suffrage movements. Jessie Mackay, who served an apprenticeship under Sheppard in the Christchurch suffrage campaign, exemplified the link between the old and the new. Alongside Sheppard, she rebuilt the National Council of Women in 1918, then forged a career as a freelance writer, contributing articles on New Zealand to overseas periodicals and keeping *White Ribbon*'s readers abreast of international women's issues.[16] Despite the depths of her despair in 1920, Mackay longed for the day when 'the far-wandered reformer w[ould] again lay his flowers at the feet of New Zealand women'. Although she conceded that they had 'much to learn from the graduates in Dame Necessity's hard Old World School', she was convinced that New Zealanders had 'much to give when the linked hands of women hurl most of the old blatant necessities back into limbo. Resolute Canadian, strong South African, vivid Australian, Pan-Britannia needs us all!'[17]

Beyond the histories of suffrage and feminist activism in New Zealand and Australia, this book also casts new light on the international women's movement before the First World War. Building on the push to situate Australasian histories in their wider regional, imperial, and global contexts, it shows that such stories can also be used to better understand the operation of transnational reform movements. While the Pacific's 'neo-Europes' are usually appended to the standard, progressive Euro-American narrative of the pre-war international women's movement, considering Australasian women's forays on to the international stage reveals a more contingent history. Only by examining its antipodes, as well as its metropoles, can a comprehensive story of Western women's internationalism be written. Examining organisations like the World's WCTU and IWSA from their margins offers new insights about their politics as well as, crucially, the difficulties of international organisation. Reading the World's WCTU's records against antipodean branch archives reveals the degree to which it marginalised suffrage activism. In the same vein, the correspondence between Vida Goldstein and Rose Scott questions the periodisation and geographic limitation of the scholarship on debates about nationality in the international women's movement. As I have shown, it was in resolving the

'Australian question' – not in their discussions with national groups within the Hapsburg Empire – that the ICW and IWSA first codified their membership criteria. These organisations' decisions, made in concert with Australian women's groups, 'contributed in important ways to the globalization of strategies that shaped the relation between the international and the national'.[18]

In addition to stressing the value of an antipodean perspective, this book has displayed the utility of delving beneath as well as across colonial and national borders. Where the archives permit, I have demonstrated where Australian and New Zealand women fit within the emerging international women's suffrage movement, while also showing where this movement extended beyond a coterie of mobile settler elites and permeated the everyday lives of the women's movement's rank and file. By focusing as much on places as monolithic nations – colonial cities like Auckland and Adelaide, for example – and using the archives of 'layered' organisations like the ICW and WCTU that linked branch, region, nation, and globe, we can reach a closer understanding of how the suffragists fit within the wider world. Such an approach is becoming more common, yet much more remains to be done.[19] Unearthing local and regional histories of feminist internationalism from specific locales in the Americas, the north of England, or Central and Northern Europe will no doubt further complicate the existing narrative of the early international women's movement. So, too, would more work heeding Patricia Grimshaw's call for suffrage historians to reorient the field away from its Atlantic centres to decipher patterns at its Pacific frontiers.[20] We can anticipate that the resultant histories will not follow a linear or progressive narrative. By extending the field of vision to include individuals marginalised within mainstream feminist circles like Mary Steadman Aldis, as well as the usual cast of insiders, this book has illuminated the disruptive effects of cross-border networks as well as the lingering imperial feminism of the British that stunted the growth of a truly trenchant form of internationalism until after the First World War.

Whatever the obstacles impeding their thought and action beyond the colonial and national spheres before 1914, the Australasian suffragists' sense of hope and their desire to build cross-border connections cannot be diminished. From their actions, it was clear that they believed the suffrage struggle had multiple valences, which behoved them to either create or join networks channelling ideas, personnel, and money between regional and international allies alike. Their efforts, in spite of the costs of travel, as well as their compatriots' indifference to the national coalition building on which international activism increasingly rested, were extraordinary. They remind us of the power of solidarity and the value of patience, industry, and curiosity in creating and sustaining international networks, as well as the importance of forming everyday connections if international bonds are to thrive. Seeking suffrage internationalism required attending to the global and the local at the same time. Antipodean suffragists' commitment to this difficult task was a major accomplishment, even if they did not always celebrate it. This challenge confronts all forms of international outreach, not only at the fin-de-siècle, but also in our time.

Notes

1 Miles Franklin to Margaret Dreier Robins, 13 March 1924, in J. Roe (ed.), *My Congenials: Miles Franklin & Friends in Letters, Volume One 1879-1938* (Sydney: Angus and Robertson, 1993), p. 169; J. Roe, *Stella Miles Franklin: A Biography* (Sydney: Fourth Estate, 2008), p. 147.
2 *Time and Tide*, 27 May 1920, in D. Spender, *Time and Tide Wait for No Man* (London: Pandora Press, 1984), pp. 18–21. See M. Lake, '1914: Death of a nation', *History Australia*, 12:1 (2015), 21–2; Magarey, *Passions of the First Wave*, pp. 171–92; M. McKinnon, *The Broken Decade: Prosperity, Depression and Recovery in New Zealand, 1928-39* (Dunedin: Otago University Press, 2016), pp. 18–19.
3 *Time and Tide*, 10 December 1920, p. 631; M. Chapman et al. (eds), *Jessie Mackay: A Woman Before Her Time* (Geraldine: Kakahu Women's Division of Federated Farmers, 1997). This sense of discontentment with the fruits of women's enfranchisement, in particular its failure to transform society, was a near universal phenomenon among post-suffrage women's movements. See Adams, *Women and the Vote*, pp. 429–31.
4 On democratic governments and suffrage myth-making, see Edwards and Roces, 'Orienting the global women's suffrage movement', in Edwards and Roces (eds), *Women's Suffrage in Asia*, pp. 5–6.
5 See Ballantyne, *Webs of Empire*, pp. 277–82.
6 G. Sluga, 'Feminisms and twentieth-century internationalisms', in G. Sluga and P. Clavin (eds), *Internationalisms: A Twentieth Century History* (Cambridge: Cambridge University Press, 2017), pp. 61–2.
7 Magarey et al. (eds), *Ever Yours*, p. 230.
8 SLNSW, A2274/381, Madge Donohoe to Rose Scott, 16 October 1908.
9 K. Pickles, 'The obvious and the awkward: Postcolonialism and the British world', *New Zealand Journal of History*, 45:1 (2011), 97; M. Everard and M. Aerts, 'Forgotten intersections: Wilhelmina Drucker, early feminism, and the Dutch-Belgian connection', *Revue Belge de Philologie et d'Histoire*, 77:2 (1999), 461–2.
10 Rupp, *Worlds of Women*, p. 48.
11 SLNSW, A2272/1017–18, Carrie Chapman Catt to Scott, 18 May 1909. On Australians' 'civic indolence', see Atkinson, 'The struggle against a single Australia', 262–79; Atkinson, *The Europeans in Australia*; Holbrook, 'What sort of nation', 1–10.

12 Rees, 'Bursting with new ideas', 382–98.
13 Sluga, 'Feminisms and twentieth-century internationalisms', p. 63.
14 Rupp, *Worlds of Women*, p. 12.
15 See especially Paisley, *Glamour in the Pacific*; Paisley, *Loving Protection*; Woollacott, 'Australian women's metropolitan activism', pp. 207–22; Woollacott, 'Inventing Commonwealth and pan-Pacific feminisms', 425–48.
16 H. Roberts, 'Jessie Mackay', *Te Ara: the Encyclopedia of New Zealand*, http://www.TeAra.govt.nz/en/biographies/2m15/mackay-jessie (accessed 7 December 2018).
17 *Time and Tide*, 10 December 1920, p. 631; 15 July 1921, p. 679.
18 Zimmermann, 'Feminist inter/national politics', 107.
19 See, for example, Bush and Purvis (eds), 'Connecting women's histories'; Midgley et al. (eds), *Women in Transnational History*.
20 Grimshaw, 'Women's suffrage in New Zealand revisited', pp. 25–41. My essay comparing Utah women's rise to prominence in American and international feminist circles after the 1893 Chicago World's Fair with New South Wales women's chequered pre-war internationalism steps in this direction, as does Ana Stevenson's work on suffrage print culture. Keating, 'International activism after the fair', pp. 192–212; Stevenson, 'Imagining women's suffrage', 638–66.

Bibliography

Primary sources

Archives (Australia)

State Library of New South Wales, Sydney

A871-1052	Sir Henry Parkes Papers, 1833-96.
A2260-2284	Scott Family Papers, c. 1790-1924.
AL24	Letters from Mary Lee to Lady Windeyer, 1891-92.
AW44	Prospectus relating to the monthly journal, the *Woman's Voice*, 1905.
M2291-2314	Collections held by the Fawcett Library relating to Australia and New Zealand, 1858-1967.
MLB693	Women's Literary Society Minute Book, 1892-93, with Annual Reports 1893, 1896.
MLMSS38	Scott Family manuscript and pictorial material, 1777-1925.
MLMSS186	Windeyer Family Papers, 1829-1943.
MLMSS364	Miles Franklin Papers, 1841-1954.
MLMSS2109	Mary Booth Papers, 1869-1957.
MLMSS2160 ADD-ON 1317	United Associations of Women Further Records, 1930-78.
MLMSS3641	Woman's Christian Temperance Union of New South Wales Records, 1882-1978.
MLMSS3739	National Council of Women of New South Wales Records, 1895-1976.
MLMSS7312	Rose Scott Journal, 1889-93.
PXA1023	Scott Family Collection of Studio Portrait Photographs, c. 1865-1921.
SV/80	*Just Out of Reach* (sketch by B. E. Minns), 1891.
Z396.3/S	Papers on Women's Suffrage Compiled by Rose Scott, 1884-1902.

Women's College Archive, University of Sydney, Sydney

SC Box 1	Louisa Macdonald Papers, 1891-1907.

State Library of South Australia, Adelaide

PRG88	Catherine Helen Spence Papers, 1866-1910.
SRG186	Woman's Christian Temperance Union Records, 1886-1999.
SRG690	Women's League, Minutebook and Papers, 1895-97.

University of Melbourne Archives, Melbourne

ACC101/85   Woman's Christian Temperance Union of Victoria Records, 1887–1999.

Archives (New Zealand)

Archives New Zealand, Wellington

AGGO 8333   Department of Internal Affairs, Central Filing System, c. 1840–c. 1982.

Auckland Public Library, Auckland

920 ALD   A. L. Aldis, 'William Steadman Aldis: A brief biography', 1940.

University of Auckland Library, Auckland

MSS2009/6   Minutes and other records of the Auckland Women's Political League, 1892–1916.

Auckland War Memorial Museum, Auckland

MS94   Amey Daldy Letters, 1901–5.

Alexander Turnbull Library, Wellington

fMS-Papers-4923   Waitangi Foundation: Bringing the Records Home Fellowship Papers, 1892–1919.

MS-Group-0033   Sir John Hall Papers, 1836–1907.

MS-Group-79-057   New Zealand Women's Christian Temperance Union Records, 1886–*c.* 1970.

MS-Group-0225   National Council of Women of New Zealand Records, 1896–2007.

MS-Papers-1376   Hilda Kate Lovell-Smith Papers, 1886–1973.

MS-Papers-3969   International Council of Women: Correspondence relating to National Council of Women of New Zealand, 1896–1926.

MS-Papers-4331   Greta Faulbaum Papers relating to International Council of Women Conference, Berlin, 1904.

PER DAY   Prospectus of the Daybreak Newspaper Company, 1895.

Canterbury Museum, Christchurch

ARC176.53   Catherine (Kate) Wilson Sheppard Papers, 1869–1938.

ARC1992.50   Catherine (Kate) Wilson Sheppard (nee Malcolm) later Lovell-Smith Papers, 1893–1920.

ARC2008.144   New Zealand Women's Christian Temperance Union Collection.

Hocken Collections, University of Otago, Dunedin

ARC-0021　　　　　　Lady Anna Stout Papers, 1831–1930.

ARC-0379　　　　　　Catherine Henrietta Elliot Fulton (nee Valpy) Papers, 1849–1919.

Archives (United Kingdom)

British Library, London

Add.MS47449–47455　　Elizabeth C. Wolstenholme Elmy Papers, 1881–1914.

Girton College Library, Cambridge

P396　　　　　　　　Blackburn Collection.

Women's Library, London School of Economics, London

2NWS　　　　　　　Records of the National Union of Women's Suffrage Societies, 1896–1919.

3BGF　　　　　　　British Committee of the Continental and General Federation for Abolition of Government Regulation of Prostitution Records, 1874–1915.

3JBL　　　　　　　　Josephine Butler Letters Collection, c. 1816–1935.

Manchester Libraries, Information and Archives, Manchester

GB127.M50　　　　　Papers of Millicent Garrett Fawcett, 1871–1919.

Archives (United States)

New York Public Library, New York

MSSCol2703　　　　　Schwimmer-Lloyd Collection, 1852–1980.

Newspapers and periodicals (Australia)

Advertiser (Adelaide)
Alliance and Temperance News (Adelaide)
Argus (Melbourne)
Australian Christian Commonwealth (Adelaide)
Australian Home Journal (Sydney)
Australian News of Ladies' Politics (Sydney)
Australian Woman (Sydney)
Australian Woman's Sphere (Melbourne)
Border Watch (Mount Gambier)
Bulletin (Sydney)
Brisbane Courier
Christian Colonist (Adelaide)

Cosmos (Sydney)
Daily Telegraph (Sydney)
Dawn (Sydney)
Evening Journal (Adelaide)
Evening News (Sydney)
Freeman's Journal (Sydney)
Home Queen (Sydney)
Ladies' Own Paper (Sydney)
Mercury (Hobart)
Morning Bulletin (Rockhampton)
Newcastle Herald and Miners' Advocate
New Idea (Sydney)
Our Federation (Adelaide)
Queenslander (Brisbane)
Quiz and the Lantern (Adelaide)
Republican (Sydney)
South Australian Register (Adelaide)
Southern Times (Bunbury)
Standard (Sydney)
Sunday Times (Sydney)
Sydney Morning Herald
Table Talk (Melbourne)
Telegraph (Brisbane)
West Australian (Perth)
White Ribbon Signal (Sydney)
Woman's Suffrage Journal (Sydney)
Woman's Voice (1894–95) (Sydney)
Woman's Voice (1905) (Sydney)
Worker (Brisbane)

Newspapers and periodicals (France)

Figaro (Paris)

Newspapers and periodicals (Germany)

Der Tag (Berlin)

Newspapers and periodicals (New Zealand)

Auckland Star
Bay of Plenty Times (Tauranga)
Daily Southern Cross (Auckland)
Daybreak (Wellington)

Evening Post (Wellington)
Evening Star (Dunedin)
Hawke's Bay Herald (Napier)
Lyttelton Times
New Zealand Herald (Auckland)
Oamaru Mail
Otago Daily Times (Dunedin)
Press (Christchurch)
Prohibitionist (Christchurch)
Star (Christchurch)
Wanganui Chronicle
White Ribbon (Christchurch)

Newspapers and periodicals (Netherlands)

De Telegraaf (Amsterdam)
Evolutie: Veertiendaagsch Blad voor de Vrouw (Amsterdam)
Het Nieuws van den Dag (Amsterdam)
Jus Suffragii (Rotterdam)
Rotterdamsch Nieuwsblad (Rotterdam)

Newspapers and periodicals (United Kingdom)

Chronicle of the London Missionary Society
Dawn (London)
Dundee Courier
Englishwoman's Review (London)
Ethical World (London)
Fortnightly Review (London)
Journal: Official organ pro tem of the British Women's Temperance Association (London)
Lady's Realm (London)
Morning Post (London)
Personal Rights Journal (London)
Scottish Women's Temperance News (Edinburgh)
Sentinel (London)
Shafts (London)
Time and Tide (London)
Woman's Herald (London)
Woman's Signal (London)

Newspapers and periodicals (United States)

Boston Post
Harper's New Monthly Magazine (New York)

New York Times
New York Tribune
San Francisco Chronicle
Union Signal (Evanston, IL)
Woman's Journal (Boston)
Woman Suffrage Leaflet (Boston)
Woman's Tribune (Beatrice, NE)

Published official papers (Australia)

Commonwealth of Australia, Parliamentary Debates, House of Representatives

Published official papers (New Zealand)

Appendices to the Journals of the House of Representatives
New Zealand Parliamentary Debates

Published primary sources (International Council of Women)

International Council of Women, Report of Transactions of the Second Quinquennial Meeting. London: T. Fisher Unwin, 1900.
Memorandum on the Meeting of the Executive Committee of the International Council of Women. London: Reform Press, 1901.
International Council of Women, Report for 1907–1908. Aberdeen: Rosemount Press, 1908.
International Council of Women, Report of Transactions during the Third Quinquennial Term Terminating with the Third Quinquennial Meeting, Volume I. Boston: International Council of Women, 1909.
International Council of Women, Report of Transactions during the Third Quinquennial Term Terminating with the Third Quinquennial Meeting, Volume II. Boston: International Council of Women, 1909.
International Council of Women, First Annual Report of the Fifth Quinquennial Period 1909–1910. Berlin: Langenscheidtsche Buchdruckerei, 1910.
International Council of Women, Report of Transactions of the Fourth Quinquennial Meeting. London: Constable & Co., 1910.
International Council of Women, Third Annual Report of the Fifth Quinquennial Period 1911–1912. Berlin: Langenscheidtsche Buchdruckerei, 1912.
International Council of Women, Fourth Annual Report of the Fifth Quinquennial Period 1912–1913. Berlin: Langenscheidtsche Buchdruckerei, 1913.
International Council of Women, Report on the Quinquennial Meetings, Rome 1914. Karlsruhe: G. Braunsche Hofbuchdruckerei und Verlag, 1914.
International Council of Women, Report on the Quinquennial Meeting, Kristiania 1920. Aberdeen: Rosemount Press, 1920.

BIBLIOGRAPHY

Published primary sources (International Woman Suffrage Alliance)

Report, First International Woman Suffrage Conference. New York: International Woman Suffrage Headquarters, 1902.
Report, Second and Third Conferences of the International Womanhood Suffrage Alliance. Copenhagen: Bianco Luno, 1906.
The International Woman Suffrage Alliance, Report of Fourth Conference. Amsterdam: F. van Rossen, 1908.
International Woman Suffrage Alliance, Report of the Fifth Conference and First Quinquennial. London: Samuel Sidders & Co., 1909.
The International Woman Suffrage Alliance, Report of Sixth Congress. London: Women's Printing Society, 1911.
The International Woman Suffrage Alliance, Report of Seventh Congress. Manchester: Percy Brothers, 1913.

Published primary sources (Woman's Christian Temperance Union)

Minutes of the National Woman's Christian Temperance Union at the Thirteenth Annual Meeting. Chicago: Woman's Temperance Publication Association, 1886.
Minutes of the New Zealand Women's Christian Temperance Union at the First Annual Meeting. Wellington: Lyon & Blair, 1886.
Second & Third Years Report of the Women's Christian Temperance Union of South Australia. Adelaide: T. S. Carey & Co., 1888.
Ten Reasons Why the Women of New Zealand Should Get the Vote. Christchurch: n.p., 1888.
Minutes of First Annual Convention of the Woman's Christian Temperance Union of South Australia, Held in Adelaide, August 13, 1889. Adelaide: George Hassell, 1890.
Report of the National Women's Christian Temperance Union of New Zealand Fifth Annual Meeting. Dunedin: Munro, Hutchinson, & Co, 1890.
The World's Woman's Christian Temperance Union. Chicago: World's Woman's Christian Temperance Union, 1890.
Minutes of the National Woman's Christian Temperance Union at the Eighteenth Annual Meeting. Chicago: Woman's Temperance Publishing Association, 1891.
Sixteen Reasons for Supporting Woman's Suffrage. Christchurch: Smith, Anthony, Sellars & Co., 1891.
The Woman's Christian Temperance Union of Australasia, Minutes & Proceedings of First Intercolonial Woman's Christian Temperance Union Convention. Melbourne: J. J. Howard, 1891.
Is It Right? Christchurch: Smith, Anthony, Sellars & Co., 1892.
Minutes of Fourth Annual Convention of the Woman's Christian Temperance Union of South Australia. Adelaide: Hussey & Gillingham, 1892.
Sixteen Reasons for Supporting Woman's Suffrage. Adelaide: Holden & Strutton, 1892.
Minutes of Fifth Annual Convention of the Woman's Christian Temperance Union of South Australia. Adelaide: Vardon and Pritchard, 1893.

Minutes of the Second Biennial Convention of the World's Woman's Christian Temperance Union. Chicago: Woman's Temperance Publishing Association, 1893.

Australasian Woman's Christian Temperance Union, Minutes of the Second Triennial Convention. Sydney: n.p., 1894.

Eighth Annual Report of the Adelaide Woman's Christian Temperance Union. Adelaide: G. Hassell & Son, 1894.

Minutes of Sixth Annual Convention of the Woman's Christian Temperance Union of South Australia. Adelaide: G. Hassell & Son, 1894.

Minutes of the New Zealand Woman's Christian Temperance Union at the Ninth Annual Meeting. Invercargill: Ward, Wilson and Co., 1894.

Minutes of the Third Biennial Convention and Executive Committee Meetings of the World's Woman's Christian Temperance Union. London: White Ribbon Company, 1895.

Woman's Christian Temperance Union of New South Wales Annual Report of the Fourteenth Convention. Bathurst: National Advocate, 1896.

Report of the Fourth Biennial Convention and Minutes of the Executive Committee Meetings of the World's Woman's Christian Temperance Union. London: White Ribbon Company, 1897.

Report of the National Woman's Christian Temperance Union at the Twenty-Fourth Annual Meeting. Chicago: Woman's Temperance Publishing Association, 1897.

Woman's Christian Temperance Union of Australasia, Minutes of the Third Triennial Convention. Adelaide: Shawyer & Co., 1897.

Report of the National Woman's Christian Temperance Union at the Twenty-Fifth Annual Meeting. Chicago: Woman's Temperance Publishing Association, 1898.

Twenty-Fifth Annual Meeting of Woman's Christian Temperance Union of the State of Indiana. n.c.: n.p., 1898.

Woman's Christian Temperance Union of South Australia, Minutes of Eleventh Annual Convention. Adelaide: A. & E. Lewis, 1899.

Report of the Fifth Biennial Convention of the World's Woman's Christian Temperance Union. London: White Ribbon Company, 1900.

Woman's Christian Temperance Union of Australasia, Minutes of the Fourth Triennial Convention. Adelaide: Hussey & Gillingham, 1900.

Woman's Christian Temperance Union of New South Wales, Annual Report of the 20th Convention. Sydney: n.p., 1902.

Australasian Woman's Christian Temperance Union, Minutes of the 5th Triennial Convention. Melbourne: Green & Fargher, 1903.

Report (Illustrated) of the [Sixth] Convention of the World's Woman's Christian Temperance Union. London: The Union, 1903.

Australasian Woman's Christian Temperance Union, Minutes of the 6th Triennial Convention. Brisbane: Outridge Printing Co., 1906.

Report of the Seventh Convention of the World's Woman's Christian Temperance Union. Evanston: Woman's Temperance Publishing Association, 1906.

Report to the Eighth Convention of the World's Woman's Christian Temperance Union. London: John Heywood, 1910.

Report of the Ninth Convention of the World's Woman's Christian Temperance Union. London: White Ribbon Company, 1913.

BIBLIOGRAPHY

Published primary sources (Womanhood Suffrage League of New South Wales)

Womanhood Suffrage League of New South Wales, Seventh Annual Report and Balance Sheet for the Year ending June 1st, 1898. Sydney: Christian World Printing and Publishing House, 1898.
Womanhood Suffrage League of New South Wales, Ninth Annual Report and Balance Sheet for the Year ending June 1st, 1900. Sydney: John Sands Printer, 1900.
Womanhood Suffrage League of New South Wales, Tenth Annual Report and Balance Sheet for the Year ending June 1st, 1901. Sydney: S. D. Townsend & Co. Printers, 1901.

Other published primary sources

A Letter of Earnest Appeal and Warning from Josephine E. Butler to the Members of the British, Continental and General Federation for the Abolition of the State Regulation of Prostitution. London: Pewtress & Co., 1895.
A Second Letter of Appeal and Warning from Josephine E. Butler to Members of the British, Continental, and General Federation for the Abolition of the State Regulation of Prostitution. London: Pewtress & Co., 1895.
English Opinion Evoked by the Recent Resolution of the Auckland Women's Liberal League. Auckland: H. Brett, 1896.
Englishwoman's Year Book 1903. London: Adam & Charles Black, 1903.
Fédération Britannique, Continentale et Générale Cinquième Congrès International. Geneva: Secrétariat Général de la Fédération, 1890.
Fémmina. An Appeal to the Men of New Zealand. Nelson: J. Hounsell, 1869.
Fourteen Reasons for Supporting Women's Suffrage. London: National Union of Women's Suffrage Societies, c. 1913.
Hearing before the Select Committee on Woman Suffrage, United States Senate. Washington, DC: Government Printing Office, 1902.
National Council of Women: Report of the Interstate Conference. Melbourne: A. H. Macdonald, 1905.
Official Report of the National Australasian Convention Debates, First Session: Adelaide 1897. Sydney: University of Sydney Library, 1999.
Report of Meeting on 'Proportional Representation,' or Effective Voting, held at River House, Chelsea. London: John Bale & Sons, 1894.
Report of the Women's Suffrage League of South Australia. Adelaide: W. K. Thomas & Co, 1894.
South Australian Woman's Suffrage League. Report, 1891. Adelaide: G. Hassell, 1891.
Twenty-Fourth Annual Report of the Ladies National Association for the Abolition of Government Regulation of Vice for the Years 1894 and 1895. London: J. W. Arrowsmith, 1896.

Secondary sources

Published

Ackermann, J. A. The World through a Woman's Eyes. Chicago: Woman's Temperance Publishing Association, 1896.

BIBLIOGRAPHY

———. *Australia from a Woman's Point of View*. London: Cassell & Company, 1913.
Adams, J. *Women and the Vote: A World History*. Oxford: Oxford University Press, 2014.
Allen, J. 'The "feminisms" of the early women's movements, 1850–1920.' *Refractory Girl*, 17 (1979), 10–16.
———. *Rose Scott: Vision and Revision in Feminism*. Melbourne: Oxford University Press, 1994.
Anderson, B. *Joyous Greetings: The First International Women's Movement 1830–1860*. Oxford: Oxford University Press, 2000.
———. *Imagined Communities: Reflections on the Origins and Spread of Nationalism*, rev. edn. London: Verso, 2006.
Anderson, W. 'Liberal intellectuals as Pacific supercargo: White Australian masculinity and racial thought on the boarder-lands.' *Australian Historical Studies*, 46:3 (2015), 425–39.
Arnold, R. 'Some Australasian aspects of New Zealand life, 1890–1913.' *New Zealand Journal of History*, 4:1 (1970), 54–76.
———. 'The Australasian peoples and their world, 1888–1915.' In *Tasman Relations: New Zealand and Australia, 1788–1888*, edited by K. Sinclair, 52–70. Auckland: Auckland University Press, 1987.
———. *New Zealand's Burning: The Settlers' World in the Mid 1880s*. Wellington: Victoria University Press, 1994.
Atkinson, A. 'Federation, democracy and the struggle against a single Australia.' *Australian Historical Studies*, 44:2 (2013), 262–79.
———. *The Europeans in Australia, Volume 3: Nation*. Sydney: UNSW Press, 2014.
Bain, W. S. *The International Council of Women. The Berlin Congress*. Christchurch: Lyttelton Times Company, 1904.
Baker, J. 'Australian women journalists and the "pretence of equality."' *Labour History*, 108 (2015), 1–16.
Bakewell, R. H. 'New Zealand under female franchise.' *Nineteenth Century*, 35 (February 1894), 268–75.
Ballantyne, T. *Orientalism and Race: Aryanism in the British Empire*. New York: Palgrave, 2002.
———. 'Rereading the archive and opening up the nation state: Colonial knowledge in South Asia and beyond.' In *After the Imperial Turn: Thinking with and Through the Nation*, edited by A. Burton, 102–24. Durham: Duke University Press, 2003.
———. 'The state, politics, and power, 1769–1893.' In *The New Oxford History of New Zealand*, edited by G. Byrnes, 99–124. Melbourne: Oxford University Press, 2009.
———. 'Reading the newspaper in colonial Otago.' *Journal of New Zealand Studies*, 12 (2011), 47–63.
———. *Webs of Empire: Locating New Zealand's Colonial Past*. Wellington: Bridget Williams Books, 2012.
———. 'Mobility, empire, colonisation.' *History Australia*, 11:2 (2014), 7–37.
———. *Entanglements of Empire: Missionaries, Māori, and the Question of the Body*. Auckland: Auckland University Press, 2015.
———. 'From colonial collection to tribal knowledge base: Herries Beattie, Ngāi Tahu Whānui and the many lives of an archive.' *Journal of Colonialism and Colonial History*, 20:2 (2019), 1–29.

BIBLIOGRAPHY

Ballantyne, T. and A. Burton. 'The politics of intimacy in an age of empire.' In *Moving Subjects: Gender, Mobility, and Intimacy in an Age of Global Empire*, edited by T. Ballantyne and A. Burton, 1–28. Chicago: University of Illinois Press, 2009.

Ballara, A. 'Wāhine rangatira: Māori women of rank and their role in the women's Kotahitanga movement of the 1890s.' *New Zealand Journal of History*, 27:2 (1993), 127–39.

Barnes, F. *New Zealand's London: A Colony and its Metropolis*. Auckland: Auckland University Press, 2012.

Barrow, M. 'Teetotal feminists: Temperance leadership and the campaign for women's suffrage.' In *A Suffrage Reader: Charting Directions in British Suffrage History*, edited by C. Eustance, J. Ryan, and L. Ugolini, 69–89. London: Leicester University Press, 2000.

Barrow, R. J. 'Rape on the railway: Women, safety, and moral panic in Victorian newspapers.' *Journal of Victorian Culture*, 20:3 (2015), 341–66.

Bashford, A. 'On nations and states: a reflection on "Thinking the Empire Whole."' *History Australia*, 16:4 (2019), 638–41.

Bayly, C. A. 'Informing empire and nation: Publicity, propaganda and the press 1880–1920.' In *Information, Media and Power through the Ages*, edited by H. Morgan, 179–98. Dublin: University College Dublin Press, 2001.

Beers, L. 'Feminism, internationalism and the Women's International League for Peace and Freedom.' *History & Policy*. www.historyandpolicy.org/dialogues/discussions/women-peace-and-transnational-activism-a-century-on (accessed 9 July 2018).

Belich, J. *Paradise Reforged: A History of the New Zealanders from the 1880s to the Year 2000*. Auckland: Allen Lane, 2001.

———. *Replenishing the Earth: The Settler Revolution and the Rise of the Anglo-World, 1783–1939*. Oxford: Oxford University Press, 2009.

Bellanta, M. 'Rethinking the 1890s.' In *The Cambridge History of Australia, Volume 1: Indigenous and Colonial Australia*, edited by A. Bashford and S. Macintyre, 218–41. Melbourne: Cambridge University Press, 2013.

Berger, S. and S. Scalmer. 'The transnational activist: An introduction.' In *The Transnational Activist: Transformations and Comparisons from the Anglo-World Since the Nineteenth Century*, edited by S. Berger and S. Scalmer, 1–30. Cham: Palgrave Macmillan, 2018.

Berkovitch, N. *From Motherhood to Citizenship: Women's Rights and International Organizations*. Baltimore: The Johns Hopkins University Press, 1999.

———. 'The emergence and transformation of the international women's movement.' In *Constructing World Culture: International Nongovernmental Organisations Since 1875*, edited by J. Boli and G. M. Thomas, 100–26. Stanford: Stanford University Press, 1999.

Berry, F. '"Home allies": Female networks, tensions, and conflicted loyalties in India and Van Diemen's Land, 1826–1849.' *Journal of World History*, 26:4 (2015), 757–84.

Binney, J., with V. O'Malley. 'The quest for survival, 1890–1920.' In *Tangata Whenua: An Illustrated History*, edited by A. Anderson, J. Binney, and A. Harris, 290–317. Wellington: Bridget Williams Books, 2014.

Bishop, C. 'Women on the move: Gender, money-making and mobility in mid-nineteenth-century Australasia.' *History Australia*, 11:2 (2014), 38–59.

———. *Minding her own Business: Colonial Businesswomen in Sydney*. Sydney: NewSouth, 2015.

Blackburn, H. *Women's Suffrage: A Record of the Women's Suffrage Movement in the British Isles*. London: Williams & Norgate, 1902.
Bohlmann, R. E. '"Our 'house beautiful'": The Woman's Temple and the WCTU effort to establish place and identity in downtown Chicago, 1887-1898.' *Journal of Women's History*, 11:2 (1999), 110-34.
Boisseau, T. J. 'Forging the transnational out of the international: Feminist internationalism at world's fairs and international exhibitions.' In *Women in International and Universal Exhibitions 1876-1937*, edited by R. Rogers and M. Boussahba-Bravard, 234-54. Oxford: Routledge, 2018.
Bomford, J. M. *Vida Goldstein: That Dangerous and Persuasive Woman*. Melbourne: Melbourne University Press, 1993.
Bones, H. *The Expatriate Myth: New Zealand Writers and the Colonial World*. Dunedin: Otago University Press, 2018.
Bordin, R. *Woman and Temperance: The Quest for Power and Liberty, 1873-1900*. Philadelphia: Temple University Press, 1981.
———. *Frances Willard: A Biography*. Chapel Hill: University of North Carolina Press, 1986.
Bosch, M. 'Colonial dimensions of Dutch women's suffrage: Aletta Jacobs' travel letters from Africa and Asia, 1911-1912.' *Journal of Women's History*, 11:2 (1999), 8-34.
Bosch, M., with A. Kloosterman (eds). *Politics and Friendship: Letters from the International Woman Suffrage Alliance, 1902-1942*. Columbus: Ohio State University Press, 1990.
Botting, E. H., C. C. Wilkerson, and E. N. Kozlow. 'Wollstonecraft as international feminist meme.' *Journal of Women's History*, 26:2 (2014), 13-38.
Brett, A. 'Colonial and provincial separation movements in Australia and New Zealand, 1856-65.' *Journal of Imperial and Commonwealth History*, 47:1 (2019), 51–75.
Brookes, B. 'A weakness for strong subjects: The women's movement and sexuality.' *New Zealand Journal of History*, 27:2 (1993), 140-56.
———. *A History of New Zealand Women*. Wellington: Bridget Williams Books, 2016.
Brookes, B., A. Cooper, and R. Law (eds). *Sites of Gender: Women, Men & Modernity in Southern Dunedin, 1890-1939*. Auckland: Auckland University Press, 2003.
Brooks, C. and G. Simpkin. *A Bibliography of Articles Published in the White Ribbon, the Official Organ of the New Zealand Women's Christian Temperance Union 1895-1919*. Wellington: National Library of New Zealand, 1975.
Brown, L., B. de Crespigny, M. P. Harris, K. K. Thomas, and P. N. Watson (eds). *A Book of South Australia: Women in the First Hundred Years*. Adelaide: Women's Centenary Council of SA, 1936.
Buhle, M. J. *Women and American Socialism, 1870-1920*. Urbana: University of Illinois Press, 1981.
Bunkle, P. 'The origins of the women's movement in New Zealand: The Woman's Christian Temperance Union, 1885-1895.' In *Women in New Zealand Society*, edited by P. Bunkle and B. Hughes, 55-68. Auckland: Allen and Unwin, 1980.
Burton, A. *Burdens of History: British Feminists, Indian Women, and Imperial Culture, 1865-1915*. Chapel Hill: University of North Carolina Press, 1994.

Burton, A. and I. Hofmeyr. 'The spine of empire? Books and the imperial commons.' In *Ten Books that Shaped the British Empire: Creating an Imperial Commons*, edited by A. Burton and I. Hofmeyr, 1–28. Durham: Duke University Press, 2014.

Bush, B. and J. Purvis (eds). 'Connecting women's histories: The local and the global.' Special issue, *Women's History Review*, 25:4 (2016).

Butler, J. E. *Personal Reminiscences of a Great Crusade*. London: Horace Marshall & Son, 1896.

Butterss, P. 'Building literary Adelaide, 1836–1860.' *Journal of Australian Studies*, 39:3 (2015), 344–61.

Caine, B. 'Beatrice Webb and the "woman question."' *History Workshop Journal*, 14:1 (1982), 23–44.

———. 'Vida Goldstein and the English militant campaign.' *Women's History Review*, 2:3 (1993), 363–76.

———. 'International links.' In *Australian Feminism: A Companion*, edited by B. Caine, M. Gatens, E. Grahame, J. Larbalestier, S. Watson, and E. Webby, 158–67. Melbourne: Oxford University Press, 1998.

———. 'Feminism, journalism, and public debate.' In *Women and Literature in Britain 1800–1900*, edited by J. Shattock, 99–118. Cambridge: Cambridge University Press, 2001.

Camiscioli, E. and J. H. Quataert. 'Editorial note: Suffrage and beyond: Celebrating women's history.' *Journal of Women's History*, 32:1 (2020), 7–10.

Campo, N. and M. Lake. 'International activism and organisations.' *The Encyclopedia of Women & Leadership in Twentieth-Century Australia*. www.womenaustralia.info/leaders/biogs/WLE0200b.htm (accessed 27 August 2018).

Carey, J. '"Wanted! A real white Australia": The women's movement, whiteness and the settler colonial project, 1900–1940.' In *Studies in Settler Colonialism: Politics, Identity and Culture*, edited by F. Bateman and L. Pilkington, 122–39. Basingstoke: Palgrave Macmillan, 2011.

Carlier, J. 'A forgotten instance of women's international organising: The transnational feminist networks of the Women's Progressive Society (1890) and the International Women's Union (1893–1898).' In *Gender History in a Transnational Perspective: Biographies, Networks, Gender Orders*, edited by O. Janz and D. Schönpflug, 101–26. New York: Berghahn, 2014.

'Census: 1871–1916.' *Statistics New Zealand*. www.stats.govt.nz/browse_for_stats/snapshots-of-nz/digitised-collections/census-collection (accessed 5 May 2018).

Chapman, H. 'The New Zealand campaign against Kate Marsden, traveller to Siberia.' *New Zealand Slavonic Journal* 34 (2000), 123–40.

Chapman, M., P. O'Leary, G. Talbot, B. Lyon, and J. Goodwin (eds). *Jessie Mackay: A Woman Before Her Time*. Geraldine: Kakahu Women's Division of Federated Farmers, 1997.

Clark, C. and M. Ledger-Lomas. 'The Protestant international.' In *Religious Internationals in the Modern World: Globalization and Faith Communities since 1750*, edited by A. Green and V. Viaene, 23–52. New York: Palgrave Macmillan, 2012.

Clarke, P. *Pen Portraits: Women Writers and Journalists in Nineteenth Century Australia*. Sydney: Allen and Unwin, 1988.

Clarsen, G. *Eat My Dust: Early Women Motorists*. Baltimore: Johns Hopkins University Press, 2008.

———. 'Gender and mobility: Historicizing the terms.' In *Mobility in History: The State of the Art in the History of Transport, Traffic and Mobility*, edited by G. Mom, G. Pirie, and L. Tissot, 123–8. Neuchatel: Editions Alphil, Presses Universitaires Suisses, 2009.

———. 'Revisiting "Driving While Black": Racialized automobilities in a settler colonial context.' *Mobility in History*, 8:1 (2017), 51–60.

Coleborne, C. 'Mobility stopped in its tracks: Institutional narratives and the mobile in the Australian and New Zealand colonial world, 1870s–1900s.' *Transfers*, 5:3 (2015), 87–103.

Coleman, D. (ed.). *Women Writing Home, 1700–1920, Volume 2: Australia*. London: Pickering & Chatto, 2006.

Coleman, J. 'Apprehending possibilities: Tracing the emergence of feminist consciousness in nineteenth-century New Zealand.' *Women's Studies International Forum*, 31:5 (2008), 464–73.

———. *Polly Plum: A Firm and Earnest Woman's Advocate, Mary Ann Colclough 1836–1885*. Dunedin: Otago University Press, 2017.

Coleman, P. J. *The Antipodean Connection: New Zealand Liberalism and American Progressivism*. Lawrence: University Press of Kansas, 1987.

Coney, S. *Every Girl: A Social History of Women and the YWCA in Auckland*. Auckland: Auckland YWCA, 1986.

———. *Standing in the Sunshine: A History of New Zealand Women Since They Won the Vote*. Auckland: Viking, 1993.

Cookson, J. 'How British? Local government in New Zealand to *c.* 1930.' *New Zealand Journal of History*, 41:2 (2007), 143–60.

Cooper, A., E. Olssen, K. Thomlinson, and R. Law. 'The landscape of gender politics: Place, people and two mobilisations.' In *Sites of Gender: Women, Men & Modernity in Southern Dunedin, 1890–1939*, edited by B. Brookes, A. Cooper, and R. Law, 15–49. Auckland: Auckland University Press, 2003.

Cooper, J. 'In the beginning were words: Aboriginal people and the franchise.' *Journal of Australian Studies*, 42:4 (2018), 428–44.

Coote, A. 'Out from the legend's shadow: Re-thinking national feeling in colonial Australia.' *Journal of Australian Colonial History*, 10:2 (2008), 103–22.

Cordell, R. 'Reprinting, circulation and the network author in antebellum newspapers.' *American Literary History*, 27:3 (2015), 417–55.

Cott, N. F. 'What's in a name? The limits of "social feminism"; or, expanding the vocabulary of women's history.' *Journal of American History*, 76:3 (1989), 809–29.

Cousins, S. 'Drunken, selfish "boors?" Images of masculinity in the *Dawn*.' *Hecate*, 25:2 (1999), 85–96.

Cowman, K. *Women of the Right Spirit: Paid Organisers of the Women's Social and Political Union 1904–18*. Manchester: Manchester University Press, 2007.

Cresswell, T. 'Mobilising the movement: The role of mobility in the suffrage politics of Florence Luscomb and Margaret Foley, 1911–1915.' *Gender, Place & Culture*, 12:4 (2005), 447–61.

Crozier-De Rosa, S. 'The national and the transnational in British anti-suffragists' views of Australian women voters.' *History Australia*, 10:3 (2013), 51–64.

———. *Shame and the Anti-Feminist Backlash: Britain, Ireland and Australia, 1890-1920*. New York: Routledge, 2018.

Crozier-De Rosa, S. and V. Mackie. *Remembering Women's Activism*. Oxford: Routledge, 2019.

Curless, G., S. Hynd, T. Alanamu, and K. Roscoe. 'Editors' introduction: Networks in imperial history.' *Journal of World History*, 26:4 (2015), 705-32.

Curthoys, A. 'Does Australian history have a future?' *Australian Historical Studies*, 33:118 (2002), 140-52.

———. 'We've just started making national histories and you want us to stop already?' In *After the Imperial Turn: Thinking with and Through the Nation*, edited by A. Burton, 70-89. Durham: Duke University Press, 2003.

Curthoys, A. and M. Lake. 'Introduction.' In *Connected Worlds: History in Transnational Perspective*, edited by A. Curthoys and M. Lake, 5-20. Canberra: ANU Press, 2005.

Curtin, J. 'New Zealand: A country of firsts in women's political rights.' In *The Palgrave Handbook of Women's Political Rights*, edited by S. Franceschet, M. L. Krook, and N. Tan, 129-42. London: Palgrave Macmillan, 2019.

Dalley, B. 'Lolly shops "of the red-light kind" and "soldiers of the King": Suppressing one-woman brothels in New Zealand, 1908-1916.' *New Zealand Journal of History*, 30:1 (1996), 3-23.

Dalziel, R. 'Presenting the enfranchisement of New Zealand women abroad.' In *Suffrage & Beyond: International Feminist Perspectives*, edited by C. Daley and M. Nolan, 42-64. Auckland: Auckland University Press, 1994.

Damousi, J. *Women Come Rally: Socialism, Communism and Gender in Australia 1890-1955*. Melbourne: Oxford University Press, 1994.

———. 'An absence of anything masculine: Vida Goldstein and women's public speech.' *Victorian Historical Journal*, 72:2 (2008), 251-64.

Dampier, H. '"Going on with our little movement in the hum drum-way which alone is possible in a land like this": Olive Schreiner and suffrage networks in Britain and South Africa, 1905-1913.' *Women's History Review*, 25:4 (2016), 536-50.

Deacon, D., P. Russell, and A. Woollacott (eds). *Transnational Ties: Australian Lives in the World*. Canberra: ANU E Press, 2008.

———. *Transnational Lives: Biographies of Global Modernity, 1700-Present*. New York: Palgrave Macmillan, 2010.

Deakin, A. *Federated Australia: Selections from Letters to the Morning Post 1900-1910*, edited by J. A. La Nauze. Melbourne: Melbourne University Press, 1968.

de Haan, F. 'A "truly international" archive for the women's movement (IAV, IIAV now Aletta): From its foundation in Amsterdam in 1935 to the return of its looted archives in 2003.' *Journal of Women's History*, 16:4 (2004), 148-72.

de Haan, F., M. Allen, J. Purvis, and K. Daskalova. 'Introduction.' In *Women's Activism: Global Perspectives from the 1890s to the Present*, edited by F. de Haan, M. Allen, J. Purvis, and K. Daskalova, 1-12. Oxford: Routledge, 2013.

Delap, L. 'The Freewoman, periodical communities, and the feminist reading public.' *Princeton University Library Chronicle*, 61:2 (2000), 233-76.

———. *The Feminist Avant-Garde: Transatlantic Encounters of the Early Twentieth Century*. Cambridge: Cambridge University Press, 2007.

———. 'The "woman question" and the origins of feminism.' In *The Cambridge History of Nineteenth-Century Political Thought*, edited by G. Steadman Jones and G. Claeys, 319-48. Cambridge: Cambridge University Press, 2011.

Delap, L. and M. DiCenzo. 'Transatlantic print culture: The Anglo-American feminist press & emerging "modernities."' In *Transatlantic Print Culture, 1880-1940*, edited by A. Ardis and P. Collier, 48-65. London: Palgrave Macmillan, 2008.

della Porta, D. and S. Tarrow. 'Transnational processes and social activism: An introduction.' In *Transnational Processes and Global Activism*, edited by D. della Porta and S. Tarrow, 1-17. Oxford: Rowman & Littlefield, 2005.

Denoon, D. and P. Mein-Smith, with M. Wyndham. *A History of Australia, New Zealand and the Pacific*. Oxford: Blackwell, 2000.

Devaliant, J. *Kate Sheppard: A Biography*. Auckland: Penguin Books, 1992.

Deverall, K. 'They did not know their place: The politics of Annie Golding and Kate Dwyer.' *Labour History*, 87 (2004), 31-48.

DiCenzo, M., with L. Delap and L. Ryan. *Feminist Media History: Suffrage, Periodicals and the Public Sphere*. London: Palgrave Macmillan, 2011.

Docker, J. *The Nervous Nineties: Australian Cultural Life in the 1890s*. Melbourne: Oxford University Press, 1991.

———. 'The feminist legend: A new historicism?' In *Debutante Nation: Feminism Contests the 1890s*, edited by S. Magarey, S. Sheridan, and S. Rowley, 16-26. Sydney: Allen and Unwin, 1993.

DuBois, E. C. 'Woman suffrage around the world: Three phases of suffragist internationalism.' In *Suffrage & Beyond: International Feminist Perspectives*, edited by C. Daley and M. Nolan, 252-74. Auckland: Auckland University Press, 1994.

———. *Woman Suffrage and Women's Rights*. New York: New York University Press, 1998.

Edwards, H. 'Our Australian chieftain.' In *Torchbearers: The Woman's Christian Temperance Union of South Australia 1886-1948*, edited by I. McCorkindale, 5-23. Adelaide: Woman's Christian Temperance Union of South Australia, 1949.

Edwards, L. 'Chinese feminism in a transnational frame: Between internationalism and xenophobia.' In *Women's Movements in Asia: Feminisms and Transnational Activism*, edited by M. Roces and L. Edwards, 53-74. Oxford: Routledge, 2010.

Edwards, L. and M. Roces. 'Orienting the global women's suffrage movement.' In *Women's Suffrage in Asia: Gender, Nationalism and Democracy*, edited by L. Edwards and M. Roces, 1-23. New York: Routledge, 2004.

Eldershaw, F. S. (ed.). *The Peaceful Army: A Memorial to the Pioneer Women of Australia, 1788-1938*. Sydney: Women's Executive Committee and Advisory Council of Australia's 150th Anniversary Celebrations, 1938.

Eldred-Grigg, S. *Pleasures of the Flesh: Sex and Drugs in Colonial New Zealand 1840-1915*. Wellington: A. H. & A. W. Reed, 1984.

Evans, R. J. *The Feminists: Women's Emancipation Movements in Europe, America and Australasia 1840-1920*. London: Croon Helm, 1977.

Everard, M. and M. Aerts. 'Forgotten intersections: Wilhelmina Drucker, early feminism, and the Dutch-Belgian Connection.' *Revue Belge de Philologie et d'Histoire*, 77:2 (1999), 440-72.

Favret, M. A. *Romantic Correspondence: Women, Politics, and the Fiction of Letters*. Cambridge: Cambridge University Press, 1993.

Fawcett, M. 'Introduction to the new edition.' In M. Wollstonecraft, *A Vindication of the Rights of Woman*, edited by M. Fawcett, 1–30. New York: Scribner and Welford, 1890.

Fletcher, I. C., P. Levine, and L. E. Nym Mayhall (eds). *Women's Suffrage in the British Empire: Citizenship, Nation, and Race*. London: Routledge, 2000.

Franklin, M. 'Rose Scott: Some elements of her personality and work.' In *The Peaceful Army: A Memorial to the Pioneer Women of Australia, 1788-1938*, edited by F. Eldershaw, 90–107. Sydney: Women's Executive Committee and Advisory Council of Australia's 150th Anniversary Celebrations, 1938.

Gaido, D. and C. Frencia. '"A clean break": Clara Zetkin, the socialist women's movement, and feminism.' *International Critical Thought*, 8:2 (2018), 277–303.

Garner, J. *By His Own Merits: Sir John Hall – Pioneer, Pastoralist & Premier*. Hororata: Dryden Press, 1995.

Garner, J. and K. Foster (eds). *Letters to Grace: Writing Home from Colonial New Zealand*. Christchurch: Canterbury University Press, 2011.

Garvey, E. G. *Writing with Scissors: American Scrapbooks from the Civil War to the Harlem Renaissance*. New York: Oxford University Press, 2013.

George, D. *Mary Lee: The Life and Times of a 'Turbulent Anarchist' and Her Battle for Women's Rights*. Adelaide: Wakefield Press, 2018.

Gere, A. R. *Intimate Practices: Literary and Cultural Work in US Women's Clubs, 1880-1920*. Chicago: University of Illinois Press, 1997.

Gifford, C. D. S. 'Frances Willard and the Woman's Christian Temperance Union's conversion to woman suffrage.' In *One Woman, One Vote: Rediscovering the Woman Suffrage Movement*, edited by M. S. Wheeler, 117–34. Troutdale: New Sage Press, 1995.

Goldstein, V. *Woman Suffrage in Australia*. London: International Woman Suffrage Alliance, 1908.

———. *To America and Back: January-June 1902*. Sydney: Australian History Museum, 2002.

Gordon, A. A. *The Beautiful Life of Frances E. Willard*. Chicago: Woman's Temperance Publishing Association, 1898.

———. *The World's Woman's Christian Temperance Union*. Chicago: Ruby I. Gilbert, 1900.

Gordon, A. D. (ed.). *The Selected Papers of Elizabeth Cady Stanton and Susan B. Anthony: Volume VI, An Awful Hush, 1895 to 1906*. New Brunswick: Rutgers University Press, 2013.

Gordon, L. 'What's new in women's history.' In *Feminist Studies/Critical Studies*, edited by T. De Lauretis, 20–30. Bloomington: Indiana University Press, 1986.

Gorman, D. *The Emergence of International Society in the 1920s*. Cambridge: Cambridge University Press, 2012.

Green, B. 'Complaints of everyday life: Feminist periodical culture and correspondence columns in *The Woman Worker*, *Women Folk*, and *The Freewoman*.' *Modernism/Modernity*, 19:3 (2012), 461–85.

Green, N. *The Limits of Transnationalism*. Chicago: University of Chicago Press, 2019.

Griffin-Foley, B. 'From *Tit-Bits* to *Big Brother*: A century of audience participation in the media.' *Media, Culture & Society*, 26:4 (2004), 533–48.

Griffiths, J. 'Were there municipal networks in the British World c. 1890–1939?' *Journal of Imperial and Commonwealth History*, 37:4 (2009), 575–97.

Grigg, A. R. 'Prohibition and women: The preservation of an ideal and a myth.' *New Zealand Journal of History*, 17:2 (1983), 144–65.

Grimshaw, P. *Women's Suffrage in New Zealand*, rev. edn. Auckland: Auckland University Press, 1987.

———. 'Women's suffrage in New Zealand revisited: Writing from the margins.' In *Suffrage & Beyond: International Feminist Perspectives*, edited by C. Daley and M. Nolan, 25–41. Auckland: Auckland University Press, 1994.

———. 'Colonising motherhood: Evangelical social reformers and Koorie women in Victoria, Australia, 1880s to the early 1900s.' *Women's History Review*, 8:2 (1999), 329–49.

———. 'Settler anxieties, indigenous peoples, and women's suffrage in the colonies of Australia, New Zealand, and Hawai'i, 1888 to 1902.' *Pacific Historical Review*, 69:4 (2000), 553–72.

———. 'Reading the silences: Suffrage activists and race in nineteenth century settler societies.' In *Women's Rights and Human Rights: International Historical Perspectives*, edited by P. Grimshaw, K. Holmes, and M. Lake, 1–48. Basingstoke: Palgrave MacMillan, 2001.

Gring-Pemble, L. M. 'Writing themselves into consciousness: Creating a rhetorical bridge between the public and private spheres.' *Quarterly Journal of Speech*, 84:1 (1998), 41–61.

Haley, J. 'Otago's albums: Photographs, community and identity.' *New Zealand Journal of History*, 52:1 (2018), 23–40.

Hannam, J. 'International dimensions of women's suffrage: "At the crossroads of several interlocking identities."' *Women's History Review*, 14:3–4 (2005), 543–60.

Hansord, K. 'The literary *Dawn*: Re-reading Louisa Lawson's poetry and politics.' *Hecate*, 39:1 (2014), 188–201.

Harper, I. H. (ed.). *The History of Woman Suffrage, Volume 5 1900–1920*. New York: National American Woman Suffrage Association, 1922.

Harrison, P. *Connecting Links: The British and American Woman Suffrage Movements, 1900–1914*. Westport: Greenwood Press, 2000.

Harsant, F. *They Called Me Te Maari*. Christchurch: Whitcoulls Limited, 1979.

Harvey, E. '"Layered networks": Imperial philanthropy in Birmingham and Sydney, 1860–1914.' *Journal of Imperial and Commonwealth History*, 41:1 (2013), 120–42.

Harvey, R. 'Bringing the news to New Zealand: The supply and control of overseas news in the nineteenth century.' *Media History*, 8:1 (2002), 21–34.

'He tohu: About.' *The National Library of New Zealand*. https://natlib.govt.nz/he-tohu/about (accessed 2 May 2019).

'He tohu rangatira – Māori women & the 1893 suffrage petition.' Archives New Zealand. https://archives.govt.nz/discover-our-stories/he-tohu-rangatira-maori-women-and-the-1893-suffrage-petition (accessed 13 March 2020).

Hearn, M. '"Originally French but afterwards cosmopolitan": Australians interpret the fin de siècle.' *Journal of Australian Studies*, 43:3 (2019), 365–80.

Henderson, J. R. *The Strength of White Ribbon: A Year-by-Year Record of the Centennial History of the Woman's Christian Temperance Union of Western Australia*. Perth: The Union, 1992.

Hill, R. 'Settler colonialism in New Zealand.' In *The Routledge Handbook of Settler Colonialism*, edited by E. Cavanagh and L. Veracini, 391-408. London: Routledge, 2016.

Hirst, J. 'South Australia and Australia: Reflections on their histories.' In *Turning Points: Chapters in South Australian History*, edited by R. Foster and P. Sendziuk, 118-30. Adelaide: Wakefield Press, 2012.

'Historical and colonial census data archive.' *Australian Data Archive Dataverse*. https://dataverse.ada.edu.au/dataset.xhtml?persistentId=doi:10.26193/MP6WRS (accessed 12 April 2020).

Holbrook, C. '"What sort of nation?" A cultural history of Australians and their Federation.' *History Compass*, 15:11 (2017), 1-10.

Holt, B. *Women in Council: A History of the National Council of Women of New Zealand*. Wellington: National Council of Women, 1980.

Hore, J. 'Capturing terra incognita: Alfred Burton, "Maoridom" and wilderness in the King Country.' *Australian Historical Studies*, 50:2 (2019), 188-211.

Horne, J. *The Pursuit of Wonder: How Australia's Landscape was Explored, Nature Discovered and Tourism Unleashed*. Melbourne: Miegunyah Press, 2005.

Hunt, K. 'Transnationalism in practice: The effect of Dora Montefiore's international travel on women's politics in Britain before World War I.' In *Crossing Boundaries: Women's Organizing in Europe and the Americas, 1880-1940s*, edited by P. Jonsson, S. Neunsinger, and J. Sangster, 73-94. Uppsala: Acta Universitatis Upsaliensis, 2007.

———. '"Whirl'd through the world": The role of travel in the making of Dora Montefiore, 1851-1933.' *Österreichische Zeitschrift für Geschichtswissenschaft*, 22:1 (2011), 41-62.

Hyslop, A. 'Temperance, Christianity and feminism: The Woman's Christian Temperance Union of Victoria, 1887-97.' *Historical Studies*, 17:66 (1976), 27-49.

Irving, H. 'A gendered constitution? Women, Federation and heads of power.' In *A Woman's Constitution? Gender and History in the Australian Commonwealth*, edited by H. Irving, 98-107. Sydney: Hale & Iremonger, 1996.

———. 'Fair federalists and founding mothers.' In *A Woman's Constitution? Gender & History in the Australian Commonwealth*, edited by H. Irving, 1-20. Sydney: Hale & Iremonger, 1996.

———. *To Constitute a Nation: A Cultural History of Australia's Constitution*. Melbourne: Cambridge University Press, 1997.

Janz, O. and D. Schönpflug. 'Introduction.' In *Gender History in a Transnational Perspective: Biographies, Networks, Gender Orders*, edited by O. Janz and D. Schönpflug, 1-24. New York: Berghahn, 2014.

Jerry, E. C. 'The role of newspapers in the nineteenth-century woman's movement.' In *A Voice of their Own: The Woman Suffrage Press, 1840-1910*, edited by M. M. Solomon, 17-29. Tuscaloosa: University of Alabama Press, 1991.

Johnson, M. 'Chiefly women: Queen Victoria, Meri Mangakahia, and the Māori Parliament.' In *Mistress of Everything: Queen Victoria in Indigenous Worlds*, edited by S. Carter and M. Nugent, 228-45. Manchester: Manchester University Press, 2016.

Johnson, P. 'Nineteenth-century feminism: A study of "the Dawn."' *Australia 1888 Bulletin*, 13 (1984), 71-81.

Jolly, M. 'Delicious moments: The photograph album in nineteenth-century Australia.' In *The Photograph and Australia*, edited by J. Annear, 234–5. Sydney: Art Gallery of New South Wales, 2015.

Jordan, J. *Josephine Butler*. London: John Murray, 2001.

Keating, J. '"The defection of women": The New Zealand Contagious Diseases Act repeal campaign and transnational feminist dialogue in the late nineteenth century.' *Women's History Review*, 25:2 (2016), 187–206.

———. 'International activism after the fair: New South Wales, Utah, and the 1893 World's Columbian Exposition.' In *Women in International and Universal Exhibitions 1876–1937*, edited by R. Rogers and M. Boussahba-Bravard, 192–212. Oxford: Routledge, 2017.

———. 'Piecing together suffrage internationalism: Place, space, and connected histories of Australasian women's activism.' *History Compass*, 16:8 (2018), 1–15.

———. 'Review article: Denise George, *Mary Lee: The Life and Times of a 'Turbulent Anarchist' and her Battle for Women's Rights*; Myra Scott, *How Australia Led the Way: Dora Meeson Coates and British Suffrage*; Clare Wright, *You Daughters of Freedom: The Australians Who Won the Vote and Inspired the World*.' *Australian Journal of Biography and History*, 2 (2019), 135–45.

King, M. *The Penguin History of New Zealand*, rev. edn. Auckland: Viking, 2004.

Kirkby, D. *Alice Henry, The Power of Pen and Voice: The Life of an Australian-American Labor Reformer*. Melbourne: Cambridge University Press, 1991.

———. '"Those knights of the pen and pencil": Women journalists and cultural leadership of the women's movement in Australia and the United States.' *Labour History*, 104 (2013), 81–100.

Lacqua, D. (ed.). *Internationalism Reconfigured: Transnational Ideas and Movements Between the World Wars*. London: I. B. Tauris, 2011.

Laidlaw, Z. 'Breaking Britannia's bounds? Law, settlers, and space in Britain's imperial historiography.' *The Historical Journal*, 55:3 (2012), 807–30.

Laing, K. 'World war and worldly women: The Great War and the formation of the Women's International League for Peace and Freedom in Australia.' *La Trobe Journal*, 96 (2015), 117–34.

———. '"The White Australia nettle": Women's internationalism, peace, and the White Australia Policy in the interwar years.' *History Australia*, 14:2 (2017), 218–36.

Lake, M. 'The politics of respectability: Identifying the masculinist context.' *Historical Studies*, 22:86 (1986), 116–31.

———. 'Mission impossible: How men gave birth to the Australian nation – nationalism, gender, and other seminal acts.' *Gender & History*, 4:3 (1992), 305–22.

———. 'Feminist history as national history: Writing the political history of women.' *Australian Historical Studies*, 27:106 (1996), 154–69.

———. 'Women and nation in Australia: The politics of representation.' *Australian Journal of Politics and History*, 43:1 (1997), 41–52.

———. 'A history of feminism in Australia.' In *Australian Feminism: A Companion*, edited by B. Caine, M. Gatens, E. Grahame, J. Larbalestier, S. Watson, and E. Webby, 132–42. Melbourne: Oxford University Press, 1998.

———. 'State socialism for Australian mothers': Andrew Fisher's radical maternalism in its international and local contexts.' *Labour History*, 102 (2012), 55–70.
———. 'Women's international leadership.' In *Diversity in Leadership: Australian Women, Past and Present*, edited by J. Damousi, K. Rubenstein, and M. Tomsic, 71–90. Canberra: Australian National University Press, 2014.
———. '1914: Death of a nation.' *History Australia*, 12:1 (2015), 7–24.
———. *Progressive New World: How Settler Colonialism and Transpacific Exchange Shaped American Reform*. Cambridge, MA: Harvard University Press, 2019.
Lake, M. and H. Reynolds. *Drawing the Global Colour Line: White Men's Countries and the International Challenge of Racial Equality*. Cambridge: Cambridge University Press, 2008.
Lake, M. *The Bible in Australia: A Cultural History*. Sydney: NewSouth, 2018.
Lambert, D. and A. Lester (eds). *Colonial Lives across the British Empire: Imperial Careering in the Long Nineteenth Century*. Cambridge: Cambridge University Press, 2006.
Lamme, M. O. 'Shining a calcium light: The WCTU and public relations history.' *Journalism & Mass Communications Quarterly*, 88:2 (2011), 245–66.
Laurie, A. J. 'A transnational conference romance: Elsie Andrews, Hildegarde Kneeland, and the Pan-Pacific Women's Association.' *Journal of Lesbian Studies*, 13:4 (2009), 395–414.
Lawson, O. (ed.). *The First Voice of Australian Feminism: Excerpts from Louisa Lawson's The Dawn 1888–1895*. Sydney: Simon and Schuster, 1990.
Leavitt, M. C. *Report Made to the First Convention of the World's Women's Christian Temperance Union*. Boston: Alfred Mudge & Son, 1891.
Lester, A. 'Imperial circuits and networks.' *History Compass*, 4:1 (2006), 124–41.
Levine, P. '"The humanising influences of five o'clock tea": Victorian feminist periodicals.' *Victorian Studies*, 33:2 (1990), 293–306.
———. *Prostitution, Race & Politics: Policing Venereal Disease in the British Empire*. London: Routledge, 2003.
Liebich, S. 'Connected readers: Reading networks and community in early twentieth-century New Zealand.' *Mémoires du Livre/Studies in Book Culture*, 2:1 (2010), 1–11.
Lloyd, J. 'Women's pages in Australian print media from the 1850s.' *Media International Australia*, 150 (2014), 61–5.
Loughheed, A. 'International transactions and foreign commerce.' In *Australians: Historical Statistics*, edited by W. Vamplew, 188–209. Sydney: Fairfax, Syme, and Weldon, 1987.
Lovell-Smith, M. *Plain Living High Thinking: The Family Story of Jennie and Will Lovell-Smith*. Christchurch: Pedmore Press, 1995.
Lucas, R. and C. Forster (eds). *Wilder Shores: Women's Travel Stories of Australia and Beyond*. Brisbane: University of Queensland Press, 1993.
Lyons, M. 'Love letters and writing practices: On *ecritures intimes* in the nineteenth century.' *Journal of Family History*, 24:2 (1999), 232–9.
Macdonald, C. 'The "social evil": Prostitution and the passage of the Contagious Diseases Act (1869).' In *Women in History: Essays on European Women in New Zealand*, edited by B. Brookes, C. Macdonald, and M. Tennant, 13–33. Wellington: Allen and Unwin/Port Nicholson Press, 1986.

———. *The Vote, the Pill and the Demon Drink: A History of Feminist Writing in New Zealand, 1869–1993*. Wellington: Bridget Williams Books, 1993.

———. 'Introduction.' In *Women Writing Home, 1700–1920, Female Correspondence Across the British Empire, Volume 5: New Zealand*, edited by C. Macdonald, xi–xxvi. London: Pickering & Chatto, 2006.

———. 'Intimacy of the envelope: Fiction, commerce, and empire in the correspondence of friends Mary Taylor and Charlotte Brontë, c. 1845–55.' In *Moving Subjects: Gender, Mobility, and Intimacy in an Age of Global Empire*, edited by T. Ballantyne and A. Burton, 89–109. Chicago: University of Illinois Press, 2009.

———. 'People of the land, voting citizens in the nation, subjects of the Crown: Historical perspectives on gender and law in nineteenth-century New Zealand.' *Law & History*, 2 (2015), 32–59.

Magarey, S. *Passions of the First Wave Feminists*. Sydney: UNSW Press, 2001.

———. 'Feminism as cultural renaissance.' *Hecate*, 30:1 (2004), 231–46.

———. *Unbridling the Tongues of Women: A Biography of Catherine Helen Spence*, rev. edn. Adelaide: University of Adelaide Press, 2010.

Magarey, S., B. Wall, M. Lyons, and M. Beams (eds). *Ever Yours, C. H. Spence: Catherine Helen Spence's An Autobiography (1825–1910), Diary (1894), and Some Correspondence (1894–1910)*. Kent Town: Wakefield Press, 2005.

Magarey, S., S. Sheridan, and S. Rowley (eds). *Debutante Nation: Feminism Contests the 1890s*. Sydney: Allen and Unwin, 1993.

Malcolm, J. 'A house of one's own.' *New Yorker*, 5 June 1995, 58–78.

Malone, J. E. 'What's wrong with Emma? The feminist debate in colonial Auckland.' In *Women in History: Essays on European Women in New Zealand*, edited by B. Brookes, C. Macdonald, and M. Tennant, 69–85. Wellington: Allen and Unwin/ Port Nicholson Press, 1986.

Marilley, S. M. 'Frances Willard and the feminism of fear.' *Feminist Studies*, 19:1 (1993), 123–46.

Marino, K. M. 'Transnational Pan-American feminism: The friendship of Bertha Lutz and Mary Wilhelmine Williams, 1926–1944.' *Journal of Women's History*, 26:2 (2014), 63–87.

Marks, R. 'The left and Australian nationalism since the 1960s: A history of rejection and ambivalence.' *Journal of Australian Studies*, 43:2 (2019), 145–59.

Marsden, K. *On Sledge and Horseback to Outcast Siberian Lepers*. London: Record Press, 1892.

Matters, L. W. *Australasians Who Count in London and Who Counts in Western Australia*. London: Jas. Truscott & Son, 1913.

Matthews, J. J. 'Modern nomads and national film history: The multi-continental career of J.D. Williams.' In *Connected Worlds: History in Transnational Perspective*, edited by A. Curthoys and M. Lake, 157–70. Canberra: ANU E Press, 2005.

Matthews-Jones, L. '"Granny thinking what she is going to write in her book": Religion, politics and the Pontefract by-election of 1872 in Josephine Butler's *Personal Reminiscences of a Great Crusade* (1896).' *Women's History Review*, 26:6 (2017), 935–52.

Mayer, H. *The Press in Australia*. Melbourne: Lansdowne, 1964.

McAloon, J. *No Idle Rich: The Wealthy in Canterbury & Otago 1840-1914*. Dunedin: University of Otago Press, 2002.

McDowell, L. *Gender, Identity and Place: Understanding Feminist Geographies*. Cambridge: Polity Press, 1999.

McFadden, M. *Golden Cables of Sympathy: The Transatlantic Sources of Nineteenth-Century Feminism*. Lexington: University Press of Kentucky, 1999.

McGirr, L. *The War on Alcohol: Prohibition and the Rise of the American State*. New York: W. W. Norton & Company, 2016.

McGregor, R. *Imagined Destinies: Aboriginal Australians and the Doomed Race Theory, 1880-1939*. Melbourne: Melbourne University Press, 1997.

McIntyre, J. and J. Conway. 'Intimate, imperial, intergenerational: Settler women's mobilities and gender politics in Newcastle and the Hunter Valley.' *Journal of Australian Colonial History*, 19 (2017), 171–84.

McKeever, J. L. 'The Woman's Temperance Publishing Association.' *Library Quarterly*, 55:4 (1985), 365–97.

McKenzie, T. 'William Pember Reeves, 1857-1932.' *Kōtare: New Zealand Notes & Queries*, 7:3 (2008), 40–51.

McKinnon, M. *The Broken Decade: Prosperity, Depression and Recovery in New Zealand, 1928-39*. Dunedin: Otago University Press, 2016.

McKinnon, M., with B. Bradley and R. Kirkpatrick (eds). *Bateman New Zealand Historical Atlas: Ko Papatuanuku e Takoto Nei*. Auckland: David Bateman, 1997.

McNamara, H. 'The *New Zealand Tablet* and the Irish Catholic Press worldwide, 1898–1923.' *New Zealand Journal of History*, 37:2 (2003), 153–70.

Mead, R. *How the Vote was Won: Woman Suffrage in the Western United States 1868-1914*. New York: New York University Press, 2004.

Mein Smith, P., P. Hempenstall, and S. Goldfinch. *Remaking the Tasman World*. Christchurch: Canterbury University Press, 2008.

Midgley, C., A. Twells, and J. Carlier. 'Introduction.' In *Women in Transnational History: Connecting the Local and the Global*, edited by C. Midgley, A. Twells, and J. Carlier, 1–10. London: Routledge, 2016.

Millar, C. 'The making of a feminist: Bessie Rischbieth encounters the English suffragettes.' *Lilith*, 12 (2003), 78–94.

Millar, G. 'Women's lives, feminism and the *New Zealand Journal of History*.' *New Zealand Journal of History*, 52:2 (2018), 134–52.

Morrison, H. *Pushing Boundaries: New Zealand Protestants and Overseas Missions 1827-1939*. Dunedin: Otago University Press, 2016.

Morrison, I. 'Cook's choice: Reflections on trans-Tasman literary culture.' In *Books and Bibliography: Essays in Commemoration of Don McKenzie*, edited by J. Thomson, 160–75. Wellington: Victoria University Press, 2002.

Mukherjee, S. *Indian Suffragettes: Female Identities and Transnational Networks*. Oxford: Oxford University Press, 2018.

———. 'Locating race in suffrage: Discourses and encounters with race and empire in the British suffrage movement.' In *From Suffragette to Homesteader: Exploring British and Canadian Colonial Histories and Women's Politics through Memoir*, edited by E. van der Meulen, 95–109. Halifax: Fernwood Publishing, 2018.

Mune, M. 'Elizabeth Webb Nicholls (1850-1943).' *Australian Dictionary of Biography.* http://adb.anu.edu.au/biography/nicholls-elizabeth-webb-7839/text13613 (accessed 20 September 2018).

Murray, J. H. and A. K. Clark. *The Englishwoman's Review of Social and Industrial Questions: An Index.* New York: Garland Publishing, 1985.

Nicholls, R. *The Women's Parliament: The National Council of the Women of New Zealand 1896-1920.* Wellington: Victoria University Press, 1996.

Nolan, M. and C. Daley. 'International feminist perspectives on suffrage: An introduction.' In *Suffrage & Beyond: International Feminist Perspectives*, edited by C. Daley and M. Nolan, 1-22. Auckland: Auckland University Press, 1994.

Nugent, A. 'Nellie Alma Martel and the Women's Social and Political Union, 1905-09.' *Hecate*, 31:1 (2005), 142-59.

O'Brien, A. 'Sins of omission? Women in the history of Australian religion and religion in the history of Australian women. A reply to Roger Thompson.' *Australian Historical Studies*, 27:108 (1997), 126-33.

Offen, K. *European Feminisms, 1700-1950: A Political History.* Stanford: Stanford University Press, 2000.

―――. 'Overcoming hierarchies through internationalism: May Wright Sewall's engagement with the International Council of Women.' In *Women's Activism: Global Perspectives From the 1890s to the Present*, edited by F. de Haan, M. Allen, J. Purvis, and K. Daskalova, 15-27. Oxford: Routledge, 2013.

Oldfield, A. *Woman Suffrage in Australia: A Gift or a Struggle?* Cambridge: Cambridge University Press, 1992.

Olssen, E. *Building the New World: Work, Politics and Society in Caversham 1880s-1920s.* Auckland: Auckland University Press, 1995.

Oosterman, A. 'Inky wayfarers: New Zealand journalism and the Australian connection in the early 20th century.' *Australian Journalism Review*, 27:1 (2005), 77-91.

Osterhammel, J. *The Transformation of the World: A Global History of the Nineteenth Century*, trans. P. Camilleri. Princeton: Princeton University Press, 2014.

Page, D. 'Women and nationality: Feminist organisations in the inter-war period.' In *Women in History: Essays on European Women in New Zealand*, edited by B. Brookes, C. Macdonald, and M. Tennant, 157-75. Wellington: Allen and Unwin/Port Nicholson Press, 1986.

Paisley, F. 'No back streets in the bush: 1920s and 1930s pro-Aboriginal white women's activism and the trans-Australia railway.' *Australian Feminist Studies*, 12:27 (1997), 119-37.

―――. *Loving Protection? Australian Feminism and Aboriginal Women's Rights 1919-1939.* Melbourne: Melbourne University Press, 2000.

―――. 'Performing "New Zealand" Maori and Pakeha delegates at the Pan-Pacific Women's Conference, Hawai'i, 1934.' *New Zealand Journal of History*, 38:1 (2004), 22-38.

―――. 'White settler colonialisms and the colonial turn: An Australian perspective.' *Journal of Colonialism and Colonial History*, 4:3 (2004), http://doi.org/10.1353/cch.2004.0008.

―――. *Glamour in the Pacific: Cultural Internationalism and Race Politics in the Women's Pan-Pacific.* Honolulu: University of Hawai'i Press, 2009.

———. 'The spoils of opportunity: Janet Mitchell and Australian internationalism in the interwar Pacific.' *History Australia*, 13:4 (2016), 575–91.

Parkinson, N. G. 'Impersonating a voter: Constructions of race, and conceptions of subjecthood in the franchise of colonial New South Wales, c. 1850–1865.' *Journal of Imperial and Commonwealth History*, 47:4 (2019), 652–75.

Patterson, L. and A. Wanhalla. *He Reo Wāhine: Māori Women's Voices from the Nineteenth Century*. Auckland: Auckland University Press, 2017.

Paulson, R. E. *Women's Suffrage and Prohibition: A Comparative Study of Equality and Social Control*. Glenview: Scott, Foresman, and Company, 1973.

Pawson, E. 'Time-space convergence in New Zealand: 1850s to 1990s.' *New Zealand Journal of Geography*, 94:1 (1992), 14–19.

Pearce, S. *Shameless Scribblers: Australian Women's Journalism*. Rockhampton: Central Queensland University Press, 1998.

Pedersen, S. 'Comparative history and women's history: Explaining convergence and divergence.' In *Comparative Women's History: New Approaches*, edited by A. Cova, 117–42. Boulder: Social Sciences Monographs, 2006.

Perry, L. 'The carte de visite in the 1860s and the serial dynamic of photographic likeness.' *Art History*, 36:4 (2012), 728–49.

Perryman, N. *How We Won the Franchise in New Zealand*. Wellington: New Zealand Women's Christian Temperance Union, 1924.

Pesman, R. *Duty Free: Australian Women Abroad*. Melbourne: Oxford University Press, 1996.

Pesman, R., D. Walker, and R. White (eds). *The Oxford Book of Australian Travel Writing*. Melbourne: Oxford University Press, 1996.

Phillips, J. O. C. 'Musings in Maoriland – or was there a *Bulletin* school in New Zealand?' *Historical Studies*, 20:81 (1983), 520–35.

Pickles, K. 'The obvious and the awkward: Postcolonialism and the British world.' *New Zealand Journal of History*, 45:1 (2011), 85–101.

———. 'Transnational history and cultural cringe: Some issues for consideration in New Zealand, Australia and Canada.' *History Compass*, 9:9 (2011), 657–73.

Piggin, S. and R. D. Linder. *The Fountain of Public Prosperity: Evangelical Christians in Australian History 1740–1914*. Melbourne: Monash University Publishing, 2018.

Pike, R. M. 'National interest and imperial yearnings: Empire communications and Canada's role in establishing the Imperial Penny Post.' *Journal of Imperial and Commonwealth History*, 26:1 (1998), 22–48.

Porter, F. and C. Macdonald, with T. MacDonald (eds). *My Hand Will Write What My Heart Dictates: The Unsettled Lives of Women in Nineteenth-Century New Zealand as Revealed to Sisters, Family and Friends*. Auckland: Auckland University Press, 1996.

Potter, S. J. *News and the British World: The Emergence of an Imperial Press System, 1876–1922*. Oxford: Clarendon Press, 2003.

———. 'Webs, networks, and systems: Globalization and the mass media in the nineteenth- and twentieth-century British Empire.' *Journal of British Studies*, 46:3 (2007), 621–46.

Quartly, M. and J. Smart. 'Making the National Councils of Women national: The formation of a nation-wide organisation in Australia 1896–1931.' In *Suffrage, Gender and Citizenship:*

International Perspectives on Parliamentary Reform, edited by I. Sulkunen, P. Markkola, and S. L. Nevala-Nurmi, 339–57. Cambridge: Cambridge Scholars Press, 2009.

———. 'Mainstream women's organisations in Australia: The challenges of national and international co-operation after the Great War.' *Women's History Review*, 21:1 (2012), 61–73.

———. *Respectable Radicals: A History of the National Council of Women of Australia 1896-2006*. Melbourne: Monash University Publishing, 2015.

Rees, A. '"Bursting with new ideas": Australian women professionals and American study tours, 1930–1960.' *History Australia*, 13:3 (2016), 382–98.

———. 'Rebel handmaidens: Transpacific histories and the limits of transnationalism.' In *Transnationalism, Nationalism, and Australian History*, edited by A. Clark, A. Rees, and A. Simmonds, 49–68. Singapore: Palgrave Macmillan, 2017.

Reeves, W. P. *State Experiments in Australia and New Zealand, Volume 1*. London: Grant Richards, 1902.

Rei, T. *Maori Women and the Vote*. Wellington: Huia Publishers, 1993.

Reid, J. A. *The Australian Reader: Selections from Leading Journals on Memorable Historic Events*. Melbourne: J. Whitelaw and Son, 1882.

Reinisch, J. 'Introduction: Agents of internationalism.' *Contemporary European History*, 25:2 (2016), 195–205.

Rendall, J. 'Friendship and politics: Barbara Leigh Smith Bodichon (1827–91) and Bessie Rayner Parkes (1829–1925).' In *Sexuality and Subordination: Interdisciplinary Studies of Gender in the Nineteenth Century*, edited by S. Mendus and J. Rendall, 136–70. London and New York: Routledge, 1989.

Rickard, J. *Australia: A Cultural History*, 3rd edn. Melbourne: Monash University Press, 2017.

Roberts, H. 'Jessie Mackay.' *Te Ara: the Encyclopedia of New Zealand*. http://www.TeAra.govt.nz/en/biographies/2m15/mackay-jessie (accessed 7 December 2018).

Roberts, J. *Maybanke Anderson: Sex, Suffrage & Social Reform*. Sydney: Hale & Iremonger, 1993.

Robinson-Tomsett, E. *Women, Travel and Identity: Journeys by Rail and Sea, 1870–1940*. Manchester: Manchester University Press, 2013.

Roe, J. (ed.). *My Congenials: Miles Franklin & Friends in Letters, Volume One 1879–1938*. Sydney: Angus and Robertson, 1993.

———. *Stella Miles Franklin: A Biography*. Sydney: Fourth Estate, 2008.

Rosenberg, E. S. (ed.). *A World Connecting, 1871–1945*. Cambridge: Belknap Press, 2012.

Ross, W. M. 'Votes for women in Western Australia.' *Western Australian Historical Society Journal and Proceedings*, 4:4 (1952), 44–54.

Rupp, L. J. *Worlds of Women: The Making of an International Women's Movement*. Princeton: Princeton University Press, 1997.

Rupp, L. J. and V. Taylor. 'Forging feminist identity in an international movement: A collective identity approach to twentieth-century feminism.' *Signs*, 24:2 (1999), 363–86.

———. 'Loving internationalism: The emotion culture of transnational women's organizations, 1888–1945.' *Mobilization: An International Journal*, 7:2 (2002), 141–58.

Sandell, M. 'Regional versus international: Women's activism and organisational spaces in the inter-war period.' *The International History Review*, 33:4 (2011), 607–25.

———. *The Rise of Women's Transnational Activism: Identity and Sisterhood Between the World Wars*. London: I. B. Tauris, 2015.

Sanders, J. *Dateline-NZPA: The New Zealand Press Association, 1880-1980*. Auckland: Wilson and Horton, 1979.

Sangster, J. 'Crossing boundaries: Women's organizing in Europe and the Americas, 1880s-1940s.' In *Crossing Boundaries: Women's Organizing in Europe and the Americas, 1880-1940s*, edited by P. Jonsson, S. Neunsinger, and J. Sangster, 9-19. Uppsala: Acta Universitatis Upsaliensis, 2007.

———. 'Political tourism, writing, and communication: Transnational connections of women on the left, 1920s-1940s.' In *Crossing Boundaries: Women's Organizing in Europe and the Americas, 1880-1940s*, edited by P. Jonsson, S. Neunsinger, and J. Sangster, 95-116. Uppsala: Acta Universitatis Upsaliensis, 2007.

———. 'Exporting suffrage: British influences on the Canadian suffrage movement.' *Women's History Review*, 28:4 (2019), 566-86.

Sato, C. '"A picture of peace": Friendship in interwar Pacific women's internationalism.' *Qui Parle*, 27:2 (2018), 475-510.

Sawer, M. and M. Simms. *A Woman's Place: Women and Politics in Australia*, 2nd edn. Sydney: Allen and Unwin, 1993.

Scalmer, S. 'The history of social movements in Australia.' In *The History of Social Movements in Global Perspective*, edited by S. Berger and H. Nehring, 325-52. London: Palgrave Macmillan, 2017.

Scanlon, J. *Inarticulate Longings: The Ladies' Home Journal, Gender, and the Promises of Consumer Culture*. New York: Routledge, 1995.

Scates, B. *A New Australia: Citizenship, Radicalism and the First Republic*. Cambridge: Cambridge University Press, 1997.

Schrader, B. *The Big Smoke: New Zealand Cities, 1840-1920*. Wellington: Bridget Williams Books, 2016.

Schwartz, L. *Feminism and the Servant Problem: Class and Domestic Labour in the Women's Suffrage Movement*. Cambridge: Cambridge University Press, 2019.

Scott, A. F. *Natural Allies: Women's Associations in American History*. Urbana: University of Illinois Press, 1991.

Scott, D. 'Woman suffrage: The movement in Australia.' *Journal of the Australian Royal Society*, 53:4 (1969), 299-322.

Scott, M. *How Australia Led the Way: Dora Meeson Coates and British Suffrage*. Melbourne: Arcadia, 2018.

Sewall, M. W. *Genesis of the International Council of Women and the Story of Its Growth, 1888-1893*. Indianapolis: International Council of Women, 1914.

Sharp, I. and M. Stibbe (eds). 'Women's international activism during the inter-war period, 1919-1939,' Special issue, *Women's History Review*, 26:2 (2017).

Sheppard, K. *Woman Suffrage in New Zealand*. London: International Woman Suffrage Alliance, 1907.

Sheridan, S. 'Transvestite feminism: The politics of the *Australian Woman*, 1894.' *Women's History Review*, 3 (1993), 349-61.

———. *Along the Faultlines: Sex, Race and Nation in Australian Women's Writing 1880s-1930s*. Sydney: Allen and Unwin, 1995.

———. 'Women's magazines.' In *Companion to Women's Historical Writing*, edited by M. Spongberg, B. Caine, and A. Curthoys, 607–8. New York: Palgrave Macmillan, 2005.

Simmonds, A., A. Rees, and A. Clark. 'Testing the boundaries: Reflections on transnationalism in Australian history.' In *Transnationalism, Nationalism and Australian History*, edited by A. Clark, A. Rees, and A. Simmonds, 1–14. Singapore: Palgrave Macmillan, 2017.

Simpson, H. M. *The Women of New Zealand*. Wellington: Department of Internal Affairs, 1940.

Sinclair, K. *A History of the University of Auckland 1883–1983*. Auckland: Auckland University Press, 1983.

Sinha, M., D. J. Guy, and A. Woollacott. 'Introduction: Why feminisms and internationalism?' *Gender & History*, 10:3 (1998), 345–57.

Sluga, G. *Internationalism in the Age of Nationalism*. Philadelphia: University of Pennsylvania Press, 2013.

———. 'Feminisms and twentieth-century internationalisms.' In *Internationalisms: A Twentieth Century History*, edited by G. Sluga and P. Clavin, 61–84. Cambridge: Cambridge University Press, 2017.

Smith, R. *The Ladies Are At It Again: Gore Debates the Women's Franchise*. Wellington: Victoria University Department of Women's Studies, 1993.

Smith, S. *Moving Lives: Twentieth Century Women's Travel Writing*. Minneapolis: University of Minnesota Press, 2001.

Smith, W. S. *Outlines of the Women's Franchise Movement in New Zealand*. Christchurch: Whitcombe & Tombs, 1905.

Smith-Rosenberg, C. 'The female world of love and ritual: Relations between women in nineteenth-century America.' *Signs*, 1:1 (1975), 1–29.

Smitley, M. *The Feminine Public Sphere: Middle-class Women in Civic Life in Scotland, c. 1870–1914*. Manchester: Manchester University Press, 2009.

Sneider, A. L. *Suffragists in an Imperial Age: U.S. Expansion and the Woman Question, 1870–1929*. New York: Oxford University Press, 2008.

———. 'The new suffrage history: Voting rights in international perspective.' *History Compass*, 8:7 (2010), 692–703.

Solomon, M. M. 'The role of the suffrage press in the woman's rights movement.' In *A Voice of Their Own: The Woman Suffrage Press, 1840–1910*, edited by M. M. Solomon, 1–16. Tuscaloosa: University of Alabama Press, 1991.

Sontag, S. *On Photography*. Harmondsworth: Penguin Books, 1979.

Spence, C. H. *A Plea for Pure Democracy: Mr Hare's Reform Bill Applied to South Australia*. Adelaide: W.C. Rigby, 1861.

———. 'South Australia's victory for adult suffrage.' *Canadian Magazine*, 5:3 (1895), 276–7.

———. *State Children in Australia: A History of Boarding Out and Its Developments*. Adelaide: Vardon and Sons, 1907.

———. *An Autobiography*. Adelaide: W. K. Thomas & Co, 1910.

———. *A Week in the Future*. Sydney: Hale & Iremonger, 1987.

Spender, D. *Time and Tide Wait for No Man*. London: Pandora Press, 1984.

Steel, F. 'Via New Zealand around the world: The Union Steam Ship Company and the trans-Pacific mail lines, 1880s–1910s.' In *Coast to Coast: Case Histories of Modern*

Pacific Crossings, edited by P. Ahrens and C. Dixon, 59–76. Newcastle: Cambridge Scholars Publishing, 2010.

———. *Oceania under Steam: Sea Transport and the Cultures of Colonialism, c. 1870–1914*. Manchester: Manchester University Press, 2011.

Stenhouse, J. 'Religion and society.' In *The New Oxford History of New Zealand*, edited by G. Byrnes, 323–56. Melbourne: Oxford University Press, 2009.

Stevenson, A. 'Harriet Clisby's "Sketches of Australia": Travel writing and colonial refigurations in Boston's *Woman's Journal*.' *Women's History Review*, 27:5 (2018), 837–57.

———. 'Imagining women's suffrage: Frontier landscapes and the transnational print culture networks of Australia, New Zealand, and the United States.' *Pacific Historical Review*, 87:4 (2018), 638–66.

Stoler, A. L. 'Tense and tender ties: The politics of comparison in North American history and post (colonial) studies.' *Journal of American History*, 88:3 (2001), 829–65.

———. *Along the Archival Grain: Epistemic Anxieties and Colonial Common Sense*. Princeton: Princeton University Press, 2010.

Stout, A. *Woman Suffrage in New Zealand*. London: The Woman's Press, 1911.

Stuart, L. *Australian Periodicals with Literary Content, 1821–1925: An Annotated Bibliography*. Melbourne: Australian Scholarly Publishing, 2003.

Studdert, H. 'Women's magazines.' In *A History of the Book in Australia, 1891–1945: A National Culture in a Colonised Market*, edited by M. Lyons and J. Arnold, 276–81. Brisbane: University of Queensland Press, 2001.

Summers, A. *Damned Whores and God's Police: The Colonization of Women in Australia*. Melbourne: Penguin Books, 1975.

Summers, A. 'Liberty, equality, morality: The attempt to sustain an international campaign against state regulated prostitution 1875–1906.' In *Politische Netzwerkerinnen: Internationale Zusammenarbeit von Frauen 1830–1960*, edited by E. Schöck-Quinteros, A. Schüler, A. Wilmers, and K. Wolff, 289–309. Berlin: Trafo, 2007.

Swain, S. 'In these days of female evangelists and hallelujah lasses: Women preachers and the redefinition of gender roles in the churches.' *Journal of Religious History*, 26:1 (2002), 65–77.

Tetrault, L. 'The incorporation of American feminism: Suffragists and the postbellum lyceum.' *Journal of American History*, 96:4 (2010), 1033–48.

Threlkeld, M. 'Twenty years of *Worlds of Women*: Leila Rupp's impact on the history of US women's internationalism.' *History Compass*, 15:6 (2017), 1–13.

Tolerton, J. 'Nicol key to women's suffrage.' *Otago Daily Times*. www.odt.co.nz/lifestyle/magazine/nicol-key-womens-suffrage (accessed 23 September 2019).

Towns, A. 'Global patterns and debates in the granting of women's suffrage.' In *The Palgrave Handbook of Women's Political Rights*, edited by S. Franceschet, M. L. Krook, and N. Tan, 3–19. London: Palgrave Macmillan, 2019.

Traue, J. E. *New Zealand Studies: A Guide to Bibliographic Resources*. Wellington: Victoria University Press, 1985.

———. 'But why Mulgan, Marris and Schroder? The mutation of the local newspaper in New Zealand's colonial print culture.' *Bulletin*, 21:2 (1997), 107–15.

———. 'The public library explosion in colonial New Zealand.' *Libraries & the Cultural Record*, 42:2 (2007), 151–64.

Trethewey, L. and K. Whitehead. 'Beyond centre and periphery: Transnationalism in two teacher/suffragettes' work.' *History of Education*, 32:5 (2003), 547–59.

Tusan, M. E. *Women Making News: Gender and Journalism in Modern Britain*. Chicago: University of Illinois Press, 2005.

Twain, M. *Following the Equator: A Journey around the World*. Hartford: American Publishing Company, 1897.

Tyrrell, I. 'International aspects of the women's temperance movement in Australia: The influence of the American WCTU, 1882–1914.' *Journal of Religious History*, 12:3 (1983), 284–304.

———. *Woman's World/Woman's Empire: The Woman's Christian Temperance Union in International Perspective, 1880–1930*. Chapel Hill: University of North Carolina Press, 1991.

———. *Deadly Enemies: Tobacco and Its Opponents in Australia*. Sydney: UNSW Press, 1999.

———. *Transnational Nation: United States History in Global Perspective since 1789*. New York: Palgrave Macmillan, 2007.

———. *Reforming the World: The Creation of America's Moral Empire*. Princeton: Princeton University Press, 2010.

———. 'The Woman's Christian Temperance Union and internationalism.' *Women and Social Movements, International*. https://search.alexanderstreet.com/view/work/bibliographic_entity%7Cbibliographic_details%7C2476955 (accessed 5 May 2018).

van Voris, J. *Carrie Chapman Catt: A Public Life*. New York: The Feminist Press, 1987.

von Oertzen, C. 'Whose world? Internationalism, nationalism and the struggle over the "language question" in the International Federation of University Women, 1919–1932.' *Contemporary European History*, 25:2 (2016), 275–90.

Wainwright, R. *Miss Muriel Matters*. Sydney: HarperCollins, 2017.

Wallace, C. P. *Manual of the Franchise Department*. Melbourne: Dunn & Wilkinson, 1891.

Wanhalla, A. *Matters of the Heart: A History of Interracial Marriage in New Zealand*. Auckland: Auckland University Press, 2013.

Warne, E. 'Learning from the League: Supra-national women's groups and the League of Nations.' *Lilith*, 17–18 (2012), 54–67.

———. *Agitate, Educate, Organise, Legislate: Protestant Women's Social Action in Post-Suffrage Australia*. Melbourne: Melbourne University Press, 2017.

Wernitznig, D. 'Out of her time? Rosika Schwimmer's transnational activism after the First World War.' *Women's History Review*, 26:2 (2017), 262–79.

Wevers, L. 'Reading and literacy.' In *Book & Print in New Zealand: A Guide to Print Culture in Aotearoa*, edited by P. Griffith, K. Maslen, and R. Harvey, 212–20. Wellington: Victoria University Press, 1997.

———. *Country of Writing: Travel Writing and New Zealand, 1809–1900*. Auckland: Auckland University Press, 2002.

White, R. 'British travellers and the invisibility of Australia's past, 1868–1910.' In *The British Abroad Since the Eighteenth Century, Volume 1: Travellers and Tourists*, edited by M. Farr and X. Guégan, 139–58. New York: Palgrave Macmillan, 2013.

White, R. *The Republic for Which It Stands: The United States during the Reconstruction and the Gilded Age, 1865–1896*. New York: Oxford University Press, 2017.

Wikander, U. *Feminism, Familj och Medborgarskap: Debatter på Internationella Kongresser om Nattarbetsförbud för Kvinnor 1889-1919*. Gothenburg: Makadam, 2006.

Willard, F. E. *Home Protection Manual: Containing an Argument for the Temperance Ballot for Woman, and How to Obtain It, As a Means of Home Protection*. New York: The Independent Office, 1879.

———. *Do Everything: A Handbook for the World's White Ribboners*. Chicago: Woman's Temperance Publishing Association, 1895.

———. 'Address at Exeter Hall, January 9, 1893.' In *Let Something Good Be Said: Speeches and Writings of Frances E. Willard*, edited by C. D. S. Gifford and A. R. Slagell, 170-7. Urbana: University of Illinois Press, 2007.

Wolstenholme, M. E. 'Le mouvement féministe en Australie.' *Revue Politique et Parlementaire*, 15 (January-March 1898), 520-45.

Woolf, V. *A Room of One's Own*, rev. edn. London: Hogarth Press, 1935.

Woollacott, A. 'Inventing Commonwealth and pan-Pacific feminisms: Australian women's internationalist activism in the 1920s-30s.' *Gender & History*, 10:3 (1998), 425-48.

———. 'Australian women's metropolitan activism: From suffrage, to imperial vanguard, to Commonwealth feminism.' In *Women's Suffrage in the British Empire: Citizenship, Nation, and Race*, edited by I. C. Fletcher, P. Levine, and L. E. Nym Mayhall, 207-22. London: Routledge, 2000.

———. *To Try Her Fortune in London: Australian Women, Colonialism and Modernity*. New York: Oxford University Press, 2001.

———. *Race and the Modern Exotic: Three 'Australian' Women on Global Display*. Melbourne: Monash University Press, 2011.

———. *Settler Society in the Australian Colonies: Self-Government and Imperial Culture*. Oxford: Oxford University Press, 2015.

Wright, C. *The Forgotten Rebels of Eureka*. Melbourne: Text Publishing, 2013.

———. '"A splendid object lesson": A transnational perspective on the birth of the Australian nation.' *Journal of Women's History*, 26:4 (2014), 12-36.

———. *You Daughters of Freedom: The Australians Who Won the Vote and Inspired the World*. Melbourne: Text Publishing, 2018.

Wright, M. '"An impudent intrusion?" Assessing the life of Elizabeth Wolstenholme Elmy, first-wave feminist and social reformer (1833-1918).' *Women's History Review*, 18:2 (2009), 243-64.

———. '"The perfect equality of all persons before the law": The Personal Rights Association and the discourse of civil rights in Britain, 1871-1885.' *Women's History Review*, 24:1 (2014), 72-95.

Young, N. 'The truth about female suffrage in New Zealand.' *Westminster Review*, 142 (December 1894), 666-72.

Young-Lee, P. 'The Temperance Temple and architectural representation in late nineteenth-century Chicago.' *Gender & History*, 17:3 (2005), 793-825.

Zimmermann, S. 'The challenge of multinational empire for the international women's movement: The Hapsburg monarchy and the development of feminist inter/national politics.' *Journal of Women's History*, 17:2 (2005), 87-117.

Unpublished theses

Anderson, R. J. 'Te kāinga tapu: Māori cultures of travel, 1888–1918.' MA thesis, University of Auckland, 2018.

Cobb, J. E. 'The women's movement in New South Wales, 1880–1914.' PhD thesis, University of New England, 1966.

Donovan, J. 'The intellectual traditions of Australian feminism: Women's clubs and societies, 1890–1920.' PhD thesis, University of Sydney, 2004.

Dreaver, K. 'Women's suffrage in Auckland, 1885–1893.' MA thesis, University of Auckland, 1985.

Hirst, J. B. 'Adelaide and the country, 1870–1914.' PhD thesis, University of Adelaide, 1970.

Keating, J. 'Manufacturing consensus? New Zealand press attitudes toward the labour movement in 1890.' MA thesis, Victoria University of Wellington, 2011.

Langlois, P. 'The feminine press in England and France: 1875–1900.' PhD thesis, University of Massachusetts, 1979.

Simic, Z. 'A hall of selective mirrors: Feminism, history and identity 1919–1969.' PhD thesis, University of Sydney, 2003.

Sykes, G. E. 'The new woman in the new world: Fin-de-siècle writing and feminism in Australia.' PhD thesis, University of Sydney, 2002.

Tucker, M. V. 'The emergence and character of women's magazines in Australia 1880–1914.' PhD thesis, University of Melbourne, 1975.

Webb, M. R. 'Anna Patterson Stout: Portrait of a New Zealand lady.' MA thesis, Massey University, 2015.

Wiles, D. 'As high as heaven: The Woman's Christian Temperance Union in South Australia, 1886–1915.' BA Hons thesis, University of Adelaide, 1978.

Index

[Note: page numbers in *italic* refer to illustrations; literary works can be found under authors' names]

Aberdeen, Ishbel 69, 79, *86*, 208
Aboriginal people
   citizenship 2–3, 19n.5, 19–20n.8, 204
   missions 2, 157, 189
   suffrage movements and 2, 15, 157, 188, 190
   the WCTU and 37, 189–90
   welfare efforts 15, 89
Ackermann, Jessie 74, 192
   Australia 35, 41, 48, 185
   Elizabeth Nicholls and 102, 110, 171, 184, 190
Adams, Jad 22n.28
Adams, Louisa 139–40, 146–7
Adelaide 15–16, 29, 31, 33–6, 39, *44*, 51, 110, 140, 150, 152, 172–3, 177–8, 183–4, 186, 188, 191–2, 194, 210
   suffrage movement 40–1, 43–5
   see also Adelaide WCTU; Women's Suffrage League of South Australia
Adult Suffrage Bill 1894 (South Australia) 41
African Americans
   Australasian suffragists and 113, 189–90, 201n.99
age of consent 140
Aldis, Mary Steadman 101, 115, 205, 210
   libertarianism 118
   opposition to *Contagious Diseases Act 1869* (New Zealand) 117–22
   postal activism 119–22, 124, 206
Aldis, William Steadman 117–22
Alexander, Mary Hirst 83–4

Allan, Stella 88, 136
Alliance Record 103, 106, 150
'All-Red' route 38–9
America *see* United States of America
Anthony, Susan B. 64, 68, 174
anti-suffragist sentiment 12, 69, 72, 92n.43, 104, 115, 181–2, 202n.110
archives and archival material 103, 111, 113, 139, 149, 203, 210
   digitisation 69
   indigenous women and 15
   limitations of 15, 27n.61, 31, 100
   nationalism and 14
   suffrage organisations and 102, 160, 163n.25
   the WCTU and 15–16, 31–3, 57n.28, 102, 209
   see also Canterbury Museum; Girton College Library; National Library of New Zealand
Armenian massacres 31, 40, 203
Association Internationale des Femmes 68–9
Atkinson, Alan 36, 86
Auckland 16, 29, 31, 33–9, 48, 51, 108, 146, 210
   the *Contagious Diseases Act* (1869) and 117–18, 120
   suffrage 33, 40–3, 54
   see also Auckland WCTU
Auckland University College 117, 119
Auckland Women's Liberal League (AWLL) 120–3
Auckland Women's Political League (AWPL) 36, 38

INDEX

Australasia 2–3, 5–7, 28, 38, 40, 46–9, 53, 65, 76, 88–9, 104–5, 108, 110, 115, 120, 124, 135–7, 140–1, 145–8, 152, 5, 177, 186, 197n.15, 204, 206, 209
  historiography 8, 13, 18
  neglect of 3–4, 8–9
  as a 'social laboratory' 8, 89n.2, 172–3, 176, 203
Australasian Home Reading Union 145–6
Austral Club (London) 84
Australia (Commonwealth of) 28, 37, 41, 54, 66–7, 69, 71–3, 76–84, 87–9, 139, 141–2, 145–8, 152–4, 156–7, 170, 174–6, 184–6, 188–9, 203, 207, 209–10
  geography 79–80, 145, 187
  history 5–7
  suffrage 1–2, 15, 29–30, 44, 64–5, 80, 104, 107, 153, 184, 205–6
    historiography 8–11, 32, 82–3, 172
  see also federation, Australian
Australian Federation of Women Voters 88
Australian Home Journal 141–2, 146
Australian News of Ladies' Politics 138, 143–4
Australian Women's National League 18–19n.3, 88, 97n.126, 144
Australian Woman's Sphere (AWS) 1, 81, 138, 141–3, 145–7, 151
  race and 157
  subject matter 139, 152–6, 164n.45

Bain, Wilhelmina Sherriff 70–1, 77, 79, 177, 189
Ballantyne, Tony 13, 15, 133–4, 192
Barton Ministry 80
Bayly, C. A. 133
Berlin 53, 70–1, 78–9, 84, 86, 144, 177, 182
Berry, Agnes 43

Berry, Joseph 43
Billings, Minnie 39, *193*
Birks, Rosetta 36, 82
Bishop, Catherine 38
Blackburn, Helen 14–15, 109–10, 113, 180
Bosch, Mineke 9, 99, 109
Boston 37, 74–5, 105, 136–7, 144, 189
Brisbane 43, 49
British, Continental, and General Federation for the Abolition of Government Regulation of Prostitution 68, 119–22
British Commonwealth League 24n.42, 89
British Dominions Women's Suffrage Union 89
British Empire 5–7, 30, 35, 45, 77, 88, 99, 101, 103, 106, 112, 117, 119–20, 125–6n.17, 133–5, 148–9, 151, 188–9, 210
  Australasian suffragists and 1–2, 18n.3, 83–4, 89, 111, 154, 176–8
  historiography 8, 13, 99, 108–9, 170, 172
British New Guinea 39
British Woman's Temperance Association (BWTA) 32, 50, 180–2
  suffrage and 32, 50, 180
Bulletin 145
Bunkle, Phillida 37
Burton, Antoinette 148
  see also imperial commons
Butler, Josephine 136
  interest in New Zealand 119–22, 124

Caine, Barbara 65, 136
Canada 11, 54, 69, 73, 149, 154, 168n.110
Canterbury Museum 14–15
Canterbury Women's Institute 146

Cape Colony 154
Carlisle, Rosalind 104
cartes-de-visite 110–11, 123
   see also photographs
Catt, Carrie Chapman 54–5
   interest in Australia 64–5, 72, 77, 81, 85–7
   Rose Scott and 64–5, 72, 85–6, 114, 208
Ceylon (Sri Lanka) 179
Champion, Henry Hyde 142
Chewings, Hannah 41, 43
Chicago 16, 28–9, 33, 49, 51, 52, 70, 74, 104, 173–5, 189, 203, 212n.20
   see also Woman's Temple; World's Columbian Exposition (1893)
China 39, 54, 110
Christchurch 33, 113, 121, 140, 146, 149, 152, 179, 181, 207
   suffrage 101, 104, 106, 209
   see also New Zealand International Exhibition (1906)
class 12, 90n.16, 110, 164–5n.50, 202n.111
   mobility and 191
   newspapers and 135, 143
   suffrage and 3, 33, 42, 205
   the WCTU and 32–3, 42, 51, 191
Cleveland, Grover 46
Coates, Dora Meeson 82, 198n.38
Cobbe, Frances Power 108
Coit, Adela Stanton 111
Colclough, Mary Ann 108, 136
colonisation 192
   Australia 2–3, 5–6, 15
   New Zealand 2–3, 5–6, 15
   the WCTU and 37–8, 188–90, 201n.92
   women and 171, 189–90, 201n.99
Commonwealth Franchise Act 1902 (Australia) 1, 77, 88
   racial exclusions of 2, 19n.5, 190
communication and transportation networks

   see 'All-Red' route; letters; newspapers; postal services; telegraph; travel
Contagious Diseases Acts 124n.5
   repeal campaigns, imperial 39–40, 119–22
   repeal campaigns, New Zealand 101, 117–22, 206
Cowie, Bessie Lee 74–6
Cridge, Alfred 173
cultural cringe 11, 24n.42, 177, 198n.38

Daldy, Amey 42, 72
Daley, Caroline 24n.41, 100
   see also 'Suffrage and Beyond' (1993)
Dawn (Australia) 16–17, 81, 137–43, 150–1
   interpretations of 134–5
   race and 157
   readership 144, 146–7, 166n.78
   subject matter 151–5, 158–60
Dawn (UK) 119–20, 131n.110
Daybreak 138–40, 142, 146, 158, 160
Deakin, Alfred 80, 188–9
Delap, Lucy 135, 163n.32
depression, long (1879–95) 6, 35, 139
Det Hvite Bånd 155
Dewar, Helen 38, 43, 45
DiCenzo, Maria 135, 163n.32
divorce 88, 155–6, 167n.102
Dobson, Emily 76, 84–5, 191
   the ICW and 70–1, 73, 79, 86
Do-Everything policy 59–60n.76
   in Australasia 40, 42
   discontent with 46, 50–2, 55, 87
   see also Frances Willard; Woman's Christian Temperance Union
Donohoe, Madge 55, 67, 82–3, 89, 95n.99, 96n.104, 170, 205–6
   the ICW and 70, 84, 86, 87
   the IWSA and 71–2, 84–5, 87
   the NUWSS and 83–4
   travel 77, 84
Douglass, Frederick 189

dress reform 140
DuBois, Ellen Carol 5
Dunedin 15, 33, 42, 110, 121, 126n.19
Dyer, Alfred 120–1

economic independence 51, 72, 155, 174
Edmonds, Emmeline 146
elections 85, 174
   New Zealand 1–2, 9, 42, 53, 151, 179, 181
   South Australia 43, 175
   Victoria 80, 82, 84
Elmy, Elizabeth Wolstenholme 98–9, 108, 124n.5
Englishwoman's Review 14, 136–7, 149, 159, 180
   New Zealand and 109–10
Equal Rights International 89

Fawcett, Millicent Garrett 108, 110
   Kate Sheppard and 109, 113
federation, Australian 6–7, 67, 77–8, 88, 147, 152
   New Zealand and 6–7, 19n.5
   opposition to 67, 79–80, 86–7, 98, 152, 207
   support for 67, 80, 172, 184, 186–8, 190, 194–5
   the WCTU and 47, 49, 186–7, 190, 194–5
feminism 18n.1, 83–4, 88, 136–7, 145, 176, 182, 184, 203, 206–7
   anti-feminism 18–19n.3, 122
   historiography 5, 8–11, 24n.41, 25n.45, 27n.62, 30, 65–6, 78, 99, 123, 134–5, 144, 151, 171, 206
   history 6–9, 22n.30, 107–8, 139–40, 183, 189
   imperial feminism 119, 210
   internationalism and 3, 9–10, 65, 68, 73, 89, 99, 109–10, 114–15, 204–5, 207–8, 210

nationalism and 8–9, 67, 88, 184, 186, 194–5
socialism and 40, 51, 77, 90–1n.16, 205
Franklin, (Stella) Miles 17, 96n.113, 176, 203–4, 208
friendship 9, 17, 103
   internationalism and 50, 54, 60, 99–101, 106, 109–10, 112–15, 123, 205, 207–9
   see also intimate practices

gender roles 34, 99, 109, 136–7
   churches and 173, 197n.15
   respectability and 177, 184, 190–2, 194
George, Mary 4, 43, 45
Girton College Library 14
Glasgow 75, 189
Goldstein, Vida 2, 5, 10–11, 22n.28, 73, 81, 129n.73, 144, 151, 171, 204
   Australian federation and 80, 88, 207
   expenses 45, 78, 142, 176
   internationalism 1–4, 64–6, 89, 209
   the IWSA and 1, 45, 46–8, 81–2, 84–7, 208
   journalism 134, 139, 142, 147, 155, 187
   political career 82, 86, 203
   race 157, 189–90
   Rose Scott and 64, 81, 84–7, 96n.110, 103, 114, 209
   To America and Back (1902) 80–1
   travel 1, 4, 16, 64–5, 71, 82, 89n.2, 191
   see also Australian Woman's Sphere; National Australian Women's Political Association; Women's Federal Political Association
Gordon, Maria Ogilvie 111
Great Britain 5–8, 73, 103, 107, 116, 136–7, 141, 155, 159, 184

the IWSA and 111
social purity 117–22, 124n.5
suffrage 1, 3, 44, 82–4, 103–4,
 106–10, 112, 135, 158–60,
 180–2, 199n.57
travelling 'home' to 11, 14, 25n.44,
 83, 90n.16, 113, 123, 170–1,
 173, 175–83, 195, 199n.57,
 204, 208
Griffiths, John 108
Grimshaw, Patricia 9, 11, 22n.31,
 157, 210

Hall, John 103–4, 105, 106, 114–15,
 126n.33
 Kate Sheppard and 101–2,
  126n.19, 179–80
Hapgood, Isabel 116
Harper, Frances 189
Harper's New Monthly Magazine 174
Harris, Flora 48
Henry, Alice 82, 173–4, 176–7, 208
Hewett, Ellen 116
Hodge, Margaret 71, 82, 97n.123,
 189–90
Hofmeyr, Isabel 148
 see also imperial commons
Hughes-Drew, Anderson (née
 Hughes) 75–6
Hunt, Karen 170, 174

imperial commons 106, 135, 148–9,
 151
India 40, 119, 122, 149, 189
International Council of Women
 (ICW) 58, 76–7, 86–7, 89,
 210
 Australia and 15–16, 65–6, 69–71,
  78–81, 100, 113–15, 206–8
 congresses and meetings 70
  Berlin (1904) 53, 78–9, 84, 86,
   177, 182
  Copenhagen (1902) 79, 84
  London (1899) 78
  Toronto (1909) 69, 73

conservatism 69, 88–9
'Council idea' 66, 68, 78–80,
 209–10
expenses 73, 76, 84
New Zealand and 15–16, 53, 65–6,
 70, 72–3, 77, 88–9, 98–9, 111,
 177, 206–8
suffrage and 69, 72, 89
see also Ishbel Aberdeen; May
 Wright Sewall
International Federation of Working
 Women 90n.16
internationalism 17, 68, 108, 110–11,
 114–15, 123, 135, 206,
 209–10
 barriers to 11–12, 73–4, 77–82,
  158–9, 207
 everyday internationalism 15–16,
  28–9, 31, 37, 46
 historiography 9–11, 65–6, 99, 151
 nationalism and 9–10, 16, 50, 55,
  66–7, 77–82, 84, 87, 187–8,
  207, 209–10
 suffrage and 3–5, 16–17, 41, 43,
  45, 54–5, 64–7, 82, 124, 157,
  159–61, 204–6, 211
International Socialist Women's
 Conferences 90n.16
International Woman Suffrage
 Alliance (IWSA) 15–16, 54–5,
 77, 88–9, 111, 204, 208–9
 Australia and 64–7, 69, 71–3,
  77–8, 80–5, 87–9, 114–15,
  123, 207–10
 conferences and meetings 71
  Amsterdam (1908) 85
  Berlin (1904) 69, 81
  Copenhagen (1906) 81, 84–5
  Geneva (1920) 194
  London (1909) 87
  Washington, DC (1902) 64, 81
 culture 85
 expenses 78, 84–5
 historiography 9–10, 99–100,
  109–10

membership criteria 66–7, 80–2, 207, 209–10
New Zealand and 64, 66–7, 69, 73, 89
see also Carrie Chapman Catt; Madge Donohoe; Rose Scott
International Women's Union 104
intimate practices 17, 100–1, 108–12, 115, 123
Isitt, Leonard 45

Jacobs, Aletta 111
journalism *see* newspapers; travel writing
Jus Suffragii 77

Kirkby, Joseph 44–5
Kramers, Martina 77

Labor Party (New South Wales) 4, 81
Ladies' Home Journal 141, 164n.39
Ladies' National Association for the Repeal of the Contagious Diseases Acts (LNA) 119, 122
Ladies' Own Paper 86, 138, 144
Lake, Marilyn 22n.30, 65
Lake, Serena 41, 116, 123
languages
  internationalism and 65, 77, 83–4, 155
  Māori language 37, 158
Lawson, Louisa 16, 27n.61, 152, 157
  as a businesswoman 137, 143, 146, 151
  journalism 81, 134, 137, 139, 143, 150–1, 155, 159
  see also Dawn; *Republican*
League of Nations 89, 208
Leavitt, Mary Clement 188, 192
  Australasian organising tour (1885–86) 33–5, 40–1, 115
  see also World's Woman's Christian Temperance Union
Lee, Bessie Harrison 74–6
  see also Bessie Lee Cowie

Lee, Mary 36, 102, 104, 111
  interest in New Zealand 3–4
  suffrage 41
  see also Women's Suffrage League of South Australia
letter writing 14–15, 17, 85, 98–124, 146–7, 149, 173–4, 176, 189
  epistolary networks 38, 99–106, 108–10, 129n.72
  intimacy and 98–100, 110–14
  postal activism 115–23
libraries and reading rooms 108, 140, 149
literacy 101, 125–6n.17, 139
London 10, 70–2, 74, 78, 83, 87, 104, 107–8, 116, 121, 134, 136, 149, 160, 176–83, 207
London Society for Women's Suffrage 107
Love, Mary 48, 74

Macdonald, Charlotte 123, 168n.119
Macdonald, Louisa 111, 149
  see also Women's College, University of Sydney
Mackay, Jessie 17, 158–9, 177, 203–4, 209
Main, Hannah 38, 43, 45, 205
Manoramabai 189
Māori 6, 19n.5, 19n.7, 209
  Kotahitanga 2, 15, 157, 168n.119
  niupepa 158
  and the suffrage movement 2, 37, 115, 157, 168n.119, 180
  the WCTU and 37–8, 45, 157–8
marriage 107, 156
  law reform 88, 139, 155, 208
  respectability and 191–2, 194
Marsden, Kate 116
Masterman, Alice 147
Matters, Emilie 84
Matters, Muriel 82, 171
Melbourne 1, 4, 34, 43, 47–9, 61n.115, 80–1, 86, 103, 106,

250

INDEX

108, 137, 139, 142, 144–5, 150–2, 173, 198n.38
Methodist church 36, 43, 68, 184, 191
Mill, Harriet Taylor 108
Mill, John Stuart 107–8
Minns, Benjamin 150
missionaries 5, 10, 38–9, 76, 116, 157
  the WCTU and 32, 34–5, 50, 55–6n.6, 76–7, 104, 149, 158, 171–2, 183, 187–8, 192
Montefiore, Dora 83, 90n.16, 95n.95, 174, 178
Müller, Mary Ann 107–8, 127–8n.47, 204
  An Appeal to the Men of New Zealand (1869) 107

Napier, Isabel 12, 53, 70, 74
National American Woman Suffrage Association 54
National Council of Women (NCW)
  Australia 65–6, 69, 76, 78–80, 88, 92n.38, 185
  New South Wales 69, 78, 114–15, 128n.53, 129n.74, 141, 143–4
  New Zealand 7, 69, 72–3, 98, 122, 209
  South Australia 7, 69, 79
  Tasmania 69, 78, 191
  see also Emily Dobson
  Victoria 69, 79–80
nationalism 97n.126, 137
  feminism and 8–9, 67, 88, 184, 186, 194–5
  internationalism and 9–10, 16, 50, 55, 66–7, 77–82, 84, 87, 187–8, 207, 209–10
  opposition to 49–50, 67, 72–3, 77–82, 85–8, 98, 152, 207
  suffrage historiography and 5, 8, 110–11, 25n.44, 204–5
National Library of New Zealand 26n.59
National Union of Women's Suffrage Societies (NUWSS) 83–4

networks, colonial and imperial 12–14, 29–30, 108–9
Newcomb, Harriet 71, 82, 97n.123, 189–90
news cartels 144, 148
New South Wales 38–9, 78, 83, 85, 88, 97n.123, 98, 102, 104, 145–7, 152–5, 157, 187, 190
  Australian federation and 86–7, 152
  history 5–6
  suffrage 2–4, 13, 44, 48, 55, 83–4, 101, 114, 152, 156, 159–60, 178, 186, 188, 212n.10
newspapers 47, 84, 133–4
  Australasian market for 17, 144–5
  clipping 133, 136, 139, 149–50, 158–60
  scissors and paste journalism 148–9, 152, 159
  women's advocacy press 12, 16, 28, 102, 108, 133–6, 138–44, 146–61, 172, 176
  advertising 142, 164–5n.50, 165n.51
  business models 133, 141–3
  circulation 141, 145–9
  exchange system 103–5, 149–51
  internationalism and 149, 152–5, 158–61
  women's commercial press 137, 141
  women's pages 136
New York 4, 28, 75, 176, 183
New York Tribune 77
New Zealand 34–5, 73, 98, 103, 107, 116–23, 139, 142, 145–8, 152–5, 157, 159–60, 177, 182, 203, 208–9
  Australian federation and 6–7, 19n.5
  geography 33, 38, 101, 207
  historiography 4, 8–11, 14, 22n.31, 25n.45, 29–30, 205
  history 5–7, 21n.21, 21n.25, 72–3
  suffrage 1–3, 15, 40, 42, 48, 53, 65, 99, 101–4, 108–10,

113, 150, 172, 178–83, 195,
199n.57, 203
New Zealand International
Exhibition (1906–7) 111, *113*
Nicholls, Alfred 184, 188, 191–2,
193, 194
Nicholls, Elizabeth Webb 17, 102,
108, 110, 120, 161, *193*
Australian federation 186–7, 190,
194, 207
expenses 176, 188, 191
Our Federation 49, 133, 141–2,
147, 149–50, 153, 155, 157,
165n.51, 171, 184, 186–7,
190n.112
public perception of 172, 187,
190–2, 194
race 188–90
suffrage 43–4, 47, 49, 53, 55, 106,
116, 128n.53, 157, 172, 184–6
travel 153, 170–2, 179, 183–8, 190,
194–5
the WCTU of Australasia 44, 49,
74, 133, 183–5, 191–2
the WCTU of South Australia
43–4, 106, 116, 184, 194
Nicol, Helen 126n.19
Nolan, Melanie 24n.41, 100
see also 'Suffrage and Beyond' (1993)
Nolan, Sara 75, 142

Oldfield, Audrey 196n.9
organised labour 6, 67–8, 137,
173, 203
suffrage and 15
Our Federation 49, 138, 142, 147,
150, 187, 192, *193*
circulation 141, 147, 149
finances 133, 143, 165n.51
ideology 140, 186–7, 194
race and 157, 188, 190
subject matter 152–7, 171, 184

pacifism *see* peace activism
Packe, Emma 172, 195, 205

anti-suffragism 181–3
Paisley, Fiona 14
pamphlets and propaganda 119–21
circulation of 3, 29–30, 38, 41–2,
47, 102–9, 119–21, 175, 205,
209
suffrage 41, 45, 47–9, 73, 103–7,
109, 127n.40, 179
temperance 41, 108
Pan-Pacific Women's Association 10,
24n.42, 89, 123, 207
Paris 79, 84
Parkes, Henry 104, 126n.33
parliament, women in
Australia 1, 80, 86, 203
New South Wales 98
New Zealand 12, 98, 140, 157, 203
peace activism 3, 8, 10, 77, 82,
95n.90, 140, 177, 204, 208
Personal Rights Association 118
photographs 28–9, 85, 96n.110, *105*,
112, 115, 192, 202n.111
internationalism and 110–11, *112*
photograph albums 111–12,
129n.69
see also cartes-de-visite
political tourism 17, 161, 170–2,
174
Polyglot Petition 46
postal services 98, 101, 125–6n.17
Powell, Mary 39, 74
Primrose League 103
print culture *see* libraries and
reading rooms; newspapers;
pamphlets and propaganda;
reading and reading cultures
Prohibitionist 42–3, 107, 110, 117,
138, 140, 149–50
circulation 103, 106
subject matter 151–4, 156
public speaking 50, 80–2, 173, 176,
179, 184, 197n.15
suffrage and 43, 49, 77, 84, 172,
175, 180–1, 185
as a vocation 109, 175, 188

Queensland 2, 6, 27n.61, 38–9, 43, 49, 54, 146–7, 153–4, 180, 185, 190
Quiz and the Lantern 192

race 188, 192
   feminism and 119, 135, 157–8, 171–2, 188–90, 206
   internationalism and 79, 154, 180, 204, 206–7
   suffrage and 2–3, 11, 15, 19n.5, 45, 157, 168n.119, 180
   the WCTU and 37–8, 45, 157–8, 188–91, 201n.92
rape 139
reading and reading cultures 17, 134–5, 137, 139–40, 143, 145, 148–9, 158, 198
   as a communal practice 37, 43, 100, 102, 146, 161, 208
   feminism and 108–9, 147, 155, 159–60, 206
   scripture reading 37
   see also libraries and reading rooms; literacy
Reeves, William Pember 8, 110
Republican 137
Rupp, Leila 9–10, 65
Ryan, Leila 135, 163n.32

San Francisco 38, 172, 176
San Francisco Chronicle 80, 96n.110
Sangster, Joan 170
Schnackenberg, Annie 37, 39, 43, 182
Schreiner, Olive 143
Scott, Rose 4, 83, 96n.110, 98–9, 102, 126–7n.33, 129–30n.76, 144, 186
   anti-federalism 67, 79, 86–8, 207
   archives and collections 15, 111–12, 127n.34
   correspondence 100, 102–5, 108, 123, 128n.53
   the ICW and 79–80, 84, 114–15, 129n.74
   the IWSA and 64–5, 72, 82, 84, 86–7, 114–15, 208
   journalism 135–7, 159–60
   travel 86, 96n.113, 175–6
   Vida Goldstein and 64, 81, 84–7, 96n.110, 103, 114, 209
Scottish Christian Union 53
scrapbooks 111, 115, 123, 139
Seddon, Richard 12, 42, 145
   Contagious Diseases Act repeal 121–2
Sentinel 120
Sewall, May Wright 68, 84, 98–9
   and Australian admission to the ICW 78–9
sex trafficking 3, 204
Shaw, Anna Howard 64, 69, 111, *112*
Sheppard, Kate 1–5, 12, 18–19n.3, 77, 121, 149, 187, 204, 206–7, 209
   correspondence 14–15, 102–13, 123, 126n.19, 145–6, 150
   the ICW and 72–3, 111, 182, 208
   Is it Right? (1892) 105–6
   the IWSA and 22n.28, 55, 73
   journalism 137, 140, 145–6, 150, 155, 157, 161
   the New Zealand WCTU and 42, 48, 101–2, 104–5, 111, 140, 181
   public speaking 180–3
   Sixteen Reasons Why the Women of New Zealand Should Get the Vote (1891) 104–6, 126n.40
   travel 170–2, 178–83, 194–5
   the World's WCTU and 53, 74, 180, 182, 189
Siam (Thailand) 110
Sievwright, Margaret 27n.61, 98–101, 123
Smith, Lucy 121
Smith, May Wood 79, *86*
Smith, William Sidney 22n.28, 110
Snow, Helen 116
socialism
   Christian socialism 40, 51, 63n.136
   internationalism and 90n.16

INDEX

'state socialism' 22n.30
Somerset, Isabella (Lady Henry) 180–2
  Frances Willard and 50–2, 59–60n.76
South Africa 54
  see also Cape Colony
South Australia 6, 33, 39, 117, 147, 153–5, 159–60, 173, 184, 190–1
  exceptionalism 44–5
  suffrage 2, 4, 33, 40–1, 44, 47–8, 54, 105–6, 151, 173, 186
South Australian Register (*SAR*) 173
Spectator 136, 162n.16
Spence, Catherine Helen 14, 17, 36, 45, 78, 86, 161, 170, 179, 206, 208
  A Week in the Future (1888–89) 177–8
  expenses 14–5, 180, 182, 197n.14
  journalism 136, 171, 173–4, 176–7
  proportional representation 173–5, 178, 197n.25
  suffrage 22n.28, 158, 175, 178, 197n.12
  travel (Great Britain) 175–8, 195
  travel (United States) 171–8, 189, 195, 197n.18, 197n.21
Stanton, Elizabeth Cady 68, 98, 154
State Children's Council of South Australia 174–5
Sterling, Antionette 179
Stevens, Lillian 28
Stout, Anna 27n.61, 72–3, 75, 82, 171, 180
Stout, Robert 181
Suez Canal 188
'Suffrage and Beyond' (1993) 9–10
suffrage petitions 46, 137
  criticism of 47, 116
  New Zealand 26n.59, 42, 47, 101–2, 111, 118, 126n.19, 168n.119
  South Australia 41, 46, 116
  Victoria 46–7, 61n.115

suffragettes 9, 12
  see also Women's Social and Political Union
Sydney 4, 15, 33, 38, 43–4, 48, 55–6n.6, 64, 67, 81–3, 86, 95n.95, 104, 106, 108, 134, 136–7, 139–40, 142–5, 149–51, 159–60, 203, 206

Tasmania 2, 6, 21n.20, 27n.61, 35, 61n.113, 78, 92n.38, 105, 153–4, 159, 184, 185, 192, 194
Tasman World 3, 7, 50, 160
telegraph 7, 144, 148, 159, 174, 192
temperance movement 3, 140, 149, 155–7, 184, 186, 191, 194–5
  global 9, 32, 34, 39, 46, 50–4
  Great Britain 32, 34, 50–1, 179–80
  New Zealand 35–6, 41–2, 118
  South Australia 36
  United States 29, 34, 40, 50
  Victoria 34, 103
  see also Woman's Christian Temperance Union; World's Woman's Christian Temperance Union
Tetrault, Lisa 175
Theobald, J. H. 139, 141–2
  Kate Sheppard and 145, 150–1
Time and Tide 203
transnationalism 29, 68, 76
  historiography 4–5, 10–11, 26n.55, 30, 205–6, 208–9
  limitations of 5, 10, 13–14, 183
  suffrage and 3–4, 10, 12, 77, 103, 111, 170, 204–6
travel 12, 17, 38–9, 43, 65, 69, 196n.9, 205–6, 208
  expense 15, 39, 48, 73, 76, 78, 80–1, 84, 88, 109, 173–6, 210
  as political activism 170–95
  respectability and 190–2, 195
  by sea 38, 179, 188, 190–1
travel writing 170, 177, 182, 194, 196n.9

economic imperatives for 80–1, 176–7
as political activism 170–1, 174, 177, 186–8, 190–1, 194
Twain, Mark 190
Tyrrell, Ian 29, 106
Woman's World/Woman's Empire (1991) 30

Union Signal 34, 42–3, 47, 187
circulation 116, 140, 147
as a conduit for local grievances 115–16, 124, 181–2
internationalism and 40, 207–8
Unitarianism 173
United Associations of Women 88, 164–5n.50
United Council for Woman Suffrage 78, 155
United Kingdom *see* Great Britain
United States of America 8, 10, 14, 16, 28, 34, 40, 67, 82, 136–7, 141–2, 147, 149, 152–5, 170–2, 175–7, 191, 195, 197n.18, 197n.25, 208
the ICW and 77, 79, 98–9
interest in Australasia 50, 64–5, 89n.2, 147, 171–6, 195, 197n.10
the IWSA and 50, 64, 81
race and 113, 189–90, 201n.97
suffrage 1–3, 8–9, 40–2, 44, 50–1, 54, 98–9, 104, 106–7, 129n.73, 159–60, 172, 179, 186–7, 208
temperance 28–9, 34, 50–1, 108, 134
United States' Senate Select Committee on Woman Suffrage (1902) 64

Vale, John 103, 150
see also Alliance Record
Valverde, Maria 37–8
Victoria 6, 27n.61, 81–2, 145, 147, 153–5, 159

suffrage 1, 21, 41, 45, 47–8, 61n.115, 80, 84, 97–8, 103, 105, 139, 160, 188, 194
von Beschwitz, Olga 114
von Oertzen, Christine 68

wage equality 40, 88, 208
Wallace, Catherine 47–9
Wardrobe see Australian News of Ladies' Politics
Washington, DC 4, 64, 68, 71, 81, 189
Webb, Beatrice 70, 72
Wellington 33, 116, 140
Wells, Ida B. 113, 189, 201n.97
Western Australia 2–3, 6, 27n.61, 80, 92n.38, 106, 153–4, 183–4, 185, 187, 190
White Australia Policy 188, 190
White Ribbon 104, 111, 121, 137–8, 140–1, 143, 146–7, 152, 155, 165n.62, 167n.98, 182
Māori readers 158
subject matter 142, 153–4, 156–7
White Ribbon Signal (New South Wales) 138, 140, 165n.62, 167n.101
White Ribbon Signal (Victoria) 138, 140–1, 165n.62, 167n.101
white slave trade *see* sex trafficking
Willard, Frances 37, 63n.136, 149, 192
feminism 29, 40, 59–60n.76
funeral ceremonies 28–30, 32
internationalism 29, 34, 45–6
Kate Sheppard and 182, 189
suffrage 32, 40, 46, 50, 52–3, 55, 63n.139, 180
the Woman's Temple and 28–9, 50
the World's WCTU and 21–22n.27, 34, 45–6, 50–3, 189, 205
writing 28, 36–7, 140
see also Do-Everything policy; Polyglot Petition; *Union Signal*; World's Woman's Christian Temperance Union
Wilson, Teresa 68

INDEX

Windeyer, Margaret 27n.61, 70, 178, 199n.44
Windeyer, Mary 27n.61, 48, 102
Wollstonecraft, Mary 108–9
Wolstenholme, Maybanke 27n.61, 134, 139, 146, 156, 160
  see also Woman's Voice (1894–95)
Womanhood Suffrage League of New South Wales 64, 71–2, 78, 83–4, 90n.16, 102, 114, 139, 141, 149, 155–6, 186, 199n.44
  Annual Reports 159–60
  parochialism 85–6, 159–60
  see also Dora Montefiore; Madge Donohoe; Mary Windeyer; Rose Scott
Woman's Christian Temperance Union (WCTU) 7, 15–16, 18, 21–2n.27
  Adelaide WCTU 29, 31, 33–7, 39–41, 43, 57n.28
  Auckland WCTU 29, 31, 33–9, 41–3, 45, 57n.28, 57n.36, 118, 121
  ideology 37–8, 40, 183, 186–8, 194, 201n.92
    see also Do-Everything policy
  United States WCTU 28–9, 32, 34, 50–2, 113, 189
    suffrage 50–2
    see also Woman's Temperance Publishing Association; Woman's Temple
  WCTU of Australasia 35, 47, 54–5, 108, 133, 138, 140–1, 143, 149, 152, 170, 172, 183–4, 186–7, 191–4
    conventions 37, 39, 43, 48–9, 133, 186–7, 192
    international representation 50, 53, 74–6, 179, 187–8
    New Zealand and 48, 61–2n.118, 147, 208
    parochialism 47, 49, 133, 147, 153

  race 188–9
  suffrage 31, 41–5, 47–9, 157, 185–6, 195, 205, 209
    see also Our Federation
  WCTU of New South Wales 55–6n.6, 57n.28, 83, 138, 140, 142, 147, 165n.62, 167n.101
  WCTU of New Zealand 34, 40–2, 45, 54–5, 55–6n.6, 108, 113, 116–17, 120–2, 137–8, 140–1, 143, 149–52, 181
    international representation 39, 50, 53, 67, 74–6, 180–2
    Māori and 37–38, 45, 157–8
    suffrage 22n.28, 41–2, 101–2, 104–6, 127n.18, 157, 179–82, 205, 209
    see also White Ribbon
  WCTU of Queensland 38, 43
  WCTU of South Australia 35, 37, 39–40, 44, 102, 124, 194
    suffrage 41, 43–5, 48, 106, 116–17
  WCTU of Victoria 48–9, 138, 140–1, 165n.62, 167n.101
  WCTU of Western Australia 58n.45
  see also British Woman's Temperance Association; Scottish Christian Union; Frances Willard; World's Woman's Christian Temperance Union
Woman's Herald 149
Woman's Journal 105, 136, 149
Woman's League (South Australia) 44
Woman's Signal 121, 149, 180
Woman's Suffrage Journal 106, 138–9, 141–2, 145, 147, 150, 155
  see also J. H. Theobald
Woman's Temperance Publishing Association 104
Woman's Temple (Chicago) 28–9, 46, 51, 52

INDEX

Woman's Voice (1894–95) 108, 138–40, 142, 145–6, 151–3, 156, 158
Woman's Voice (1905) 138, 143–4
Woman Voter 138, 144
women's advocacy press *see* newspapers
Women's College, University of Sydney 111, 149
Women's Federal Political Association (WFPA) 80–1
Women's Franchise League (New Zealand) (WFL)
 Auckland 33, 36, 42–3, 45, 120
 Dunedin 42, 120–1, 126n.19
Women's International League for Peace and Freedom 89
Women's Liberation 9, 144
women's literary societies 40, 108, 137, 149
Women's National Liberal Association 121
Women's Political Association of Victoria (WPA) 82
Women's Political Educational League 81
Women's Progressive Association 81
Women's Progressive Society 104
Women's Social and Political Union 82, 199n.57
Women's Suffrage League of South Australia 33, 36, 41, 43–4, 102, 175
 see also Mary Lee

women's suffrage movement *see* suffrage
Women's Trade Union League 173, 203
Woolf, Virginia 114
Woollacott, Angela 4
World's Columbian Exposition, Chicago (1893) 70, 174, 199n.44, 212n.20
World's Woman's Christian Temperance Union 7, 10, 21–2n.27, 28–34, 38, 66, 180, 208
 Australia and 34–5, 49, 53, 74–6
 conventions
  Boston (1891) 37, 74
  Chicago (1893) 49, 59–60n.76, 63n.139, 74
  Edinburgh (1900) 39, 74, 187–8
  London (1895) 74, 180, 182, 189
  Toronto (1897) 53, 74
 New Zealand and 34–5, 37, 39, 48, 53, 74–6, 182
 race and 37, 188–9, 201n.97
 rituals 46
 'round-the-world' missionaries 33–5, 40–1, 55–6n.6, 76, 115, 188, 192
 suffrage 47, 50–5, 68, 87, 204–5, 207, 209
Wright, Clare 25n.44, 64

Young Women's Christian Association (YWCA) 36, 82, 176

EU authorised representative for GPSR:
Easy Access System Europe, Mustamäe tee 50,
10621 Tallinn, Estonia
gpsr.requests@easproject.com

www.ingramcontent.com/pod-product-compliance
Lightning Source LLC
Chambersburg PA
CBHW051607230426
43668CB00013B/2016